Wildlif

X

ASPECTS OF TOURISM

Series Editors: Professor Chris Cooper, *University of Queensland, Australia*
Dr C. Michael Hall, *University of Otago, Dunedin, New Zealand*
Dr Dallen Timothy, *Arizona State University, Tempe, USA*

Aspects of Tourism is an innovative, multifaceted series which will comprise authoritative reference handbooks on global tourism regions, research volumes, texts and monographs. It is designed to provide readers with the latest thinking on tourism world-wide and in so doing will push back the frontiers of tourism knowledge. The series will also introduce a new generation of international tourism authors, writing on leading edge topics. The volumes will be readable and user- friendly, providing accessible sources for further research. The list will be underpinned by an annual authoritative tourism research volume. Books in the series will be commissioned that probe the relationship between tourism and cognate subject areas such as strategy, development, retailing, sport and environmental studies. The publisher and series editors welcome proposals from writers with projects on these topics.

Other Books in the Series
Managing Educational Tourism
    Brent W. Ritchie
Recreational Tourism: Demand and Impacts
    Chris Ryan
Coastal Mass Tourism: Diversification and Sustainable Development in Southern Europe
    Bill Bramwell (ed.)
Sport Tourism Development
    Thomas Hinch and James Higham
Sport Tourism: Interrelationships, Impact and Issues
    Brent Ritchie and Daryl Adair (eds)
Tourism, Mobility and Second Homes
    C. Michael Hall and Dieter Müller
Strategic Management for Tourism Communities: Bridging the Gaps
    Peter E. Murphy and Ann E. Murphy
Oceania: A Tourism Handbook
    Chris Cooper and C. Michael Hall (eds)
Tourism Marketing: A Collaborative Approach
    Alan Fyall and Brian Garrod
Music and Tourism: On the Road Again
    Chris Gibson and John Connell
Tourism Development: Issues for a Vulnerable Industry
    Julio Aramberri and Richard Butler (eds)
Nature-Based Tourism in Peripheral Areas: Development or Disaster?
    C. Michael Hall and Stephen Boyd (eds)
Tourism, Recreation and Climate Change
    C. Michael Hall and James Higham (eds)
Shopping Tourism, Retailing and Leisure
    Dallen J. Timothy

For more details of these or any other of our publications, please contact:
Channel View Publications, Frankfurt Lodge, Clevedon Hall,
Victoria Road, Clevedon, BS21 7HH, England
http://www.channelviewpublications.com

ASPECTS OF TOURISM 24
Series Editors: Chris Cooper (*University of Queensland, Australia*),
C. Michael Hall (*University of Otago, New Zealand*)
and Dallen Timothy (*Arizona State University, USA*)

Wildlife Tourism

David Newsome, Ross K. Dowling and Susan A. Moore

With Joan Bentrupperbäumer,
Mike Calver and Kate Rodger

CHANNEL VIEW PUBLICATIONS
Clevedon • Buffalo • Toronto

To our partners and children
Jane, Ben and Rachel Newsome
Wendy, Jayne, Simon, Mark, Tobias, Aurora and Francis Dowling
Warren, Jessica and Samuel Tacey
     and
for all those people who love to see animals in the wild

Library of Congress Cataloging in Publication Data
Newsome, David
Wildlife Tourism/David Newsome, Ross K. Dowling, and Susan A. Moore; with Joan Bentrupperbäumer, Mike Calver, and Kate Roger. 1st ed.
Aspects of Tourism: 24
Includes bibliographical references and index.
1. Wildlife-related recreation. 2. Tourism. I. Dowling, Ross Kingston. II. Moore, Susan A. III. Title. IV. Series.
SK655.N49 2004
338.4'759–dc22   2004022939

British Library Cataloguing in Publication Data
A catalogue entry for this book is available from the British Library.

ISBN 1-84541-007-6 (hbk)
ISBN 1-84541-006-8 (pbk)

Channel View Publications
An imprint of Multilingual Matters Ltd

UK: Frankfurt Lodge, Clevedon Hall, Victoria Road, Clevedon BS21 7HH.
USA: 2250 Military Road, Tonawanda, NY 14150, USA.
Canada: 5201 Dufferin Street, North York, Ontario, Canada M3H 5T8.

Typeset by Archetype-IT Ltd (http://www.archetype-it.com).
Printed and bound in Great Britain by the Cromwell Press.

Contents

Preface

This is the 24th book in Channel View Publications *Aspects of Tourism* series and the second in the series on which the three authors have collaborated. The first, *Natural Area Tourism: Ecology, Impacts and Management* (2002), defined natural area tourism as an applied science. This book is a research monograph which reflects our thinking on what constitutes wildlife tourism specifically in natural areas especially in relation to its ecological base. It also highlights our understanding of impacts and current views on management. While we acknowledge that the first major contribution in this field is the pioneering text *Wildlife Tourism* by Myra Shackley (1996), this book represents the first major contribution on the subject in the new millennium. Its strengths include its scientific base, its integration of science and social science perspectives as well as its global scope with examples from polar to tropical regions and from rain forests to dry land environments. Although this is primarily a research text it is also a valuable resource for wildlife managers and advocates of wildlife tourism around the world.

Humans have always had close contact with animals and our overall appreciation of wildlife dates back to times when human lives were linked with the animals that lived around them. Wildlife co-exist with humans but have generally been viewed as a resource by them. Traditional approaches to the conservation of wildlife have centred around their use to humankind in what has been named an 'anthropocentric' or 'human-centred' worldview. In recent times, however, the appreciation of wildlife solely for their attributes, rather than their resources, has led to the emergence of an 'ecocentric' or 'life-centred' view in which humans believe that it is useful to recognise biodiversity as a essential element of life on earth. This recognition of the intrinsic value of all forms of life, regardless of their potential or actual use to humans, introduces a new aspect of our relationship with wildlife and helps to explain the unprecedented recent increase in wildlife tourism.

The underpinning base of our approach to the subject is embedded firmly in our shared belief that wildlife tourism is an exciting venture based on the twin goals of fostering wildlife conservation and natural area tourism development. In recent years there has been a shift away from viewing animals in captivity to viewing them in the wild. Wildlife tourism fundamentally comprises the viewing of wild animals and our views of wildlife, from a Western world perspective, have been influenced largely through television documentaries focusing mainly on large vertebrates. By extension, and in line with general convention, in this book we exclude invertebrates and plants from our definition of wildlife and focus solely on non-domesticated vertebrates. This is based on our general observation that it is the vertebrates that usually are the focus of wildlife tourism interest and operations.

We also make a distinction between consumptive and non-consumptive wildlife tourism. The former generally is regarded as including hunting and fishing while the latter focuses mainly on viewing. It is recognised that both form parts of a continuum in which there is often some overlap, but in this book we put the spotlight on non-consumptive wildlife tourism as we assign more value to the wildlife than viewing them merely as a resource for human consumption and destruction. However, it is recognised that wildlife tourism also results in potential and actual impacts across a range of wildlife, habitats and interactive situations. Impacts are dependent on the numbers of tourists, number and resilience of the wildlife under view, and the nature of the tourism activity. A range of other factors also influence the impacts of tourists on wildlife. These include habitat factors, seasonal factors and breeding status, all of which will be discussed in the book.

The viewing of wild animals in the wild is the focus of this book. While clearly accepting that wildlife viewing in captive or semi-captive situations forms one end of a spectrum of wildlife tourism, we confine our discussion to the sustainable viewing of wildlife in the wild. Wildlife tourism embraces all three types of natural area tourism. It is partly adventure travel, is generally nature based, and involves ecotourism's key principles of being sustainable and educative as well as supporting conservation. Our definition of wildlife tourism is that it is 'tourism undertaken to view and/or encounter wildlife. It can take place in a range of settings, from captive, semi-captive, to in the wild, and it encompasses a variety of interactions from passive observation to feeding and/or touching the species viewed'.

The book has been written for a broad audience including students pursuing university and training programmes, tourism industry professionals, planners and managers in natural area management, and finally government agency employees. As a general text, it should be useful to students in a range of disciplines including tourism, environmental science, geography, planning and regional studies. As a specific text it provides a practical guide for natural area managers, such as national and marine park managers, as well as tour operators. The applied approach to ecology and understanding of environmental impacts makes this book also suitable for those from business, communications and marketing backgrounds as well as those with more scientific leanings. The foundation on ecology and impacts is valuable, but of even greater value is the explanation on the practical aspects of managing natural area tourism. This includes planning frameworks for natural area tourism as well as a number of management strategies with special attention paid to interpretation and monitoring. The book also has been written as a contribution to research and as such it brings together the essential elements of ecology, impacts and management to comprehensively address the provision of sustainable natural area tourism.

Finally, we would like readers to note that this book has been enriched immeasurably by the contributions of three other academics: Joan Bentrupperbäumer, Mike Calver and Kate Rodger, who together bring significant expertise to the book from their natural and social science backgrounds. They have authored Chapter 3 – Human Dimension of Wildlife Interactions (Joan Bentrupperbäumer); Chapter 7 – Natural Science and Wildlife Tourism (Kate Rodger and Mike Calver); and Chapter 8 – Researching Ecological Impacts (Mike Calver). The work of these contributors adds substantially to this text: however, the overall book was conceived, researched and compiled by the authors who view this book as a logical extension of their original volume in this series on *Natural Area Tourism: Ecology, Impacts and Management*. Thus the final responsibility for the text lies with the book's primary authors and we are the ones responsible for its final form.

We trust that you enjoy this book.

David Newsome
Ross Dowling
Susan Moore

Perth, Western Australia
February 2005

Acknowledgements

The authors would like to thank a number of people who contributed to this book. They include the contributors, reviewers and publishing staff. Firstly the contributors, Associate Professor Mike Calver, Dr Joan Bentrupperbäumer and Ms Kate Rodger, are thanked for their willing participation in this project. All three are experts in their recognised fields and we believe that this book has been enriched by their contributions.

Comments and suggestions by a number of people significantly enhanced the calibre and comprehensiveness of this publication. They included Professor Michael Hall, University of Otago; Associate Professor Mike Calver, Murdoch University; Ms Kate Rodger, Murdoch University and Ms Sabrina Genter, Murdoch University.

The authors also wish to acknowledge the cartographic skills of Alan Rossow, Colin Ferguson, Mike Roeger and Stephen Goynich of Murdoch University who prepared the diagrams and maps for this book. We think the work of these people adds considerable value to the book.

Noella Ross, Secretary, School of Environmental Science, Murdoch University, diligently formatted the text and assisted with the compilation of the references. This is the second book that she has assisted us with and we thank her for her continued support. We also thank Ross Lantzke for providing technical expertise in the use of various computer software packages.

We wish to acknowledge the enthusiasm and support of the publishers Mike, Marjukka and Sami Grover, Ken Hall and the entire team at Channel View Publications. Finally we wish to thank the *Aspects of Tourism* Series Editors, Professors Michael Hall, Chris Cooper and Dallen Timothy, for once again working with them on this progressive series of books which advances our knowledge of tourism.

David Newsome would like to thank Ross Dowling and Sue Moore for their intelligent input and enthusiasm in the second book that we have collaborated on. I thank my wife Jane for her love and not only for managing family affairs, but also for helping search and document the literature on wildlife tourism. I would also like to extend gratitude to family and friends who helped with transport and accommodation while I was collecting field data for this book. They are Ken and Paul

Newsome, Mick and Margaret Willis, Robert Whittaker and Richard Baker. Above all I acknowledge the interest and enthusiasm of my children who show wonder and delight in this planet's extraordinary wildlife and who share my passion for the natural environment.

Ross Dowling would like to thank his fellow authors for their collegial spirit and immense knowledge freely shared throughout the gestation of this book. He also wishes to acknowledge the professionalism and hospitality granted to him while he was a Visiting Research Scholar at Murdoch University's School of Environmental Science during the period July–December 2003, when much of the text for this book was written.

A number of colleagues at Edith Cowan University have encouraged me throughout my career and I would like to thank them for their ongoing professional support. They are Professor Millicent Poole (Vice Chancellor), Professor John Wood (Deputy Vice Chancellor), Professor Robert Harvey (Executive Dean, Faculty of Business & Law), Dr Kandy James (Head, School of Marketing, Tourism & Leisure), and Thandarayan Vasudavan (Lecturer in Tourism). In addition Julie Connolly (Senior Administration Officer, School of Marketing, Tourism & Leisure) also helped to keep me going with her professional input during the time I was Head of the School from 2001 to 2003.

I also wish to thank a number of close academic colleagues from around the world who have in some small way contributed to my own thoughts on wildlife tourism through discussion, debate and dialogue over time. They are David Fennell (Brock University), Dallen Timothy (Arizona State University, USA), Allan Fyall (Bournemouth University, England), Michael Hall (University of Otago, NZ), Bruce Prideaux (James Cook University, Australia) and Stephen Page (University of Stirling, Scotland). Thanks also to Tony Charters (Tourism Queensland, Australia) who is without doubt my ecotourism mentor. He has contributed more to the development of Australian ecotourism, including wildlife tourism, then any other person and he is always a great source of knowledge and professionalism. To him I owe a big debt of gratitude for his support over the past 15 years.

Finally I wish to thank my wife Wendy for her unfailing love and support through this my fifth book in the last three years. I could not have achieved this without her. I also wish to acknowledge my children Aurora, Francis, Jayne, Mark, Simon and Tobias as well as my three grand-daughters Helena, Paige and Shenee. This book is part of my legacy for you all.

Susan Moore would like to thank her co-authors for their enthusiasm, organisational abilities and knowledge of wildlife tourism. As with all her work, she recognises the support provided by her partner, Warren Tacey and children, Jessica and Samuel.

Authors and Contributors

Authors

David Newsome is Senior Lecturer in Environmental Science in the School of Environmental Science, Murdoch University, Perth, Western Australia. He holds degrees in natural resources and environmental science. His general research interests include wildlife tourism, ecotourism and geotourism with a specific emphasis on the assessment and management of the biophysical impacts of recreation and tourism in natural areas. He is co-author of the book *Natural Area Tourism: Ecology, Impacts and Management*.

Ross Dowling is Foundation Professor of Tourism in the School of Marketing, Tourism & Leisure, Edith Cowan University, Joondalup, Western Australia. He holds degrees in geology, geography and environmental science. His environment–tourism research interests include wildlife tourism, ecotourism and geotourism. He is co-author of the books *Natural Area Tourism: Ecology, Impacts and Management and Ecotourism,* and is co-editor of *Ecotourism Policy and Planning* and *Tourism in Destination Communities*.

Sue Moore is Senior Lecturer in Environmental Science in the School of Environmental Science, Murdoch University, Perth, Western Australia. She holds degrees in natural resources. Her environment–tourism interests include wildlife tourism, ecotourism and tourism policies and planning. She is co-author of the book *Natural Area Tourism: Ecology, Impacts and Management*.

Contributors

Joan Bentrupperbäumer is a Senior Research Fellow and Project Leader with the Rainforest CRC and Lecturer at Tropical Environmental Science and Geography and the School of Psychology, James Cook University, Cairns, Queensland. She holds degrees in biological and behavioural sciences. Her current research incorporates an interdisciplinary approach exploring reciprocal relationships indigenous and non-indigenous people have with the natural/built/social/cultural environment in World Heritage Areas and the implications of such relationships for environmental management, tourism and local communities in the region.

Kate Rodger is currently undertaking a PhD in wildlife tourism in the School of Environmental Science, Murdoch University, Perth, Western Australia. She has degrees in conservation biology and environmental science and is currently investigating ways to improve the use of science in the sustainable management of wildlife tourism.

Mike Calver is an Associate Professor in the School of Biological Sciences and Biotechnology at Murdoch University, Perth, Western Australia, where he teaches and researches in animal ecology. He holds degrees in animal ecology and education. He has published extensively on both vertebrate and invertebrate ecology, including both theoretical topics such as food selection and practical applications such as pest control. He is currently on the editorial board of the journal *Pacific Conservation Biology*.

Chapter 1
Viewing Animals in the Wild

Introduction

Human fascination with animals has been around as long as the two have co-existed on planet earth. Relationships between humans and animals can take many different forms including being a source of food, clothing or shelter; use for scientific and medical research; as sport or entertainment; as a form of companionship; and/or a point of connection with the natural world. Understanding this relationship with animals is important because it shapes our feelings and actions towards them. This has a direct bearing on our view of animals in and for tourism.

According to Malcom Hunter's lively short history, the term 'wildlife' is less than a century old and was not included in major dictionaries before 1961 in the United States and before 1986 in the United Kingdom (Hunter, 1990). Ominously, its first use was in a book published in 1913 called *Our Vanishing Wild Life*, which foreshadowed the conservation crisis apparent during the second half of the 20th century. While this work defined wildlife primarily in terms of game species, it also included vertebrate species not regarded as game but perceived as subject to human harvesting or culling. Later definitions of wildlife often emphasise game animals, while others include all non-domesticated vertebrates and, in some cases, invertebrates and plants. This ambiguity creates problems when stakeholders with differing understandings of what is included under the term 'wildlife' debate management issues (Hunter, 1990: 4–5).

In this chapter wildlife is taken to mean all non-domesticated vertebrates, in keeping with the scope of recent major monographs (e.g. Berwick & Saharia, 1995: Bolon & Robinson, 2003; Bookhout, 1996). Although invertebrates and plants are excluded, this does not imply that interactions between them and wildlife species are unimportant in the overall well-being of wildlife populations, nor that these groups are unlikely to gain interest in wildlife tourism operations.

The development of the term wildlife was accompanied by the growth of the interrelated academic disciplines of wildlife biology, wildlife management and wildlife conservation. There are now specialist societies (e.g. The Wildlife Society http://www.wildlife.org/, East African Wildlife Society http://www.eawildlife.org/) and journals (e.g. *Wildlife Research* http://www.publish.csiro.au/

1

journals/wr/, *Journal of Wildlife Management* http://www.wildlife.org/publications/, *South African Journal of Wildlife Research* http://journals.sabinet.co.za/wild/) devoted to the study of wildlife and academic courses in wildlife biology at many universities.

Wildlife co-exist with humans but have generally been viewed as a resource by them. Traditional approaches to the conservation of wildlife have centred around their use to humankind. Even today the medicinal, agricultural and industrial importance of wildlife is stressed alongside the aesthetic and ethical value. The viewing of wildlife as part of nature is generally regarded as being either restorative or as a competence builder. These two themes seem to derive their origins in the overall view that humans have of the world. Generally there are two worldviews and people differ over how serious our environmental problems are due to their different worldviews. Worldviews come in many forms but the two most common vary according to whether or not they put humans at the centre of things.

Two examples are the human-centred or anthropocentric worldview that underlies most industrial societies such as in Australia and the ecocentric or life-centred worldview (Miller, 2004). An ethic of 'use' is the normative or dominant mode of how human beings relate to nature, where nature is viewed predominantly as a set of resources which humanity is free to employ for its own distinct ends. It is an instrumental and anthropocentric view (Wearing & Neil, 1999).

Key principles of the human-centred worldview are that humans are the planet's most important species and that humans are apart from, and in charge of, the rest of nature. It assumes the earth has an unlimited supply of resources to which access is gained through use of science and technology. Other people believe that any human-centred worldview, even stewardship, is unsustainable. It is suggested that human worldviews must be expanded to recognise inherent or intrinsic value to all forms of life, that is, value regardless of their potential or actual use to humanity. This is a life-centred or ecocentric worldview in which humans believe that it is useful to recognise biodiversity as a vital element of earth for all life.

The ecocentric worldview believes that nature exists for all of earth's species and that people are not apart from or in charge of the rest of nature. According to Miller (2004), people need the earth, but the earth does not need people. He suggests that some forms of economic growth are beneficial and some are harmful and that human goals should be to design economic and political systems that encourage sustainable forms of growth and discourage or prohibit forms which cause degradation or pollution. A healthy economy depends on a healthy environment as human survival, life quality, and economies are totally dependent on the rest of nature.

Human–wildlife encounters

Reverence for, the use of, and the appreciation of wildlife probably goes back to prehistoric times when human lives were linked with the animals that lived around them. Throughout human history various species have been domesticated and kept as pets and it is clear that animals play a diverse and crucial role in human society today. In more recent times people's appreciation of animals has become linked to issues concerning human related impacts on the natural world such as environmental degradation, ecological sustainability and the loss of biological diversity. Urban living, which isolates many people from natural ecosystems, their deep relationship with and interest in various species, natural history documentaries, concerns for the environment, relative affluence, increased transportation and technology and global conservation initiatives, all contribute to an ever-increasing interest in wild animals.

There also appears to be a strong desire within humans to have close contact with animals. Children appear innately fascinated with a plethora of animal species. At one level this is evidenced by the enormous interest in domestic pets. Moreover, over the last 20 years or so there has been an extension from traditional pets to more exotic animals such as snakes, lizards and large invertebrates, indicating that our interest in animal life has broadened.

All of this combines to explain the unprecedented increase in wildlife tourism (Table 1.1). The various approaches and attitudes that people have in relation to wildlife tourism also vary according to levels of education, interests and experience, cultural differences and according to the species of human interest. Different species illicit different responses from people, depending on whether they are seen as being dangerous, rare, large and powerful; 'furry and cuddly'; anthropomorphic in behaviour; or seen as being intelligent.

Wildlife tourism fundamentally comprises the viewing of wild animals but, as considered above, the desire to view wild animals sits within a complex framework that may result in target species being influenced in an unnatural and negative way. Chapter 2 explores this situation according to the 'wildlife tourism paradigm' and highlights a hierarchy of possible influences, commencing with the relatively simple action of finding wildlife through to a situation where wildlife may be fed, touched and manipulated through ignorance or even malicious intent. The paradigm (see Table 2.1) thus facilitates an overview and provides avenues where potential problems might be anticipated in a wildlife tourism situation.

People's views of the world form one part of their approach to wildlife and their encounters with them. The influence of television documentaries has particularly shaped the views of wildlife of people in the Western world. For many urban dwellers their view of natural areas and the animals within has almost been exclusively shaped by their view of the world as seen through the media of television, and to a lesser extent, motion pictures. Thus it could be argued that this virtual experience often represents their first, and sometimes their only, encounter with wildlife. Other encounters may be gained from viewing wildlife in captive or semi-captive situations such as zoos, aviaries or aquariums. These settings vary in themselves from small enclosed pens to larger

Table 1.1 Spectrum of wildlife tourism: Selected examples

Animal group of principal interest	Tourism activity	Example of location
Insects	Butterfly viewing	Baynes Reserve, Berkshire, England
Insects	Glow-worm viewing	Springbrook National Park, Australia
Crustaceans	Red crab migration	Christmas Island, Indian Ocean
Fish	Snorkel in freshwaters	Bonito, Prata River, Brazil
Fish and invertebrates	Snorkel/scuba dive coral reefs	Ningaloo Reef and Great Barrier Reef, Australia
Fish	Snorkel with whale sharks	Ningaloo Reef, Australia
Fish	Feeding and close interaction with stingrays	Cayman Islands, Maldives, Western Australia
Fish	Underwater viewing/feeding of sharks	Dyer Island, South Africa
Reptiles	Observing Komodo dragons	Komodo Island, Indonesia
Reptiles	Viewing turtle egg laying process	Exmouth and Mon Repos, Australia
Reptiles and birds	Observe pythons and birds	Bharatpur, India
Reptiles	Observe crocodiles via boat tours	Kakadu National Park, Australia
Birds	Independent or organised visits to reserves for birdwatching	UK, India, USA, Europe, Africa, Australia, South America
Birds	Visits to seabird breeding islands	UK, Australia, USA
Birds	Lodges catering for birdwatchers and offering guided tours	Peru, Costa Rica, Australia
Birds and reptiles	Boats trips on wetlands	Kakadu National Park, Australia; Pantanal, Brazil
Birds and mammals	Islands containing rare, endangered and/or rehabilitated populations	Kapati Island, New Zealand; Rottnest Island, Australia
Birds	Independent travellers and coach tours to see breeding albatross colony	Taiaroa Head, New Zealand
Mammals	Vehicle safari to see large concentrations of mammals	Masai Mara, Kenya; Ngorongoro Crater, Tanzania
Mammals	Tiger viewing from hides or elephant back. Forest lodges.	Chitwan National Park, Nepal, India

Table 1.1 (*cont.*) Spectrum of wildlife tourism: Selected examples

Animal group of principal interest	Tourism activity	Example of location
Mammals	Mountain trek and camping in order to observe habituated gorillas	Virunga National Park, West Africa
Mammals	Overnight stay in forest hides in order to view mammals attending a salt lick	Taman Negara National Park, Malaysia
Mammals	Guided tour to observe nocturnal species	Atherton Tableland, Australia (vehicle access and night walk)
Mammals	Boat and/or shore based observation of cetaceans and pinnipeds	Australia, South Africa, Argentina, USA
Mammals	Independent travellers and coach tours attending structured feeding programme. Resort facilities	Monkey Mia, Shark Bay, Western Australia

fenced areas. These are described as setting preferences for human–wildlife encounters within containment lines where the experience is mediated, but none the less rewarding for the viewers. Settings beyond containment lines occur when the wild animal is viewed in its own environment. Here the encounter is usually both natural and emotional for the viewer. Accepted examples of human–wildlife encounters in the wild usually include photography, feeding and hunting where the first two are labelled as 'non-consumptive' and the last as 'consumptive'.

Sport hunters, hunting groups and game officials believe that humans should be allowed to hunt animals as long as they do not damage wildlife resources. Some of this sport hunting falls into the category of tourism with tourists paying to visit places specifically to hunt and kill wildlife. Examples include sport fishing and big game hunting. Such hunting is tacitly supported by some environmental groups as a way of preserving biological diversity by helping prevent depletion of other native animal species (Miller, 2004). Other groups oppose such hunting altogether on the basis that it reduces the genetic quality of remaining wildlife populations because hunters are most likely to kill the largest and strongest animals. By contrast, natural predators tend to improve population quality by eliminating weak and sick individuals. However, an underlying principle of wildlife tourism is that is should be fostering conservation of species, and therefore, the hunting of wildlife as a tourism activity seems to be inconsistent, unjustified and unnecessary.

Weaver (2001a,b) makes a distinction between consumptive and non-consumptive wildlife tourism. The former embraces tangible products while the latter focuses on experiences. He states that consumptive activities include hunting and fishing whereas non-consumptive wildlife tourism includes birdwatching. By extension this also includes other forms of wildlife viewing as well as wildlife photography. Both form parts of a continuum in which there is often some overlap. Weaver (2001a,b) illustrates this by suggesting that most hunting excursions end without a kill being achieved and the experience of being 'in the wild' is valued just as highly by hunters as the hunting/kill element itself. Conversely he notes that non-consumptive wildlife experiences may include several forms of consumption such as the deterioration of the environment through erosion, trampling of vegetation and the establishment of facilities. He also suggests that the keeping of checklists of wildlife species is a form of consumption because once birders have checked off the species sighted it is no longer sought and is thus 'consumed'. Other forms of consumption include that of fossil fuels and the purchase of material souvenirs, both of which require at least some degree of resource consumption. However, the authors agree with Duffus and Dearden (1990) who suggest that there is a fundamental difference between touristic activities which seek to destroy and remove an animal and those that do not (Box 1.1).

Box 1.1   Is fishing wildlife tourism?

An interesting debate has occurred over whether bill-fish fishing constitutes an ecotourism (or in this case, a wildlife tourism activity. Holland *et al.* (1998) explored the boundaries of ecotourism by suggesting that bill-fish 'catch-and-release' fishing was an ethical treatment of the fish and as such it could qualify to be classified as an ecotourism activity. This brought a response from Fennell (2000) who challenged this assertion and suggested that fishing generally was not able to be viewed as being part of ecotourism as it was consumptive in nature. He argued that 'catch-and-release' fishing was only slightly more non-consumptive than consumptive along a broad continuum. In conclusion he stated that although ecotourism was founded on respect for plants and animals, along the way pseudo ecotourism has materialised which no longer affords such respect. He suggests that we need to better conceptualise and define ecotourism to ensure that such consumptive activities cannot be defined as ecotourism. This challenge brought a response from the original authors who redoubled their assertion that bill-fish angling is ecotourism (Holland *et al.*, 2000). They argued that not all fishing is consumptive and that fishers and wildlife tourists often shared the same values in regard to the environment. The authors concluded that Fennell was placing too narrow a definition on ecotourism and that if this was applied to other activities then ecotourism would become a term reserved for a narrow range of behaviours with limited benefits for all.

(From Holland *et al.*, 1998, 2000; Fennell, 2000)

Recently an economic argument has been made for the exploitation of wildlife for non-consumptive tourism to support long-term conservation (Wilson & Tisdell, 2001). Wilson and Tisdell (2001) illustrate their point through the case of the sea turtles which are harvested for their shell and meat in a range of countries. In addition turtle tourism can adversely impact on their breeding due to the increasing pressure by tourists wanting to watch nesting turtles. However, through managed and improved encounters it is suggested that sea turtle based tourism will provide educational, economic and conservation benefits.

Wildlife viewing in the wild

The immense scope afforded by wildlife tourism involves many actual and potential species occurring in a diverse range of environments. Some examples are noted in Table 1.1. Other aspects of wildlife tourism that could be added to such a table include the viewing of polar wildlife as in the case of cruise ships visiting the Antarctic Peninsula and tourism access into mountain and cave environments around the world (Plate 1.1).

Research carried out on tourist preferences in viewing wildlife has shown that the majority of people surveyed were interested in seeing mammals, then birds

Plate 1.1 Tourist group moving towards elephant seals and penguins on the Antarctic Peninsula
Source: Ross Dowling

next, with reptiles and invertebrates being consistently ranked lower (Bart, 1972, cited in Shackley, 1996). Research carried out in Australia also confirms the popularity of mammals with the general tourist public (Green *et al.*, 2001; Moscardo *et al.*, 2001). Furthermore, there is much interest in mammals as they display many features of appearance and behaviour that is of positive appeal to tourists. Primates and many marsupials fall into such a grouping.

People also like to see dangerous animals such as predators and aggressive herbivores. These traits, coupled with easy viewing, explain why the observation of wildlife in African savannah ecosystems is so popular. By contrast tourism in tropical rain forest environments has been much slower to develop because it is more difficult to see animals due to the presence of dense vegetation, and the nocturnal habits of many species. Despite this, specialist tourism operations centring on large charismatic rain forest primates have been developed in Africa and to a lesser extent in Indonesia.

Reptiles, invertebrates and other groups of animals, although generally less popular than mammals and birds, also feature as tourist attractions in their own right. Specific reptile attractions include turtle nesting areas, Komodo dragons, Galapagos iguanas and crocodiles and alligators at various sites around the world. Fish feeding can take place at coral reef sites as in the case of the Ningaloo and Great Barrier Reefs in Australia. Excursions to view dangerous sharks from the safety of dive cages are offered in South Africa. Invertebrates can also be a specific focus of attention as seen in glow-worm cave tourism in New Zealand and Australia and in the red crab migration on Christmas Island in the Indian Ocean.

Many wildlife tourism situations are unique in terms of sensitivity to and response to potential impacts. Potential impact situations are strongly dependent on the nature of the tourism activity and the numbers of people accessing the site. The situation is further complicated by factors such as the timing, extent and frequency of access. Other factors that add further variables in affecting potential impacts include habitat factors, seasonal factors, variations in the weather, breeding status of the target species, population size and other stressors that may emanate from the wider landscape matrix.

Tourism activities range from visitation from local and regional urban centres and free independent travellers accessing wildlife areas, the operation of small party guided tours through to regular coach party access potentially involving large numbers of people. Modes of access vary from walking, cycling, car and bus access on sealed roads, use of off-road vehicles, through to the use of animals such as dogs pulling sleds, horse trekking and camel and elephant back safaris. Water bodies and offshore islands require boat access. Occasionally spotter planes are used to locate species as in the case of whale shark and manta ray tourism in Western Australia. The tourism component may involve camping as in the case of wildlife centred guided walks/tours in Africa, Alaska and Australia. In many cases tourist hides / shelters and or accommodation will have been constructed in natural areas in order to cater for wildlife tourism and facilitate viewing opportunities (Table 1.1) It is also important to realise that wildlife tourism frequently does not sit in isolation from management, supervision and restrictions on access. Management exists in response to perceived impacts or is in place as a precaution where the impacts situation is not altogether well understood (see Chapter 6). It is important to point out, however, that negative impacts may still occur in the presence of management if management is ineffective or ignored by the visitor.

In recent years there has been a shift away from viewing animals in captivity to viewing them in the wild. This has been clearly illustrated in the case of dolphin viewing in the United Kingdom which has changed through the efforts of animal welfare and animal rights campaigners concerned about dolphinaria (Hughes, 2001). Their concerns focused on the issues of harm to the dolphins during transport to their artificial homes, the confining nature of the captive environment, and the encouragement of unnatural behaviours for entertainment. Through a campaign of education and direct action all UK dolphinaria were closed in the 1990s and these have been replaced by a growing wild dolphin watching industry based in sites in England, Scotland and Wales. Of the three the Scottish one in Moray Firth (Figure 1.1) has developed most strongly based on a population of relatively rare Atlantic bottlenose dolphins. The industry was regulated by a set of guidelines established under the Scottish Natural Heritage's Dolphin Space Programme's Code of Conduct but in recent times this has been replaced by an industry led voluntary code of practice. Hughes (2001) concludes that dolphin tourism in the UK represents a clear case where wildlife tourism has been transformed through a shift from anthropocentric to ecocentric views on wildlife.

The viewing of wild animals in the wild is the focus of this book. While clearly accepting that wildlife viewing in captive and semi-captive situations forms one end of a spectrum of wildlife tourism, this will be left to other scholars to define, characterise and interpret. Thus the approach taken here is grounded on an ecocentric worldview in which the human – wildlife encounter occurs in the wild or natural environment of the species under view. It is also focused on non-consumptive encounters and thus delimits the killing of wildlife for sport as lying outside of both our interest and writings. Therefore discussion of touristic and recreational trophy hunting and fishing has not been included in this book as it was felt that they fall outside the authors' ecocentric view of wildlife. This discussion has been canvassed by others and is left to them and others to pursue. Thus the overriding view of wildlife tourism is that it is best carried out in the wild and should be non-consumptive in approach.

Sustainability

The concept of sustainability has become a mediating term in bridging the ideological and political differences between the environmental and development lobbies, a bridge between the fundamentally opposed paradigms of eco- and anthropocentrism (Wearing & Neil, 1999). MacLellan (1999) argues that wildlife tourism may be a sustainable form of tourism development in relatively undeveloped regions. Provided it is well managed he suggests that it can deliver economic benefits, community involvement, and support for and preservation of the environment. He illustrates the rapid growth of wildlife tourism in Scotland over the past decade with a surge of interest in visitors wanting to undertake guided tours to areas where interesting birds and animals can be viewed in close proximity. The tourists spent almost their entire holiday in some form of wildlife study either through viewing the wildlife and / or photographing it. In the case of Minch, in north-western Scotland, a significant industry is growing around whale watching. While still in its infancy the industry is expanding and there is increasing demand from visitors. Consequently a management plan is being drawn up incorporating sustainable management strategies, codes of conduct (for tourists) and practice (for operators), regulations and licensing. MacLellan (1999) concludes that a key for the future development of the industry is the inclusion of conservation organisations in the decision-making process, and where possible, the management of the wildlife sites. He also suggests that environmental education is important to promote wildlife tourism as a contribution to conservation rather than as a tour to 'tick off' the species under view.

In wildlife tourism the focus is on sustaining the features that attract tourists against their alteration by tourism itself (Williams, 2001). However, he suggests that sustainability is a fallacious concept because it relies on the traditional worldview of progressive materialism. It assumes the natural world exists primarily to meet human needs and therefore it implies some form of determinable limit on the carrying capacity of local and regional ecosystems. He suggests that:

> modern science, rather than leading to greater certainty and foundational truth as forecast in enlightenment thought, ends up producing greater uncertainty ... and in ecology this uncertainty has moved to centre stage. Ecological thinking has shifted from a view of the natural world as dominated by harmony and order to one of instability and catastrophe. (Williams, 2001: 363)

He notes that 'modern' ecology espouses change, disequilibrium and chaos and thus the concept of carrying capacity, which assumes stable ecosystems, is now discredited. He concludes that sustainability is ultimately a cultural concept.

Development cannot take place upon a deteriorating environmental resource base, neither can the environment be protected when development excludes the cost of its destruction (Holden, 2000). He asserts that the application of the concept of sustainable development to tourism has led to different perspectives in its meaning. The major difference lies in the manner in which 'sustainable tourism' is applied more to the sustenance of tourism then to the resources from which it derives its benefits.

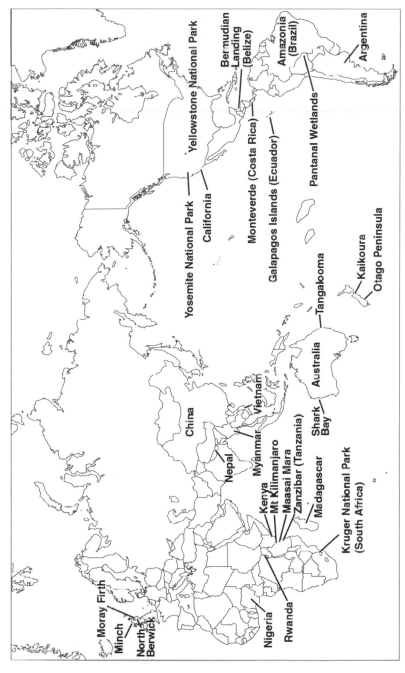

Figure 1.1 Location map of wildlife tourism destinations referred to in this chapter

The concept of sustainability is today understood as resting on the notion of the triple bottom line (Elkington, 1997). This triple bottom line is achieved by having solutions to problems or actions that are not only biologically and physically possible but are also economically feasible and socially acceptable. Even more recently, sustainability has been defined as 'meeting the needs of current and future generations through an integration of environmental protection, social advancement, and economic prosperity' (Government of Western Australia, 2003: 24). This definition goes beyond the triple bottom line through emphasising the integration between these factors and achieving them synergistically. The underlying importance of this new approach is its emphasis on how synergies can be found to provide mutually reinforcing solutions. Thus the development of wildlife tourism not only provides benefits to biodiversity conservation but also has direct community and economic benefits. This process has been referred to as 'bioprospecting' and often includes the additional benefit of preserving and/or enhancing traditional cultural knowledge (Government of Western Australia, 2003).

Tourism

Tourism is a temporary short-term movement of people to destinations outside their normal environment and their activities (Medlik, 2003). It generally concerns travel which is predominantly for leisure and which involves at least an overnight stay. All tourism comprises either mass tourism or alternative tourism. The former is characterised by large numbers of people seeking replication of their own culture in institutionalised settings with little cultural or environmental interaction in authentic settings. Williams (2001) states that tourism represents an instrument for preservation of various features of a material system (e.g. natural landscapes, wildlife, culture, etc). He notes that while tourism can help preserve wildlife, natural landscapes and cultures on the one hand, on the other tourism can transform landscapes and habitats as well as the dilution of their traditional meaning.

Tourism can also be viewed as a form of 'conspicuous consumption' relaying cultural messages about lifestyle and identity (Holden, 2000). Tourist behaviour in destinations will not be uniform, and will be representative of a mix of a range of individual motivations with wider cultural forces, which shape beliefs and attitudes. Holden (2000) notes that in Kenya the development of tourism has placed both the land and waters under threat. In the parks the insatiable appetite of tourists wanting to see the 'Big Five' game animals of elephant, rhino, buffalo, lion and leopard, has brought about widespread disruption of wildlife breeding and eating patterns (Visser & Njuguna, 1992). At coastal locations the coral reef is under threat from sewage pollution from hotels, tourists walking on the coral, boats dragging their anchor chains through it and locals breaking pieces off to sell to tourists.

Alternative tourism, however, is usually taken to mean alternative forms of tourism which place emphasis on greater contact and understanding between hosts and guests as well as between tourists and the environment. Alternative tourism can be defined as forms of tourism that set out to be consistent with natural, social and community values and which allow both hosts and guests to enjoy positive and worthwhile interaction and shared experiences (Wearing & Neil, 1999).

There are a number of dimensions to tourism in the natural environment. Travel to natural areas is categorised in a number of ways according to the relationship between specific tourism activities and nature. They include activities or experiences for which the natural setting is incidental, those that are dependent on nature, and those that are enhanced by nature. These three dimensions of natural area tourism equate to the environmental education equivalents of education – in, about, and for the environment (Dowling, 1977). Thus by extension it is possible to characterise natural area tourism as:

- tourism in the environment – e.g. adventure tourism;
- tourism about the environment – e.g. nature-based tourism;
- tourism for the environment – e.g. ecotourism.

In adventure tourism the emphasis is on the activity, for example, white water rafting or scuba diving, whereas nature-based tourism is more concerned with the viewing of nature. Here the focus is upon the study and/or observation of the abiotic (non-living) part of the environment, e.g. the rocks and landforms as well as the biotic (living) component of it, e.g. fauna and flora. Where it differs from wildlife tourism is that nature-based tourism has a broader focus than purely the viewing of wildlife only. In nature-based tourism the whole landscape and surrounds is the primary focus for tours and it is more holistic in its embrace of the environment. It tends towards small-scale, but it can become mass or incipient mass tourism in many national parks (e.g. Yosemite, Figure 1.1). It is sometimes perceived as synonymous with ecotourism since one of its aims is to protect natural areas, but it also differs in its lack of overt environmental interpretation and/or education.

Ecotourism

Ecotourism is a subset of natural area tourism and may combine elements of both nature-based tourism and adventure travel. However, it is also characterised by a number of other features, notably its educative element and conservation-supporting practice. Ecotourism is nature-based tourism that involves education and interpretation of the natural environment and is managed to be ecologically sustainable. The definition recognises that 'natural environment' includes cultural components and that 'ecologically sustainable' involves an appropriate return to the local community and long-term conservation of the resource. There are five key principles which are fundamental to ecotourism; these are that ecotourism is nature-based, ecologically sustainable, environmentally educative, locally beneficial and generates tourist satisfaction (Dowling, 2001). The first three characteristics are deemed to be essential for a product to be considered ecotourism while the last two characteristics are viewed as being desirable for all forms of tourism.

Ecotourism is based on the natural environment with a focus on its biological, physical and cultural features. Ecotourism occurs in, and depends on, a natural setting and may include cultural elements where they occur in a natural setting. The conservation of the natural resource is essential to the planning, development and management of ecotourism. All tourism should be sustainable – economically, so-cially and environmentally. The sustainability of natural resources has been recognised by the national and state governments in Australia as a key guiding principle in the management of human activity. Ecotourism is ecologically sustain-able tourism undertaken in a natural setting. The challenge for ecotourism in any country or region is to develop its tourism capacity and the quality of its products without adversely affecting the environment that maintains and nurtures it. This involves ensuring that the type, location and level of ecotourism use does not cause harm to natural areas.

The educative characteristic of ecotourism is a key element which distinguishes it from other forms of nature-based tourism (Dowling & Wood, 2003). Environmen-tal education and interpretation are important tools in creating an enjoyable and meaningful ecotourism experience (Plate 1.2). Ecotourism attracts people who wish to interact with the environment in order to develop their knowledge, awareness and appreciation of it. By extension, ecotourism should ideally lead to positive action for the environment by fostering enhanced conservation awareness. Ecotourism education can influence tourist, community and industry behaviour and assist in the longer-term sustainability of tourist activity in natural areas. Edu-cation can also be useful as a management tool for natural areas. Interpretation helps tourists see the big picture regarding the environment. It acknowledges the natural and cultural values of the area visited as well as other issues such as resource management.

The involvement of local communities not only benefits the community and the environment but also improves the quality of the tourist experience. Local communi-ties can become involved in ecotourism operations, and in the provision of knowledge, services, facilities and products. These benefits should outweigh the cost of ecotourism to the host community and environment. Ecotourism can also generate income for resource conservation management in addition to social and cultural benefits. The con-tribution may be financial with a part of the cost of the tour helping to subsidise a conservation project. Alternatively it could consist of practical help in the field with the tourists being involved in environmental data collection and/or analysis. Finally the satisfaction of visitors with the ecotourism experience is essential to long-term viability of the ecotourism industry. Included in this concept is the importance of visitor safety in regard to political stability. Information provided about ecotourism opportunities

Plate 1.2 Guide interpreting hippopotamus footprints, in the World Heritage Region, Greater St Lucia Wetland Park, South Africa
Source: Ross Dowling

should accurately represent the opportunities offered at particular ecotourism destinations. The ecotourism experience should match or exceed the realistic expectations of the visitor. Client services and satisfaction should be second only to the conservation and protection of what they visit.

It has been suggested that ecotourism has a number of characteristics with it involving travel to natural destinations, minimising impact, building environmental awareness, providing direct financial benefits for conservation, providing financial benefits and empowerment for local people, respecting local culture, and supporting human rights and democratic movements (Honey, 1999). She then defines ecotourism as travel to fragile, pristine, and usually protected areas that strive to be low impact and (usually) small scale and adds that it helps educate the traveller, provides funds for conservation, directly benefits the economic development and political empowerment of local communities, and fosters respect for different cultures and for human rights.

Honey (1999) suggests that even places such as Myanmar, which once was wary of tourism, the former Soviet Union, eastern Europe, China, and Vietnam, which once tightly controlled tourism; are now on the ecotourism bandwagon. Some entire countries, such as Costa Rica and Belize, are billed as ecotourism destinations. Elsewhere, pockets are promoted such as Zanzibar (Figure 1.1), Mount Kilimanjaro, and the game parks in Tanzania; Amazonia, and the Galapagos Islands in Ecuador, the habitat of the mountain gorillas in Uganda and, before its civil war, Rwanda. In 1998, the World Tourism Organisation predicted that developing countries would continue to gain from the tourism boom and that international travellers would remain 'interested in visiting and maintaining environmentally sound destinations' WTO (1998: 3). While ecotourism and wildlife tourism are not synonymous, neither are they mutually exclusive as there is a good deal of overlap between the two.

Wildlife Tourism

Wildlife tourism embraces all three types of natural area tourism. It is partly adventure travel, is generally nature based, and involves ecotourism's key principles of being sustainable and educative as well as supporting conservation. An early conceptual framework for wildlife tourism focused on three dimensions of wildlife–human interaction (Duffus & Dearden, 1990). These include hunting and fishing (consumptive use), zoos and aquaria (low-consumptive) and wildlife observation and photography (non-consumptive). It also embraces the recreational use of wildlife which was based on three elements: ecology, the recreational user and the historical context of human–wildlife interactions. Permeating the original framework is the evolution of change of tourists over time, based on the categories of tourists in the tourist area lifecycle concept of Butler (1980), as well as their impacts on the site/species visited, based on the Limits of Acceptable Change management planning framework of Stankey *et al.* (1985). A study of the dynamics between tourists and albatrosses in New Zealand upheld the conceptual framework in its application to a bird colony and concluded that site users, contact wildlife species and the natural habitat of the focal species all demonstrate various dimensions of change over time (Higham, 1998). A further finding was that in the absence of deliberate management intervention, wildlife tourism attractions evolve over time to the detriment of both the visitor experience as well as to the wildlife observed. All three dimensions demonstrate widely varying qualities of experience, management demands and potential impacts upon the wildlife setting and the focal species (Higham, 1998).

Several other researchers have characterised wildlife tourism. Orams (1996, 2002) emphasised a spectrum of tourist–wildlife opportunities with a number of

Table 1.2 Wildlife–tourist spectrum

Category	Setting	Example	Human influence
Captive	Aviaries	Gondwanaland, Qld, Australia	Completely human constructed
	Zoos	San Diego Zoo, California, USA	
	Oceanariums	SeaWorld, Florida, USA	
	Aquariums	Monterey Bay, California, USA	
Semi-captive	Wildlife parks		Partially human constructed
	Rehabilitation centres		
	Sea pens	Dolphins Plus, Florida, USA	
Feeding wildlife		Dolphins, Monkey Mia, Shark Bay, Western Australia	Natural environment
		Reef Sharks, Bahamas	
		Kea (parrots), South Island, New Zealand	
Wild	National parks	Kruger National Park, South Africa	
	Migratory routes	Cape Cod, Massachusetts, USA (whales)	
	Breeding sites	Mon Repos, Australia (sea turtles)	
	Feeding/drinking sites		

Source: Orams (2002)

components: interaction opportunities (how tourists might come into contact with wildlife), management strategy options, and outcome indicators for tourists and wildlife (Table 1.2). Wildlife tourism has also been defined as an area of overlap between nature-based tourism, ecotourism, consumptive use of wildlife, rural tourism, and human relations with animals (Reynolds & Braithwaite, 2001). They included in their definition a wide range of activities catering for a wide range of

Table 1.3 The wildlife tourism product

No.	Wildlife-based product	Description
1	Specialist animal watching	Birdwatching or whale watching
2	Habitat specific tours	Usually diverse and/or rich in wildlife
3	Nature-based tours	Which focus in part on wildlife viewing
4	Eco accommodations	Located in wildlife rich habitats
5	Thrill seeking tours	Where large or dangerous wildlife are encouraged to engage in spectacular behaviour by tour operators
6	Artificial wildlife attractions	Viewing of species kept in captivity
7	Hunting/fishing tours	Consumptive use of wildlife

Source: Reynolds and Braithwaite (2001)

needs in a variety of ways. To them, wildlife-based products include specialist animal watching, nature-based tours, thrill seeking tours, artificial wildlife attractions and hunting and fishing tours (Table 1.3).

However, as previously noted, this book focuses on wildlife tourism in the wild, which is non-consumptive, sustainable and conservation supporting. Major wildlife experience destinations around the world include the Masai Mara, Serengeti and Kruger National Parks in Africa; Kakadu National Park in Australia; Chitwan National Park in Nepal; the Galapagos Islands and the Pantanal Wetlands in South America. Spectacular and charismatic species are also the focus of specific tourism activity as seen in gorilla tourism in Africa; orangutan viewing in Indonesia; lemurs in Madagascar, swimming with whale sharks in Western Australia; observing elephant seals in the USA and Argentina and whale watching in Australia, New Zealand, South Africa and North America (Newsome *et al.*, 2002). Besides those people who seek out specific species and concentrations of wildlife, the presence and observation of wildlife plays an important part in the recreational experience of hikers, campers and other natural area users.

Definition
Wildlife tourism is defined as the following:

> Wildlife tourism is tourism undertaken to view and/or encounter wildlife. It can take place in a range of settings, from captive, semi-captive, to in the wild,

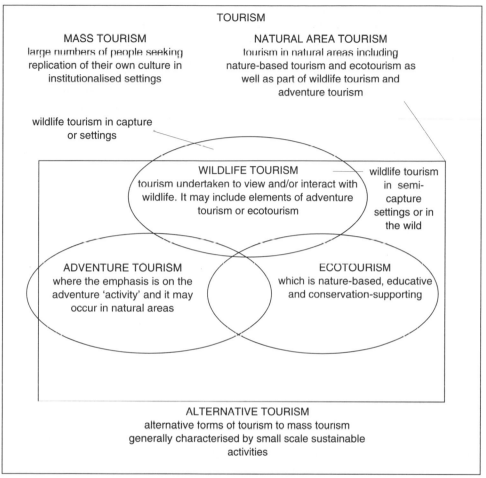

Figure 1.2 An overview of wildlife tourism's position within tourism

and it encompasses a variety of interactions from passive observation to feeding and/or touching the species viewed.

As noted previously, wildlife tourism is partly nature-based, may involve and element of adventure travel, and shares some of the key characteristics of ecotourism (Figure 1.2). When wildlife tourism occurs in natural areas it is referred to as tourism in the wild. Often there is an element of adventure for the tourist when travel occurs to relatively remote regions to view animals, some of which may be perceived as being dangerous. Wildlife tourism also shares some of the characteristics of ecotourism when it takes place in natural areas, is educative and/or interpretive, and fosters conservation supporting practices.

Some commentators include the killing of wildlife as wildlife tourism. Examples of this include fox hunting, wildfowling, sport fishing, poaching and big game hunting (e.g. see Shackley, 1996: 74). The rationale for including these activities as a part of the tourism experience is that they are sometimes undertaken by tourists. One argument is that hunting is lucrative and contributes considerable revenues to conservation programmes, as in the case of the CAMPFIRE Programme in Zimbabwe. However, we neither condone nor accept this practice and have deliberately delimited our definition of wildlife tourism to exclude any activity which results in the killing of wildlife as it does not sit comfortably with the ecocentric worldview that engenders respect for all living creatures. By extension the culling (killing) of 'overabundant' species by tourists is also excluded from the authors' view and definition of wildlife tourism.

Thus the definition of wildlife tourism we have advanced above is that it is a sustainable tourist activity undertaken to view and/or interact with wildlife in a range of settings.

Wildlife tourism growth

Tourism based on interactions with wildlife is increasing in popularity across the world (Reynolds & Braithwaite, 2001). The Ecotourism Society (1998) considered the scale of this market, estimating that between 40 and 60% of international tourists were nature tourists, of whom 20–40% of these were wildlife-related tourists. It also estimated that in 1994 there were between 106 million and 211 million wildlife-related tourists worldwide, although this could have included tourists who took a wildlife or nature-based trip as part of their holiday experience.

In the United States over 75 million people watch wildlife each year and it is now the country's number one outdoor recreational activity (Ceballos-Lascurain, 1998). In response to this growth, a national group of governmental agencies and conservation organisations created the Watchable Wildlife Initiative in 1990. Its goals are to promote wildlife viewing, conserve biodiversity, foster environmental education and generate economic opportunities based on ecotourism. California's Watchable Wildlife Programme was established in 1992 and is now the largest and most successful programme through its promotion of 'six steps to sustainable success' (Garrison, 1997). They include selecting sites based on regional diversity, biological sustainability and quality viewing as well as ensuring that each site provides adequate visitor services and resource protection. Another key goal is to provide 'seamless' recreational and educational opportunities focusing on quality products and a state-wide programme of visibility shared between all agencies. Other goals include establishing partnerships, identification of market segments, and the development of cooperative market strategies (Garrison, 1997).

Cater and Cater (2001) describe the explosive growth of whale watching through the examples of the industry in Kaikoura, New Zealand and Puerto Piramide in Argentinian Patagonia. Both destinations registered a 15–20 fold increase in visitation during the 1990s with over 60,000 visitors undertaking whale watching in Kaikoura by the late 1990s and in excess of 80,000 at Puerto Piramide. There has also been an increase in underwater observatories and semi-submersibles for the passive viewing of marine life. Such facilities have proliferated in recent years and are marketed as being environmentally friendly while providing visitors with the opportunity to observe and appreciate marine life in its natural setting (Cater & Cater, 2001). An integral part of such experiences is the interpretation provided by the experience so that visitors are motivated to protect the marine environment.

Wildlife tourism is on the increase in China. Many nature reserves, forest parks and scenic sites are now targeting tourists. The Chinese State Tourism Administration China designated 1999 as the national Year of Ecotourism with the theme of 'Touching, Understanding and Protecting Nature'. A survey of 100 provincial and national nature reserves across 29 provinces found that 82% were engaged in nature-based, predominantly wildlife, tourism (Nianyong & Zhuge, 2001).

Wildlife tourists

Often it is the quality of a natural area's living or biotic element, that is, the fauna and flora or wildlife that plays a primary role in attracting tourists to specific destinations (Newsome *et al.*, 2002). Wildlife tourists seek an experience that will enable them to explore, no matter for how short a time, a new ecosystem and its inhabitants. Some tourists are lifelong wildlife enthusiasts and others merely take day trips to a wilderness area from a luxury hotel base. Many such visitors seek to be informed and educated although others wish primarily to be entertained. There are many different kinds of wildlife-watching holidays; tourists can choose between a luxury hotel-based safari in Kenya, wilderness backpacking in the Rockies or an Antarctic cruise to watch penguins and killer whales.

Balantine and Eagles (1994) suggest that ecotourists, and by extension wildlife tourists, generally demonstrate the following psychographic characteristics. They possess an environmental ethic, focus on intrinsic rather than extrinsic motivation, are biocentric rather than anthropocentric in orientation, aim to benefit wildlife and the environment, strive for first-hand experience with the natural environment, and expect an educative and interpretative element. Besides those people who seek out specific species and concentrations of wildlife the presence and observation of wildlife plays an important part in the recreational experience of hikers, campers and other natural area users. Surveys in the USA (Hendee & Schoenfeld, 1990) and Australia (Smith, 1998) have shown that observing wildlife in natural settings ranked high with hikers and campers and added to their outdoor experience. Additionally, much of the scuba diving that occurs in kelp beds and off rocky shores and around coral reef systems is centred around viewing animal life. Given this sustained and increasing interest in seeing animals in the wild and the large number of different species involved there is a risk of negative impacts occurring.

Impacts are not just one way, created by the tourist on the wildlife, and they are not necessarily negative. Wildlife tourism also impacts greatly on the tourist, often as a peak emotional experience (Box 1.2). A study of whale watchers focusing on the observers rather than the wildlife, revealed some interesting findings (Orams, 2000a). A survey was made of 704 passengers on whale watch cruises at Tangalooma, Australia, and the findings revealed that a range of factors influenced their enjoyment including the number of whales viewed and their behaviour, the number of fellow passengers, cruise duration, boat construction and seasickness. However, the major finding was that the geographical proximity of the whales was not a major influence on the tourists' level of satisfaction with their wildlife encounter, and Orams (2000b) concludes that whale watching is not just about watching whales.

Box 1.2   The wildlife tourist experience at the Penguin Place, Otago Peninsula, New Zealand

An in-depth survey of 40 visitors to the Penguin Place, Otago Peninsula, New Zealand, was undertaken in order to find out how the wildlife tourism experience had impacted them. The Penguin Place is a private conservation reserve trying to save the world's most endangered penguin species, the yellow-eyed penguin (*Megadyptes antipodes*), from extinction. Virtually all of the international visitors described their visit very positively and most believed that their satisfaction stemmed from being able to get very close to the penguins. The most frequent experience reported by visitors was their 'enjoyment of viewing wildlife in their natural environment'. The main beneficial experiences reported were enhanced environmental awareness (cognition) and 'mood' benefits (affection). The authors report that as such, emotion played an integral part in the birdwatching experience, suggesting that the experience of wildlife viewers is a complex, sensory encounter. This is related to the viewing issues of proximity (being up front and close to wildlife), authenticity (viewing the birds in their natural habitat) and wonder (beneficial experiences of aesthetic appreciation). This understanding of human encounters with wildlife can assist in the development of sustainable wildlife viewing and may lead to increased conservation and the preservation of endangered animal species.

(From Schanzel & McIntosh, 2000; see Figure 1.1)

Stakeholders

There are a range of stakeholders in wildlife tourism. These include host communities, tourists, operators and managers as well as a whole range of other groups, organisations, businesses and government bodies. Importantly it also includes any person or group who expresses an interest and/or involvement in wildlife tourism. Thus working with stakeholders to advance the goals of wildlife tourism is a complex issue but one which must be addressed if successful wildlife tourism is to occur.

Involvement of the local community is based on the objective that local communities should benefit from wildlife tourism occurring in their locality. Benefits can be financial, employment, increased provision of services and facilities, and better planning, management and operation of wildlife tourism. Involvement can be as operators, providers of goods and services, employees, guides, and trainers; and participation in wildlife tourism planning, management and operation, interaction of the community with visitors or as recipients of income (e.g. the CAMPFIRE Programme in Zimbabwe).

People in local communities should have opportunities for involvement in wildlife tourism development, should have protection of their lifestyles, and should have interaction with visitors if desired. The attitude of the local community towards visitors is important to the tourist's experience, visitor satisfaction and, ultimately, the image of the destination visited. Cultural interaction is often sought by wildlife visitors and may or may not be welcomed by local communities. Local communities should be able to determine their preferred form and level of interaction with visitors.

Stakeholder involvement in wildlife tourism can occur in two ways, by being involved in decisions regarding its development as well as enjoying some of its benefits (Newsome *et al.*, 2002). Stakeholder involvement may occur in the planning process when local communities are acknowledged as a key group. However, the inclusion of other stakeholders is neither widely accepted nor practised. The second way in which stakeholders can be involved is in the benefits of wildlife tourism which can include both quality of life and financial benefits. Providing information and training for residents about wildlife tourism should help them maximise their benefits from such activities. In order to access such benefits residents may receive professional, vocational and entrepreneurial training as well as knowledge of the industry and its workings.

Involvement in decision making for wildlife tourism in natural areas, such as national parks, can range from manipulation of stakeholders by planners, through partnerships, to stakeholder control. These levels of involvement are explicitly described in Arnstein's (1969) ladder of citizen participation. The individual rungs of the ladder are:

(1) Manipulation
(2) Therapy
(3) Informing
(4) Consultation
(5) Placation
(6) Partnership
(7) Delegated power
(8) Citizen control

The ladder summarises a progression in the amount of stakeholder influence in decision making from non-participation (manipulation) to comprehensive participation (citizen control). For wildlife tourism to fully reflect the active involvement of stakeholders, then frameworks such as Arnstein's ladder of citizen participation must be included in the development process.

The integration of stakeholders in the development of sustainable tourism in the Arctic has been explored by Mason *et al.* (2000). Tourism in the Arctic is nature based and focuses largely on wildlife. The number of tourists is increasing each year and adverse impacts such as tourist litter and waste are becoming a problem. The environmental non-governmental organisation the World Wide Fund for Nature (WWF) has joined other stakeholders to integrate conservation with Arctic tourism. The collaboration includes tour operators, scientists, academics and NGOs as well as representatives of local, regional and national governments. The goal of the project was to integrate conservation ideals into tourism in Arctic locations to enable communities, tourists and operators to work towards a more sustainable form of tourism. According to the authors the project has been successful due to considerable consultation and negotiation thus providing all stakeholders with a feeling of project ownership. Outcomes of the project include the publication of a set of principles and codes in several languages as well as the initiation of pilot projects in a number of Arctic locations. The whole process has shown the value of including an environmental organisation in the development of tourism in natural areas.

An example of the initiative of the local community as key stakeholders in wildlife tourism development has occurred in the well-documented Community Baboon Sanctuary in Belize (Ryel & Grasse, 1991; Horwich *et al.*, 1993; Miller, 2004; Box 1.3).

Impacts, Policies and Management

Ecotourism provides economic benefits for many countries. Although nearly every country in the world, including the United States, Canada, Germany, Australia, and other developed countries, is now engaged in ecotourism and wildlife tourism, perhaps its most exciting potential is in its use as a tool for economic development and environmental protection in developing countries. Once, some of the world's oldest and most prized nature destinations, including the Galapagos Islands, Nepal, and even Monteverde in Costa Rica were visited by only the most physically rugged and intellectually curious. Now, however, with improved air and ground transportation, better accommodations, and extensive publicity, these destinations are being marketed to a mass audience (Honey, 1999). Wildlife tourism delivers only marginal benefits when it is poorly planned and unregulated. Therefore care must be taken to ensure that wildlife tourists do not damage or disturb wildlife and ecosystems, especially in popular or particularly sensitive areas. In Kenya's well visited Amboseli National Park, Maasai Mara Game Reserve, and Nairobi National Park, hordes of camera-carrying tourists packed in minivans have endangered the cheetahs,

---

Box 1.3   The Community Baboon Sanctuary, Bermudian Landing, Belize

The Central American country of Belize is home to black howler monkeys (*Alouatta nigra*). These primates live in troops headed by a dominant male. Vegetarians, they travel slowly among the treetops, feeding on leaves, flowers and fruits. This species is the centrepiece of an experiment recruiting peasant farmers to preserve nearby tropical forests and wildlife. The project is the brainchild of American Robert Horwich who met with the 300 people of Bermudian Landing (Figure 1.1) in 1985 and suggested that the villagers establish a sanctuary that would benefit both the monkeys and themselves. He proposed that the farmers leave thin strips of forest along the edges of their fields to provide food for the howler monkeys and allow them to travel through the sanctuary's patchwork of active garden plots and young and mature forest. Leaving strips of forest along the river, he noted, would also reduce soil erosion and river silting, yielding more fish for the villagers.

To date more than 100 farmers have done this, and the 47-square-kilometre (18 square mile) sanctuary is now habitat for an estimated 1100 black howler monkeys. The idea has subsequently spread to seven other villages. Now as many as 6000 wildlife tourists visit the sanctuary each year to catch glimpses of its monkeys and other wildlife. Villagers serve as tour guides, cook meals for the visitors, and lodge tourists overnight in their spare rooms. So as long as wildlife tourism does not grow so big that it negatively impacts on the monkeys, this experiment can demonstrate the benefits of integrating ecology and economics by allowing local villagers to make money by helping sustain the forest and its wildlife.

(From Miller, 2004)

which must hunt during the day to avoid having their kills snatched by lions and hyenas. During the 1990s the cheetah population in Amboseli had dropped to fewer than eight (World Resources Institute, 1993: 150, cited in Honey, 1999).

Impacts

In the context of wildlife tourism, nothing is more important than ensuring that wildlife is not impacted adversely by tourism. Achieving this goal can only be carried out by appropriate policies, planning and management that maximises the symbiotic relationship between wildlife and tourism and minimises any deleterious impacts by tourism. Avoiding negative impacts is essential for a sustainable wildlife tourism industry which is conservation supporting. This book characterises such impacts in three categories which are related to access, observation and close contact/feeding. Access issues differ according to the type of access whether by foot, road, off-road, boat or aircraft. Additional impacts on wildlife can occur when prolonged access comes about through camping and built facilities.

The impacts of observing wildlife vary according to the differing attitudes held by tourists toward wildlife. It is here where the importance of tour operators and guides comes in as they can help shape the visitors' views through increased awareness and knowledge. This can lessen tourists' disruption of the normal activities of wildlife and reduce the possibility of negative habituation traits.

Species vary in their degree of tolerance to human intrusion; for example, some species are shy and move away at the slightest detection of a human by sound, smell or eyesight. Previous experience, however, plays an important part in determining the response of a species to disturbance. The vulnerability of an animal to disturbance depends on its life-history traits and evolutionary strategies such as longevity, degree of parental care and reproductive effort (Hammit & Cole, 1998). Some animals, for example bears in the USA and elephants in Africa, are known to produce a more dramatic response to disturbance when caring for very young offspring. Tolerance levels can also vary with age, breeding season, time of year and habitat type. Furthermore, species with specialised food or habitat requirements are additionally more vulnerable than generalist animals. In contrast to this, species that live in large groups generally respond less to disturbances than solitary animals.

There are a number of direct and indirect negative impacts on wildlife caused by tourism ranging from motor vehicle accidents to disease transfer and behaviour modification. Direct impacts include death from vehicle accidents. For example, in Nigeria's Yankari and Kainji Lake national parks (Figure 1.1) the most common wildlife road fatalities are of bushbuck, roan, antelope and hartebeest. In Yellowstone National Park, USA, animals killed by motorists include elk, mule deer and wolves. Health issues for wildlife caused by humans include the risk of disease transference. Other direct impacts result from disturbance to animals hunting, feeding or undertaking other daily routines. Lilieholm and Romney (2000) state that other sensitive species may forgo the use of critical habitat for nesting or foraging, resulting in increased mortality and reduced health, fecundity and population levels. Other problems sometimes created by tourism include poor waste management, food refuse and feeding of animals, all of which can lead to an imbalance in the park ecosystem as well as a safety issue for tourists (Box 1.4). Increased contact with tourists can reduce the wildlife's fear of humans and lead to greater problems for local communities through crop raiding or personal threat. Indirect impacts of tourism occur through fire, vehicle impaction of soils, noise, and the construction and operation of tourist facilities and associated infrastructure. However, there are a number of management strategies to assist in the mitigation of adverse impacts on wildlife caused by tourists (Figure 1.3)

The impacts created by tourists getting close to and feeding wildlife can be significant. A critical issue are the expectations of visitors that may have been heightened through marketing and promotion. The feeding of wildlife often evokes polarised views with tourists actively seeking such experiences and conservationists decrying the practice. Solving such a situation is often complex and in many cases involves a considerable amount of science, management and understanding.

Increasingly, tourism is often used to provide an economic rationale to preserve natural areas rather than developing them for alternative uses such as agriculture or forestry. In current analyses of natural or protected areas it is this element that has become central, pushing debate onto the question of maintaining an area in its natural state as opposed to exploiting the resources it contains. This economic valuation is increasingly being used to justify the existence of protected areas through the demonstrable 'value' of both the wildlife and ecosystem features. Tourism is becoming increasingly central to these strategies given that tourists are willing to pay to experience these natural areas (Wearing & Neil, 1999).

Ecotourism generates as much as $20 billion in revenues each year. It is especially important to the economy of some lesser developed countries such as Kenya, Rwanda and Tanzania (Figure 1.1) (Miller, 2004). Kenya has developed national guidelines for ecotourism. All revenue raised by Kenyan national parks and reserves remains under the jurisdiction of the Kenyan Wildlife Service and is used mostly to provide better conservation of the protected areas. The government requires that tourist lodges give Kenyans preferential employment treatment for all but the most senior positions and use Kenyan food products as much as possible. Furthermore, every game-lodge visitor pays a $5 tax that is put into a trust fund for local use. Parks without lodges deposit a percentage of gate

Box 1.4   The impact and management of wildlife tourism on the Galapagos Islands, Ecuador (From Honey, 1999)

The Galapagos, originally known as the Enchanted Isles, is often cited as the place where wildlife tourism originated. This archipelago is universally viewed as one of the most unusual and precious ecosystems on earth: 95% of the reptiles, 50% of the birds, 42% of the land plants, 70 to 80% of the insects, and 17% of the fish on the Galapagos live nowhere else in the world. Since the 1960s, scientific research, sound park management, well-trained naturalist guides, and a fairly well regulated and responsible nature tourism industry have helped ensure that the wildlife of the Galapagos has been little disturbed by the steep rise in visitors (Table 1.4). But since the late 1980s, the Islands have had to cope with a variety of complex problems – new immigrants, introduced species, illegal fishing, and conflicts between towns people and park people – that have come in the wake of the wildlife tourism boom.

By 1997, tourism was providing an income for an estimated 80% of the people living on the Galapagos Islands and generating 60% of all tourism revenues earned by the Ecuadorian government. The Islands raise more money from tourism than does any other location in Ecuador, as much as $60 million annually in the mid-1990s, and in recent years there has been much debate over how to keep more of the profits on the Islands for the benefit of both the park and the local community.

The ecotourism industry's contribution to conservation efforts on the Galapagos has, on the whole, been positive because the industry recognises that its long-term success is based on a healthy and well-protected environment. Keeping footprints off the Galapagos means carefully controlling all visitors. Tourists visiting any of the 54 designated land sites and 62 marine sites must be accompanied by naturalist guides; about a dozen sites are the most visited, and the vast majority of the islands are off limits to tourists. Although the guides work for the tour companies, they must attend special training courses given by the park service and Charles Darwin Biological Research Station. Most are not Galapaguenos, and many hold degrees in biology or natural sciences and speak several languages. They function as both educators and guards. The guides make sure people stay on the narrow gravel paths, do not touch or take anything, do not take food onto the islands, do not litter, and do not disturb the animals. Before leaving an island, everyone carefully washes shoes off so as not to transport anything, even grains of sand, from one island to another.

Alleviate crowding in national parks
Limit visitation through higher entry fees or quotas
Control visitor use and access within national parks
Promote tourism at alternative public and private reserves
Create new national parks
Improve the design of park facilities
Improve habitat and wildlife protection
Introduce animal habituation
Create educational tours
Attract sensitive tourists and volunteers

Figure 1.3 Strategies for mitigating adverse tourist impacts on wildlife
(Lilieholm & Romney, 2000)

Table 1.4 Visitors to Galapagos National Park

	Number of visitors (in thousands)								
	1972	1975	1979	1985	1989	1990	1993	1994	1996
Foreigners	6.7	7	10	12	27	26	37	41	46
Nationals	0.1	0	2	6	15	15	10	13	16
Total	6.8	7	12	18	42	41	47	54	62

Source: Honey (1999)

receipts into local trusts. Money from these trusts is used to fund schools and hospitals, and to compensate local landowners. Each year, for example, almost 700,000 visitors pass through Kenya's national parks and protected areas, spending nearly half a billion dollars and making ecotourism the country's leading industry. A wildlife economist has estimated that in Kenya one male lion living to age 7 generates $515,000 in tourist dollars. By contrast, if killed for its skin, the lion would only bring about $1000. Similarly each of Kenya's 20,000 elephants brings in about $20,000 per year in tourist income. Over a lifetime of 60 years a Kenyan elephant is worth close to $1 million in tourist revenue (Olindo, 1991).

Another example of a country that has benefited from ecotourism is Rwanda, where tourism is largely responsible for saving the nation's mountain gorillas from extinction by poaching and habitat loss. A wildlife reserve created by Diane Fossey, who was murdered by a poacher because of her efforts to protect the mountain gorilla, has become an international attraction and contains 150 of the country's 320

remaining gorillas. The reserve has brought $4 million annually into the area sur-
rounding the gorillas' home giving local people an important incentive to protect
the gorillas.

Policies

According to McLaren (1998), thousands of communities around the world are
attempting some form of tourism development. Many people in communities
where abrupt transformations are taking place have little information about the
forces changing their lives. What is apparent, though, is that most of the communities are going through almost entirely the same process: fairly well-defined cycles of
expectation and disappointment. Yet tourism continues to grow haphazardly, often
to the detriment of local people, communities, and the environment, with little
long-term integrated planning.

The key strategy for wildlife tourism planning and development is that priority
must be given to ecological sustainability. The overall goal of planning for wildlife
tourism is the protection and enhancement of the wildlife tourism situation. Thus
it is important to identify wildlife resource values and the integration of these
values into decision-making processes which determine the location, the size and
type of permitted wildlife tourism activities. These decisions are primarily made
within the framework of management plans, zoning plans and systems for issuing
permits in natural areas. The policy of appropriate levels of use is therefore concerned with the identification of levels of acceptable change which are compatible
with the protection of wildlife together with associated natural and cultural
resource values.

In this book the focus is on policies rather than planning although both are essential for the sustainable management of wildlife tourism. Planning has been
recognised as 'a process of human thought and action based on that thought . . .
which is a very general human activity' (Chadwick, 1971: 24). This definition makes
planning a broad, over-arching human activity within which policies sit. Policies
are also defined as actions, while most definitions emphasise the decision-making
element of policies and policy making. Most definitions make it very clear that policies involve both a process of policy making as well as, but not always, a policy
document. A number of useful texts address planning in relation to natural area
tourism and by default are relevant also to wildlife tourism (e.g. Hall, 2000a;
Newsome *et al.*, 2002; Fennell & Dowling, 2003).

Understanding policies for managing or affecting the delivery of wildlife
tourism is essential if humans are to sustainably manage this form of tourism. Policies occur at, and are an expression of, the intersection of politics, society and
management. Because wildlife tourism is an interface between private enterprise
and public management and enjoyment, it is important to consider and understand
both public and 'private' policy, the latter encompassing policy developed by the

tourism industry and its members. Few policies specific to wildlife tourism exist; however, many affect the management and delivery of wildlife tourism, even if only in an indirect manner.

Management

Tourism management in natural areas serves three main objectives: the reduction of adverse environmental impacts, contributions to local communities, and the enhancement of tourist experiences. To be acceptable to tourists, management intervention should be low key and persuasive. Explanation and education through interpretation is the key to affecting tourist behaviour in ways considered to be environmentally and socially acceptable. Tourist management measures have been described as involving a spectrum of approaches from soft, to intermediate and hard (Jim, 1989). Soft techniques are aimed at influencing user behaviour, intermediate techniques focus on redistributing use, and hard techniques are those that are regimented and aim at rationing use (Table 1.5). Such a spectrum of tourist management approaches is offered for consideration and possible application at individual sites within a region.

A recent approach is to differentiate management into two broad groups of strategies and associated actions based on site management and visitor management (Newsome *et al.*, 2002). Site management actions seek to influence visitor use through manipulating the natural environment and facilities. Visitor management, on the other hand, relies on controlling visitor numbers and group size and education. Factors influencing the choice of actions by managers, such as cost and extent of impacts, are explored.

The development of wildlife tourism in natural settings brings with it an inherent responsibility to ensure that the animals are not adversely impacted. One form of tourism development policy in natural areas is to contain facilities and activities in specified areas in contrast to allowing dispersion of development and/or activities throughout a region. These development zones should be located where they do not pre-empt areas more suitable for other types of development for wildlife and/or environmental preservation. The tourists either remain within the cluster or take day tours to attractions outside the area. With regard to built facilities, clustering is superior to dispersal in terms of benefits to visitors and reduction of unacceptable impacts to the wildlife and host communities. The environmental argument for clustering is two edged. The argument in favour is that it can leave much of the environment (between clusters or nodes) in a relatively natural state and thus, by implication, enjoyable, renewable and cheap to maintain. The alternative, that of continuous strip development, is usually regarded as unsatisfactory for both environmental and practical reasons.

Another strategy used to reduce the negative environmental impacts of wildlife tourism is to separate out land use zones. The monitoring of impacts is important

Table 1.5 The tourism management spectrum

Measure	Management objectives	Techniques
SOFT Influencing use behaviour	To change user attitudes and behaviour Determination of tourist preference by market research Determination of tourist use by observation, visitor books, etc.	Using environmental information and education Establishment of a Code of Ethics
INTERMEDIATE Redistributing use	To reduce the contrast between heavily used and lightly used areas over time To raise lower use levels to match carrying capacity levels To redistribute uses so that their desired preference is matched by more appropriate settings	Concentration versus dispersion Information dissemination
HARD Rationing use	Controlling tourist numbers relative to type, place and time	Information dissemination Advanced reservation by permit Differential pricing, fees and queuing

After Jim (1989)

with the need to adapt and fine-tune management strategies in response to feedback on progress and performance. It is particularly important as part of the process of determining appropriate levels of use.

In most cases judgements will have to be made on the basis of best available information as to what are and are not 'appropriate' levels of use. In making these judgements, the precautionary principle should apply (Box 1.5).

Within the overall broad sweep of wildlife tourism there are many management approaches. These include managing access to wildlife, wildlife viewing and wildlife feeding. In addition wildlife education and interpretation is concerned with the extent to which education and interpretation can be designed not only to meet immediate on-site needs, but also contribute to enhanced wildlife conservation awareness which visitors may take with them when they return to their normal lives or visit some other natural area in the future.

Box 1.5   The planning and management of wildlife tourists at Monkey Mia, Shark Bay, Western Australia

Shark Bay is located on the eastern edge of the Indian Ocean at the most westerly point of the Australian continent. The bay is the largest enclosed marine embayment in Australia and covers 22,000 square kilometres of which 66% is marine. The bay straddles the tropical and temperate boundary of the world's climatic zones. The most unique aspect of the bay is the marine fauna and flora. It contains a large assemblage of large marine life including sharks, whales, dolphins and manta rays (*Manta birostris*). Shark Bay also provides a habitat for the world's largest herd of dugongs (*Dugong dugon*) that graze on vast seagrass beds covering 400 sq kms of the bay. In 1991 Shark Bay was inscribed on the World Heritage List. It was nominated on the basis of its natural values and when listed it was one of only 11 (out of approximately 400) World Heritage Sites to be inscribed on the basis of meeting all four natural criteria for listing.

The bay is also home to a pod of wild bottlenose dolphins that have been swimming into a beach at Monkey Mia to interact with people since the early 1960s (Plate 1.3). A recreation reserve has been created at Monkey Mia to guide the development and use of the area. The main goals of the reserve are to protect the dolphin population and their habitat, enhance visitor experiences with the dolphins, increase visitor awareness of the conservation values of the area, and maintain the area's conservation values while providing and encouraging recreation and tourism activities.

The dolphins are the prime destination for visitors to the area that generates a considerable contribution to the region's economy. In the early 1990s the dolphins were visited by over 100,000 tourists per year. Although visitor numbers fluctuate they appear to have stabilised at around 100,000 per year with July being the most popular month with approximately 15,500 visitors or 500 per day. The tourism industry is a rapidly growing component of the Shark Bay economy. A resort has been built at Monkey Mia and marine tour ventures include two catamarans which offer marine wildlife tours, a glass bottomed boat which visits a nearby pearl farm as well as boats for hire, ground and aerial tours.

Some 60% of Shark Bay's tourists are Western Australians. Others include interstate or international tourists (up to 40%). The most popular form of tourist accommodation in the area is in caravan parks. Perth people travel to the area principally by private car, a smaller number visit by commercial bus or air whereas interstate and international visitors usually visit either by coach or rental vehicle.

A management plan for the area has been prepared and its major focus is to maintain the interaction experience between humans and dolphins. A review of

dolphin management introduced regular beach feeding and a number of education, interpretation and research programmes. Over the next few years the resort
proposes to increase its capacity from 550 to 1375 persons. This increase will
place even greater pressure on the dolphin–human interaction experience.
However, using the precautionary principle, a study undertaken to review the
extent and type of possible future development at Monkey Mia has suggested
that the dolphin interaction area could cater for approximately 700 people per
day, 200 more than the present peak of 500 per day.

The population of Shark Bay is about 1500 and a survey of residents indicates that tourism generates more money for the local people than other
commercial activities suggesting that it distributes economic benefits 'more
evenly' than commercial fishing, mining or pastoralism. As tourism in the
area increases so does the number of outsiders coming to either invest or
work in the industry. The World Heritage strategy makes several provisions
for wildlife tourism within the area and recognises the need to provide a
range of tourism and visitor opportunities. The primary tourism development strategy is to ensure that conservation values are protected while
providing a range of tourism development opportunities. Wildlife tourism
provides the future for Shark Bay Region provided that it is well planned to
ensure that environmental and community goals are not displaced by economic imperatives.

(Dowling, 2001, 2003)

Science and Wildlife Tourism

In advocating an ecocentric approach to wildlife tourism, it is natural to want to
understand what natural science has to say about such encounters. This is usually
determined by wildlife biology which is concerned with how animals behave in
their natural environment. From this knowledge an understanding can be gained
of wildlife conservation and management specifically in the areas of species conservation, interaction and impact management, as well as education and
interpretation. However, it is argued that conventional wildlife biology with its
focus on animal behaviours does not provide adequate answers to the crisis that
many species are in because of the human impacts on them. Thus a new science
has emerged called 'conservation biology' which focuses on investigating such
impacts as well as developing appropriate management strategies to conserve
threatened species. However, application of this science to tourism is only in its
infancy and therefore it is an area of research which should be fast-tracked in
order to bring scientific knowledge to wildlife tourism so that wildlife can be supported by tourism.

Plate 1.3 Human–dolphin interaction at Monkey Mia, Shark Bay World Heritage Region, Western Australia
Source: Ross Dowling

Wildlife Tourism's Contribution to Conservation

Wildlife tourism is more than travel to enjoy or appreciate wildlife, it also includes contributions to conservation and community projects in developing countries, and environmental education and awareness through the establishment of codes of conduct for wildlife tourists as well as the various components of the travel industry (Kutay, 1993). One of the important contributions that wildlife tourism makes is its contribution to conservation. This is an ideal that is not always reached, but is one that underpins this type of tourism. The imperative for conservation advocates becomes how to conserve rather than whether or not to conserve. An economic rationale has been made for the exploitation of wildlife for non-consumptive tourism in order to bring about their long-term conservation (Wilson & Tisdell, 2001). In this way wildlife tourism is increasingly being used as part of a sustainable political philosophy for protected area managers and conservation agencies as a means of providing practical outcomes in order to fund continued protection for these areas (Wearing & Neil, 1999).

The tourism industry regards wildlife tourism and ecotourism as exciting new products to market whereas environmental and conservation groups tend to see them more as a means of conservation and protection (McLaren, 1998). A number of environmental groups and socially responsible organisations have joined the wildlife tourism industry looking for ways to promote and finance conservation efforts. They developed the first models of wildlife tourism conservation by using tourist fees to support conservation in wildlife areas and national parks. International laws were implemented to protect endangered species and large parcels of land were set aside as protected areas. Many of these conservation projects have been successful in generating funds for both wildlife conservation and local communities. Ideally, wildlife tourism's profits will help local people who in turn will participate in integrated, regional planning. The protection of natural areas for tourism encourages land use planning and through this rural communities will receive the economic benefits of wildlife tourism. In some cases it will support a range of activities from small-scale accommodations built by local people to large community tourism industries (see Box 1.6).

Outline of the Book

This book is intended to provide a review of wildlife tourism as part of the *Aspects of Tourism* series. It develops the subject of wildlife tourism as an applied science, and furthermore, the reader will be able to gain a feel for the scope of suc-

---

Box 1.6   The conservation value of birdwatching

There are a number of activities for improving the conservation value of birdwatching. One of the first requirements is the accurate provision of information on its financial contribution. Sekercioglu suggests that Costa Rica, a small Central American country that has promoted wildlife tourism, generated US$410 million from birdwatching alone per annum. Another positive activity is the hosting of birdwatching festivals. Over 240 such festivals in the USA generate millions of dollars each year for rural communities. Other suggestions include the education of citizens, businesses and governments on the potential adverse impacts of birdwatching and ways to minimise these, as well as the encouragement of birdwatching tour companies to financially support conservation of their tour destinations.

Birdwatching is a good form of ecotourism because birdwatchers are educated, wealthy and conservation supporting and they represent a large and growing segment of low impact tourists. It is suggested that they have the highest potential to contribute to local communities, educate local people about the value of biodiversity, and create local and national incentives for successful protection and preservation of natural areas.

(After Sekercioglu, 2002)

---

cessful wildlife tourism developments, primarily in natural areas, as well as the complexities arising from the range of different styles, types and levels of development. One objective of the book is to overcome the existing perception that wildlife tourism in natural areas is inherently adverse and that rather it offers a view that with adequate foresight, planning and management it represents a sound opportunity to bring about increased awareness and conservation of wildlife. The book is written in three parts. The first examines wildlife from the standpoints of ecology and human interactions. The second part reviews a number of aspects of wildlife tourism including stakeholder engagement, governing policies and impact management. The final part of the text introduces the role that science has to play in contributing to stakeholder understanding and management of wildlife tourism. This final section separates this book from the others that have been written on the subject and stresses the importance of a scientific understanding of wildlife through wildlife biology. It then suggests that a synthesis of science and management together should underpin the future of wildlife tourism development.

This book offers a number of useful points for further research on the intersection of wildlife and tourism. One underlying theme is that wildlife tourism, like ecotourism, is an appropriate vehicle to bring about greater ecological understanding. For this reason such tourism separates itself out from other forms of tourism. If people in the developed world seek to ascribe some form of legacy to the earth then one of the best ways of doing this is by gaining an understanding of our environment leading to its appreciation that inspires action for protection of the natural environment of which wildlife is a part.

Chapter 2 provides an overview of the key elements of the ecological impacts of human interactions with wildlife. Readers should note that the scope of this book does not address the social, cultural and / or economic impacts of wildlife tourism although references to these are made in a number of places throughout the text. In this chapter impacts are classified impacts into three categories – gaining access to and locating wildlife, observing wildlife and getting close to and feeding wildlife. The first is subclassified into impacts arising from access gained by foot, domesticated animals, vehicles or boat as well as prolonged access caused through camping and built facilities. Impacts attributed to observation including disruption and habituation are examined along with a special section on the searching for and observing wildlife at night. Finally the impacts associated with feeding wildlife are outlined. The chapter notes that it is impossible to provide an overall account of wildlife tourism's potential ecological impacts due to the diversity in site characteristics, types of tourists and species viewed. However, the chapter concludes by summarising the major impact issues and providing a framework for anticipating and understanding all of the major sources of negative impact in wildlife tourism.

The third chapter, written by Dr Joan Bentrupperbäumer, provides an account of the human impacts of wildlife interactions. Drawing from a range of disciplines the chapter extracts a number of underlying threads which are relevant to understanding human–wildlife relations in the context of wildlife tourism. It begins with an examination of why humans are interested in and attracted to wildlife through a range of characteristics including our similar natures, aesthetic appeal and our attraction to rare and endangered species. This is followed by an account of a number of differing views (e.g. dominionistic, utilitarian, moralistic) and encounters (e.g. actual and virtual) that people may have of wildlife in a tourism context. Actual encounters described include those within and beyond containment lines, photographing wildlife, feeding wildlife and hunting. Virtual representations of wildlife discussed are media representations, popular cultural images, marketing, interpretation as well as monitoring and managing the virtual landscape.

Having examined the ecological base and human dimensions of wildlife tourism, the following three chapters reflect on the conduct of wildlife tourism from a development perspective. Chapter 4 tackles the important aspect of stakeholder engagement – who they are, examples of engagement and the role of stakeholders in community wildlife tourism development. Engaging stakeholders in wildlife tourism development is a complex task often including government agencies, non-government organisations, protected area managers, conservation organisations, the tourism industry, local communities, tourists and individuals with a specific perceived or vested interest. Their engagement in wildlife tourism ideally should represent a partnership between local communities, the private sector and government so as to develop a conservation grounded, community based tourist attraction, accommodation or tour. In order to achieve this the importance of communications is stressed. A number of examples of stakeholder engagement are presented at a range of levels from local (park based), regional to international. The special considerations of indigenous peoples are also noted with an example of community involvement in wildlife tourism in Belize. A key contribution is coverage of the challenges involved in developing community wildlife tourism and the role of adaptive management. This type of management takes place when management responds to monitoring.

A monitoring programme is designed to detect impacts when a management strategy is already in place. If monitoring indicates any negative change then in the adaptive management approach there is provision to respond and adjust the management programme accordingly. Management is adapted to deal with and mitigate negative change in condition. This approach to the management of wildlife tourism is championed throughout the book and is one of its central unifying themes.

Chapter 5 describes wildlife tourism policies from the standpoint of both biodiversity conservation as well as tourism development. These policies are noted as sitting within a policy landscape in which it is important to have ownership established, otherwise there is the potential for open access and a 'tragedy of the commons' may result. It is suggested that this should be addressed before sustainable wildlife tourism can be achieved. As with the previous chapter this one describes policies at a range of levels from local to international including policies addressing both public and private involvements. Policy instruments are then classified and described with motivational, self-regulatory, economic and regulatory examples. Finally the factors influencing the choice of policy instruments for wildlife tourism are reviewed.

Chapter 6 provides an account of the various approaches that can be used in managing wildlife tourist interactions. It notes that specific tourism management plans are not widespread and, where management plans exist, aspects of tourism management tend to be incorporated within the general management planning process. Indirect techniques are concerned with influencing and modifying human behaviour and include various site and visitor management techniques. Site management includes the physical design of the setting such as the use of walkways, barriers and hides which influence visitor behaviours and actions. However, management may also involve the use of fees and permits, regulations, education and interpretation, all of which are described. A framework for managing negative impacts is presented that involves a number of specified objectives and actions designed to meet clearly identified objectives. The final section of the chapter explores the management of visitors' desires to feed wildlife and recommends guidelines for the structured feeding of wildlife.

In the third and final section of the book, the focus shifts to the role of science in understanding the impacts of wildlife tourism. Chapter 7, written by Kate Rodger and Mike Calver, describes the nature of science then introduces wildlife biology and its place in wildlife tourism. It examines the contribution of science to the sustainable management of wildlife tourism. It argues that through science data can be collected and analysed through the scientific process but at best, science can only predict the most likely consequences of management actions. This is best carried out through wildlife biology which can contribute to a greater understanding of impact management, monitoring processes, education and conservation, and problem prediction. The chapter concludes by noting a number of perceived barriers that impede research into wildlife tourism as well as the lack of, and the complexity and cost of research on wildlife tourism. Addressing this in the following Chapter 8 Mike Calver presents a research framework for answering questions about the impacts of wildlife tourism. The framework is described and integrated with major research approaches and field techniques. Key points are illustrated with examples from the literature on wildlife tourism and the chapter concludes with a consideration of how the results of well-designed impact studies provide the strong inference necessary for adaptive management of the wildlife tourism experience.

The final chapter reviews some of the key arguments presented throughout the book. It briefly examines the importance of understanding differing worldviews and the ecological base in understanding wildlife tourism. Planning for wildlife tourism development is then presented in relation to expanding the usual 'involvement of communities' to the more active 'engaging of stakeholders'. This is followed by advancing the platform of adaptive management in the ongoing sustainable management of wildlife tourism. The importance of science and wildlife biology is then explored in relation to providing a firmer base to make decisions for tourism planning as well as impact management and monitoring. Finally, future research directions are briefly noted.

Chapter 2
Ecological Impacts

Introduction

The introduction of the idea of ecodevelopment by the World Conservation Strategy (IUCN, 1980) led to the Bruntland Commission's (WCED, 1987) concept of sustainable development with its recognition of the interdependencies among environmental conservation, social responsibility and economic development. Now well accepted and advanced by many nations, the idea of sustainability champions the existence of ecological and social conditions necessary to support the increasing quality of human life through future generations. The objective of such stewardship should be to pass on to future generations a stock of natural resources no less in quantity and quality than that inherited by the present generation. In a tourism context this has a considerable validity because it calls into question the logic of unbridled tourism growth based on mass numbers without any concern for the impact on the environment, particularly in natural areas.

As already noted in Chapter 1, the advancement of wildlife tourism is underpinned by its sustainable base. Thus wildlife tourism, as a type of niche tourism, aims to meet the needs of present tourists and host regions while protecting and enhancing environmental, social and economic values for the future. By extension, sustainable wildlife tourism development should incorporate the management of its resources in such a way that it can fulfil economic and social needs while maintaining cultural integrity, essential ecological processes, biological diversity and life support systems (Page & Dowling, 2002).

A natural consequence of advancing sustainable approaches to wildlife tourism is to try to understand the impacts caused by wildlife tourists. These impacts can be classified as economic, social and environmental in nature and may be either positive (good), neutral (no net impact) or negative (adverse). For example, tourism can create economic opportunities for communities involved in wildlife tourism but it can also result in an economic overdependence on tourism and encourage price inflation (Holden, 2000). In a similar way there are also a range of social/cultural benefits for communities involved in wildlife tourism such as capacity building, job generation and the continuation of cultural traditions. The opposite occurs through limited participation, the establishment of menial jobs, and community intrusion and cultural disruption. While all of these impacts are important and warrant further scrutiny (see Chapter 4), this book and the focus of this chapter places emphasis on the ecological impacts of wildlife tourism, especially in the identification of its adverse ecological impacts.

The approach taken here is in accordance with the wildlife tourism paradigm presented in Table 2.1. The importance of understanding negative environmental impacts relates to the maintenance of viable tourism and consequent implications for planning and management. The main objective of this chapter, therefore, is to provide an overview of the potential negative ecological impacts of tourism on wildlife. Moreover, because of the wide range of species, situations and potential impacts (see accounts provided by Boyle & Samson, 1985; Green & Higginbottom, 2000; and Reynolds & Braithwaite, 2001) the main emphasis will be on some of the most widely recognised situations that include birdwatching and tourism centred on some mammals. The justification for this approach is that bird observation is carried out in many countries and that certain species of mammal represent wildlife icon status. It should be recognised, however, that there is an increasing interest in experiencing certain species of fish, reptiles and invertebrates in a range of locations around the world. Finally because of the complex nature of wildlife tourism (e.g. some situations may involve several modes of access and several tiers of disturbance, such as that indicated in Table 2.1) the examples provided here will at times cross over and often be transferable from one section to another.

Gaining Access to and Locating Wildlife

An overview of the various forms of access and the tourism implications of such access into natural areas is contained in Table 2.2. A very large proportion of wildlife tourism occurs in reserved areas such as national/marine parks and nature reserves and these areas usually have controlled access. Despite this a number of problems are detectable depending on whether visitors walk, use domestic animals for transport or enter through the use of vehicles.

Access on foot and/or in combination with the use of domesticated animals

Various studies have provided insight into the nature of disturbance caused by humans accessing natural areas on foot or in the company of pets/pack animals (e.g. Burger, 1981; Yalden & Yalden, 1990; Griffiths & Van Schaik, 1993). Burger (1981) examined the effects of human activity on birds at Jamaica Bay in the north-west part of the USA (Figure 2.1); the reserve comprises sandy shoreline, mudflats, salt marsh and freshwater ponds. The nature of avian response was found to depend on the type of disturbance, the location of various species and the species involved. For example, the rapid movements of people running in the refuge caused birds to flush from adjacent ponds. Despite their rapid movements

Table 2.1 The wildlife tourism paradigm

Elements of the wildlife tourism paradigm	Potential impact
Accessing natural areas to see wildlife	Construction of roads Noise and disturbance Road kill Barriers Pollution Facilities constructed in natural areas and close to wildlife habitat
Locating wildlife	Focus on breeding colonies and islands Locating migratory movements Targeting of rare and endangered species
Observing wildlife	Animal response to intrusion varies according to species, breeding status, sex, age, habitat and experience Focal activities such as spotlighting Can occur in sensitive environments (e.g. cave habitats)
Photographing wild animals	Potential for extended visitor–wildlife interaction Risk of close approach Disturbance to feeding animals (e.g. encirclement of predators by vehicles in African national parks) Animals may be followed May be attempts to manipulate and feed Focus on breeding birds and/or adults with young Small animals may be captured
Feeding wildlife	Disruption of normal feeding activities Nutritional problems for target species Attraction of scavenging species Habituated/attracted species a potential danger to visitors Risky and dangerous animals may have to be destroyed
Touching and close interaction	Risk of disease transmission Visitor conflict in relation to differing values regarding appreciation of wildlife (manipulative versus authentic) Habituated/attracted species a potential danger to visitors Risky and dangerous animals may have to be destroyed

Table 2.2 Accessing natural areas to see wildlife

Mode of access	Type of access commonly utilised	Advantages for the visitor	Potential disadvantages for wildlife
Walk	Trail	Absence of vehicle noise and more authentic experience	Off-trail access and increased disturbance. Damage to adjoining habitats
Riding another animal	Trail	More authentic experience. May be able to get much closer to target spp	Some species may disturb wildlife. Risk of disease transmission from domesticated animals
Use of off-road vehicle	Unsealed road	Access to remote and relatively inaccessible places. Increased search area	Off-road access and increased disturbance. Damage to adjoining habitats
Two-wheel drive and coach access	Sealed road	Increased access	Potential for increased speeds and larger numbers of people entering the area. Larger cross-section of visiting public and behaviours. Noise, pollution and road kill
Use of boats	Need for launching ramps Long trips require cruise ship facilities	Access to islands and aquatic environments	Wildlife disturbance and pollution
Camping as part of the activity	Trails and roads	Can stay in natural area overnight	Habitat damage and pollution. Some species may be attracted to the campsite
Construction of permanent tourist accommodation (hotel, resort or lodge). Vehicle access normally present	Road construction is usual but access can vary depending on location and potentially involve cars, off-road vehicles buses and/or boats and/or aircraft	Already on site for wildlife viewing opportunities	Habitat loss as a result of site clearing and development of infrastructure. Risk of pollution from waste disposal and energy usage. Some species may be attracted to the site

birds were tolerant of horse riders and birds only flushed when horses were close enough to trample them. The study showed that fewer birds were present when people were around. Gulls, terns and ducks were much more tolerant of human presence than migratory shorebirds which completely vacated areas where disturbance took place. This work clearly demonstrates that human access on foot has the potential to disturb the daily living activities of wildlife (see Table 2.3). It would also appear that wildlife is much more tolerant when access is gained through the use of animals.

Some areas may be accessed on foot in order to see species that arrive for the breeding season. The Peak District National Park in England (Figure 2.1) is one such area, as well as being subject to other heavy recreational pressures mainly from hikers. Yalden and Yalden (1990) studied the impact of hikers and walkers with dogs on the golden plover (*Pluvialis apricarius*) on a popular stretch of the Pennine Way footpath. The footpath traverses peat bogs that are an important breeding habitat for the golden plover. They found that the plovers were susceptible to being disturbed at all stages in the breeding cycle. Reactions included alarm behaviour and displacement of adults into adjacent territories. The incubation period was interrupted especially when dogs were present. Adult birds were also flushed from nests containing chicks. These reactions are energetically demanding, result in reduced feeding time, increase aggressive conflict between birds guarding adjacent territories and prevent birds from returning to nests containing eggs and chicks. These stresses are also likely to be significant contributing factors in declining breeding success and abandonment of the area as a breeding site.

People leaving designated trails will magnify these responses, as wildlife is likely to be disturbed further. Problems are also associated with wider environmental damage such as trampling of vegetation and damage to soils that may result in a reduction in the quality of wildlife habitat (detailed in Newsome *et al.*, 2002).

Access via roads

Roads are vital assets in the successful operation of wildlife tourism but also a potential source of negative impact (Plate 2.1). The landscape ecology of roads in the tourism context is documented by Newsome *et al.* (2002) who identify two levels of impact; the first is concerned with clearing and construction, and the second, which operates on a more or less permanent basis, largely involves noise disturbance, barrier effects and road kill. It is difficult to single out noise disturbance as the prime source of negative impact for wildlife but it is likely to contribute to stress, disorientation and avoidance behaviour. The avoidance of roads by wildlife will also help to reduce natural dispersal as well as acting as a barrier to migration. Conversely noise can help to prevent road death. Clevenger *et al.* (2003) found that road noise and disturbance played a significant part in being a deterrent to small mammals crossing busy roads.

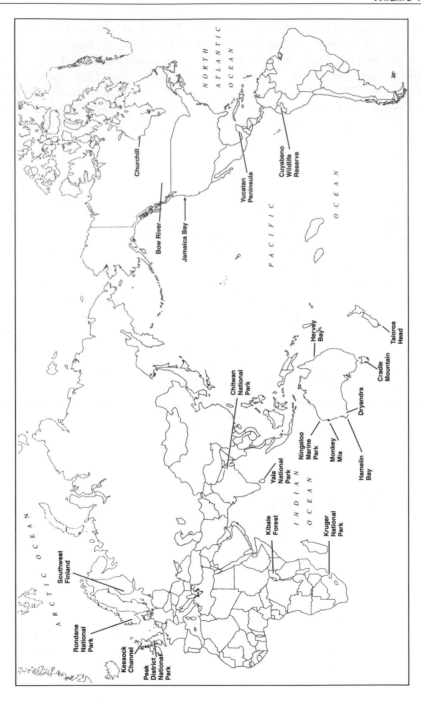

Figure 2.1 Map of sites referred to in this chapter

Table 2.3 Potential impacts of tourism on activities of daily living of wildlife

Activity	Aspects of tourism impact	Wildlife groups potentially affected
Navigation and orientation	Migrating species may be target of tourism interest. Disturbance at resting and refuge sites	Birds Bats Cetaceans
Communication to attract mates, deter predators, show fear, keep in contact with others	Noise Smell of humans and pet dogs	Birds Whales Wildlife with a high dependence on olfaction for communication
Finding food	Disrupted feeding patterns/ hunting behaviours Food provisioning	Wide range of species especially birds and mammals
Escaping from danger	Initiation of frequent escape responses resulting in stress and disruption to other normal activities	Wide range of species
Social behaviour in relation to colonial breeding, concentrations of wildlife and interaction within family groups	Disturbance can cause increased intra-specific competition and aggression between species	Birds Primates
Courtship and mating	Disrupted courtship displays and egg laying in birds	Birds
Breeding and egg laying activity/Rearing young	Disturbance that increases predation and mortality of young	Turtles Birds
Hibernation and aestivation	Disturbance (e.g. bat caves) resulting in additional and expensive energy expenditure	Bats and some other mammals Amphibians and fish that are dug out of dry water bodies are at risk
Moulting behaviour	Birds need safe refuges to undergo plumage moults. Moulting reduces normal activities and increases susceptibility to impact	Birds

Plate 2.1 Lions crossing a sealed road in the Kruger National Park, South Africa. There is a 2000 km sealed road and track network in the Kruger National Park. A wide variety of species can be seen crossing the roads. During the peak holiday and visitation period traffic congestion can occur when people stop to observe and photograph wildlife that is crossing or on the road. Some species appear to be habituated to the presence of traffic which without speed restrictions increases the risk of road kill. The speed limit in the park is 50 km/hr on sealed roads but the recommended speed limit is 25 km/hr. Fines are imposed for exceeding the limit and visitors may be expelled from the park.
Source: David Newsome

A more readily detectable impact, however, is the loss of wildlife that is killed as a result of crossing road corridors. Accordingly, road death as a result of vehicle collisions can be a significant problem in natural areas. Jones (2000) reports that the widening and sealing of an access road into the northern part of the Cradle Mountain–Lake St Clair National Park (Figure 2.1) resulted in a dramatic decrease in the populations of resident eastern quoll (*Dasyurus viverrinus*) and Tasmanian devils (*Sarcophilus harrisii*). Trombulak and Frissell (2000) maintain that traffic volume and vehicle speed are likely to be the most important factors in relation to wildlife deaths on roads. Furthermore, recent research has found that road kill is not random but spatially clustered and that road kill aggregations can be linked to types of land use, certain vegetation types, proximity to wetlands that attract wild-life, stretches of fast road, high traffic volume and according to whether fencing is present or not (Jones, 2000; Clevenger *et al.*, 2001; Clevenger *et al.*, 2003).

Clevenger *et al.* (2003) report on the complexity surrounding the road kill situation as evidenced in their Bow River Valley study in Canada (Figure 2.1). They found that for small vertebrates, mammals made up 46% of the road kill tally while 47% comprised birds, and amphibians accounted for 7% of deaths. It was noted that the greatest number of road kills occurred in summer. Mammals were most affected in April, birds during May to August and amphibians were most impacted from June to August. The seasonally aggregated nature of road kill is explained by the breeding and dispersal activity of small mammals and birds during the short summer season, the increased levels of activity making them more susceptible to road kill. The proximity of roads to wetlands is of particular significance as water attracts many species of animal. In particular large numbers of amphibians can be killed as in the case of migrating frogs, toads and salamanders (e.g. Van Gelder, 1973).

Clevenger *et al.* (2003) found topography, such as level and low-lying sections of road, to be a significant factor in explaining road kills of ravens (*Corvus corax*) and snowshoe hares (*Lepus americanus*). Snowshoe hares were also more likely to be killed when away from safe road passage such as culverts and when close to cover. Additionally mammals were more susceptible to being killed on the quieter and narrower roads while bird deaths were more prevalent on the wider, higher traffic volume roads. Clevenger *et al.* (2003) maintain that large busy roads actually deter small mammals from attempting to cross and the problem is more of a road barrier issue than road kill problem. Birds, on the other hand, because of their abundance and flight activity are more likely to be killed when crossing large and busy roads.

Off-road access and car parks

Where access roads take visitors to a focal point of interest car parking facilities may be provided. The car park itself may attract wildlife if animals are fed. Opportunistic and scavenging species may congregate as a result of this (Edington & Edington, 1986). Car park location can be important especially on beachfronts where marine turtles nest, as car headlights can disturb nesting adults and disorientate hatchling turtles (Waayers & Newsome, 2003). Moreover, when vehicles are driven along beaches for access and sightseeing purposes non-target species such as crabs and their burrows may be crushed (e.g. Wolcott & Wolcott, 1984). Furrows left in the sand by off-road vehicle tyres may act as barriers, slowing down the progress and increasing the predation mortality of turtle hatchlings that are making their way to the sea (Waayers & Newsome, 2003).

Off-road access allows the visitor to penetrate a natural area beyond the road network. The wider problems associated with this have been discussed by

Newsome *et al.* (2002) in the context of arid, arctic-alpine and tropical environments. In terms of wildlife tourism such activity allows greater penetration and coverage of wildlife habitat and increases the risk of disrupting the normal activities of wildlife (see Table 2.3). This can be problematical if there are no refuge areas or when wildlife is under some form of natural stress due to seasonal weather conditions. For example, in the USA, access from snowmobiles can be significant because wildlife is often under stress and in poor condition during the northern winter period. Impacts of disturbance to wildlife consist of damage to habitats and displacement from foraging and resting areas. Disturbance from snowmobiles can force animals to expend more energy in avoiding humans. Animals coping with severe winter conditions survive under conditions of reduced physiological activity. Any additional energy expenditure that is forced upon them may lead to a decreased capacity to survive the winter. This is especially so when food is scarce (Olliff *et al.*, 1999).

The potential impacts associated with both sealed and unsealed road access into natural areas constitutes a serious planning issue and necessary management actions are considered in Chapter 6.

Access via boat

Boats of various types and sizes are used to access concentrations of wildlife on islands, to observe wildlife along rivers and lakeshores and to view marine wildlife at sea. Most of the information on the potential effects of boat traffic on wildlife relates to the effects of general recreational activity but the impacts documented here are relevant to the wildlife tourism situation. Birds are a focus of attention worldwide and, at the same time, there has been a phenomenal growth in boat-based trips to observe whales and dolphins.

Marine mammals

Accessing wildlife by boat comprises two main issues akin to the terrestrial situation. The first is the potential risk of collision and the second is disturbance of wildlife resulting in avoidance behaviour (see Disruption of the normal activities of wildlife, p. 58). In relation to the former, cetaceans, pinnipeds, dugong and manatee are at risk depending on the situation. Collision with watercraft is a hazard for wildlife as exemplified by data on manatees compiled from Florida and Puerto Rico by Mignucci-Giannoni *et al.* (2000). In many instance it is not tourism but general recreational activity that constitutes the problem as in the case of excessive speeds associated with powerboat and jet-ski usage. Mignucci-Giannoni *et al.* (2000) noted that manatees had died as result of direct impact rather than propeller cuts, although they did find live animals with lacerations caused by boat propellers. Damage to wildlife in this way can be significant. For example in Florida, between

1974 and 1995, 25% (*n* = 644) of manatee deaths were cased by watercraft collision. In Puerto Rico it was 18% (*n* = 14) for the same period.

Boat-based watching of large whales remains the dominant component of an industry that involved 9 million people in 1999 (cited in Weaver, 2001a). Whale watching is thus a very important dimension of the marine based wildlife tourism situation. Various studies have explored the impact situation. For example, Blane and Jaakson (1994) investigated the response of beluga whales (*Delphinapterus leucas*) to boat traffic in the St Lawrence River estuary. Beluga responses to boats included spending more time underwater, increasing their swimming speed and bunching into groups. It was noticed that these activities intensified when there were more and closer boats and with faster boat speeds.

Other work also documents an avoidance response to boat traffic and whale watching activities. Grey whales (*Eschrichtius robustus*) have been documented moving away from the main whale watching centre at Tofino in Canada (Duffus, 1996) while humpback whales (*Megaptera novaeangliae*) in Hervey Bay, Australia, have been recorded to dive in response to boats within a range of 300m (Corkeron, 1995) (Figure 2.1).

Lutkebohle (1995) studied the way boats affected the behaviour and distribution of bottlenose dolphins (*Tursiops truncates*) in the Kessock Channel, Scotland (Figure 2.1). Dolphins were seen to engage in stops, changes of direction from the boat and carried out prolonged dives when boats were present. Lutkebohle (1995) also noticed (2 out of 23) positive responses where dolphins were attracted to boats. He concluded that it was not possible to determine whether dolphins would be negatively affected by boat traffic in the longer term.

Other investigators have explored different aspects of whale watching and boat interaction. Given the importance of song in communication, especially in the breeding season, Au and Green (2000) investigated if the noise emanating from whale watching boats might impact on humpback whales. It was concluded that boat motor sounds are unlikely to impact on the hearing function of the whales.

It would appear, therefore, that while avoidance behaviour is well documented some authors (e.g. Lutkebohle, 1995) remain cautious as to defining the long-term significance of such reactions on whales. The complexity surrounding how boat traffic might impact on whales is illustrated in recent work by Williams *et al.* (2002). In their study of behavioural responses of killer whales (*Orcinus orca*) to whale watching boats they recognised that boat noise can mask communication signals in killer whales, that killer whales give avoidance responses to boat traffic and that such avoidance responses (increased swim speeds, diving) can have energetic costs for the animals. They also note that the way a whale responds to boats could change over time as a result of habituation. The situation is complicated further in that there is some evidence of variations in response to whale watching activities according to different individuals and different groups of whales within the same species (Hoyt,

1996). Moreover, the long-term effects of cumulative short-term avoidance behaviour remain to be demonstrated. There is no evidence as yet to show that a population of whales has declined as a result of whale watching tourism.

Birds

Tuite *et al.* (1984) explored how recreational use affected wildfowl utilising inland freshwater bodies in England and Wales. They found that recreation resulted in short-term disturbance and brought about a change in distribution of birds either on the water body or in the local area. However, because of the mobility of wildfowl, the widespread availability of water bodies, the fact that many species have crepuscular feeding habits and that recreation occurred at a low intensity during the main over-wintering season for the birds, the level of disturbance was deemed to be minimal.

The situation, none the less, is different with species with breeding requirements. Many lakes and waterways in New Zealand are increasingly being accessed for recreational purposes. Bright *et al.* (2003) report on the effects of boat passes on the New Zealand dabchick (*Poliocephalus rufopectus*). It was found that a single boat pass caused a significant change in dabchick behaviour and this effect was amplified with further boat passes. Birds spent more time out of sight and in alert posture. Even though the dabchick does not fly, when disturbed the observable responses are considered to have energetic implications because of reduced feeding time, particularly when birds are displaced into neighbouring territories which results in conflict. Bright *et al.* (2003) also found that there was evidence of habituation at high boat use sites. In this case dabchicks spent less time responding to boat passes. The authors, however, maintain that habituation is not necessarily benign due to costly physiological responses (e.g. Regal & Putz, 1997; Fowler, 1999; see Figure 2.2). Moreover, other studies have shown that habituated birds still show reduced breeding success in high disturbance situations (Keller, 1989).

In terms of the marine environment two studies are described that demonstrate the potential effects of boat access on birds. They are particularly relevant in relation to tourist visits to seabird breeding colonies and boat based birdwatching trips. Mikola *et al.* (1994) examined the effects of recreational boating on the velvet scoter (*Melanitta fusca*) in south-west Finland (Figure 2.1). They found that the passage of a boat < 30 m from the birds caused the female to leave her ducklings and either swim towards or in front of the boat. The approach of boats caused the ducklings to dive. This forces the birds to use more energy and disrupts normal feeding activity. It took 20 minutes for the birds to recover and resume normal behaviour. Such a reduction in feeding activity could be especially significant in years of poor seasonal weather conditions. It was also observed that boating disturbance as described above increases the chance of opportunistic predation of ducklings by gulls.

The work of Ronconi and St Clair (2002) raises some important points regarding the sensitivity of different species and the relative importance of the characteristics of the boating activity. They identify the black guillemot (*Cepphus grylle*) as a particularly sensitive bird because it naturally forages close to the breeding colony. It was found that the birds were more likely to flush as the distance from the shore increased. This observation probably relates to the black guillemots' preference for 'cover'. Foraging near the cliffs offers refuge (cover) while foraging further out to sea means there is less 'cover'. The characteristics of the boating activity also influenced disturbance. Birds were more easily flushed when boats approached rapidly but boat speed alone was not a reliable predictor of disturbance. Small boats were more likely to flush birds than medium sized boats but no significant difference was found between small and large boats. Small boats were observed to generally travel faster than other sized boats and tended to have closer approach distances. It was concluded that approach distance was the most significant factor affecting flushing probability.

The work of Galicia and Baldassarre (1997), which is a study of tour boat visits to view wildlife, reflects the impact scenarios previously described. The study undertaken on the American flamingo (*Phoenicopterus ruber ruber*) in Mexico (Figure 2.1) demonstrates the effects of tour boat activity. Feeding time was reduced from 40% to 24% and alert behaviour increased by 400%. Recovery from loss of normal feeding rates took 10–20 minutes. In undisturbed conditions the flamingos would engage in courtship behaviour for 23% of the time. This dropped to 7% during a boat based disturbance event. Of 291-tour boat events 75% of these caused a change in activity in around 50% of the flock. Birds (30% of the flock) were actually caused to fly in 35% of cases. In relation to approach distance 23% of birds would be alert at a boat distance of > 100 m while this figure was 2% when no disturbance. The significance of this disturbance is that the increase in alert time translates into loss of feeding time. This in turn can impact on the nutrient status of the birds and thus compromises the birds in terms of the demands of pair formation, courtship and egg production.

Prolonged access through camping and built facilities

The provision of overnight and longer-term permanent accommodation in natural areas can facilitate the location and viewing of wildlife. Buckley (2003) details the nature of many such facilities from around the world. Potential impacts are noted but there are also social, conservation and economic benefits. In particular there is scope for environmental interpretation, guiding and the fostering of positive attitudes towards wildlife both from a local community and visitor perspective.

Site clearance and infrastructure development can, however, change conditions for wildlife (Buckley *et al.*, 2000; Newsome *et al.*, 2002). Loss of habitat through construction, erosion or physical damage to vegetation can result in the loss of habitat effectiveness in supporting various species. This is caused by either a loss of cover for a prey species to hide and / or loss of suitable habitat for a predator (e.g. Olliff *et al.*, 1999).

A change in conditions brought about by tourist resorts can result in avoidance or attraction of susceptible species (see later section: Disruption of the normal activities of wildlife, p. 58). When wildlife avoids an area this can translate into increased search effort on behalf of resort management and visitor alike. In other situations the attraction of wildlife may pose a risk to the visitor as in the case of Yala National Park in Sri Lanka (Figure 2.1) where an Indian elephant (*Elephas maximus*) has been observed to be attracted to visitors who were providing food. The situation is dependent upon the scale of development and the activities undertaken as well as the environment and the species involved. Some resorts cater entirely for the wildlife visitor while others may cater for a range of recreational interests.

An example of how a wild animal might be affected because it avoids an area is provided by Nellemann *et al.* (2000). Their work examined the avoidance of a tourist resort by wild reindeer (*Rangifer tarandus tarandus*) in the Rondane National Park in Norway (Figure 2.1). They found that although male reindeer were more tolerant, maternal reindeer tended to avoid the resort by a 10 km zone. Such avoidance could potentially impact on the productivity of the herd because of reduced available habitat and forage intake during the winter.

Some further issues associated with tourist developments can be drawn from the work of Lindsay *et al.* (2002) who investigated the impacts of lakeshore development on birds in Wisconsin, USA. They found that insect eating and ground nesting birds declined and seed eating birds increased where lakeside developments had taken place. Sensitive species (e.g. *Gavia immer*) were significantly associated with undeveloped lakes. It was thus concluded that lakeshore development had the potential to either improve or degrade bird habitat according to the ecology of the species involved. Those species (e.g. cowbirds) that are tolerant of, or benefit from, disturbance can affect the breeding success of other birds.

In some cases the owners and managers of tourist lodges / resorts engage in the supplemental feeding of wildlife. This occurs at O'Reilly's Guesthouse in Australia (Buckley, 2003). Here parrots are hand fed and visitors enjoy close contact with the birds. Supplemental feeding such as this, however, remains a contentious issue because of the risk for inappropriate foods being given out by uninformed visitors and the potential to attract opportunistic and predatory species that can affect the reproductive output of other species. The issues surrounding the feeding of wildlife are further discussed in p. 76, Box 2.4 and Chapter 6).

Summary of key points

This section demonstrates that the process of accessing wildlife habitats for tourism purposes has the capacity to result in negative impacts, the nature of which varies depending on the mode of access. The evidence points to wildlife being more tolerant of intrusion when humans use animals as a means of transport. Although many species can be approached more closely when vehicles are used the impact of roads via road kill and other impacts can be significant. The construction of accommodation facilities and use of car parks can further extend impacts when wildlife is attracted to food indirectly or directly supplied by humans. Moreover the use of off-road vehicles can extend impacts into less frequently accessed areas.

Access by boat can result in collisions and precipitate avoidance behaviour. Although the latter has been noted in relation to tourism focused on cetaceans long-term ecological impacts on these animals have not been proven. Birds are susceptible to disturbance when breeding but also show a capacity to habituate to the situation. Apparent tolerance to human intrusion should, however, not be taken as a neutral impact because of possible costly physiological responses and the energetic implications of reduced feeding activity.

It is important to note that some species are more sensitive to disturbance than others. Impacts can manifest as fatal accidents, attraction or avoidance or as all three in any given tourism situation.

Observing Wildlife

Human approaches and attitudes in wildlife tourism

From a tourist's point of view, the observation of many species of free-ranging terrestrial mammal is relatively straightforward, such as in the case of the savanna ecosystems in Africa, observing wild kangaroos in Australia or when viewing ungulates in North American national parks. Some mammals can, however, be somewhat more difficult to observe than others, requiring a more concerted tourism effort. This is the case with nocturnal species or low visibility species such as those that occur in tropical rain forests. Many large mammals can be shy, solitary, exist in low populations or be located in relatively inaccessible environments. Nevertheless, depending on the situation, the viewing of free-ranging terrestrial mammals can often be undertaken by individuals as an unguided walk or drive. It can also be coordinated in a group as in the case of safari tours or as a boat tour. Guided spotlighting activities are often aimed at predominantly nocturnal species and are a well established means of tourists viewing wildlife in Australia and in the Kruger National Park in South Africa (Figure 2.1). As more and more people are interested in, and taking, commercial tours the role of tour operators and guides becomes very important in ensuring that the wildlife experience is rewarding and sustainable in the longer term. Large, impressive species and apex carnivores are always a focal point of interest but can pose safety issues for visitors. For example, in Chitwan National Park, Nepal (Figure 2.1) the main focus of attention is to see a tiger (*Panthera tigris*) from a hide or go for a guided walk/elephant ride in search of the Indian rhinoceros (*Rhinocerous unicornis*).

In many cases there is often a desire for close contact and an interest in feeding wildlife (explored in more detail on p. 76 and in Chapter 3). Most visitors seem to approach wildlife cautiously at first. This could reflect some awareness that disturbance is possible but perhaps the single most important factor is the perception that they themselves may be at risk of being bitten or injured in some way. Children especially need guidance as they are self-exploring and unaware of any risk to wildlife or themselves. In unsupervised/self-touring situations there are always people who are uncertain how to react and there are others that exhibit some form of negative behaviour. Negative behaviour frequently entails trying to provoke some sort of response (Plate 2.2). More rarely deliberate destructive behaviour is seen resulting in the injury and death of wildlife.

Negative behaviours can occur in the presence of tour operators. In a study of tourism concerned with wild kangaroos in Australia, Higginbottom *et al.* (2001a) report the results of a tour operator survey in which operators identified the following problems that occurred when supervision of visitors was not always possible:

- visitor being wounded at one site;
- a single case of a visitor firing an arrow at a kangaroo;
- visitors throwing missiles in order to make the animals move;
- children chasing kangaroos;
- visitors rushing towards kangaroos;
- close approach of visitors for photography.

Inappropriate and/or ignorant behaviours appear to be common problems where supervision of large numbers of visitors is not possible and/or where, for some reason tour operators/managers cannot supervise all people for all of the time. (e.g. Butynski & Kalina, 1998; Litchfield, 2001; Lewis & Newsome, 2003; Newsome *et al.*, 2004).

Additionally, the increased operational activity and management of wildlife viewing as a result of increasing awareness of the attraction can bring about a change in visitor profile. The consequences of this are that the awareness and expectations of the majority of visitors can change over time. Duffus and Dearden (1990) describe an expert–novice continuum in which during the early phases of wildlife tourism development the visitors are likely to be well informed, appropriately motivated, few in number and conferring minimal impact on the target species and its environment. Over time and with a wider awareness of the wildlife attraction they describe the emergence of less informed, less motivated, more generalist visitors who are more likely to impact on the attraction (Plate 2.3). Moreover, such a trend increases the demand for facilities, the provision of more basic types of information and reduces the attractiveness of the site for the more specialist and genuine wildlife enthusiast (see Box 2.1).

Plate 2.2 Visitors engaging in inappropriate behaviour while visiting Carnac Island near Perth, Western Australia. Carnac Island is an important haul out site for Australian sealions. Visitors need to understand that sealions are hauled out and resting following physiologically demanding foraging activities. Orsini (2004) maintains that people need to understand this in order to fully appreciate the viewing experience. He maintains that otherwise there is a risk that people make attempts to elicit a reaction in order to get the sealion to do something.
Source: Jean-Paul Orsini

Higham (1998) details the nature of a changing visitor profile at Taiaroa Head in New Zealand (Box 2.1 and Figure 2.1). Similar trends have also been observed at Monkey Mia in Western Australia (Figure 2.1) where the food provisioning of dolphins takes place. Monkey Mia was a small-scale informal dolphin-feeding situation some 30 years ago. Initially only a few locals and a small number of tourists fed the dolphins that were attracted to fish discarded by fishermen. Now the dolphin feeding attracts some 100,000 visitors a year. Along with the increase in vis-

Please DO NOT
annoy, pester, torment,
plague, molest, worry,
badger, harry, harass,
heckle, feed, persecute,
irk, vex, bother, tease,
nettle, ruffle, irritate,
frighten, or shout at
the animals!

Plate 2.3 Public information sign outside the gorilla enclosure at London Zoo, UK. The sign illustrates the point that some members of the public may engage in inappropriate behaviour either deliberately or through ignorance. It serves the point of illustrating what may happen when an unsupervised and/or uninformed public comes into contact with wildlife.
Source: David Newsome

itors there has been resort development, the risk of increased impacts, and the need to manage and supervise the site according to a structured feeding programme (see p. 76).

Disruption of the normal activities of wildlife

The response of wildlife to human intrusion varies according to the animal's sensitivity and response to human presence (Plate 2.4), characteristics of the tourist activity and the effectiveness of any management that is in place (Table 2.4). General aspects of wildlife responses to humans are discussed by Newsome *et al.* (2002) and summarised in Figures 2.2 and 2.3. An example in support of the relationships depicted in Figure 2.2 is provided by Mullner *et al.* (in press). They examined the effects of ecotourists on the reproductive success of hoatzins

---

Box 2.1   The significance of an evolving visitor profile: The case of the Taiaroa Head Royal Albatross colony

Taiaroa Head contains the only colony of mainland breeding northern royal albatross (*Diomedea epomophora sandfordi*). Initially only visited by local residents and a few wildlife enthusiasts the colony was declared a fauna reserve in 1964. Guided tours of the reserve commenced in 1972 comprising two afternoon tours of up to 10 people on three days a week. From about 1980 onwards, visitor numbers, tours and days of operation were increasing and an albatross-viewing centre was opened in 1983. By 1991 a new reception facility was in operation, tour group size had increased to 15 and as many as 21 tours could take place on a daily basis. Higham (1998) notes that following the opening of the new reception centre the number of people on tours had increased significantly, especially in response to the arrival of tour coaches.

Visitor numbers had increased from a few hundred in 1972 to nearly 40,000 by 1990. The change in demographics coincided with a shift in visitor expectations. The novice visitors now far outweighed the wildlife enthusiast and birdwatchers. While these latter visitors would be able to achieve a high level of visitor satisfaction the expectations of the novice are different. Higham (1998) documents expectations of visitors desiring to walk among large numbers of nesting birds and showing interest in feeding and handling albatrosses. Such a situation, coupled with large numbers, noise problems and the use of flash photography, necessitates policing. The need to police inappropriate behaviour also impacts on guide satisfaction as the information that is delivered becomes more basic with less ecological content.

Long-term observations of the Taiaroa Head colony have shown that the nesting distribution of the albatrosses has shifted to areas further from the human activity where the birds are more exposed to the sun and at greater risk of heat stress. Increased nest temperatures can increase the hatching period and increase chick mortality due to fly strike. It has also been observed that where tourists are present chicks move up to 47 m from their nests as compared to only 12 m in the absence of disturbance. The former situation could interfere with the important activity of wing exercising and jeopardise chick survival in the longer term. Thus while in the short term the birds appear tolerant of human activity there is the possibility of longer-term impact.

Source: Higham (1998)

Plate 2.4 Elephant seal–human interaction on Macquarie Island in the sub-Antarctic. Close contact between a southern elephant seal (*Mirounga leonina*) and researcher on Macquarie Island in the sub-Antarctic. It has been reported that there are no significant detectable impacts from the presence of researchers and that these animals are very tolerant to the presence of humans on land (Engelhard *et al.*, 2001, 2002; Burton & van den Hoff, 2002). In a tourism situation, however, such close encounters should be avoided altogether as repeated disturbance may cause stress (increased cardiac output and production of stress hormones) and pose a risk for the visitor.
Source: Stuart Harris

(*Opisthocomus hoazin*) in the Cuyabeno Wildlife Reserve in Ecuador (Figure 2.1). It was found that hatchling success was higher in undisturbed nests as compared to those nests exposed to visitation by tourists. Juvenile birds at tourist exposed sites had lower body mass and a stronger corticosterone response to stress. Guides who reported that hoatzins occurred in larger numbers prior to regular tourism activity had noticed the lower survival of hoatzin chicks at tourist sites. The observed reduced breeding success can be linked to increased vigilance, increased levels of stress and energy expenditure, displacement of chicks from the nesting tree and reduced parental attention.

Table 2.4 Factors influencing the nature and degree of potential impact on wildlife

Environmental conditions	*Aspects of relevance to anticipating tourism impact*
Mode of access and implications for habitat alteration and wildlife disturbance	Walking on trail networks Walking off trail networks Use of vehicles on sealed roads Use of vehicles on unsealed roads Use of vehicles off roads Pollution and infrastructure factors associated with use of cars, buses, boats and aircraft
Environmental sensitivity	Scope for wildlife habitat damage in ecosystems exhibiting low levels of resistance and resilience
Sensitivity of target species	Sensitive species may be difficult to see or more readily impacted
Visitor pressures	Large versus small numbers of tourists per day
Frequency of visits	High versus low frequencies of potential disturbance
Human behaviour (also refer to Chapter 3)	Unsupervised versus supervised wildlife tourism as it relates to harassment, feeding and interaction with wildlife
Existing management (also refer to Chapter 6)	Rangers in attendance Education and interpretation Controls on visitation Site management Separation from wildlife Safe havens for wildlife Penalties for inappropriate behaviours
Adaptive management (also refer to Chapter 6)	Management response/s to evolving visitor profile. (e.g. change from specialist to mass tourism scenarios)
Political factors such as adequate suitable legislation and development control (also refer to Chapter 5)	Adequate planning and natural resource protection policy development
Empowerment of local communities (also refer to Chapters 4 and 5)	Local community interest in protecting wildlife and recognition of value of tourism as a sustainable use

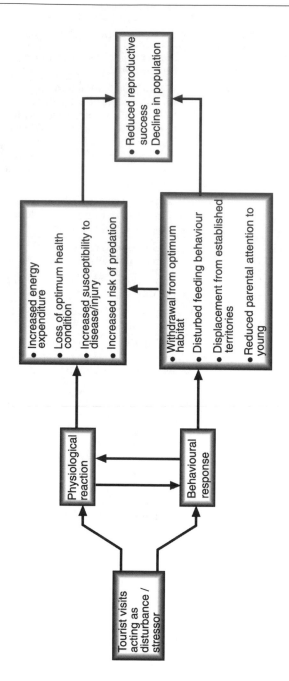

Figure 2.2 The potential linkages between an animal's reaction to humans and flow on ecological effects

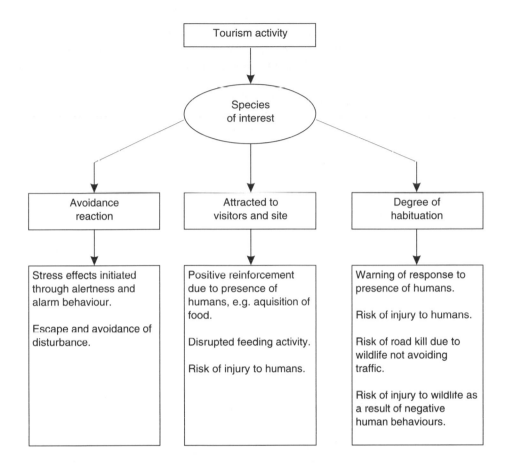

Figure 2.3 Potential response of wildlife to disturbance

As already noted, one of the first responses of many animals to human presence is increased vigilance or alertness, which can then result in avoidance behaviour. Avoidance is recognised as a potentially stressful reaction as reflected by a disruption of daily activity. The aspects of an animal's life that can be disrupted are indicated in Table 2.3. Avoidance behaviour, at the same time, is also a means by which shy and wary species keep a distance between themselves and close human contact.

Vigilance is a normal behavioral response especially in relation to the detection and observation of potential predators (Elgar, 1989). It also relates to prey detection

(Lima, 1994) and in observing others of the same species in regard to mating behaviour (Cowlishaw, 1998). Vigilance involves head lifting and visual scanning and interrupts other activities such as feeding and resting (Quenette, 1990). The implications of increased vigilance behaviour due to wildlife tourism are that other activities are reduced and hormonal responses can take place that increase heart rate and metabolic activity (e.g. Gabrielsen & Smith, 1995; Fowler, 1999). Any physiological response associated with the stress of ongoing vigilance that occurs in a sustained fashion (such as when there are continuous visits by tourists) can be detrimental to the species concerned (Saprolsky *et al.*, 2000).

Dyck and Baydack (2004) examined the vigilance behaviour of polar bears (*Ursus maritimus*) in response to tourist viewing from tundra vehicles at Churchill in Canada (Figure 2.1). They found that vigilance responses of male bears increased in the presence of tourist vehicles and that continued vigilance could translate into metabolic costs. They recommended that further work be undertaken to establish whether noise, vehicle activity and distance between bears and vehicles increased vigilance behaviour.

These latter points raised by Dyck and Baydack (2004) illustrate some of the factors that need to be taken into consideration in establishing degree of impact and developing a management plan for the situation. A further complexity that surrounds the perceived risk of physiologically stressing wildlife in tourism situations is brought out by Romero and Wikelski (2002). In their work on Galapagos iguanas (*Amblyrhynchus cristatus*) they found that baseline corticosterone levels were indistinguishable in iguanas at undisturbed sites as compared with tourist-visited sites. Moreover they found that the iguanas visited by tourists had 50% of the levels of known stressed animals. This difference can be explained as being attributable to habituation in the tourist-visited areas and that the iguanas are not chronically stressed as a result of tourism. As noted earlier, physiological change is a normal survival mechanism and the corticosterone release in iguanas is a survival mechanism designed to elicit a behavioural response in the face of natural environmental stress. Romero and Wikelski (2002) thus conclude that, because short-term hormone release is beneficial to the animal in bringing about physiological and behavioural responses to stressful conditions, the lowered corticosterone levels in habituated iguanas may reduce their capacity to cope with other stressors such as reduced food supply and oil spills.

In terms of vulnerability to disturbance Figure 2.4 shows the spectrum of tourism and biological factors that contribute to increased risks. Clearly if a tourism situation is characterised by a constant stream of large groups of people then this has the potential to make species concerned more vulnerable to disturbance. What people do and the way they conduct themselves can be critical in terms of reducing potential impacts. This is where management is so important in reducing impacts by providing sanctuary areas, keeping people at safe distances and supervising visitors via the

Figure 2.4 Factors increasing vulnerability of an animal to disturbance

presence of on-site wardens. There are several biological factors that increase risks to both wildlife and visitors alike. Wildlife is more sensitive to disturbance and potentially more aggressive when caring for young. Seasonal factors are important in terms of disturbance at migratory bird rest areas and when food supply is short due to difficult weather conditions. The habitat an animal is viewed in can determine its sensitivity to disturbance. For example, primates can feel safer if large trees are available to escape into and hippos can be approached more closely if they are in water. One of the most important factors to consider is the animal's previous experience with humans, hence the significance of habituation (Figure 2.3).

Habituation is when an animal learns to become less sensitive to a particular stimulus. This results in the animal reacting less and less and then not at all to the

---

Box 2. 2   Habituation: The case of the North American Elk

Elk (*Cervus elaphus*) habituate to non-threatening and predictable disturbance. Thompson and Henderson (1998) note that elk habituation can result in biologically meaningful effects that benefit the reproductive success of the species. Habituation means that elk are able to conserve energy during the normally physiologically demanding winter period. This is achieved by them accessing supplementary feed in some reserves resulting in the persistence of elk in areas where humans are present. Roads and trails that have been cleared of snow also allow easier access for elk reducing the expenditure of energy while foraging. Elk that preferentially use national parks and other protected areas and become habituated to humans may also be advantaged when faced with competition from other elk. All of these traits will help to reduce mortality and favour increases in population size. Thompson and Henderson (1998) caution that increases in a habituated elk population could result in an increased incidence of disease that could spread to domestic animals and even humans. The attraction of habituated elk to supplemented food also potentially increases the chance of aggression directed towards humans and damage to property.

---

presence of humans. The biological basis for such a response is that there is no benefit to be had from reacting to a stimulus that poses no apparent threat or danger. Valuable energy can be conserved as otherwise the animal would be in a constant state of tension (Box 2.2). This enables the filtering of stimuli that then do need a response.

Sometimes habituation is employed as a deliberate strategy in order to develop tourism around a highly valued wildlife experience. Because of their complex behaviour, intelligence and high degree of manual dexterity it is not surprising that monkeys and apes are highly sought after wildlife tourism experiences. Primates are either a focal point of tourism or form an integral part of wildlife tourism in Central and South America, Africa, Madagascar, India, China, Nepal, Japan and Southeast Asia.

In central Africa gorillas (*Gorilla gorilla berengei*) have been deliberately habituated in Rwanda, Uganda and the Democratic Republic of Congo. Butynski and Kalina (1998) report that the process of habituation can involve daily contact for as much as 24 months and that during the habituation period gorillas exhibit strong avoidance behaviours, suffer stress related diarrhoea and there is a risk of injury to staff. When people are in frequent and close contact with gorillas there is the risk of disruption to activities of daily living, especially social activities. Butynski and Kalina (1998) maintain that this is the case in well-habituated gorillas. Litchfield

(2001) highlights the problems associated with visitors wishing to be photographed (see Table 2.1) with wild gorillas. Park staff can come under pressure to allow visitors close contact with the animals or there may be attempts to bribe the guides so that they allow close access. Brochures that show tourists in close proximity to gorillas exacerbate expectations of close contact. A significant problem with deliberately habituating apes for tourism purposes lies in the risk of them contracting diseases, such as intestinal infections, respiratory infections and measles, from humans, especially where group sizes are larger, there is close approach and when visits are frequent (Litchfield, 2001; Woodford *et al.*, 2002).

Attraction (Figure 2.3) is where animals learn by association. This is where the animal links two or more sets of stimuli and then changes its behaviour to bring about a specific result. The presence of tourists may be associated with food and animals are attracted accordingly. Attraction can be associated with aggression because aggression has evolved to enable various species gain control of resources such as habitat, food, mates or territory. Thus where animals are attracted to tourist sites wildlife may exhibit aggressive behaviour to one another and to humans because there is an abnormal mix of humans and wildlife and/or concentration of animals that are competing for food. Where such aggression emerges and impacts on humans, the offending animals will have to be removed, relocated or destroyed by management (see pp. 76–77).

Impacts associated with watching wildlife: The case of birds

Bird watching is a very popular hobby and forms a significant part of wildlife tourism (Jones & Buckley, 2001; Sekercioglu, 2002) principally because birds are relatively easy to observe anywhere in the world, they are present in virtually all-natural areas and most are active during the day. Their attractiveness to humans lies in the diversity of plumage, behaviour and the wide range of sounds they make. Publishers have actively responded to this interest and birdwatchers are extensively catered for with support literature such as magazines and 'where to find' books. Furthermore there is a plethora of excellent field guides. There are more identification books and membership of bird conservation organizations than for any other group of animals. There are also many companies, based in Australia, the UK and North America that organise guided tours to birdwatching sites all over the world. Such tours help to promote ecotourism and have fostered an increased interest in the protection of natural areas in the developing world. Birdwatching is still increasing in popularity, takes place in many different situations (unguided self-exploration, guided tours) and is frequently associated with hiking, boat trips, car touring and camping.

Despite the fact that most bird enthusiasts will be well educated, conservation minded and committed to minimising their impact on the environment a number of problems have been reported (Table 2.5). Negative impacts can be associated with

Table 2.5 Negative impacts associated with birdwatching and birdwatching tourism

Activity	Impact	Significance
Close approach	Disturbance resulting in flushing of birds	Physiological cost of bird being flushed
Close approach	Reduced use of preferred habitat	Reduced breeding success
Close approach	Nest abandonment	Reduced breeding success
Close approach	Increased risk of nest predation	Reduced breeding success
Desire to see and record rare and endangered birds	Increased pressure on rare and threatened species	Birds may be more sensitive to disturbance and placed further at risk
Tape playing	Disruption of birds' social organisation	May cause stress and leave eggs and chicks exposed to predators
Accessing the site	Trampling and damage to vegetation	Reduced habitat effectiveness for some birds
Car parking and camping at popular sites	Pollution and littering	Attraction of scavanging species and displacement of species intolerant of disturbance
Large group size	Noise	Physiological costs of birds being flushed

Derived from Burger *et al.* (1995); Jones and Buckley (2001); Sekercioglu (2002)

self-exploration birdwatching and where there are organised visits to specific sites and breeding colonies (e.g. Anderson & Keith, 1980; Klein, 1993; Burger *et al.*, 1995; Klein *et al.*, 1995; Rodgers & Smith, 1997; Sekercioglu, 2002). This work shows that, even in protected areas, the apparently benign processes of observation and photography have the potential to disturb birds. Even where birds are viewed under guided conditions problems can arise. This aspect has been discussed in the context of changing visitor profiles and where a bird attraction evolves from one that is visited by enthusiasts to one that approximates to a mass tourism situation (see Box 2.1).

Birds are especially at risk when they are displaced from resting and feeding areas or when nesting birds are closely approached (see Box 2.3, Plate 2.5). Despite the general good level of awareness and care taken, some birdwatchers are careless in their desire to record and/or photograph a species that they have not seen before. For example, many self-exploration birdwatchers who visit natural areas in the

---

Box 2.3 Human visitation to colonies of breeding birds

A number of authors have reported on the actual and potential disruptive effects of recreation and tourism on colonial nesting birds in both island and mainland settings (e.g. Anderson & Keith, 1980; Burger *et al.*, 1995; Rodgers & Smith, 1995; Nisbet, 2000; Bolduc & Guillemette, 2003). Many species of nesting birds are susceptible to disturbance during the early parts of the breeding season which can lead to reduced reproductive efficiency. Those species that show low site fidelity are particularly susceptible because they tend to desert their nests in response to human intrusion. Mixed tern and black skimmer (*Rynchops niger*) colonies, for example, were found to exhibit a greater sensitivity to the presence of humans than other species (Rodgers & Smith, 1995).

Anderson and Keith (1980) observed brown pelicans (*Pelecanus occidentalis*) to be severely impacted by a single disturbance at the start of the nesting season. Eggs and young are mostly lost through predation. The authors observed western gulls (*Larus occidentalis*), attracted by the presence of humans, predated and damaged eggs. It was also observed that newly arrived birds did not construct nests in areas where disturbance had taken place. The situation was found to be more critical for Heerman's gulls (*Larus heermanni*) as, at the time, around 95% of the adult population nested on one island in the Gulf of California. Heerman's gulls are fiercely territorial and do not move until humans are only a few metres away. If humans succeed in disturbing the birds, for example by walking through the colony, severe displacement and confusion results in the destruction of eggs and aggressive attacks on the young by neighbouring birds.

Burger *et al.* (1995) report that human entry into heron colonies can result in higher chick mortality due to young and immature birds escaping the nest and losing the protection of parent birds. Additionally, the same species of bird can react differently to similar types of disturbance. This is illustrated by work carried out by Rodgers and Smith (1995) who found, in contrast to the findings of Anderson and Keith (1980) discussed earlier, that the brown pelicans (*Pelecanus occidentalis*) they studied were reasonably tolerant of human disturbance.

---

developing world are subject to offers of informal guiding or the assistance of 'guides' who are strongly motivated by cash in exchange for pointing out and providing tourists with a wildlife experience. Goodwin *et al.* (1998) report that unregulated guiding has impacted on birds in Keoladeo National Park in India. Rare species which visit the park, and nesting birds, are targets for close access and

Plate 2.5 Researcher taking photographs of penguins on Macquarie Island in the sub-Antarctic. In contrast to research activities tourism situations can result in a high frequency of contact between visitors and wildlife. Moreover, tourists are less likely to have knowledge about the wild animals they are viewing. Continued stimulation caused by the presence of tourists can lead to physiological responses in the absence of postural change in the species under observation and being photographed. Possible reactions include hormonal responses (Fowler, 1999) and increases in cardiac output (Culick *et al.*, 1990; Culick & Wilson, 1995).
Source: Stuart Harris

photography by birdwatchers. Goodwin *et al.* (1998) provide the example of attention being focused on a barn owl (*Tyto alba*) sighting, apparently an unusual observation in Keoladeo. As a result many visitors were shown and photographed the bird. It was then reported to have left the park the very same day. This example brings out the issues associated with photographing wildlife. As indicated in Table 2.1 the act of photographing a species can be disruptive especially if the bird is approached closely and flash photography is used.

Searching for and observing wildlife at night

The search for animals that are active at night includes sitting by badger (*Meles meles*) setts in England, supervised night drives in the Kruger National Park in South Africa and guided walks in Australian National Parks. Self-drive searching or walking at night has also become established in reserves noted for their wildlife as in the case of Dryandra Woodland in Western Australia (Figure 2.1). Marine turtle nesting beaches, for example, in Australia, Malaysia, North, Central and South America are also focal points of night viewing activities as people seek to observe marine turtles coming ashore to lay their eggs.

Spotlighting from vehicles in the Kruger National Park

Personal observation of wildlife during spotlighting tours in the Kruger National Park (Figure 2.1) by Newsome (2000) showed that small mammals generally tried to get away from the light. Larger mammals were slower to respond with some species, such as lions tolerating the spotlighting activity and not moving away. Spotlighting excursions occur virtually every night and are concentrated around rest camps in many parts of the park. They are coordinated by park staff and include educational commentary. Any disturbance of foraging or hunting is reduced because the total area of habitat subject to spotlighting activities is < 10% of the total reserved area. The night drives operate for only three hours each night and the activity is confined to proximity of the rest camps. Moreover the large size of the Kruger National Park means that extensive areas of the park are inaccessible to tourist related activity.

Observing marine turtles at night

Turtle viewing can take place as an independent activity or within an organised and structured programme. Impacts can occur primarily as result of ignorance as to how to observe a nesting turtle. Documented impacts include torchlight and noise discouraging turtles to ascend beaches or causing turtles to abandon the construction of nest chambers (Wilson & Tisdell, 2001). Other potential problems include the use of camera flash, touching and the blocking of turtles attempting to return to the sea (Jacobson & Lopez, 1994). Johnson *et al.* (1996) reported that organised and guided turtle watches in Florida affected loggerhead turtle (*Caretta caretta*) nesting behaviour because females were aware of tourist presence and did not spend sufficient time camouflaging their nests. The implications of not adequately camouflaging a nest may be that such nests are more prone to predation. In terms of the night viewing of hatchling emergence Jacobson and Lopez (1994) report on the digging and movement by tourists close to nests and trampling and handling of hatchlings by tourists. Without management in place it is possible that disturbance of this nature could negatively affect breeding populations of marine turtles (see Chapter 6).

Guided spotlighting tours and walks in the Australian Wet Tropics

Spotlighting tours focus on observing nocturnal mammals, birds and reptiles and in some cases invertebrates. The activity involves traveling to a suitable site and then walking with a guide, who searches for, locates and interprets wildlife. In many cases the tour party, comprising up to 15 individuals, are also issued with torches. Research carried out by Wilson (2000) provides some insight into the potential effects of spotlighting on mammals. In exploring the behavioural responses of rain forest possums (e.g. *Hemibelideus lemuroides*) to light she argued that bright light has the potential to temporarily degrade the night vision of a nocturnal species and noted that such an occurrence is particularly significant in the case of arboreal species that need to judge distances between trees when moving through the canopy of a forest. Wilson (2000) also found the noise (loud talking, snapping of vegetation, boisterous behaviour of children and crunching of footwear on gravel pathways) made by visitors had the potential to disrupt the social and foraging behaviour of possums. This is because human made sounds can mask those sounds that are meaningful to nocturnal wildlife. Disturbance from both light and noise is thus likely to result in vigilance and agitation with consequent avoidance behaviour that results in a decline in the numbers of possums sighted at night. Wilson (2000) also observed that the Herbert River ringtail possum (*Pseudochirulus herbertensis*) was more sensitive to spotlighting than other species and that the lemuroid ringtail possum (*Hemibelideus lemuroides*) avoided bright light more, this was relative to when lower light intensities were used for viewing. Approaches to the management of spotlighting activities in the Australian Wet Tropics are considered in Chapter 6.

Summary of key points

The impacts of wildlife observation can be strongly linked to the attitude and behaviour of wildlife tourists. Potential impacting behaviours consist of close approach, touching, feeding and attempting to illicit a response from the target species. Initial responses of wildlife include vigilance or alert behaviour that can lead to the displacement of an animal from normal activities or from its preferred location. Ongoing reaction of this kind can lead to chronic stress especially when avoidance of humans results in increased competition with the same or other species for cover and food and when there is a greater susceptibility to predation.

Habituation to tourism conditions may render an animal less able to cope with natural conditions and stressors. In some situations habituation may increase to risk of wildlife contracting disease from humans, put a species at risk from inappropriate human behaviours and/or promote the chance of collision with a vehicle. The attraction of wildlife to humans can result in unnatural concentrations of the same species and loss of fear of humans.

Getting Close to and Feeding Wildlife

Issues relating to visitor expectations and the manipulation of wildlife

There are two main spectra of client interest in wildlife both of which have a high negative impact potential at one end and a positive impact potential at the other (Figure 2.5). It is fortunate that deliberate vandalism is rare and there is an increasing interest in visitors seeking more natural and authentic wildlife experiences. However, as already noted, visitor profile changes can occur over time with popular attractions resulting in a shift from well-informed clients seeking an authentic experience to those that wish to control, manipulate and feed wildlife as well as wishing to amuse themselves at the same time. The most widely observed negative human behaviours include the feeding of inappropriate 'food' items, attempts to illicit a response, shouting, throwing objects and chasing wildlife. Sometimes these behaviours are the result of ignorance on behalf of adults and due to the excitement of over-enthusiastic children. Many people are simply unaware that an animal may not wish to be touched or crowded or that touching may cause harm in some way.

Visitor expectation is thus a critical issue in wildlife tourism in terms of advertising, operating and managing an attraction (also see Chapters 3 and 6). Tourism operators are often under pressure to satisfy customer demands which can encompass some or all of the following:

- a successful viewing of the target species;
- the safety and comfort of clients in close viewing situations;
- close access to target species;
- opportunities to photograph the species concerned;
- opportunities to safely touch the species concerned;
- opportunities to feed the species concerned.

Wildlife can therefore be manipulated in order to achieve the above desires and this can take the form of both informal and/or organised feeding and close interaction, the construction of artificial waterholes in order to attract and concentrate species, tour operator organised fish feeding operations (see Table 2.6), swimming and interacting with marine mammals and the deliberate habituation of species such as gorillas (see pp. 65–67). In terms of the less well informed and more generalist wildlife tourism client, problems of dissatisfaction and boredom can arise if, when at the site, they do not see the target animal; they have little awareness or no interest in the surrounding environment or they become saturated by the experience. In order to satisfy client expectation the most widespread form of wildlife manipulation is the provision of food in order to attract species for close access and/or to photograph an animal. Visitors often use feeding as an opportunity to touch an animal if it is perceived safe to do so.

Visitor Expectation Spectrum

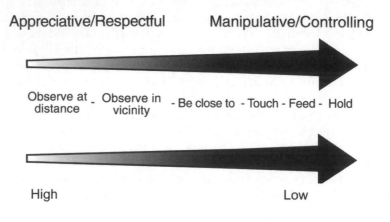

Visitor Attitude Spectrum

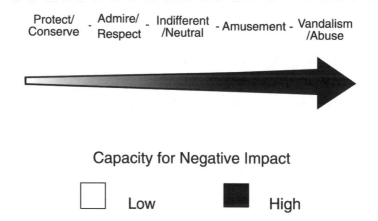

Figure 2.5 Spectrum of client interest in wildlife and its relationship to potential negative impacts on wildlife

Table 2.6 Issues and risks associated with food provisioning and the close approach to wildlife

Example of wildlife tourism situation	Risk to humans	Impacts and risks to wildlife
Formalised fish feeding (Great Barrier Reef, Australia)	Risk of being bitten. Attraction of dangerous species	Increased population of provisioned species. Fish sustaining wounds while competing for food. Pollution of local waters. Increased vulnerability to fishing. Dependence on supplemented food
Stingray tourism. Food provisioning and close interaction (Australia, Cayman Islands, Maldives)	Risk of being stung. Risk of being bitten. Attraction of dangerous species	Skin lesions from excessive handling. Dependence on supplemented food. Pollution of local waters. Increased vulnerability to fishing
Shark dive tourism (Bahamas)	Aggressive behaviour and risk of attack	Abnormal concentrations at feeding sites
Food provisioned wild cassowaries (north-east Australia)	Attraction to humans. Risk of aggression towards humans	Quality of provisioned food and health implications for the birds. Habituation to vehicles and risk of road kill
Close approach to African elephant during self-drive touring (Kruger National Park)	Breeding males may charge. Damage to vehicle and risk of injury	Stress associated with responding to human intrusion
Close approach to breeding pinnipeds (southern hemisphere)	Risk of being charged and bitten. Risk of disease transmission to humans	Increased vigilance and stress associated with avoidance behaviour. Risk of stampede. Disturbance to maternal attendance and care
Close approach to hauled out pinnipeds (southern hemisphere)	Risk of being charged and bitten. Risk of disease transmission to humans	Increased vigilance and interruption of rest period. Displacement from haul out site
Dolphins. Controlled food provisioning and close interaction (Monkey Mia, Australia)	Risk of being bitten	Risk of catching human diseases. Dependence on supplemented food. Disrupted maternal care
Dingo. Informal food provisioning and client behaving as if the dingo is a domestic dog (Fraser Island, Australia)	Risk of being bitten. Fatality recorded in 2001	Offending animal/s will have to be relocated or destroyed
Small to large sized monkeys. Close contact as part of tourism experience. Contact may include incidental or deliberate food provisioning (e.g. China, Japan, central America, Africa, India and Southeast Asia)	Risk of being bitten. Risk of damage to and/or personal items being stolen	Nuisance animal/s will have to be destroyed
Locating family groups of gorilla. Deliberately habituated groups. (e.g. Rwanda and Uganda)	Risk of client panic if a gorilla charges	Risk of catching human diseases. Increased disturbance and stress

Feeding wildlife

Feeding wildlife or food provisioning comprises the intentional or accidental supply of non-natural food sources to wild animals in their natural habitat. Accidental food provisioning is when wildlife is attracted to and acquires food from disposal areas or from discarded food wastes (e.g. bears in North America). Food can also be stolen from picnic areas or directly from tourists (monkeys in Africa and Asia). The deliberate supply of food involves tourists informally feeding wildlife (stingrays and dingoes, Australia) or via formal supervised arrangements involving guides and/or tour operators (parrot feeding, Australia). There may also be highly structured feeding situations that are directly controlled by management. This may involve the development of a special area or feeding station where controlled amounts of appropriate foods are dispensed to the public for feeding animals at specific times (dolphin feeding, Australia). In these latter situations the food provisioning activity is often supported with an interpretive programme.

Less direct forms of deliberate food supplementation occur in the form of bird feeding tables, nectar feeders, provision of waterholes and in the planting of bird-attracting flowers and shrubs (e.g. at tourist accommodation that caters for birdwatchers and bird sanctuaries). In these cases the objective is to facilitate viewing and photography of wildlife as opposed to close access, contact and the need to feed a wild animal (see Chapter 3).

Both Green and Higginbottom (2000) and Orams (2002) provide useful accounts and insights into the issues surrounding the feeding of wildlife. Table 2.7 provides some examples of the negative impacts associated with feeding wildlife. The main issues relate to dependence on humans, habituation and the attraction of species to humans in search of food. Wildlife can become dependent on supplemented food, show increased vulnerability to injury and death from various human activities and/or pose a threat when in close contact with humans. Box 2.4 provides an example of the problems associated with an emerging and increasingly popular, yet unmanaged food-provisioning situation.

Orams (2002), however, makes the point that not all of the impacts associated with feeding wildlife are negative and that the case as to whether the health of animals is impacted by food supplementation remains to be comprehensively demonstrated. He also notes the controversial nature of wildlife feeding in that the public is receiving conflicting messages. Legislation may in fact forbid feeding but contradictions occur when authorities do not enforce no-feeding regulations. In some cases feeding is allowed and in other cases it is not. Feeding may be advertised as part of a tourism package. Some species may be fed, while feeding of other species is not allowed. The same species may be fed in one situation, for example on private land, with feeding of the same species not being allowed in the conservation estate. Given its rising popularity and the strong human desire to feed wild animals

Table 2.7 Examples of potential negative impacts associated with food provisioning

Species	*Impacts*	*Source*
Fish	Aggression and attacks on humans	Perrine (1989)
Sharks	Aggression and attacks on humans	Nelson *et al.* (1986)
Birds	Dependence on supplemented food	Cannon (1984)
Birds	Altered migration patterns	Paton *et al.* (1983)
Wallabies	Dependence on humans, high local densities, road kill and harassment of visitors	Skira and Smith (1991)
White-tailed deer	Reduced foraging activity	Doenier *et al.* (1997)
Moose	Death from choking after eating foreign materials (stomach contents included a table cloth, tape, wire, plastics and pot scrubbers)	http://www.watertonpark.com/reference/wildlife.htm
Bears	Aggression towards humans	Albert and Bowyer (1991)
Bears	Increased risk of road kill	Knight *et al.* (1988)
Dingoes	Aggression and attacks on humans	Lawrance and Higginbottom (2002)
Dolphins	Low nutritional value of supplemented food	Wilson (1994)
Dolphins	Increased mortality of juveniles due to decreased parental behaviour and susceptibility to human pathogens	Wilson (1994)
Dolphins	Aggression towards humans	Orams *et al.* (1996)
Hamadryas baboons	Aggression and attacks on humans	Kamal *et al.* (1997)
Samango monkey	Harassment of visitors and stealing food from campgrounds and picnic areas	Chapman *et al.* (1998)

Box 2.4   Impacts and risks associated with food provisioning and close inter-action: The case of stingray feeding in south-west Australia

Hamelin Bay (Figure 2.1) has in recent years emerged as a stingray- provisioning site where up to 12 large stingrays (*Dasyatis brevicaudata* and *Dasyatis thedidis*), swim into shallow waters near to shore in order to be fed by visitors to the area (Plate 2.6). The site is not currently managed as a stingray feeding attraction but in the future could evolve into a permanent feeding site (Lewis & Newsome, 2003). The Hamelin Bay Caravan Park experiences locally significant visitation over the summer holiday period (Dec–Feb), with the campsite and caravan park occupancy numbering up 1500 during the peak season.

In terms of stingray–human interactions visitors are presented with an opportunity to swim or snorkel with the rays. Many people, however, wade into the shallow waters and attempt to touch and/or feed the rays with pieces of fish obtained from a nearby fish cleaning table. In terms of problematical human behaviour the following observations were made by Newsome *et al.* (2004): visitors falling on rays while attempting to touch them, rays being stepped on as people exited boats, children observed forcing their sibs to touch a ray, people touched their tails, some patrons held on to the rays and a group of children were observed to be closely surrounding a stingray. Some patrons were even observed to be placing their children on tailless (tail removed by local fishermen) stingrays' backs for photographs. In addition, as many as 20 patrons were seen to overbalance when not having strong footing, or when unexpectedly approached by a ray. Stingrays were seen to raise their tails towards humans in aggressive posture on two occasions. The first was when a young boy grabbed the pectoral fin of the ray and would not let go. The second was when a patron was teasing a ray with fish but not feeding it. Stingrays were also fed bread or had sand and rocks thrown at them or in some cases became snared on fishing lines.

Aggression between the rays themselves was also observed, with large female stingrays acting aggressively toward both the smaller males and eaglerays that were also present. Stingrays were seen to fight over large fish, shoving each other with their snouts and forcefully veering each other out of the away. Silver gulls (*Larus argentatus*) are also attracted to the site with the rays responding by raising their tails out of the water in aggressive posture. Given the combined effects of unsupervised human behaviour and the way that the wildlife is interacting with each other, the risk of a patron being stung remains high.

Other problems noted at the site were fish carcasses floating in the water, turbidity and an oily slick thought to be composed of a combination of fish oils and various oils and applications derived from human skin. Some patrons and local residents were also concerned that unconsumed fish carcasses could attract sharks, substantially increasing the risk of shark attack.

(From Lewis & Newsome, 2003; Newsome *et al.*, 2004)

Plate 2.6 Children engaging in close contact with food provisioned wild stingrays. Children often become excited and attempt to elicit a response from wildlife. Because of this and their lack of knowledge children need to be supervised. Interpretation programmes should especially focus on engaging children and in doing so create a foundation for appropriate behaviour in the presence of wildlife.
Source: Anna Lewis

food provisioning constitutes an important management problem and is considered further in Chapter 6.

Summary of key points

There is a range of visitor expectations with many clients desiring close contact but safety and the scope for successful photography. Others, for various reasons, want to touch and feed wildlife. Complexity is added given the range of situations in which people acquire close contact and feed wildlife. Feeding may be unstructured (no or little control over the amount and type of food or the way it is provided) or structured (controls over the amount and quality of food and mechanism of delivery) and a wide range of species (fish, birds, reptiles and mammals) can potentially be involved.

The impacts associated with close contact and feeding include dependence on provisioned food, an increased vulnerability of target species to ill health or death and risks of injury to visitors. The ecological impacts of feeding have, in many cases, not been adequately researched. The contradictory nature of feeding in particular where the same wildlife is fed in some situations but not in others, combined with variable management responses and regulation, means that both close contact and the feeding wildlife remains a controversial issue.

Conclusions

It is impossible to supply a totally comprehensive account of potential ecological impacts of wildlife tourism because of the great diversity in site characteristics, tourism profiles (visitor attitude, number of visitors, frequency of visits and level of manipulation) and species concerned. The reader, however, has been presented with what is believed to be a solid introduction to the major issues as they relate to possible negative impacts. The complex nature of some impact situations has also been highlighted. Most of all insight is provided into various impact situations. This in turn gives substance to a framework (the wildlife tourism paradigm) for anticipating and understanding all of the major sources of negative impact in wildlife tourism.

A number of situations, however, remain unresolved as to what the best course of action to take is in terms of allowing a particular activity. For example, it appears that habituation is not necessarily neutral to wildlife as exemplified in the case of mountain gorillas or Galapagos marine iguanas. The feeding situation remains controversial and problematical and the challenge remains as to how this human need can be best dealt with into the future. It is likely that attempting to ban feeding altogether is unrealistic and counterproductive in encouraging people to support the conservation of nature. In realising this there is a need to understand which animals can be fed, under what circumstances and where.

The challenge for the future is managing those situations where close contact and feeding takes place while minimising negative and maximising positive impacts. This will require further studies aimed at detecting impacts and monitoring which in turn is strongly dependent on political commitment, staffing and funding. The importance of these latter points cannot be understated. The case of cetacean tourism illustrates this in relation to predicting and managing impacts because in many situations the animal's ecology and the effects of tourism are not fully understood. This emphasises the need for constant data collection and revision of management practices (Chapter 6) in the light of such data.

Additional relevant texts

Sherwood *et al.* (2002) and Spellerberg (2002) provide more detail on the ecology of wildlife and roads. A number of reports produced by the Australian Cooperative Research Centre for Sustainable Tourism provide further details on general and specific wildlife tourism situations. For example, see Green and Higginbottom (2001), Green *et al.* (2001), Moscardo *et al.* (2001), Lawrance and Higginbottom (2002). An account of the impacts of recreation and tourism on various groups of animals is contained in Liddle (1997), Knight and Gutzwiller (1995) provide a number of case studies with an emphasis on birds, while Gales *et al.* (2003) provide an account of tourism issues that focus on southern hemisphere marine mammals.

Chapter 3

Human Dimension of Wildlife Interactions

Contributed by JOAN BENTRUPPERBÄUMER

Introduction

The human dimension of wildlife interactions is a topic wide in scope, essentially interdisciplinary, drawing on anthropology, psychology, sociology, ethics, medicine, human geography, environmental science and management. This chapter draws upon these disciplinary lines and extracts theoretical perspectives, themes and concepts which are particularly relevant to understanding human–wildlife relations in the context of wildlife tourism. Within this framework this analysis will explore some general issues surrounding human interest in wildlife, the development of human–wildlife relationships, the nature and role of such relationships in human life and, in the wildlife tourism context, the consequences of these interactions for humans.

Many factors behind these relationships are psychological in nature and so there is the need to explore ways in which animals (wildlife) enter psychological and cultural symbolic processes. Such a focus allows us to step back from the more explicit and mechanistic explorations of human and wildlife behaviour, management regimes and policies, and impacts and impacting processes, all of which are addressed elsewhere in this book. This in turn enables us to better understand the complex interrelationships driving human–wildlife interactions which is fundamental to identifying why nature-based tourism, and in particular wildlife tourism, exists in the first place, what is motivating and sustaining the human interest in and need to interact with wildlife, how this is manifested in the very visible and sometimes unintentionally disruptive ways humans interact with wildlife, and ultimately how such an understanding can better inform us of the most appropriate and effective human and wildlife management strategies.

This chapter is by no means exhaustive in its coverage of the human dimension of wildlife interactions and the implication for wildlife tourism. None the less, it does provide a sense of the psychological factors thought to operate in human–wildlife interactions within this context. This search for a way of understanding such interactions develops through four sections. The chapter begins by identifying the major theoretical positions relating to the broad question of how humans relate to nature, followed by a closer examination of several predominately psychological approaches central to human relations with nature and wildlife. Each of these perspectives provides important and unique insights into the psychological foundations of human interest in, attraction to, and affiliation with wildlife, the driving forces behind wildlife tourism.

This is followed in the second section with a brief exploration of factors underlying our view of wildlife, and the value dimension of human–wildlife relations in the tourism context. In the third section, the chapter presents a more in-depth analysis of the process of encountering wildlife and the many varied and sometimes controversial activities associated with these encounters. The final section of this chapter addresses the issue of virtual representations of wildlife and the implications of such representation for human–wildlife relations. Wildlife images are an extremely popular means of communicating information about the natural environment. They exist in extensive quantities in various media forms. A brief description and analysis of a spectrum of representations and contexts is presented, followed by a consideration of how such use affects public and tourist understandings of wildlife.

Psychological Foundations of Human–Wildlife Relations

Why is it that we are so attracted to and interested in nature and in particular wildlife? What is it that determines our feelings, concern and connectedness with wildlife, our behaviour towards them once we encounter them, and for many of us our preparedness to go to extreme lengths just to see, photograph, hunt, and occasionally feed and touch them?

Human need for and response to nature

In considering the development of human–wildlife relations one important perspective focuses on the human need for contact with nature which is steeped in evolutionary history. There are a number of researchers who argue that humans behave in accordance with functional-evolutionary principles (e.g. Kaplan & Kaplan, 1989; Kellert & Wilson, 1993; Ulrich, 1993; Wilson, 1984), that is, 'the function of much of human behaviour is to further our chances of survival and is guided by inherited behavioural tendencies acquired by our species through evolution' (Bell *et al.*, 2001: 40). According to this perspective humans evolved in the natural environment, changing in response to it, as well as being fascinated by it (Knopf, 1987). In order to survive humans had to be efficient assimilators of constantly changing stimuli providing information about the natural environment and thus adapt to the demands imposed by such environments.

A concept to emerge in 1984 which encapsulated this evolutionary perspective was biophilia, having been proposed by the sociobiologist, Edward Wilson, to describe the innate human need for contact with nature (Wilson, 1984). Wilson's

(1984) early interpretation of biophilia was based on the notion that a particular characteristic of humans was their 'tendency to pay attention to, affiliate with, or otherwise respond positively to nature' (Ulrich, 1993: 73). Since its inception the notion of biophilia/biophobia has created considerable debate among a wide range of scholars interested in human response to and need for nature, because, as Soulé (1993: 441) notes, this put forward the following fundamental question:

> To what degree and in what forms has evolution produced genetically based responses in humans, positive and negative, to biological and other environmental phenomena?

The biophilia hypothesis has been used by many as a framework for investigating human affiliation with nature (for example, Kahn, 1997, 1999; Ulrich, 1993), and in particular companion animals (Katcher & Wilkins, 1993), and wildlife (Kellert, 1993, 1996; Kellert & Wilson, 1993). The biophilia concept has drawn many supportive as well as critical comments (see for example, Kahn, 1999; Kellert & Wilson, 1993; Sagan & Margulis, 1993; Soulé, 1993), reigniting the debate between the neo-Darwinian or genetic basis for human affinities and reactions to nature and animals, and explanations that are 'nondeterministic, nonbiological, concerned with culture, social equity, and justice, and often influenced by Marxist thought' (Soulé, 1993: 442). Soulé (1993: 442) considers such mutually exclusive views to be unproductive, pointing out that a strict adherence to them rather than a joining of ideas is based on 'ideology being more precious than knowledge'. However, there are those who disregard this strict dichotomy of explanations and instead define biophilia simply as human affinity for other species regardless of whether learned or innate (e.g. Diamond, 1993).

In the context of wildlife tourism there are many possible applications of this hypothesis in furthering our understanding of human need for and response to wildlife, some of which will be explored later in the chapter. But, as noted, there is an alternate perspective, one that disputes the environmental/evolutionary deterministic view that the 'needs of nature run deep' and that such needs are 'innately wired into our basic design' (Knopf, 1987). This perspective emphasises the role of human perceptual and cognitive processes as powerful forces shaping how humans respond to nature. Advocates of this notion of a 'learned response' emphasise the role of past experiences and accumulated emotions and meanings.

Despite strong advocates of either the evolutionary or the learned perspective, there are many like Soulé (1993) and Knopf (1987) who propose the need for an integrative approach.

> Perhaps a more integrative view is to propose that response to nature emerges from an interaction of both innate and experiential forces. It seems logical to propose that perceptual and cognitive tendencies are strongly innately prescribed, whereas affective tendencies are strongly experientially prescribed. In

this sense, the evolutionary and cultural perspectives are both correct – each addresses a different aspect of people-nature transactions. (Knopf, 1987: 789)

Effects of nature on humans

Whether innately driven, learned, or a fusion of both, most researchers share a consistently favourable view of the outcome of the natural environmental experience for most people (Hartig & Evans, 1993; Kahn, 1999; Kellert & Wilson, 1993; Ulrich, 1993). While negative responses do occur, nature nevertheless tends to be more beneficial than not (Knopf, 1987). Currently, there are a number of theoretical frameworks that endeavour to explain these responses, most of which are founded on concerns about human health and well-being, and quality of life issues (Hartig & Evans, 1993). In the course of an extensive review of the literature, Knopf (1987) identified four broad themes which underlie the effects of nature on humans: (1) restoration; (2) competence building; (3) symbolic meaning; (4) stimulation, curiosity. The two themes perhaps most relevant to this stage of the analysis of the effects of nature on humans are 'nature as restorer', and 'nature as competence builder'. While these two themes are presented here as possible explanations of what underlies human response to wildlife they by no means are intended to exclude the consideration that 'responses are not generic but individualistic – shaped by the interacting forces of personality and experience' (Knopf, 1987: 793).

Restorative effects of nature

Many researchers have been interested in the restorative effects of the natural environment in general. Two theoretical frameworks that are relevant to this notion of 'nature as restorer' are Ulrich's (1983) stress reduction theory, and Kaplan and Kaplan's (1989) attention restoration theory. Ulrich's (1983) stress reduction theory, a psychoevolutionary model, emphasises the role of natural settings in generating psychophysicological recovery from stressful experiences associated most often with contemporary urban environments and lifestyles. An important basic assumption of this model is the 'rapid-onset of emotional responses to certain environmental configurations', responses which are 'assumed to have been adaptive in evolution' (Hartig & Evans, 1993: 440). This notion of a restorative response has been supported by a number of studies conducted in laboratory settings, hospitals, prisons and work environments (e.g. Katcher & Wilkins, 1993; Parsons, 1991; Ulrich, 1983, 1984; Ulrich *et al.*, 1991). Studies conducted in natural recreation settings, including World Heritage Areas and National Parks, also support this restorative perspective, with nature being perceived by the vast majority of local visitors and tourists as peaceful, tranquil, serene, and as an important place for respite and relaxation (Bentrupperbäumer & Reser, 2001, 2002, 2003a). Furthermore, Ulrich (1993) found in over 100 studies that the key perceived benefit of recreation in natural areas was stress reduction.

Kaplan and Kaplan's (1989) attention restoration theory provides another explanation for the restorative effects of nature by focusing on the recovery of attentional capacity following cognitive fatigue. According to Kaplan and Kaplan (1989), contemporary society puts considerable demand on directed attention which requires the individual to concentrate on the task at hand, and to ignore disruptive emotions or events. This often leads to mental exhaustion, reduced work efficiency, and a reduced sense of well-being. Because directed attention is critical to problem-solving and human effectiveness in general, and because it is so fragile, hard to uphold, and can cause considerable fatigue, respite from this state is desirable. This can be achieved by the effortless attention offered by viewing nature or wildlife, or just being in natural settings because such settings facilitate opportunities for pleasurable activities, and feelings of fascination and tranquillity.

While to date these theories have not specifically been used to account for those psychologically restorative benefits in human–wildlife encounters, they nevertheless provide important insights into the possible restorative processes underlying our need for, and attraction to wildlife. In the wildlife tourism context it would be difficult to disentangle the effects of the natural environment from the actual wildlife encounter. What is evident is that restorative benefits arise from exposure to natural settings, and by implication, from wildlife because wildlife are symbolic of and generally surrounded by the natural environment, however minimal.

In pursuit of competence

The ability of natural environments to facilitate a heightened individual sense of control, competency, self-esteem, self-reliance, and self-confidence is particularly well documented in the literature on therapeutic and outward bound style wilderness programmes (Hartig & Evans, 1993; Knopf, 1987; Reser & Scherl, 1988). In wildlife tourism, this notion of 'nature as competence builder' (Knopf, 1987) is particularly relevant to one group of wildlife tourists – hunters. As will be shown later in this chapter, for some in this group hunting is driven by the need to take part in challenging, skill enhancing, and sometimes risky behaviour as a way of increasing their personal growth and competence level. Hunting clearly takes people beyond the everyday, presenting a very different world, providing a new set of experiences, and requiring the development of new and challenging problem-solving skills. Hartig and Evans (1993) identify a number of wilderness characteristics that appear to be instrumental in encouraging adaptiveness and personal development. One that is significant for the hunter is that the novelty and threat value associated with the activity and the setting requires close attention and a preparedness to deal with unexpected situations. Such activities clearly promote competence building. Knopf (1987: 788) identifies another important outcome of this activity: 'People can be more concerned with mastering skills of their own choosing rather than trying to conform to social or institutional constraints.' Furthermore, an individual operating in nature in this way is more likely to be immediately rewarded for his or her actions (Knopf, 1987), because such actions generate immediate feedback, 'which in turn facilitates later insight concerning, for example, one's own competence or ability' (Reser & Scherl, 1988: 280).

Affiliation with animals

Understanding the nature, quality and consequences of our relationship with other animals has direct and important implications for wildlife tourism because of its role in defining our interest in, and our feelings, concerns, and behaviour toward them. This topic has become increasingly important in the last couple of decades particularly in relation to analyses of our attitudes toward, appreciation, treatment and use of, and the psychophysiological benefits derived for our affiliation with animals (Brodie & Biley, 1999; Franklin & White, 2001; Nash, 1990; Singer, 1995; Swabe, 1996). Much of this discussion has centred on the role of animals in satisfying human needs for food, entertainment, companionship, scientific and medical research (Shepard, 1996; Swabe, 1996). Embedded within these needs are a number of controversial issues, some of which are relevant to wildlife tourism, which is considered a form of entertainment (for example, blood sports, containment, behaviour modification, social isolation). While discussions on animal welfare and rights are now emerging in the wildlife tourism literature (e.g. Hughes, 2001), such discussions and debates still have a long way to go in terms of outcomes such as development and implementation of programmes, protocols and regulations, structural changes, and changed tourist and tourist operator behaviour.

Companionship

Many studies have explored the social, physiological and psychological impacts of animals, in particular pets, on humans (see Beck, 1999; Brodie & Biley, 1999 for a review; Katcher & Wilkins, 1993). Most of these studies have reported a positive or restorative effect of such relationships including, for example, decrease in depression, stress level, irritable behaviour, and loneliness, and an increase in self-esteem, social interaction and group harmony, to name but a few. This notion of social and psychophysiological benefits from human–animal encounters has resulted in the adoption of a variety of measures particularly by health care professionals in promoting optimal holistic health. In this area of research it has even been found that, 'the mere presence of animals can instigate higher levels of relaxation amongst their human companions' (Brodie & Biley, 1999: 332), which may partially explain why for some wildlife tourists just being in the presence of other animal species is sufficient to satisfy their needs at the time. The deep attraction some tourists have to wildlife may also reflect the influence of interactions with companion animals within the general population. An impressive number of analyses provide strong evidence that the presence of animals, their behaviour, their touch, their attention, has made the world a more comfortable place by reducing human isolation and maintaining human health. As noted by Kellert (1996: 22), 'Humans crave companionship'.

Bonding and emotional attachment

The psychological impact of bonding with wildlife has been articulated in a number of texts written by many who have actually worked as wildlife scientists in the field (e.g. Fossey, 2000; Galdikas, 1995; Goodall, 1990; Hogan *et al.*, 1998; Peterson & Goodall, 1993; Pinkola Estés, 1992), see Box 3.1. Emotional attachment to wildlife is a powerful psychological dimension of bonding and is the response most often discussed in these and other texts. Wilson's (1984) biophilia hypothesis has been proposed to explain the emotional attachment people feel for wildlife and how this plays an important role in determining behaviour (Kellert, 1996; Kellert & Wilson, 1993). According to the functionalist approach to attitudes and hence to emotions (Eagly & Chaiken, 1993; Lazarus, 1991; and readings in Pratkanis *et al.*, 1989), emotions are considered to play an important motivational role particularly in terms of mobilising both mental and behavioural activity. The results of a study on the endangered cassowary (*Casuarius casuarius*) lend support to this notion that emotional connection to wildlife is associated with pro-environmental behaviour (Bentrupperbäumer, 1998). However, an important caveat to this was the finding that while emotional response was necessary since it was an important determinant of behaviour, alone it was not sufficient. To be most effective it had to be experiential, and that experience had to be direct, *in* nature itself, as opposed to indirect or abstract, that is being confined to the classroom, information centres, television screens or glossy magazines. Emotional attachment to animals therefore offers a number of interesting perspectives on their possible functions in a tourist's mental and behavioural relationship with wildlife.

The other interesting debate concerning emotion is the interplay of emotion and cognition. The implication of many theoretical treatments is that emotion is post-cognitive (Edwards, 1990). However, Ittelson *et al.* (1974) view it differently. They consider the first level of response to the environment to be affective and that such a response may govern the directions that subsequent relations with the environment will take. Whether it is innate or learned, of motivational consequence or not, pre- or post-cognitive, a number of studies confirm that emotional attachment to wildlife is real and important.

Attributes of wildlife

Wildlife consists of a substantial diversity of species from invertebrates to vertebrates, all of which play a role in wildlife tourism (for example, from butterfly parks to whale watching). While the wildlife tourism literature places an emphasis on species only included within *Phylum Chordata* (Sinha, 2001), in reality, tourism that

---

Box 3.1   Bonding and emotional attachment to wildlife: A perspective from wildlife biologists

Some of the most instructive accounts of human bonding and emotional attachment to wildlife have been written by women scientists who have spent many years in the field studying animals such as the great apes, dolphins, wolves, whales, elephants, coyotes, lions. In addition to their scientific writings these wildlife biologists have written sensitively, passionately and honestly about such attachments, attachments that run so deep that they have not only devoted their life to studying and conserving such species, but some have lost their life in the process.

Another interesting aspect of this bonding and emotional attachment to wildlife for these scientists is the tension experienced between the so called 'objectivity' of science and accusations of anthropomorphism. But as noted by Hogan *et al.* (1998: xiv):

> The passion to know nature continues to motivate us as scientists and writers as we study animals, form bonds with them, and write about them. Intimacy and relationship with other animals has become one of the places we inhabit, like land, home, air, or water. In turn, we are inhabited by it, our work and lives shaped by the relationships forged by it. Because of our work, we are replacing the hard, objective eye of the past with one of a softer sight, replacing a concept of anthropomorphism with one of empathy.

For many wildlife tourists it has been these popular accounts of the human bonding and attachment to wildlife evident in the commitment of these scientists to their work and the conservation of the species that has been an important motivational factor in their desire to see such charismatic animals in the wild and through this 'tourist' activity contribute to the conservation of the species (see Box 3.2).

---

is primarily based on some form of interaction with other species suggests a need for being more inclusive of life forms other than vertebrates. Humans respond to disparate life forms in many different ways, some of which may be predictable (Kellert, 1996), and influenced by certain attributes (Eddy *et al.*, 1993; Kellert, 1996; Plous, 1993a). In order to better understand human preference for and attraction to certain wildlife species there is the need to look at the attributes of those species found to facilitate a preferential response. These include physical and behavioural characteristics such as: mental ability, phylogenic similarity, body shape and size, aesthetic appeal, means of locomotion, ability to form attachments (Eddy *et al.*,

1993; Kellert, 1996; Plous, 1993a; Tremblay, 2002). While a number of these attributes may play a more significant role for some wildlife tourists in determining their preferential response, in most instances they are not operating in a mutually exclusive way.

Similarity   Similarity to humans appears to play an important role in human preference for, attraction to, affection toward, and treatment of animals (Plous, 1993b). Research undertaken by Eddy *et al.* (1993), which proposes an extension of attribution theory to include species other than humans, suggests that humans are more likely to impute attributional capacities to animals as a function of their phylogentic group. In other words, the extent to which humans will attribute characterisitcs such as similar emotions and cognitive processing abilities to other species is dependent on the degree of their physical similarity to humans. This places primates high up on the mental ability and preference scale, which is confirmed in this and a number of other studies (e.g. Cheney & Seyfarth, 1990; Peterson & Goodall, 1993; Griffin, 1992; Plous, 1993b). Those species considered similar in terms of mental states not only implies high intelligence but also the capacity for pain and suffering. Eddy and colleagues' (1993) evolutionary explanation for this tendency to allocate cognitive processing abilities to conspecifics is that such tendencies evolved as a consequence of the need to take into account the experience and intentions of other humans. The significance of phylogenic similarity, which produces a hierarchy of mental states and preferences for wildlife, clearly has implications for how individual wildlife species will be treated, pursued, and used in wildlife tourism (Moscardo *et al.*, 2001; Tremblay, 2002). But similarity does not just include physical likeness. It can also be associated with behavioural responses such as nurturing, in particular caring for young. Wildlife engaged in nurturing activity appears to be particularly appealing and fascinating for tourists. As noted by Tremblay (2002: 168):

> The perceived capacity for affection (such as caring for young) and adherence to morally acceptable human-like behaviours (such as monogamy) is also suspected to play a role in general interest and preferences toward animals.

Aesthetic appeal   The attraction various wildlife species hold for tourists can also be linked to the aesthetic appeal of particular species (Tremblay, 2002). While aesthetic preferences can be individualistic, shaped by social and cultural processes, nonetheless it has been found that certain wildlife species 'elicit consistent aesthetic responses', found to be greatly influenced by colour, shape, movement and visibility (Kellert, 1996: 15). This would partly explain one of the most popular wildlife tourism activities, birdwatching, given the strong emphasis on visibility and the very evident aesthetic appeal of birds in terms of colour and movement. Kellert (1996) also found that aesthetic responses to wildlife was linked to size of the species, evident in the aesthetic preference humans have for very large animals. At the top end of the size class are the charismatic megafauna such as elephants, giraffes and whales which, in addition to being very large in size, are considered to be 'aesthetically pleasing and emotionally resonant wildlife' (Sagan & Marguils, 1993).

Aesthetic appeal of animals is also expressed in commonly used terms such as 'cute and cuddly', features primarily linked to age and size class, skin texture and behavioural traits (young, small, soft/furry, playful animals). Evidence suggests that the more 'cute and cuddly' an animal, the more positive the human response in terms of attraction, feelings, concerns, attitudes and treatment (Kellert, 1996). One possible explanation for the attraction to wildlife with such characteristics is that proposed by Voith (in Brodie & Biley, 1999: 330): 'Humans are predisposed to become attached to other humans, especially children, and if animals exhibit child-like behaviours and features this attachment is understandable.' Cute and cuddly are clearly childlike features, applicable to many wildlife species, in particular the young of the species which are generally small, soft and playful. Additionally, a nurturing ethic of compassion and kindness toward wildlife is more likely to be evoked for species with such features.

While there appears to be evidence of the existence of a deep attraction to certain wildlife species based on aesthetic appeal, Kellert (1996: 17) acknowledges that such a response is complex:

> The human aesthetic response to animals and nature suggests constancy and coherence rather than random fluctuation. More appears to be involved than a simple reaction to the pretty. Initially the aesthetic response to living diversity may seem casual, even trivial, but on closer inspection it embraces deeper levels of meaning.

The significance of aesthetic appeal of wildlife in the context of wildlife tourism is still not fully understood (Tremblay, 2002). Nevertheless, it is fair to assume that if the appeal of the species elicits a response, the experience based on that response has the potential to deliver important outcomes for the wildlife tourist. This is because it 'evokes a strong, primarily emotional, register in most people, provoking feelings of intense pleasure, even awe, at the physical splendour of the natural world' (Kellert, 1996: 15).

Rare, endangered   Shackley (1996) argues that a strong focus in wildlife tourism is placed on rare or endangered species. And according to Reynolds and Braithwaite (2001: 36), 'species on rare and endangered lists appear to hold a special attraction for wildlife tourists'. From a lay perspective the term rare implies something is unusual, while endangered implies something is scarce, imperil, at risk. Based on this notion of the unusual, one possible explanation for this attraction to rare and endangered species is that for the wildlife tourist an encounter with such an animal presents an exceptional, extraordinary, unique opportunity. Therefore, should such an encounter be realised it will have special significance, one which is not only restricted to the privileged few, but is also out of the ordinary, far removed from the everyday.

In a management context, terms such as rare and endangered imply low numbers, threatening processes, and possible extinction. Inherent in this are notions of irreversible loss, lasting damage, dysfunctional and finite life support systems, and critical time frames. Given this emphasis on the environmental crisis scenario, another possible explanation for the special attraction to rare and endangered species in the wild is the role such species may play as the 'miner's canary of ecosystem well-being' (Bentrupperbäumer, 1998). In other words for wildlife tourists rare and endangered species may be regarded as important symbols of a viable and functioning natural ecosystem, one which may be on the brink but nevertheless is still there and can be brought back. They are symbols of life itself (Knopf, 1987), symbols we so desperately need in a world that is in a state of rapid and uncontrollable change, be it on a global or local level, environmental or political. Research conducted on the endangered cassowary (*Casuarius casuarius*), supports this notion of the 'miner's canary'. Local residents were found to be using this species as a touchstone with respect to how things are in general and the status of the natural environment (Bentrupperbäumer, 1998). Therefore, for wildlife tourists an important part of the symbolic character of rare and endangered species could be their use as a barometer of ecosystem well-being.

Our *View* of Wildlife in a Tourism Context

For the purpose of this analysis, how we 'view' wildlife is considered an expression of our value orientations which provide us with a set of beliefs about the importance of wildlife, our relationship with them, and ultimately how we behave toward them and how we care for them. While there has been much written on value orientations toward the environment (e.g. Cosgrove *et al.*, 1994; Stern *et al.*, 1993; Rapoport, 1993), and wildlife (e.g. Kellert, 1993, 1996), this analysis is not intended to be a comprehensive overview of such values, nor is it intended to present the many different cultural perspectives, for example, Western vs. Eastern, indigenous vs. non-indigenous. This clearly would require a much more indepth examination of the psychological, sociological, philosophical and cultural perspectives on values and value orientations which is beyond the scope of this analysis. Rather, the emphasis here is on briefly addressing four key universal values considered particularly relevant to understanding our view of wildlife in a tourism context. They explore the notions of control (dominionistic), use (utilitarian), rights and responsibilities (moralistic), and conservation (protectionistic) of wildlife (Figure 3.1). Many wildlife tourism programmes comprise a combination of such views; however, the utilitarian view, while not always predominant, is nevertheless common to all.

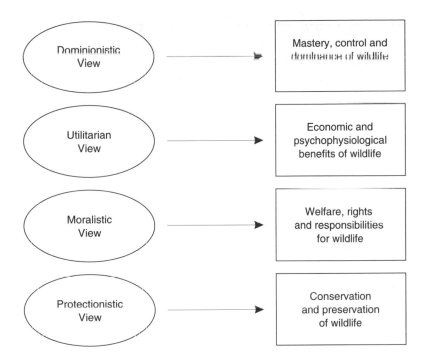

Figure 3.1 Four key determinants of our view of wildlife in a tourism context

The way in which wildlife is viewed/valued in tourism has important implications across all levels of the industry, from industry representatives to the tourism providers and individual tourists. For example, on the broadest level such views can influence the way industry represents wildlife in a promotional context and their preparedness to take on a regulatory role. On another level these views can influence the way tourism providers conduct their operation. And at an individual tourist level the nature and quality of the interaction with wildlife can be affected.

Dominionistic view: *Mastery, control and dominance*

There is a general consensus that, in reflecting a worldview common in most human societies (DuNann Winter, 1996; Kellert, 1996; Nash, 1990), the underlying philosophical position of the wildlife tourism industry is the dominant anthropocentric conviction that animals are subordinate to humans (Orams, 2002). This is a worldview based on the Judeo-Christian tradition which promotes 'dominion' over other species. For some this implies domination and control, for others, stewardship (DuNann Winter, 1996). The view that wildlife can and should be controlled is described by Kellert (1996) as 'dominionistic', and is a view held most strongly by that group of wildlife tourists, the hunters. As noted earlier, one outcome of this dominionistic experience of nature for the hunter is an increase in feelings of self-reliance because such an experience 'can sharpen mental and physical competence through testing various abilities and capacities' (Kellert, 1996: 20).

The dominionistic view of wildlife is most evident in zoos and wildlife parks where confinement in highly artificial environments and circus-like performances clearly demonstrate the mastery, control and dominance people have over animals. Of concern to many is the negative influence such wildlife settings and encounters may have on people's attitudes toward wildlife.

> The typical zoo experience appears to reinforce attitudes of mastery over animals and nature. . . . Indeed, a pervasive atmosphere of control and superiority could actually bolster the illusion of human hegemony, leaving the average visitor more arrogant than ever toward the non-human world. Kellert (1996: 87, 89)

On the other hand, as will be discussed later when addressing the protectionistic view, a primary objective of some of these settings is conservation and preservation of endangered species.

Utilitarian view: *Economic and psychophysiological benefits*

Another popular view based on this notion of control and subordination and which has been linked to wildlife tourism, is utilitianism (Hughes, 2001; Kellert, 1993, 1996; Nash, 1990). At the broadest level, if a utilitarian view is considered as reflecting a benefit to humans, clearly such a view is very descriptive of wildlife tourism on two accounts. Wildlife tourism not only provides an economic benefit to tourism providers in all instances (Reynolds & Braithwaite, 2001), but as demonstrated throughout this chapter, it provides important psychophysiological benefits to all wildlife tourists. Despite the universality of this utilitarian view of wildlife across all wildlife tourism programmes, with economic benefits to all tourism providers, the nature and quality of psychophysiological benefits is very variable. Kellert's (1993, 1996) value classification system would differentiate these into naturalistic and aesthetic value orientations. However, the encompassing anthropocentric nature of this view suggests an encompassing utilitarian perspective.

Moralistic view: *Welfare, rights and responsibilities*

Hughes (2001: 322) argues that in the wildlife tourism industry, 'animals are more often objects than subjects', being used, exploited, manipulated for the sole purpose of the enjoyment of tourists and/or the economic benefits to tourism providers. As well as reflecting a dominionistic and utilitarian view of wildlife, this anthropocentric perspective implies the absence of moralistic considerations at an industry level, that is, considerations for animal welfare, animal rights and the responsibilities of the tourist and tourism provider. However, there is some evidence of a move toward addressing animal welfare and rights in the wildlife tourism industry with the development of codes of practice, regulatory mechanisms, management policies and protocols (e.g. Reynolds & Braithwaite, 2001; Scarpaci *et al.*, 2003), and structural shifts in the way wildlife are being presented and cared for, particularly in zoos (Hughes, 2001; Beardsworth & Bryman, 2001).

This may reflect what is seen as a general shift in public value orientations toward wildlife from utilitarian to protectionist (Zinn *et al.*, 2002). Alternatively, this view may be influenced by a number of anthropocentric concerns as opposed to the emergence of an environmental/wildlife ethic, an ethic centred on animal welfare and rights. Such concerns would include the realisation that unless the resource (wildlife) is cared for it could disappear, which would have considerable economic consequences for the industry. At the wildlife tourist level, most research has indicated that the group least likely to have a moralistic view and in most instances do not value animal rights at all, is the hunters (e.g. Daigle *et al.*, 1996). While currently there is much discussion concerning environmental responsibility and its incorporation in the tourism industry, some would argue that this is still superficial, 'All debates over environmental impacts have failed to produce structural changes in tourist provision, or in tourist's values, such that all tourist experiences are environmentally responsible' (Hughes, 2001: 322).

Protectionistic view: *Conservation and preservation*

Increasingly evident in the wildlife tourism industry are those providers and consumers who have a strong protectionistic view of wildlife and consider the major purpose and outcome of their tourism activity is the conservation and preservation of species. Of particular note are the wildlife parks and zoos which are involved in captive breeding and release programmes of endangered species, and the 'in-the-wild' tourism programmes which link conservation to tourism such as the mountain gorilla ecotourism programme developed through the International Gorilla Conservation Programme (see Box 3.2).

In some cases this protectionistic view of wildlife is based on an eco or biocentric value orientation which acknowledges the inherent worth or intrinsic value of wildlife, that is, that wildlife itself does have value independent of human 'valuing', and that humans have a responsibility to ensure their survival. In other cases this protectionistic view and the subsequent initiation of wildlife tourism programmes has been linked to the notion that the 'welfare of people and conservation are one and the same thing' (Lanjouw, 2001), particularly in developing nations of the world. Wildlife tourism is seen as one way of directly and indirectly generating much needed money for those communities located in areas inhabited by the

Box 3.2 A protectionistic view: Linking science, conservation and wildlife tourism

Some of the most familiar and popular accounts of linking science, conservation and wildlife tourism are those from and about scientists living and working in remote and difficult regions of the world, such as the primatologists, Dian Fossey (Fossey, 2000), Jane Goodall (Goodall, 1990), and Biruté Galdikas (Galdikas, 1995). These deeply dedicated wildlife biologists were responsible not only for their landmark long-term animal behavioural studies, but for bringing onto the world stage the plight of the three great apes – mountain gorillas, chimpanzees, and orangutans.

Through their scientific work came the realisation that all the great apes were endangered, primarily as a result of poaching, habitat destruction and illegal logging. And while alone it would not be sufficient, nevertheless one way to achieve conservation of primates was through various types of wildlife tourism programmes.

The mountain gorilla

The first example of this protectionistic view of wildlife which links science, conservation and wildlife tourism is that devised by the Dian Fossey Gorilla Fund and the International Gorilla Conservation Programme which see 'gorillas and tourism inextricably linked'. Five gorilla tourism programmes currently exist which generates US$20 million annually both directly and indirectly for three countries, Rwanda, Uganda and the Democratic Republic of Congo. In Uganda it is estimated that park entrance and gorilla trekking fees provide up to 70% of the Uganda Wildlife Authority's budget. Despite the monetary gains to local communities, wildlife authorities, and governments, there are those who are questioning the current sustainability of such programmes and are deeply concerned about the long-term survival for gorillas given the pressures to increase the number of tourists and gorilla groups available to tourists. As noted by Butynski (1998):

> Perhaps most importantly, the concept of gorilla tourism as a sustainable activitycontributing to the survival of the Virunga gorillas would undoubtedly lose much credibility and support, not only from the international conservation community, but also from those tourists who thought they were benefiting gorilla conservation through their visits.

The orangutan

Another example of this protectionistic view of wildlife in the context of wildlife tourism is that devised by the Orangutan Foundation International which was co-founded in 1986 by Dr Biruté Galdikas. The Orangutan Study and Support Tour and the Orangutan Foundation Volunteer Programme are two initiatives which have been set up for the primary purpose of conserving this species. The first initiative contributes over £35,000 annually to fund conservation efforts in the park and is clearly targeted at those visitors who welcome the opportunity of encountering such unique animals and of their activities contributing to the conservation of the species:

> In joining this tour not only will you have the privilege of seeing these gentlest of creatures in the wild but also to help in the fight against their extinction. (The Orangutan Foundation, 2003)

While not a conventional wildlife tourism programme, the Orangutan Foundation Volunteer Programme nevertheless also offers visitors the opportunity to encounter orangutans in their own natural habitat such as the Tanjung Putting National Park, Central Kalimantan, Borneo. The main purpose of this programme is to provide a much needed workforce which assists in installing and improving infrastructure, developing facilities for conservation education and wildlife appreciation, and rehabilitation programmes.

endangered species. As well as providing alternate livelihoods for some in these local communities, such wildlife tourism programmes demonstrate how people can benefit economically from conservation.

In the context of wildlife, it has been suggested that the higher the value humans place on wildlife, and in particular certain species, the more likely efforts will be made to protect, and care for that species (Kellert, 1996). This positive relationship between value, concern and engaging in activities to conserve a species was found in research on the endangered cassowary undertaken in the Wet Tropics World Heritage Area (WTWHA) of Australia (Bentrupperbäumer, 1998).

Encountering Wildlife in a Tourism Context

Identifying what constitutes an encounter with wildlife and how this influences human–wildlife relationships will ultimately determine where intellectual discussion, theoretical consideration, research effort, and management resources need to be focused. Within the context of tourism and for the purpose of this chapter encounters with wildlife are considered to occur in both virtual and actual landscapes and places, with the virtual incorporating printed and electronic materials where the perception of the animal is mediated, and the actual, the physical environment. This definition differs somewhat to that of Beardsworth and Bryman (2001) who consider an encounter with wildlife to occur with an unrestrained animal in its own environment. Here the concept of the encounter is broadened to include both the virtual and actual landscapes because the aim is to capture a more comprehensive understanding of what influences human–wildlife interaction. While most of the emphasis has traditionally been placed on interactions in the actual landscape, as will be demonstrated, the importance of considering the virtual and its influence on the nature of human–wildlife interactions cannot be underestimated. As Beardsworth and Bryman (2001: 87) note, experiences in one landscape will clearly shape 'expectations and interpretations in relation to another'. In other words, the way people build up their knowledge of wildlife through media representations, marketing programmes, previous encounters in semi-captive and captive situations, and in the 'wild', will strongly influence their expectation of and response to future wildlife encounters.

Human–wildlife encounters in *virtual* landscapes

In terms of the virtual landscape often the representation of wildlife is the 'first encounter', for many the only wildlife encounter, and so constitutes a potent instrument of emotion and behaviour, connection and consciousness, direction and control (Cooper, 1994). For those who venture out, a sanitised, virtual world is no substitute for the intimacy with animal and wild nature. Nevertheless, the virtual, constructed, and marketed landscape of wildlife which is what many tourists are exposed to prior to departing for their vacation or leisure trip, can play a powerful role in determining where they go, what they see and do, and what their expectations of such encounters are (Bentrupperbäumer & Reser, 2001). Furthermore, striking, distressing, exotic, spectacular images via a vast array of virtual outlets (print, film, audio) can shape the human connection to wildlife, how humans feel about them, human attitude toward them, and ultimately whether or not humans are concerned about them. A greater understanding of the nature, role and consequences of the virtual representation of wildlife and popular understandings and perceptions of wildlife encounters is therefore of particular applied and management importance in tourism. For this reason this is a landscape that requires careful consideration and management, discussed later in this chapter.

Human–wildlife encounters in *actual* landscapes

In terms of the actual landscape, tourists encounter wildlife in locations that vary from remote and wild regions, such as natural wildlife habitat areas, to secure and confined enclosures, such as zoos, aviaries and aquariums. According to Orams (1996) and Shackley (1996), the whole of this landscape encapsulates 'wildlife tourism'. The actual landscape continuum from the wild to the confined, or the wild, semi-captive and captive setting, as categorised by Orams (1996), provides a variety of opportunities for tourists to encounter wildlife in a way that best suits their needs, their desired experience, their ability to control the encounter, and in particular, their preparedness to confront what for many may be their first real interaction with wild and exotic animals.

The types of encounters with wildlife in actual landscapes and the human needs associated with such encounters in wildlife tourism vary greatly. As suggested by many researchers the primary goal of most leisure trips for the majority of participants is experiential (e.g. Botterill & Crompton, 1996). This is also the case in wildlife tourism where most tourists participate in encounters with wildlife to achieve particular states (e.g. desired experiences), or outcomes (e.g. socialisation). Floyd and Gramann (1997) identified a link between setting and experience such that the type of setting in which the encounter takes place can constrain or facilitate the attainment of such desired experiences. Of particular theoretical relevance to this discussion of the setting/experience relationship for the visitors is that of stress, coping, and control. The perceived environmental demands of any particular setting and coping resources available to the participant directly relates to stress. For wildlife tourism, this would suggest that providing a variety of settings within which the human–wildlife encounter can occur would enable the participant (tourist) to choose the one most likely to facilitate their desired experiences and their control needs.

Setting preferences in human–wildlife encounters

Within the containment lines

While considered less adventurous by some, encounters with wildlife in captive or semi-captive situations can nevertheless be a rewarding experience, albeit a mediated one. This is particularly the case for those who do not have any other opportunity of encountering wild animals (Kellert, 1996; Shackley, 1996), which applies to many children and elderly, age groups least able to see animals in their natural environments (Mason, 2000; Shackley, 1996). Consequently, for many tourists such settings provide an opportunity to experience a reasonably close encounter with wildlife which otherwise may simply be unattainable due to age or economic circumstances of the observer, or, as in the case of some rare, endangered, and/or dangerous animals, an encounter not possible in the natural environment. Here in these captive or semi-captive settings, 'even the dangerous and threatening aspects of "wildness" (Bostock, 1993: 51–3) are themselves sanitized and rendered harmless and entertaining' (Beardsworth & Bryman, 2001: 98).

For other wildlife tourists it may well be the highly structured nature of the physical environment that attracts them to captive and semi-captive settings. A preference for such settings can be due to the clear and unambiguous environmental cues to which many tourists are receptive. These are cues that facilitate a heightened sense of control over the encounter, which enhances coping and reduces stress (Bell *et al.*, 2001; Sinha, 2001). In a structured environment a sense of control is achieved partially because the built features of the setting act as a channel for communication, directing people where to go, what to do. And partially because it provides the tourist with an opportunity to experience wildlife in comfort and safety (Sinha, 2001). One assumption underlying this type of wildlife encounter is that tourists participate in order to achieve their desired experience in a way that is non-threatening, anxiety avoiding. The relaxed attentional state produced by these settings through attention to safety, legibility, wayfinding, and comfort, is an attractive proposition to many who are concerned about such issues, and who do not wish to be distracted by them.

> The quality of the experience can provide greater or lesser satisfaction for an observer, and depends on the degree of control of the wildlife encounter which the observer feels he or she has. (Reynolds & Braithwaite, 2001: 36)

Beyond the containment lines

For the individual to actually be in the physical presence of a wild animal in its own environment, unrestrained, the experience for most is awesome. Human/animal proximity varies along a continuum from direct physical contact as in holding or touching to a distant mere glimpse. For many wildlife tourists the type of encounter achievable will depend on the characteristics and status of the particular wildlife species, the environmental situation, and their own sense of control. Interestingly, Cooper (1993) suggests that a more respectful relationship between humans and wildlife is likely to occur when the interaction takes place in the wild as opposed to captivity.

Types of activity, human needs and consequences

In wildlife tourism the types of activity, and the human needs and consequences associated with such activities, are many and varied. Rather than address the extensive range of activities tourists engage in when interacting with wildlife, here the focus is on some of the most popular, and in some instances controversial, and to explore the reasons why they occur. These include photography, feeding, and hunting.

Photographing wildlife

Perhaps one of the most important and popular activities associated with wildlife tourism is observation and photography which are closely intertwined events. While many view these as fairly benign and the least disturbing for wildlife (e.g. Roe *et al.*, 1997), the extremes to which some tourists go just to see and/or to get that elusive photo, particularly of animals in their natural environment, suggests otherwise (e.g. Kellert, 1996; Klein, 1993 in Sinha, 2001). Furthermore, the extremes to which some tourism providers will go given this demand is of great concern. So what is driving the human need to engage in this type of wildlife interaction given that for many photographers often the event unfolding in the actual setting is a mediated event, one seen and experienced through the lens of a camera?

In addition to considerable advances in technology and subsequent ease with which photographs can be taken, one reason for the popularity of nature-oriented and in particular wildlife photography may well have to do with the nature and characteristics of photography itself (Albers & James, 1988; Hoelscher, 1998; Sontag, 1977; Urry, 1990). Urry (1990) provides a list of eight characteristics considered central to our understanding of the role of photography in tourism. The one characteristic repeatedly discussed in the literature is linked to the notion of authenticity. Urry (1990: 139) describes this in the following way: 'Photography *seems* to be a means of transcribing reality. . . . A photograph thus seems to furnish evidence that something did indeed happen.' Many writers (e.g. Albers & James, 1988; Hoelscher, 1998; Sontag, 1977; Urry, 1990) link this 'apparent transcription of reality' to the enormous proliferation in photography and see it as being an 'immensely valuable asset for one enterprise in particular: tourism' (Hoelscher, 1998: 549). This would suggest that, 'the meanings of photographs reside both in their making and in their subsequent uses' (Rose, 2000: 556).

In terms of the act of making photographs, picture-taking, Sontag (1977: 10) argues that it has become a 'principal device(s) for experiencing something, for giving an appearance of participation'. She goes on:

> Most tourists feel compelled to put the camera between themselves and whatever is remarkable they encounter. Unsure of other responses, they take a picture. This gives shape to experience: stop, take a photograph, and move on.

Urry (1990) links photography to the notion of obligation involving both the tourist and tourism provider, with the tourist feeling obliged to not miss photo opportunities and the tourism provider feeling obliged to seek out and identify the ideal 'viewing-location'. In addition to enabling participation and creating a sense of obligation, for many, the act of picture-taking provides a purpose, a reason for visiting, thus shaping and structuring the event.

Photography also plays an important role for the wildlife tourist beyond the moment and the actual setting within which the act of picture taking occurred, one which also drives and shapes the behaviour itself. As well as documenting their experiences, the resultant photographic images provide each individual tourist with the means by which they can authenticate and celebrate their experiences, promote their achievements to others, and recall and relive the events at whatever time they choose. In other words, reconstruct the event and thereby the experience. According to Botterill and Crompton (1996: 59), such 'constructive revision', in this case through photography, 'is a stage in which all of the greater moments of life that are often recognised and labelled as growth experiences take place'.

Such important experiential outcomes associated with both the making and sub-sequent uses of photographs are powerful motivating forces driving this activity:

> Needing to have reality confirmed and experience enhanced by photographs is an aesthetic consumerism to which everyone is now addicted. (Sontag, 1977: 24)

For many wildlife tourists viewing or observing wildlife is closely intertwined with photography. Nevertheless, there are some interesting perspectives on why this activity in itself is both popular and important. One perspective put forward by Katcher and Wilson (1993) is that the activity of just simply observing wildlife may be associated with one of the two properties of events in nature, the Heraclitean motion, and a psychological association with safety or comfort. The Heraclitean motion refers to a form of movement that is 'always changing but always remaining the same' (e.g. birds flying, fish swimming, animals feeding) (Katcher & Wilkins, 1993). Motion of this kind can be hypnotic simply by being quiet and repetitive. The psychological effect of observing such quiet and repetitive motions is calming. These tranquil-type events are also associated with an absence of danger contrast-ing dramatically with events which signal danger (e.g. erratic motion of injured or dying fish, sudden movements and/or sounds of animals attempting to escape a predator). Sensitivity to such distinctive patterns of safety and danger associated with movement are clearly beneficial and hence selected for over time. Benefits as-sociated with safety include psychological and physicological relaxation, enhanced problem-solving abilities, and more creative, less stereotyped thought patterns (Katcher & Wilkins, 1993).

Feeding

Feeding wildlife is one way that ensures a close, often special, but sometimes dangerous encounter with wild animals, and is one which has been and continues to be used by many different groups of people for all sorts of reasons. Those engaged in such an activity and the reasons why vary from the backyard feeding by a community resident for reasons which include pleasure, relaxation, care and concern, to the tourist operator wishing to provide that special and sometimes sen-sational experience for their customer, and the scientist needing to obtain a particular set of data. Orams (2002) provides a comprehensive and interesting typology of the provisioning of food to other species, which includes the range of purposes behind such activity and the orientation or focus of those engaged in the activity. This typology also identifies the philosophical states underlying the provisioning of food. According to this typology, in the wildlife tourism context feeding animals is grounded in the strongly anthropocentric philosophy that animals are subordinate to humans, to be used solely for the benefit of humans.

Orams (2002) identifies three purposes of feeding wildlife in tourism: (1) permits close observations; (2) experience unusual or exciting animals; (3) education.

Besides ensuring a close encounter with wildlife and providing unusual and educational opportunities, why are people so attracted to feeding wildlife? Orams (2002: 287) argues that, 'The sharing of food is something more complex and more fundamental for humans than simply getting close to animals.' Katcher and Wilkins (1993) provide one possible explanation based on the ascription of kinship to certain animals. They claim that feeding wildlife may well be associated with a human predisposition to treat at least some animals as kin and so engage in nurturing behaviour, one aspect of which is the provision of food. Additionally, when feeding involves a close encounter it often provides the opportunity for a tactile experience. Katcher and Wilkins (1993) also argue that activities such as feeding of animals may be linked to an innate tendency of humans to attend to living things.

Hunting

Recreational and trophy hunting and fishing are other types of human–wildlife encounters providing a range of benefits and very different experiences for the tourist. In order to understand why people engage in hunting there is the need to explore the social and psychological dimensions of the activity. A number of studies, particularly from North America, have identified hunting as providing the participant with a variety of social, psychological and physical benefits in addition to the need and desire to harvest game (e.g. Daigle *et al.*, 2002; Hauteluoma & Brown, 1979).

Floyd and Gramann (1997) categorised hunters based on the psychological experiences desired from their hunting participation: *outdoor enthusiast, high-challenge harvester, low-challenge harvester, and nonharvester*. The *outdoor enthusiasts* were those who 'stressed nature enjoyment and seeing animals as important hunting experiences', whereas the *nonharvesters* were primarily interested in 'getting away', enjoying nature, and placed little importance on harvesting. In contrast, the experiences most sought by the *high-challenge harvesters* were associated with challenge, risk and skill development, and for the *low-challenge harvester*, nature enjoyment, fitness, excitement, seeing animals in their natural habitat were the most desired experiences. These researchers also found significant relationships between the hunter categories (segments) and the types of settings they preferred. For example, the *high-challenge harvesters* who were particularly interested in shooting big game animals, preferred hunting in undeveloped, remote settings which were exclusive to them as these settings maximised their chance of obtaining the outcome they desired, shooting game as well as preserving the challenge of the hunt. An interesting outcome from this research was the suggestion that in addition to the need to identify types of wildlife tourists as defined by their desired social and psychological experiences, linking these desired experiences to setting preferences provides a useful tool in marketing hunting opportunities.

Virtual Representations of Wildlife

An important issue and consideration in wildlife tourism has to do with how cultures in general *represent* wildlife and the implications of such representations for human–wildlife interaction. One perspective is that of social representations (Farr, 1987, 1993; Grauman & Kruse, 1990), where the focus is on how cultural products, such as films, books, newspapers, magazines and art, embody and express cultural understandings. These are collective or shared understandings, which not only represent but shape and inform community understandings, and ultimately individual experience and behaviour in the context of the natural environment. Another perspective is the representation of wildlife by the tourism industry and environmental management agencies where the focus is primarily on marketing and interpretation. The nature and role of all of these virtual representations of wildlife and the influence this has on environmental concern and awareness, pre-trip decision-making and expectations, and actual experience and behaviour once at the destination, are briefly discussed here in the context of media representations, popular cultural images and symbolic meanings, and marketing.

Media representations

Western media representations of the natural environment and wildlife over the past 20 years provide an informative look at the nature and magnitude of public interest in these topics. During this time there has been a constant stream of multiple, fascinating, often dramatic, sometimes frightening images of wildlife presented to us on magazine covers, television documentaries, billboards, newspapers and across the internet. As Beardsworth and Bryman (2001: 83) describe, 'The sheer volume and variety of images of wild animals in the mass media might provide us with a broad indication of the continuing interest our species has in the other species with which it shares the global environment.'

Because wildlife images are such a popular means of communicating information about the natural environment, fostering public awareness and environmental consciousness through these images is clearly an integral part of environmental education. In addition to awareness, such representations are an often-used unobtrusive measure of community or national concerns, particularly those multiple, dramatic, and alternately poignant and/or frightening images of ecosystem collapse from vanishing species, to lost habitat, to the systemic poisoning of the earth's life support systems (Reser & Bentrupperbäumer, 2000).

Champ (2002) considered wildlife media as a potential contributor to understanding the shift in public value orientation toward wildlife from utilitarian to protectionist. Of those interviewed, he found that 'They were learning about, being entertained by, and in some cases were grounding themselves in relation to images, sounds, and stories via such media outlets as film, television, and magazines' (2002: 283).

The significance of the role which media representations play in the construction of human–wildlife interrelationships is clearly articulated by Beardsworth and Bryman (2001: 86):

> It is no exaggeration to suggest that the typical television viewer's primary mode of engagement with the wild is through highly processed (and skilfully edited) electronically mediated representations of real or 'virtual' animals. Arguably, such representations, and the ideological frameworks within which they are organised, come to dominate the ways in which the 'wild' is construed in contemporary cultures. The wildlife documentary (whether composed of 'natural' or 'staged' footage, or a combination of the two) effectively replaces and supplants the encounter for the majority of individuals.

Popular cultural images and representations of wildlife

Virtual representations of wildlife are also evident in forms other than the usual mass media, and promotional and interpretive materials such as pamphlets, brochures, and signage. In contemporary societies there is the prevalent use of wildlife in a pseudo-totemic fashion, both through language and imagery; for example, sports teams, resource management agencies, trade marks (Beardsworth & Bryman, 2001). A spectrum of these representations in the form of language, images, logos, and caricatures litter the virtual landscape. In addition to the sheer volume of such wildlife representations, their role in 'identifying' and imposing 'meaning' on place, community, organisation, and individuals can create the cultural and symbolic 'space' that can impact on public perceptions, awareness, knowledge, interest and concerns for wildlife (Bentrupperbäumer & Reser, 2000).

Wildlife tourists are very much exposed to these popular cultural images both prior to their departure and once at their destination. A particularly widespread form of presentation is the anthropomorphised portrayal of wildlife, the use of caricatures and cartoon representations. These are used in all virtual media formats by a diversity of organisations in a wide variety of ways to impart an assortment of messages. In many instances the link between the caricature and the appearance and behaviour of the actual species is very tenuous (Beardsworth & Bryman, 2001). Of concern are the many occasions when cartoon animals are given human attributes which convey ambiguous, often incorrect, and sometimes inappropriate messages. When such anthropomorphism is used 'as sources of "knowledge" about the real thing' (Beardsworth & Bryman, 2001: 86), which so often happens in the case of wildlife tourists who are unfamiliar with the species, there is the potential for problems. In the case of the endangered cassowary, environmental managers consistently use caricatures of this animal to communicate conservation messages. Not only are many of the messages ambiguous and incorrect, the public found the use of cartoons to represent this species and conservation messages very inappropriate (Bentrupperbäumer, 1998).

Another very popular use of wildlife images is as logos for place and corporate identity purposes representing nations, regions, communities, organisations, groups, industries, businesses, sports teams, environmental agencies, etc. Clearly the use of logos for such identity purposes is a popular activity based on the notion that it allows for easy and quick recall of where or who the logo represents. Despite the continued faith in this ability, recent research in the WTWHA suggests otherwise. Just 5% of community residents ($n = 788$) were able to describe the logo of the key environmental management agency, a logo that has been in place for a considerable amount of time and is highly visible throughout the region (Bentrupperbäumer & Reser, 2003a). Immortalising wildlife as human caricatures is another popular marketing initiative aimed at wildlife tourists (Box 3.3). Such caricatures are widespread across the landscape and the taking of photographs of various versions, such as models and concrete structures of various species, has in many instances become the surrogate for the 'real' encounter.

Marketing

Many tourists depend on an external or secondary information source to make important travel decisions (Nielsen, 2003; Wicks & Schuett, 1991). In particular, such sources of information can play a significant role in determining visitors' choice of destination (Wicks & Schuett, 1991), the activities they will engage in once there, and their expectations of what the area has to offer (Manfredo, 1989). Active *external* information users are considered a particularly important visitor/user group because, as Manfredo (1989) suggests, since they are using external information to improve decision making and therefore already predisposed toward receiving and attending to messages, they are more likely to be susceptible to persuasive appeals. These posters, images, ads and texts influence and shape the expectations and understandings that mediate actual encounters, experiences and enjoyment (Ellen & Fukui, 1996; Everden, 1992; Moscardo *et al.*, 2001; Moscardo & Woods, 1998; Simmons, 1993).

Wildlife feature a great deal in marketing particular areas, destinations, and/or tours. In research undertaken in the WTWHA, Bentrupperbäumer and Reser (2001) found that 35% of the brochures analysed used images of wildlife to promote the area and/or tour, and 85% of these same brochures cited wildlife in the text. The wildlife images represented numerous species of birds, reptiles, amphibians, mammals and insects; however, the most frequently used image was that of the crocodile. While this is perhaps not unusual, of concern in terms of the images used was the message being presented. Often these images would depict the feeding of wildlife, an activity that is now well documented as potentially dangerous for tour-

Box 3. 3   Popular cultural and tourism images of wildlife: Examples from Northern Australia

Kakadu and crocodiles

There is little question that the crocodile has become the iconic image of Kakadu, and possibly the large Top End (Northern Territory) visitor experience and encounter. Images of crocodiles eclipse all other representations of the natural environment and wilderness character of Kakadu, and such images have been utilised and exploited by almost all commercial ventures and tourism initiatives associated with visitation to Kakadu. While there are many good and understandable reasons why such a dramatic predator species might be seen as a natural symbolic vehicle for representing the character, wildness and power of a 'wilderness' environment, there appears to be other, more humbling, reasons for the ubiquitous use and often caricaturisation of the crocodile as image and emblem.

One need only look at the spectrum of crocodile memorabilia, trivia, and images in any tourist shop along the Arnhem Highway or in Darwin or Katherine to appreciate that the fibreglass effigies, the bedroom warning signs, and the postcards are all minimising, trivialising, and ultimately sanitising a very real and present visitor danger (Plate 3.1). These products and representations are also caricaturising as well as wholly misrepresenting and distorting the nature and behaviour of this fascinating animal. There are also a number of visitor venues along the route to Kakadu which highlight crocodiles as their main event and attraction, providing crocodile 'performances' for river cruises and at riverside restaurants.

All of this sanitises the visitor risk associated with crocodiles, and by inference other threats associated with the wild, natural environment. Crocodiles are presented as amusing, unreal, even soft and comical, and ultimately and paradoxically, harmless, notwithstanding their seeming ferocity. There are recurrent and conflicting messages and meanings for visitors, but such messages are of course both dangerous and incongruent with the warning messages of the management agencies. It is instructive to note that such sanitising images and misrepresentations of this animal outnumber credible warning messages, enroute to Kakadu by a factor of approximately 40 to 1.

Wet Tropics and cassowaries

The development and use of images of the endangered species, the cassowary, as symbol, logo, and popular culture touchstone for the Wet Tropics World Heritage Area of Australia is particularly interesting given its fairly recent history, its

Plate 3.1 Trivialisation of crocodiles, Northern Territory

close association with research and conservation, and the subsequent embracing of the high profile status of the species by industry and management. Prior to the intense cassowary research and conservation initiatives of the early 1990s in the Wet Tropics, relatively little was known of the species, and the only significant cultural representation evident was confined to local indigenous communities.

However, in the last 10 years, as with the crocodile in Kakadu, the cassowary has now come to symbolise the Wet Tropics World Heritage Area (Plate 3.2). This symbolic use varies with a spectrum of cassowary images and representations evident throughout the region. The variety of formats which use cassowaries include tourist brochures and memorabilia, commercial enterprise advertising and naming, environmental management agency identity, education, conservation and interpretation initiatives, and community conservation programmes.

Examples of 'industry' representation of cassowaries:

Cassowary Mowing
Cassowary Coast Development Bureau
Cassowary Coast Employment
Cassowary Coast Investigations & Security
Cassowary Garden Service
Cassowary Ridge Bed & Breakfast

In the context of wildlife tourism, the representation of cassowaries is most often in the form of naturalistic images on tourist brochures and promotional material, used to illustrate the wildness and uniqueness of the particular programme and setting.

Plate 3.2 Use of the cassowary as logo for the Wet Tropics World Heritage Area (Extract from Bentrupperbäumer & Reser, 2003b)

ists and detrimental to wildlife (e.g. Orams, 2002). Furthermore, negligible textual information was available on behaving in an environmentally responsible way, particularly in the context of human–wildlife interaction. While this may not be seen as a role of such promotional material by those in the industry who produce it,

---

Box 3.4   Monitoring and managing the virtual landscape: A consideration for the Wet Tropics World Heritage Area of Australia

Comprehensive studies in the Wet Tropics World Heritage Area of Australia (Bentrupperbäumer & Reser, 2001, 2002, 2003b) suggest that the virtual landscape, be it specific to wildlife or more generally, the natural environment, is one that requires careful monitoring and management with respect to particular representations and products which are produced. The tourist industry and environmental management agencies in particular need to appreciate the nature and impacts of virtual representations of wildlife on visitor motivations, expectations, and actual visitation, experience and behaviours. As well this perspective provides fresh insights with respect to larger issues relating to presentation, interpretation, and education, which have their own long-term influence on managing impacts and changing behaviours.

This monitoring and managing of the representations of wildlife requires a change in the way we think about wildlife management, and a realisation that such representations have powerful 'impacts' on tourist perceptions and expectations, and ultimate environmental impacts on behaviour and natural settings. Words and images are powerful mediators and determinants of behaviour and impact.

---

nevertheless one of the management agencies responsible for the area clearly state, 'Whenever possible, marketing programs promoting use of northern Queensland and the Area should aim to foster visitor expectations and behaviour consistent with management objectives for the Area' (Wet Tropics Management Authority, 1997: 109). Despite the considerable emphasis in nature-based tourism on marketing materials such as leaflets, brochures, pamphlets, and information centres as important avenues for promoting the region and/or particular tour, research undertaken in the WTWHA found that just 6.3% of visitors to recreation sites in this region used tourist leaflets as a means of knowing about the location, and 9.1% used information centres (Bentrupperbäumer & Reser, 2002).

Conclusions

Nature-based tourism, and in particular wildlife tourism, is beginning to take centre stage at local, national and international levels. This clearly says something about the desire for human connectedness with nature and specifically the importance of wildlife in people's lives. It is critical therefore that if an analysis of wildlife tourism is to be taken seriously the human dimension of wildlife interactions must be considered. In turn this analysis must pay particular attention to the psychological and sociological processes that underlie the development of human–wildlife relations, human interest in wildlife, and the nature and role of such relations in human life.

The challenge for any such analysis is to extract from the many disciplinary perspectives those key theoretical perspectives, themes and concepts which are central to developing a better understanding of such relationships and to present these in a coherent way. With this in mind this chapter began with an exploration of the diverse discourses and research literatures which share a central concern for human relations with the natural environment, and through this, clarified and focused on how this informs us about the nature and role of human–wildlife relationships, particularly in the context of wildlife tourism. The natural environment and specifically animals are important in people's lives for reasons which have been explained using evolutionary and/or learned principles. More specifically, an understanding of our affiliation with animals is fundamental to wildlife tourism because it not only determines the extent of our interest in non-human life and hence our desire to encounter them, it inevitably shapes our feelings, concerns, and behaviour toward them. Companionship, bonding, emotional attachment and attributes of wildlife are considered key aspects of our affiliation with animals as examined in this chapter.

The way in which the tourism industry views wildlife and their willingness to accept and implement regulatory policies is often determined by the values they hold for wildlife. Such values also influence the way tourism providers conduct their operation and the nature and quality of the interaction between the individual tourist and wildlife. The examination of value orientations toward wildlife outlined in this chapter provided a brief description of the four key universal values considered particularly relevant to understanding our view of wildlife in a tourism context.

For most people, 'encountering' wildlife is an everyday event, occurring most frequently in the *virtual* landscape. In the *actual* landscape such encounters can be very varied for people in terms of setting preferences, types of activities engaged in, and the needs and consequences associated with such encounters. This section of the chapter explores these different aspects of human–wildlife encounters focusing specifically on the most popular and sometimes controversial such as photographing, feeding and hunting.

Wildlife is also an intensely marketed commodity used and represented by the tourist and various commercial industries, environmental management agencies, and community organisations in a variety of ways. The last section of the chapter describes this use and representation of wildlife within the context of the virtual landscape. The spectrum of representations, images, and contexts is considered as is the effects of such use on public understandings of wildlife. The discussion also addresses the role which popular cultural images play in the construction of human–wildlife interrelationships.

Further reading

In order to provide the reader with a deeper insight into the human dimension of wildlife tourism this chapter has drawn on the conceptual and theoretical frameworks and research findings evident in a variety of literature from a diversity of disciplines. Consequently much of what has been presented has relied on literature which, while relevant to wildlife tourism, has nevertheless not depended on this as a primary source.

Wilson's (1984) book, for example, provides an important and interesting perspective on human need for contact with nature, a need upon which wildlife tourism is based. This book presents an evolutionary basis for understanding our relationship with nature, with living biota. Such a provocative concept caught the imagination of scholars from a diverse field of disciplines and generated a considerable amount of research in the drive to provide the empirical evidence necessary to prove or disprove the proposition. A comprehensive and informative presentation of such research and the different disciplinary perspectives is available in Kellert and Wilson's (1993) edited collection. Part Four in particular explores the role of animals in human cognitive development and communication. Kahn (1997, 1999) also provides an interesting examination of the human relationship with nature from the perspective of developmental psychology.

Understanding human affiliation with animals which has important implications for wildlife tourism has also generated a considerable volume of research and writings from a diversity of disciplines. Kellert's (1996) book provides an overview of the results from his studies on human–animal relations that he had undertaken over two decades. As a leading social scientist, his research added a critical new dimension to the debate on biodiversity loss which had predominantly focused on ecological impacts. A more psychological perspective on this is presented in articles by Plous (1993b) and Eddy *et al.* (1993) who address the issue of the role of animals in human society.

The exploration of human affiliation with animals is also evident in several articles some of which focus on wildlife tourism. Tremblay (2002), for example, considers particular attributes of wildlife and their role in attracting tourists via the use of wildlife icons. This use of icons, popular cultural images and media representations of wildlife, is explored in a number of articles. Beardsworth and Bryman (2001) presents an interesting sociological perspective on the different modes of engagement through which humans experience wild animals, one of which is *representation*. Farr (1987, 1993) provides a more detailed analysis of the concept of social representations and how it reflects cultural understandings.

Chapter 4

Stakeholder Engagement

Introduction

Participation by residents in wildlife tourism planning is also fundamental to the process, so stakeholders have a buy-in and a degree of empowerment in the process of wildlife tourism development. The public now demand that their concerns be incorporated into the decision-making process. Appropriate ecoethics for resident and tourist participation in the planning process include the need for developers to take account of local community attitudes and feelings, including the way that a local unaltered environment contributes to a community's sense of place. Any wildlife tourism development should not lessen enjoyment of the local environment by the local community and where practicable, should enhance it. Wildlife tourism development at the regional level must be developed within the context of sustainable local, national and international tourism development. At both the regional and national levels, development policies, plans and programmes, laws and regulations, and marketing, all influence tourism development. The three main principles of sustainable development that can also be applied to regional wildlife tourism development planning are its concentration on ecological, social and economic issues.

There are a number of stakeholders in tourism development and management. Each group has a contribution to make to changing the nature of tourism and their own success is dependent upon the contribution of others. Tourism development involves multiple stakeholders including business and government as well as community and environmental groups. An introductory definition of stakeholder is any person, group or organisation that is affected by the causes or consequences of an issue (Bryson & Crosby, 1992). Although it is often difficult and time-consuming to involve a range of stakeholders in the planning process, this involvement may have significant benefits for sustainability including environmental, social, cultural, economic and political (Medeiros de Araujo & Bramwell, 2000).

A central task in stakeholder development is to establish who the stakeholders actually are and whether or not they adequately represent the affected stakeholders. This can be done by identification, self-nomination or referral. Once identified stakeholders can be positioned on a map according to these relationships in order to determine their power to influence the relationships between their perceived legitimacy and the urgency of their claims. These three relationships are central to how stakeholder groups become involved in an issue. Another important consideration is to limit the number of stakeholders in collaborative planning to a manageable size in order to build trust and consensus and increase the likelihood of achieving a mutually acceptable outcome.

The local community

One aspect of stakeholders' interests in tourism development is the involvement of the local or host community (Richards & Hall, 2000; Scheyvens, 2002; Singh *et al.*, 2003). When referring to natural areas, the use of the term 'community' is sometimes based on an incorrect assumption that it comprises a single homogeneous unit; however, social stratification is a common phenomenon in almost every community and different groups within it often have differing interests or stakes in the natural resource (Ashley & Roe, 1998). Thus when related to wildlife tourism in the wild, a community may not work together for its development in a harmonious way. Therefore a more appropriate approach is to expand the definition of the host community to the wider community, in this instance a set of people with a mutually recognised interest in the resources of a particular area rather than as people living in that area (Gilmore & Fisher, 1992). The community thus represents users of a resource rather than a homogeneous resident unit.

Ashley and Roe (1998) suggest that tourism can involve and affect local residents without being driven and controlled by the community and therefore there can be many forms of their involvement. These may include a range of involvement from passive to active and include lease agreements, concessions, partnerships and active involvement in businesses (Table 4.1).

Wildlife Tourism's Stakeholders

Wildlife, especially big game, was an important motivator in the creation of reserves in colonial Africa (Plate 4.1). Over time, consumptive hunting has been overtaken by non-consumptive sustainable tourism. However, in the development of wildlife tourism it is important that tourism should more equitably balance the costs and benefits of conservation, which are often borne by local communities. The authors argue that this balance can be achieved through the creation of mutually beneficial, self-sustaining mechanisms that support tourism, wildlife, institutions and communities. Ensuring the long-term success of wildlife tourism depends on creating local incentives to conserve and protect environmental amenities. In the past national parks and other protected areas have been viewed by local peoples as 'fortresses' from which they have been locked out. However, a more recent approach has been one of 'integrated community conservation' which espouses a participatory approach to park management which aims to improve the livelihoods of communities surrounding protected areas through activities such as wildlife

Table 4.1 Different forms of community involvement in tourism

No	Type of enterprise or institution	Nature of local involvement	Examples
1	Private business run by outsider	Employment Supply goods and services	Kitchen staff in a lodge Sale of food, building materials, etc.
2	Enterprise or informal sector operation run by local entrepreneur	Enterprise ownership Self-employment Supply of goods and services	Craft sales, food kiosk, campsite, home stays Guiding services Hawking, sales of fuelwood, food
3	Community enterprise	Collective ownership Collective or individual management Supply of goods and services Employment or contributed labour	Community campsite Craft centre Cultural centre
4	Joint venture between community and private sector	Contractual commitments Shares in revenue Lease/investment of resources Participation in decision-making	Revenue-sharing from lodge to local community on agreed terms Community leases of land/resources/concession to lodge Community holds equity in lodge
5	Tourism planning body	Consultation Representation Participation	Local consultation in regional tourism planning Community representatives on tourism board and in planning fora

Source: Ashley and Roe (1998)

tourism. This is partly in recognition that the costs and benefits of conservation have not been shared equally among different levels of society as well as in response to the failure of the fortress conservation approach Scheyvens (2002). She argues that unless local people gain some benefits from the conservation of wildlife they will have little incentive to sustainably manage these resources.

The local host community and wider community groups are both included in a wider group again, that of the stakeholder. In wildlife tourism this group includes the tourism industry; planners and investors; protected area managers; conservation non-government organisations; the local communities; and finally, the tourists themselves. While tourists who are on wildlife tours are primarily interested in

Plate 4.1 Big game viewing in Southern Africa
Source: Ross Dowling

viewing wildlife, they are generally also interested in interacting with local communities in a sustainable manner. This can occur when visitors view wildlife with local guides, visit villages, sample local food and drink, or watch crafts being made, music played or dances. Local guides are often especially highly valued by wildlife tourists as they can provide deeper understanding of the surrounding environment.

An important aspect of stakeholders and wildlife tourism managers is to identify just who exactly the stakeholders are. For protected area managers to work in isolation from the community is neither practical, desirable, nor usual. Apart from legal processes that prescribe formal consultation procedures, managers are interacting with the community every day on what are regarded as routine matters: cooperative firefighting, tourism management, pest animal control, weed spraying, road maintenance, school programmes, and joint interpretive displays (Worboys *et al.*, 2001).

When managers consult the public when making decisions they must ensure that the process is efficient and fair. They need to consider carefully who should be involved. The people consulted are often referred to as 'stakeholders'. There is no rigid definition of them but the term is typically used to define persons or groups

Table 4.2 Examples of stakeholders

No.	Stakeholder	Relationship
1	Neighbours	May be directly impacted by an issue (e.g. fire) or are directly responsible for one (intrusion of pets)
2	Park visitors	May be directly impacted by an issue (restriction of access) or are directly responsible for one (track erosion)
3	Employees of an industry	Whose practices may be altered or restricted (e.g. mining, grazing, fishing, logging)
4	Representatives of private companies	Whose practices may be altered or restricted (e.g. tour leaders, extractive industries)
5	The wider national and international community	Concerned with conservation or economic development
6	Various community groups	With specific concerns (e.g. frog conservation society, bird watching clubs, etc.)
7	Government agencies	With varying agendas and responsibilities (e.g. the department that controls land use around the protected area
8	Non-government organisations	Particularly those with a government focus
9	International conservation organisations	For example, World Heritage Committee, IUCN, WWF
10	Local businesses	
11	Any person or group who expresses an interest	

After Worboys *et al.* (2001)

who have an interest in or who could be affected by an issue or a situation. It should also include persons or groups who perceive themselves as affected (Forrest & Mays, 1997). According to Worboys *et al.* (2001) examples of stakeholders include the local community, visitors, business, government agencies, national and international community groups, as well as any person or group who expresses an interest (Table 4.2).

Ashley and Roe (1998) state that in recent years community involvement in wildlife tourism has increased due to its perceived local economic, social and conservation benefits. The development of wildlife tourism offers local residents income generation, jobs and skill development. It is also a way in which they can gain benefits from wildlife that in the past may have only brought them costs. In addition, most conservationists now recognise the crucial role played by local people in managing wildlife and habitat. Thus wildlife tourism is viewed as a way in which wildlife can be conserved and managed; and the tourism industry recognises the importance of local people because of their central role in maintaining natural and cultural heritage. Finally, both government and non-government organisations are funding wildlife tourism developments as a way of fostering the integration of development and conservation. Thus in wildlife tourism development there can be a number of stakeholders involved but with each holding a different perspective on the development. For example, community based wildlife management projects may combine both the development and conservations perspectives but to highly varying degrees.

Stakeholder Engagement in Wildlife Tourism

Wildlife tourism development represents a partnership between local people, the private sector and government and it is gaining acceptance because it makes good economic sense and can benefit all partners. Stakeholder involvement in wildlife tourism in Australia is varied (Box 4.1). Burns and Sofield (2001) note that the host community is an important element to consider in the concept of sustainability and that the sustainability of wildlife tourism is dependent, in part, on its support from the areas' residents. They argue that host satisfaction is related to both the involvement of local community members in wildlife tourism activities, and the benefits and disadvantages of wildlife tourism to host communities. In their research report on 'The host community: social and cultural issues concerning wildlife tourism' they define the host community as those who live in the vicinity of the tourist attraction and are either directly or indirectly involved with, and/or affected by, the wildlife tourism activities. They state that the actual and perceived impacts of wildlife tourism will influence the attitudes of the host community and ultimately have an effect on sustainability. They postulate that wildlife tourism will only be sustainable where there are benefits for the host community. These may be social and/or cultural, and environmental and will not necessarily be confined to economic benefits.

The importance of communications

Worboys *et al.* (2001) state that good communications are essential for engaging with the community and selecting the right channel of communication is often the key to having one's message understood. This includes verbal, non-verbal and visual communication. Working with other organisations within the community includes a range of techniques from conflict resolution to group decision making. The key underlying principles on groups working together are understanding, integrity and commitment.

The key to communicating with stakeholders in wildlife tourism development is through providing opportunities for a multi-level exchange of ideas and informa-

Box 4.1   Australian community involvement in wildlife

A study of 320 local councils in Australia reveals that community involvement in wildlife tourism attractions varies from some, with little involvement, to others with a high level of involvement. Because host interaction with wildlife and wildlife tourism ranges over a broad spectrum, different communities often have different attitudes towards wildlife. They may regard wildlife as a valuable resource or may have an integrated relationship with it. In some instances conflict may exist between hosts over wildlife resources and their utilisation for tourism. Factors that affect host attitudes towards wildlife tourism include the hosts' feeling of empowerment or control over the attraction and/or their economic benefits from it.

Community involvement in wildlife tourism in Australia includes a range of engagements. A low level of community involvement occurs in The Osprey House Environmental Centre at Dolhes Rocks, Queensland. The Centre is an accredited ecotourism attraction based on wetlands and mangroves and is home to many migratory shorebirds. A low level of involvement occurs with volunteers running the centre. A moderate level of community engagement occurs in the Dolphin Discovery Centre at Bunbury in Western Australia (Plate 4.2). This non-profit organisation is dedicated to promoting wildlife tourism in the interests of developing economic and employment opportunities for the local community. It has a number of volunteers who provide information for visitors and assist in the management of tourist–dolphin interactions. In Barraba Shire in New South Wales, there is a high level of community involvement in birdwatching. The community had claimed Barraba as the habitat of the Regent Honey Eater and have depicted the bird on its 'welcome to Barraba' signs. It also has been responsible for establishing birdwatching trails in the area and for promoting 'birds of the district' via the media. They have set up a birdwatchers club and members act as guides on birdwatching tours.

(Burns & Sofield, 2001)

tion as well as the development of shared solutions. One way in which this takes place is through interpretation. This is an educational activity which aims to reveal meanings and relationships through the use of original objects, by first-hand experience, and by illustrative media, rather than simply to communicate factual information (Tilden, 1982). The four roles of interpretation can be described as promotion, visitor enjoyment, management and education for conservation. Higham and Luck (2002) surveyed the Oamaru Blue Penguin Colony wildlife tourism attraction on the east coast of the South Island of New Zealand. The colony is

Plate 4.2 Dolphin viewing at the Dolphin Discovery Centre, Western Australia
Source: Bunbury Dolphin Discovery Centre

managed by a community based group and attracts over 25,000 visitors per year. Viewing facilities and physical barriers are used to manage visitors within a designated viewing area of the former harbour-side quarry. An interpretive commentary is provided and nocturnal viewing is provided. The highlight is the evening penguin parade. The penguins' welfare is undertaken by colony staff as well as members of NZ's Department of Conservation and present indications are that the penguins are breeding better than those not in the tourist colony.

A framework for public participation in sustainable development, has been advocated for Australia's natural resource management (Ross *et al.*, 2002). In this approach the key components are the agencies and participants involved as well as other factors such as the nature of the tenure, the task to be achieved and finally the duration of the process. A key ingredient of the process includes many forms of consultation based on the party taking the initiative encouraging two-way communication and being willing to shape the eventual decision according to public input. Best practice involves identifying the stakeholders who ought to be consulted, approaching them directly, and tailoring the consultation approach according to their culture, gender, social organisation and geographical constraints.

Examples of stakeholder engagement

There are a number of examples of wildlife tourism in which stakeholders have engaged in its development including small-scale examples such as parks through to larger ones such as regions, nations and international collaborative efforts. An example of a park-based development is Nepal's Annapurna Conservation Area. Nepal (2000) argues that the most desirable state of park-based tourism is the one which envisages a symbiotic relationship between tourism, parks and local communities. This relationship guarantees benefits to all elements and takes into account that tourism creates some adverse impacts. Local communities interact with tourism and national parks in a number of ways through local institutions, grassroots organisations, line agencies and local entrepreneurs, but it is expected that a balance of interactions among the three elements will provide mutual benefits for all three. Nepal (2000) champions the Annapurna Conservation Area, Nepal, as a sound example of local involvement in developing strong links between the park, tourism and the community, and suggests that this has only come about through the park's participatory approach to management. Three main principles guide the park project – sustainability, public participation and the *Lami* (catalyst approach). Various management committees have been established to engage local people in environmental and wildlife [protection of species, etc.] on the one hand, and community development on the other.

Another tourism development planning framework, which includes stakeholder engagement, has been applied to the North West Cape region of Western Australia (Dowling, 1999). It is an area of outstanding natural beauty with unique marine (e.g. whalesharks) and terrestrial wildlife protected within both national and marine parks. Tourism is the fastest growing industry in the region and increasing concern is held for the ongoing conservation of the region's environment. The planning approach to the study stemmed from its commitment to balance the competing needs of profitable development, tourism values, community lifestyles and environmental protection (Figure 4.1). Its underlying philosophy derived from the need to find options and solutions by the application of an open methodology. This was based on understanding the inputs, letting land assets and natural resources speak, gaining expert and public input, and formulating recommendations that emanated clearly from the information base.

By applying this methodology, it was considered that a long-term tourism development strategy could be implemented that is sustainable:

- politically – because the various viewpoints are properly and objectively analysed;
- commercially – because the development models are tested for long-term profitability;

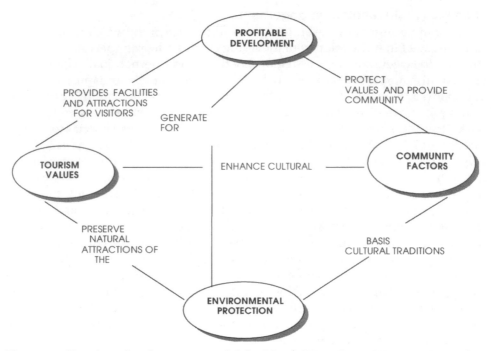

Figure 4.1 Tourism development model for North West Cape, Western Australia

- ecologically – because the impacts of the development models are examined in relation to known resource data;
- socially – because the economic, demographic and cultural impacts are established in consultation with local people; and
- technically – because the scope of the use of appropriate technologies are demonstrated in the evaluation process.

This philosophical base was translated into practical application through a methodology incorporating three phases – analysis, formulation and reporting (Figure 4.2). The analysis phase included site visits and local consultations, the formulation phase included an evaluation of options, and the reporting phase included a review with local decision makers. Key elements of the consulting process included distributing information well before discussion took place in a range of individual and public meetings. Issues were discussed in an iterative manner in order to ensure that all stakeholders had a chance to input fairly into the process. The focus was on the formulation stream of action in the centre of the diagram, where the information was brought together after analyses. Each information source was tested for relevance and processed as necessary to operate the methodology. The resulting

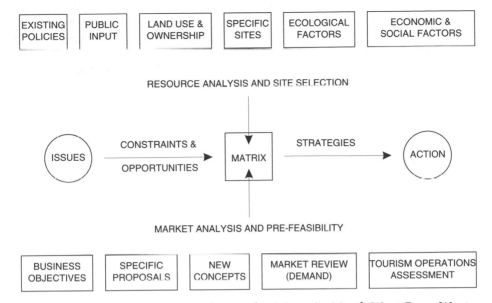

Figure 4.2 Tourism development plan methodology for North West Cape, Western Australia

stakeholders discussions and inputs have led to a workable development plan, but as of the end of 2003 this plan has not yet been implemented.

In a two-year study of the future of the Banff-Bow Valley, Canada, the numerous stakeholders were aggregated into a number of sectors including the study task force, government, national environment, local-regional environment, park users, commercial visitors services and tourist (Ritchie, 2000). Interests were then evaluated according to an Interest Based Negotiation (IBN) process which focuses on 'basic interests' and seeks to achieve a 'wise' agreement. The process is based on a set of four principles which includes:

- separation of the people from the problem;
- a focus on 'interests', not positions;
- the invention of options for mutual gain;
- the use of objective criteria.

Once the various sector interests were identified these were then summarised into three groups under the headings; (1) cultural, community, governance; (2) economic; and (3) environmental. From there a second step of the process was initiated which attempted to build on the understanding of each other's interests to develop a consensus based vision or roadmap for the future for the region. The resultant outcome was a tourism development model which positions the region as a sustainable national and international destination seeking to attract visitors who are interested in the area's unique heritage.

The integration of stakeholders in an international level includes sustainable tourism development in the Arctic (Mason *et al.*, 2000). Tourism in the Arctic is nature based and focuses largely on wildlife. The number of tourists is increasing each year and adverse impacts such as tourist litter and waste are becoming a problem. The environmental non-governmental organisation the World Wide Fund for Nature (WWF) has joined other stakeholders to integrate conservation with Arctic tourism. The collaboration includes tour operators, scientists, academics and NGOs as well as representatives of local, regional and national governments. The goal of the project was to integrate conservation ideals into tourism in Arctic locations to enable communities, tourists and operators to work towards a more sustainable form of tourism. According to the authors the project has been successful due to considerable consultation and negotiation thus providing all stakeholders with a feeling of project ownership. Outcomes of the project include the publication of a set of principles and codes in several languages as well as the initiation of pilot projects in a number of Arctic locations, and the whole process has shown the value of including an environmental organisation in the development of tourism in natural areas.

Stakeholder engagement in private wildlife tourism development

While protected areas are usually public lands, there is an increasing role for private protected areas as government funding decreases. In many countries the public sector is too financially constrained to effectively manage their existing protected areas, let alone establish new ones. In Central America it has been estimated that one-sixth of the landscape is designated as protected areas but most have little visible management and are little more than 'paper parks'. When properly established and managed, private protected areas can complement the public system. An essential element in the development of private parks is the need for a good relationship with the public sector, that is, private protected areas work best when there is some form of public policy and partnership.

One successful private protected area is the Domitila Private Wildlife Reserve in Nicaragua (Barany *et al.*, 2001). This 420 hectare site has a rich ecosystem replete with a population of howler monkeys, many tropical and migratory birds, large numbers of butterflies and a combination of forest and wetlands. The owners of the area are developing the site on wildlife tourism as a vehicle to contribute to biodiversity conservation. Surrounding the Reserve is a local population with a low standard of living, creating a reliance on subsistence agriculture. However, the Reserve owners have included the community in its plans by forming a partnership with them. The focus of the Reserve's community development initiative is to improve their living conditions through better education and the establishment of improved infrastructure.

The Role of Stakeholders in Community Wildlife Tourism

Stakeholder involvement in wildlife tourism occurs in two ways (Newsome *et al.*, 2002). The first of these is involvement in decisions regarding establishing and managing tourism in a natural area and it usually occurs through the planning process. Stakeholder involvement in planning, where local communities are acknowledged as a key group, is widely accepted in the developed world, whereas such involvement is a new concept elsewhere (Timothy, 1999). In the developing world, traditional practices precluding community involvement are often difficult to change. The second way in which stakeholders can be involved is in the quality of life and financial benefits of wildlife tourism. Providing information and training for residents about tourism should help them maximise their benefits from tourism activities. Residents may receive professional, vocational and entrepreneurial training. Involvement by local communities in tourism and accessing the benefits requires some knowledge of the industry and its working.

Involving stakeholders incurs both benefits and costs. Benefits may include better decisions, increased accountability, stakeholder acceptance, local community empowerment and clarifying visitor preferences (Newsome *et al.*, 2002). Better decisions result from stakeholders providing information that increases the number of options identified and considered, saves costs, protects the natural environment or adds interpretive value. Conflicts can be brought into the open and resolved rather than jeopardising future actions. Stakeholder involvement may empower local communities and help them to understand the purposes of wildlife tourism development strategies. It also helps make explicit the values, norms and preferences of visitors. This information as well as biophysical data can then be used to comprehensively plan for the future of wildlife tourism development. Stakeholder involvement in such processes also helps clarify the multiple goals and preferred futures associated with most natural areas. Essential to this process is the gaining of the views of the indigenous people who either live in the area or have some claims over it.

Indigenous people

Indigenous people are the original ones who have lived in an area for a long time. They are often referred to as the first 'peoples' or 'nations'. Their way of life is usually traditional and they generally enjoy a close relationship with their environment. The traditional knowledge and wisdom of indigenous peoples can help us to develop more sustainable relationships between people and wildlife. Indigenous people are often key stakeholders in planning for natural areas. They may rely on the area for their livelihood or be linked to it by strong cultural or spiritual ties. They may live within it. Often, their culture is a focus of interpretation and product sales. They may also have very different ways of consulting and reaching agreement (Newsome *et al.*, 2002). Today a number of protected areas are jointly managed by indigenous peoples and regional, state or national governments. One example is the Uluru-Kata Tjuta National Park. In 1985 the national park was handed back to its traditional owners by the Australian government. Since then the indigenous Anangu people and the Australian National Parks and Wildlife Service have jointly managed the park under the conditions that the Anangu have freehold title of the land, the area is leased back to the government, a predominantly Aboriginal board of management be established, the Anangu have rights of use and residence in the park, and a rental and part of the park fees is paid to the Anangu people.

Another good example of indigenous community involvement in the initiation of wildlife tourism development is that of the Bermudian Landing community, Belize River, Belize (Box 4.2).

Box 4.2   Community involvement in wildlife tourism, Belize

The Community Baboon Sanctuary in Belize (see Chapter 1), is upheld by the government as a model of participatory wildlife tourism development. Community participants understand the intrinsic, aesthetic and material values of the area and recognise it as an important habitat for the black howler monkeys (*Alouatta nigra*). A survey of 50 households in three of the eight villages within the sanctuary gave strong support for it and had positive feelings about its purpose and its impacts. However, not all members felt that they benefited from the Sanctuary and some key issues included the extent and nature of benefits to local residents, perceptions regarding management capabilities, and how management is responding to these issues. Despite the issues raised, a number of specific problems identified, and the fact that only 32% of residents felt that it actually benefited them personally, 90% felt that Sanctuary status should be maintained and 96% felt it was important to protect the monkeys. Alexander concludes that for local support to remain secure, management must orient its work to address the key issues identified by the residents. They are the extent of local participation, representative management structure, effective management capabilities, fair employment allocation, and education opportunities for community residents regarding the howlers, protection of their habitat, and the value of resource conservation.

(Alexander, 2000)

A similar involvement occurs in the establishment of rehabilitation sanctuaries developed for the orangutan of Borneo. Two sanctuaries have been developed in Malaysian Borneo, the Sepilok Centre in Sabah and Semenggoh in Sarawak. In both places the centres care for orangutan which have been either injured or orphaned. The Sepilok Centre was established in 1964 and has rehabilitated and successfully released over 200 orangutan back into the wild. Semenggoh, near Kuching, also has a successful rehabilitation and release programme which attracts thousands of wildlife tourists each year.

Host communities, particularly in the developing world, are increasingly counting the costs of development that has failed to put their rights and interests on a par with those of their visitors (Mvula, 2001). She reports on the impacts of wildlife tourism on local rural communities surrounding South Luangwa National Park, Zambia. The park is Zambia's most important tourism product receiving over 11,000 wildlife tourists per year with the largest international markets being from the UK and North America. The tourists are there mainly to photograph the wildlife and in the park they stay either in safari lodges and camps. The park is managed by the South Luangwa Area Management Unit (SLAMU) which is responsible for the conservation and management of wildlife and for co-ordinating the use of resources of the area. It has adopted a policy of involving the local communities in the conservation of the area. Currently all fees accrued from non-consumptive tourism activities in the park are put towards conservation. The communities have been organised into 40 Village Action Groups (VAGs) which are charged with the responsibility of how their wildlife money is utilised, either on a community development project or as household cash.

Her findings are that the experience has encouraged the community to become more involved in tourism despite the fact that at present its benefits currently reach few local people. Key benefits of wildlife tourism perceived by the locals include the creation of new businesses and jobs, publicity of the area, and increased environmental awareness. A problem for the locals was that tourists did not visit their villages so that it was relatively hard for locals to get involved in the tourism industry. However, the majority of the community members would like to run their own tourist enterprises such as selling handicrafts and local produce to tourists and tour operators as well as sharing their traditions, customs and ways of living. Mvula concludes that all of this can happen if the community is given greater access to tourists, start-up capital and relevant training and skills.

Hammitt and Symmonds (2001) describe a cautious approach to wildlife tourism development in the Republic of Cameroon. Korup National Park comprises rainforest and its formation was underpinned by the desire to conserve its biodiversity. More than one quarter of the world's primate species are found in the park and it is also an important habitat for African forest elephants. In addition it contains an abundance of birds, fish and rare plants. The park is managed by the Korup Forest

Project with assistance from a number of international non-government organisations and thus it has adopted more of a global approach to its development than many comparative parks in developing nations. Although visitation in the 1990s was relatively low, the park is expected to gain in international recognition and it has planned for a sustainable future. Meetings are held with the local community to discuss issues of conservation and buffer zones have been created in order to establish an equilibrium between potential wildlife tourism growth and the needs of the local society. The buffer zone supports and sustains local populations who are not allowed to live in the park. To reduce the potential environmental impacts of visitors to the park and its surrounding area, a number of other areas have been developed as visitor zones to reduce an overall adverse impact on Korup.

The Challenges Involved in Developing Community Wildlife Tourism

Wildlife tourism is often championed as being an effective strategy for diversifying the incomes of rural and/or remote areas in a sustainable manner as it is said to consume less resources than other rural development initiatives such as forestry or farming. However, there are a number of challenges which face community wildlife tourism development including economic, social and environmental. The underlying key is to help the community move from passive to active and individual to collective involvement in tourism. A number of strategies can be employed which increase participation including ensuring access to resources, building collective management, complementing existing livelihoods, establishing partnerships with the private sector and creating local conservation benefits (Table 4.3).

Williams (2001) states that tourism represents an instrument for preservation of various features of a material system (e.g. natural landscapes, wildlife, culture, etc.). He notes that while tourism can help preserve wildlife, natural landscapes and cultures on the one hand, on the other tourism can transform landscapes and habitats as well as the dilution of their traditional meaning. In wildlife tourism the focus is on sustaining the features that attract tourists against their alteration by tourism itself. However, he suggests that sustainability is a fallacious concept because it relies on the traditional worldview of progressive materialism. It assumes the natural world exists primarily to meet human needs and therefore it implies some form of determinable limit on the carrying capacity of local and regional ecosystems. He suggests that

> modern science, rather than leading to greater certainty and foundational truth as forecast in enlightenment thought, ends up producing greater uncertainty ... and in ecology this uncertainty has moved to centre stage. Ecological thinking has shifted from a view of the natural world as dominated by harmony and order to one of instability and catastrophe. (2001: 363)

Table 4.3 Enhancing community involvement in wildlife tourism

No	Strategies	Examples
1	Increase financial benefits for residents	Provide training in professional tourism skills Create linkages through partnerships
2	Ensure equity of cash distribution	Develop sales opportunities Expand collective income & its equitable distribution
3	Maintain access to resources	Secure wildlife resource rights
4	Complement livelihoods	Recognise existing livelihoods Adapt tourism management to them
5	Encourage active participation	Integrate social development skills with business and conservation expertise
6	Co-operate with the private sector	Make it worthwhile for the private sector to work with local communities Assist communities to know and exercise their market power effectively
7	Minimise environmental damage	Integrate wildlife impact management with community enhancement measures
8	Limit cultural intrusion	Establish visitor codes of conduct
9	Create local conservation incentives	Ensure financial benefits are sustainable, significant, widely distributed and are linked to wildlife preservation
10	Have supportive government policies	Focus policy attention on the issues, remove constraints, have a co-ordinated approach and establish a flexible process
11	Capitalise on ecotourism	Link wildlife tourism to ecotourism
12	Ensure profitability	Reduce existing costs, provide realistic expectations, ensure clarity on trade-offs

(After Ashley & Roe, 1998)

He notes that 'modern' ecology espouses change, disequilibrium and chaos and thus the concept of carrying capacity, which assumes stable ecosystems, is now discredited. He concludes that ultimately, sustainability is a cultural concept.

Ashley and Roe (1998) state that a vital first step is to focus the attention of different stakeholder groups on community involvement before addressing economic, environmental or marketing issues. If this is achieved then wildlife tourism can bring many benefits to communities in ways which contribute to secure livelihoods, generate significant local income, stimulate local participation and empowerment, and foster conservation of wildlife (Box 4.3).

Wildlife tourism can generate a range of economic benefits for local communities including revenue creation, job generation, diversification and infrastructure

Box 4.3   Community involvement in wildlife tourism at Sabi Sabi Private Game Reserve, South Africa

Sabi Sabi links the cornerstones of ecotourism, namely community, conservation and tourism, through its philosophy which is based on two principles. The first is to conserve rapidly dwindling wilderness areas and to provide a sanctuary for fauna and flora as part of South Africa's heritage. The second is the belief that the only way a wildlife sanctuary can survive the onslaught of socio-economic pressures is as an ecosystem, based on sustainable development, employing labour, and earning foreign currency. Failure to do so would inevitably make it fall into the category of 'available land' for agricultural, industrial and urban development.

Sabi Sabi Private Game Reserve has been in existence in its present form since 1979. Situated in South Africa's Eastern Transvaal region, positioned between the rural community of Gazankulu to the west and the Kruger National Park to the east, it occupies a strategic position within the greater community. Over 200 mammal species, 350 bird species and a diversity of flora greater than that of Europe, are supported within this complex ecosystem. The Reserve covers almost 70,000 hectares, has no fences and is managed as a single ecological unit. Added to the Kruger National Park, this region covers an area of over 2 million hectares.

In the modern-day South Africa, game reserves cannot exist just for their own sake. They must offer opportunities and make a tangible and positive impact on the lives of those South Africans who live in their proximity. Sabi Sabi has a holistic approach and balances environmental needs with those of people and their communities. Sabi Sabi employs 190 Shangaan people (from the nearby Shangaan tribe) ranging from unskilled labour in training to professionally trained rangers, trackers and training managers (Plate 4.3). With the ratio in the rural areas of breadwinners to dependant being 10 to 1, Sabi Sabi supports over 1800 rural inhabitants.

Sabi Sabi has embarked on two unique programmes to bring about education and understanding to all people in the area. The first programme is called 'Teach the Teachers' which involves teachers from the communities in close proximity to the Reserve. They are taught the importance of tourism to the economy and the interlinking of ecotourism, the environment and the community through workshops given by senior rangers. The second programme is the Reach and Teach Travel and Tourism Programme which is slightly more diverse but similar in content to the first, and involves teachers from the whole of South Africa.

Sabi Sabi also has in-house programmes to increase staff literacy and English proficiency. Once a staff member is proficient in English, there is no restriction on career opportunities. The Shangaan people also make and supply Sabi Sabi with curios to be sold to tourists as mementos of their trip.

Sabi Sabi has embarked on clear and specific habitat improvement pro grammes. These include such things as combating soil erosion, fire management, road maintenance and sewage and rubbish disposal. Overall, Sabi Sabi acts as a catalyst for tourism, creating a demand for the country and generating valuable revenue as a result. Sabi Sabi has made a large investment in South Africa and will continue to set the standard as a leader in the field of ecotourism.

(Basel, 1993)

Plate 4.3 Shangaan tracker with tourists at Sabi Sabi Private Game Reserve, South Africa

improvement. However, a number of challenges exist including economic leakage, menial jobs, a compromise of other livelihood activities and a drain on existing re-sources. Community involvement in wildlife tourism can result in increased pride in, and recognition of, the cultural and natural assets of the area through the devel-opment of cultural centres, the renewal of interest in traditional culture and crafts, and interpretation of the region's wildlife. Notwithstanding, tourism can also exac-erbate social conflict in communities (Ashley & Roe, 1998). Cultural intrusion, disruption, abuse, dislocation and corruption can occur through a lack of cultural appreciation and understanding on the part of tourists or their operators.

According to Ashley and Roe (1998) the benefits of wildlife tourism have been traditionally received at the international level while being borne at the local level, especially by local communities. Although the ideal is for wildlife tourism to generate economic benefits for conservation at the local level, this does not always occur. However, tourism can generate higher returns than other uses of wildlife so it has considerable potential to help fund conservation. A major problem is that the conservation of habitat or species through the management of common resources usually depends on the commitment of all members of the community whereas the direct financial benefits may only be gained by a few. Ashley and Roe (1998) suggest that collective resource conservation depends not only on a range of incentives but also on local people having rights, responsibilities, skills and appropriate management institutions. They argue that wildlife tourism requires active intervention in order to be more appropriate and offer greater benefits and involvement for local residents.

Adaptive management

Given that there are a range of challenges for stakeholders and their engagement in wildlife tourism, an emerging approach which may be of value is through the concept of adaptive management (Holling, 1978). When first applied to the environmental sciences it was devised as a means to accept and embrace uncertainty in understanding environmental impacts of new projects. Thus it aided in the prediction of how a part of an ecosystem would respond as a result of the implementation of a management decision (plan or policy). When applied to other situations the characteristics of the approach include the collaboration of interests, identification of values and continuous learning. Organisations which are adaptive have well-defined mandates, an innovative membership, a range of participatory systems, and the integration and co-ordination of related processes. Underpinning these principles is the ability of stakeholders to implement change while recognising institutional limitations; that is, once the new knowledge has been identified, do they have the will and capacity to act on the information?

Adaptive management has been applied to the community based tourism planning process in Squamish, British Columbia, Canada (Reed, 2000). Although the results are mixed, the process has shown to be a useful emergent tool in community based tourism planning, and in the Squamish case it helped the community to move away from considering tourism as a collection of products towards concerns for research, planning, logistical support, training, and coordination. In addition the final plan introduced new interpretations of tourism to the community.

The Economic and Social Costs and Benefits

Recently, tourism has emerged as an additional nature-based industry, which offers new development and employment opportunities for populations in remote regions. Net benefits from tourism accrue from the balance of economic, social and environmental interactions of tourists with a destination (Greiner *et al.*, 2004). Any wildlife tourism venture should only be considered successful if local communities have some measure of control over them and if they share equitably in the benefits emerging from wildlife tourism opportunities (Scheyvens, 2002). But wildlife tourism, like other forms of tourism, can generate both positive and negative impacts. Thus the main aim of stakeholder participation is to maximise economic, social and ecological benefits and to minimise any adverse costs. By presenting income, employment and infra-structural benefits for rural populations, wildlife tourism is often presented as a mechanism having the potential to offset the local opportunity cost of protected areas. The logic for such development is that political support for conservation is best generated where protected areas demonstrate tangible economic benefit to local peoples (Goodwin *et al.*, 1998). They argue that where people gain more from the use of wild animals through tourism, they are more likely to protect their asset and may invest further resources into it.

One of the most obvious and immediate benefits of tourism associated with local communities is the increase in employment opportunities and income generation for the last host region (Wearing & Neil, 1999). This includes:

- direct employment (associated service industries such as hotels, restaurants, concessions);
- indirect employment (generated as a result of increasing industry inputs such as employment at a retail souvenir outlet);
- induced employment (generated as a result of increased spending capacity of local residents due to increased receipts from tourism; consumption of goods for example).

Whale watching in the United Kingdom attracted 121,000 whale watchers and contributed over £6 million to the economy in 1998 (Hoyt, 2000). In Scotland it is the number one wildlife attraction and in rural areas it is estimated to provide approximately 12% of local income. A 2000 survey of 48 operators found that most were local (72%) and employed up to five full-time equivalent jobs (86%) (Woods-Ballard *et al.*, 2003). They see the potential economic value of whale watching in Scotland as being considerable, especially in remote coastal areas. Despite their confidence they conclude that the industry is Scotland is currently at a fragile stage in its development and that it needs to place greater emphasis on sustainable practice, internal regulation and marketing diversification. Tonga is another country whose economy is partially based on whale watching (Box 4.4).

A study of selected wildlife tourism attractions in New Zealand suggests that it can be successfully carried out in urban situations (Higham & Luck, 2002). The authors reported on wildlife tourism case studies which included a little blue penguin colony in Oamaru, South Island; a dolphin cruise on the Hauraki Gulf,

---

Box 4.4   The costs and benefits of whale watching, Tonga

In the middle of last century the Kingdom of Tonga in the South Pacific had a small-scale whaling industry; however, this was banned by royal decree in 1978. Since then a small whale watching industry has grown in the northern island group of Vava'u and this has been popular with visitors. There are approximately 7000 visitors per year to the islands, the majority of whom visit by air, but with a significant number visiting by sail boat to visit the Port of Refuge harbour. The whales viewed in the islands are humpbacks (*Megaptera novaeanliae*) which are classified by the IUCN as being 'vulnerable'.

In recent times there has been a call both from within Tonga as well as from without, for the nation to resume whaling and this has prompted a study of the value of whale watching to the community (Orams, 2001). The findings of a survey of 136 tourists found that the majority undertake a commercial whale watch trip on their visit. These can be separated into three groups or segments: dedicated whale watchers, whose prime motivation for visiting the region is to watch whales; general whale watchers, for whom the whale watch trip is part of an overall marine experience; and other visitors who were unaware of the presence of whales in the area but who viewed such presence as an added bonus for their trip. Like other whale watchers those who participated in the Tongan survey are well educated, well off and environmentally aware.

Virtually all visitors were opposed to the commercial hunting of whales, with lesser opposition to the indigenous hunting of whales for local consumption. Most also said that they would be less likely to visit Vava'u if whale hunting resumed there. Overall Orams concludes that the great majority of visitors are opposed to the consumptive use of whales and that the reinstatement of this industry would impact adversely on whale watching tourism, which he estimates to contribute US$550,000 per annum to the Vava'u economy. He warns that if whaling were to resume there would be an opportunity cost as the established growing whale watching industry is unlikely to co-exist with a whaling industry.

(Orams, 2001)

Auckland; and a wildlife sanctuary in Karori, Wellington. All three are bringing considerable benefits to the local wildlife, environment and economy in situations that have traditionally been thought of as either unsuitable or inappropriate for wildlife tourism or ecotourism. Delivered benefits from the penguin colony in Oamaru include the restoration of the breeding environment, comparative breeding, and predator eradication; The Dolphin experience delivers education, and the Karori Wildlilfe Sanctuary is involved in species conservation through translocation.

For any real benefits from wildlife tourism, local people must be involved at every stage, from the initial planning through to the development, monitoring, enforcement, and ownership. In Costa Rica, considered a model eco- and wildlife tourism destination, many biological reserves and stands of old-growth forest are owned by foreigners. One local community has formed an association to buy back these lands. With the development of the wildlife tourism industry, local residents have garnered some benefits as employees of ecotourism entrepreneurs, but there seems to be no example of a local resident who is owner of a successful ecotourism or wildlife tourism establishment. The locals hope some day to develop their own wildlife tourism operations (McLaren, 1998).

Conclusions

Engaging stakeholders in wildlife tourism development is a complex task. Developing tourism in ways that are more appropriate for communities takes considerable time and effort, participatory planning and conflict resolution procedures. A central consideration is that of inclusion of all relevant individuals and groups in the engagement process. This is important because those who want to participate in the planning of wildlife tourism may have either a real or a perceived stake, and each is important. Although the range of interested stakeholders may be large, those in the local community with a direct involvement in the area are very important and need not only to be heard but also to be involved in future management if desired, once the plan is enacted. Another important part of stakeholder participation is the resolution of conflicts by shifting the focus away from personal or individual goals to areas of common interest.

Further reading

There are a number of additional texts which provide more detail on stakeholder engagement and tourism generally. Sound overviews of the field are given in books by Richards and Hall (2000), Scheyvens (2002) and Singh *et al.* (2003). An excellent account of stakeholders and natural area management is provided by Worboys *et al.* (2001), and for stakeholders and natural area tourism by Newsome, Moore and Dowling (2002). The relationship between stakeholders and wildlife tourism is specifically dealt with in an excellent, practical book published by the International Institute for Environment and Development by Ashley and Roe (1998). Another book which also is practical in orientation but with a greater theoretical base, is a research text published by Australia's Cooperative Research Centre for Sustainable Tourism (Burns & Sofield, 2001).

Chapter 5

Wildlife Tourism Policies

Introduction

Wildlife tourism, in common with other forms of tourism, occurs within a political and social setting. Such settings reflect and influence the extent of interest in sustainable tourism enterprises as well as the cultural, economic and historic concerns of the society within which the tourism activities are occurring. The focus of this chapter is wildlife tourism policies, which are an expression of the intersection of politics, society and management.

This chapter begins by defining policy and refining these definitions so they are applicable to wildlife tourism. In contrast to many other approaches to studying policy, this book covers both public and to a lesser extent 'private' policy, the latter encompassing policy developed by the tourism industry and its members. Most books concentrate on one or the other but not both. Few policies specific to wildlife tourism exist and as such international, supranational, national, state, regional and local policies associated with but not specifically addressing wildlife tourism are reviewed.

Much of the chapter is devoted to exploring policy instruments, the tools available to those making and implementing wildlife tourism policies. As with other parts of this chapter, the description of policy instruments takes into account the limited attention paid to-date to the development and analysis of wildlife tourism policies. Where wildlife tourism policy instruments exist they are described. If they do not, but there are interesting developments underway in the related areas of biodiversity conservation, protected area management or tourism policy, the situation is reviewed and its applicability considered in relation to sustainable wildlife tourism. The last part of the chapter reviews the factors influencing the choice of policy instruments and provides criteria for evaluating these choices.

Defining wildlife tourism policy

The term policy is notoriously hard to define, with many policy textbooks devoting pages to its definition. Hill (1997) provides the following practical insights. He noted that most definitions emphasise action; a policy can be recognised as a course of action or inaction rather than a specific decision. Also important is recognising that policies reflect societal values, with these values allocated through 'a web of decisions and actions' (Hill, 1997: 7). Decisions are not only interrelated but they also centre on selecting goals and determining how to achieve them. Most definitions make it clear that policies involve the processes of policymaking and implementation as well as, but not always, a guiding policy document.

Given all of the above, the most useful definition of policy remains the following comment, made by Cunningham, a former senior British civil servant, and requoted by Hill (1997: 6): 'Policy is rather like an elephant – you recognise it when you see it but cannot easily define it'. In this chapter examples are provided of policies to help recognise 'the elephant'. Policies addressing or associated with wildlife tourism range from international conventions, through national policies and state-level policies, through to actions proposed by regional or local councils or communities.

For the purposes of this book, a number of attributes of policies and most specifically wildlife tourism policy can be used to help identify such policies as well as clarify the scope of this chapter (Figure 5.1). First, most if not all of the discussion of tourism policies to-date has focused solely on public policy, that is, policies made by governments. In reality, the tourism industry, and wildlife tourism as

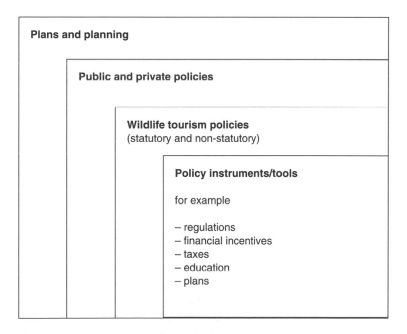

Figure 5.1 Policies, plans and wildlife tourism

part of this industry, is directed by both public and 'private' (industry-developed) policies.

Until the 1980s, environmental management was sought via public policy-making by governments, generally with a heavy reliance on a command-and-control approach and associated mandatory regulations (Kraft & Vig, 1997; Rivera, 2002). The 1980s and beyond have seen a shift to industry self-regulation, with this shift occurring in all environmental sectors including tourism (Hall, 2000a; Rivera, 2002). Thus, any analysis of wildlife tourism policy must include both public policy – the policies made by governments and with governmental involvement – and the 'private' policies made by tourism companies, industry groups and environmental non-government organisations.

Second, a general 'rule-of-thumb' can be used to help locate and identify wildlife tourism policies; these comments are also more broadly applicable to environmental policy. International conventions and legislation are clearly policies. Other policy documents, usually the result of policy processes, most often include policy, strategy or plan in their title. Searching for such terms is an easy rule-of-thumb to assist in recognising policies (i.e. 'the elephant'). Similarly, most modern policies, those written in the last decade or so, include within them one or more of the following sections: mission, vision, goal, object (if legislation), objectives, strategies, policy instruments, and increasingly monitoring and evaluation. If one or more of these words are found in a document then it is probably a policy resulting from a policy process.

The relationship between policies and plans is vexed and confusing, especially as both are ambiguous and difficult to define. Planning can be defined as a very general human activity, based on the processes of thinking and resultant actions (Hall, 2000a). This definition makes planning a broad, over-arching human activity within which policies and their construction sit. This simple relationship is confused, however, by planning and policymaking often referring to the same activity, and then the resultant plan being adopted and used as 'policy'. For this reason, it is suggested that many plans reflect policy at a given time and place and should be recognised and treated as such. A final level of complexity is planning and the resultant plans being prescribed as a tool to assist in implementing a policy, *within* a broader policy document (Figure 5.1). For example, the Commonwealth of Australia's Environment Protection and Biodiversity Conservation Act 1999 (Cth) prescribes the preparation of recovery plans for endangered species. This is an example of a policy prescribing a plan and planning process, as one of a suite of policy tools, to protect endangered plant or animal species or ecosystems.

Third, wildlife tourism policies may be statutory or non-statutory. Statutory policies are based in law and as such are the domain of governments who enact and implement laws as part of their responsibilities in managing their countries, states, provinces, shires and so on. Governments also have non-statutory policies where they rely on influencing and educating rather than regulatory means to effect change. An Australian example relevant to wildlife tourism is the National Ecotourism Strategy (CDT, 1994).

The final signpost to identifying wildlife tourism policy, and again these comments are applicable to environmental policy more generally, is that policies rely on policy instruments for their implementation. Policy instruments are the tools available to help implement a policy. These instruments sit below or within the policy. They are the means used to achieve the desired ends (Howlett & Ramesh, 1995; Bridgman & Davis, 2000). Examples include regulations, financial incentives, taxes and education programmes. Those working in the policy area or studying policy are often dogged by confusion regarding the difference between policies and their instruments. Again a useful rule-of-thumb is that policies usually contain a number of instruments. So, if a document contains a number of tools for achieving an outcome, then it is more likely to be a policy than an instrument.

The policy landscape: Wildlife as a fugitive, common-pool resource

Managing wildlife, whether it is for tourism or some other use, is a complex business. This complexity is a function both of the 'fugitive' nature of wildlife and its existence as a common-pool resource. Wildlife can be regarded as a fugitive resource (Ciriacy-Wantrup & Bishop, 1975) because many species, and especially birds, can move across and through lands and waters independent of who owns the land/water. Such fugitive status makes their management difficult, particularly in Western societies where the ability to manage is closely linked with ownership of the land or water (i.e. the property rights). This difficulty is compounded when wildlife move across ownership boundaries, for example out of a national park into surrounding private property. The same sort of fugitive movement occurs when marine animals such as turtles, which are often the focus of tourism interest, move out of marine protected areas into unprotected areas where they may be harvested for food.

Wildlife can also be considered as a common-pool resource (Briassoulis, 2002). Common-pool resources (CPRs) are those where it is extremely difficult and therefore costly to exclude users and potential users, and exploitation by one user can reduce the availability of the resource to others (Ostrom *et al.*, 1999). Widely recognised common-pool resources are air, water resources, the ocean, ecosystems, fisheries, grazing pastures, irrigation systems and wildlife. Wildlife tourism, through its dependence on wildlife, is therefore susceptible to the characteristic problems of CPRs – over use and lack of incentives for individuals to invest in maintaining or improving the resource.

Wildlife tourism, as a CPR, is faced by the 'tragedy of the tourism commons' where the eventual fate of all common resources is over-exploitation and degradation (Hardin, 1968). Wildlife can be subject to extensive viewing and/or interactions with multiple parties of tourists. It can also be subjected to and adversely impacted by non-tourism uses such as agriculture, transport, mining, and manufacturing. Additionally, these uses, both tourism and non-tourism related, may be conflicting and there may be volatility in these uses and associated institutional arrangements, and conflict between user groups. There may also be differences in the understanding of those involved about who holds the property rights in relation to the wildlife. The magnitude of the tragedy also depends on the wildlife's sensitivity to impacts and their severity, and the nature of the development and its components, especially size.

Much of the wildlife of interest to tourists is within protected areas, including national parks, marine reserves and world heritage areas. When this is the case, then the wildlife is usually, although not always, the subject of policies for that protected area. Its management is part of the bundle of property rights associated with that protected area. Additionally, in some countries such as Australia and the United States, governments have been able via legislation to assume responsibility for managing wildlife independent of where it occurs. This is particularly the case with high-value wildlife such as endangered species, where a government may prescribe that a particular species, and its habitat, must be protected. In these cases, the government has effectively resumed or at the very least adopted the property rights to that species.

This complex policy backdrop has major implications for wildlife tourism and its management. Wildlife as a fugitive resource will move across lands and waters subject to a diversity of property regimes – state, communal, private, or open access. Given that many policy responses are based on property rights and often relate to only one form of property (e.g. protected areas), this complexity of property types makes policy formulation and implementation much more complex. Additionally, given the CPR nature of wildlife a central policy question becomes how to address the problem of 'free riders' or the 'investment incentive problem'. That is, when use is unrestricted, there is no incentive for investors to engage in activities that will reduce overuse. Hence resources are overused and destroyed (Briassoulis, 2002).

A tradition response to free riding has been privatisation, the objective being to privately allocate property rights (e.g. Hardin, 1968). More recently, however, the emphasis has shifted to creating new or strengthening existing institutional arrangements. Co-management, often with strong involvement by local communities, is typical of these newer policy responses. The CAMPFIRE programme of Zimbabwe, with its community-based conservation approach, is one such example and is explored in some detail later in this chapter (Campbell *et al.*, 1999; Wynberg, 2002).

Policies for Wildlife Tourism

Few policies exist at any jurisdictional level addressing tourism or more specifically wildlife tourism. This lack is particularly apparent at international and supranational levels. The reasons for this lack of attention are unclear. Possibilities include the relative newness of tourism, lack of recognition of the need for policy guidance and other more globally pressing environmental and social concerns.

International and supranational policies

Most countries in the world are signatories to one or more international conventions. These conventions bind the signatory countries to prescribed behaviours. Such international law can have a significant influence on the domestic activities of the signatory countries. Hall (2000a) differentiates between hard and soft international law: hard law is the binding content of treaties and the provisions of customary international law, whereas soft law refers to extra-treaty obligations often emerging from annual meetings discussing treaty implementation. For example, the Convention on Biological Diversity is hard law, whereas the recommendations of the Rio de Janeiro Conference where this Convention was adopted is soft law (Hall, 2000a).

International policies of relevance include those addressing wildlife, biodiversity, sustainability, protected areas and tourism (Tables 5.1–5.3). Hall (2003) noted that one of the key lessons learned from examining tourism policies is that many of the most significant arrangements do not define or mention ecotourism although their wording may act as a major constraint on or facilitator of ecotourism activities. The same comment applies for wildlife tourism.

The most relevant international policies are those conferring some level of protection on the lands and waters where the wildlife of interest live (Table 5.2). The World Heritage and Ramsar Conventions afford the highest levels of protection. Formal sanctions are available under the World Heritage Convention for countries that do not fulfil their obligations, for example, by placing a listed site 'in danger'. Such an action places the country at risk of having its sites removed from the world heritage list (Anon, 1997). The Ramsar Convention, on the other hand, provides no formal means of penalising countries for failing to conserve protected sites (Hollis & Bedding, 1994). Social norms associated with Ramsar-listed sites, however, are now such that informal, social sanctions provide a powerful influence against site degradation.

Although no convention explicitly addresses tourism, UNEP (the United Nations Environment Programme) has been designated as the lead agency by the Commission on Sustainable Development for implementation of Agenda 21 issues on tourism (Tables 5.3 & 5.1). Objectives include promoting sustainability, developing sustainable tourism tools for protected/sensitive area management, and supporting implementation of multilateral environmental agreements related to tourism (such as biological diversity, climate change, regional seas, marine impacts from land-based activities, migratory species, Ramsar, world heritage and others) (UNEP, 2003).

Table 5.1 Examples of international biodiversity and sustainability policies relevant to wildlife tourism

Convention	Form of law	Description	Relevance to wildlife tourism
Convention on International Trade in Endangered Species of Wild Flora and Fauna (CITES) 1973	Hard	The goal is to regulate trade in wildlife using species-specific biological criteria. Included are all species threatened with extinction that are or may be affected by trade.	Only relevant to wildlife tourism if some element of tourism is related to trade and the species of interest is threatened with extinction.
Convention on Biological Diversity 1992	Hard	The objectives are the conservation of biological diversity, the sustainable use of its components, and the fair and equitable sharing of the benefits arising out of the utilisation of genetic resources.	Protects the biota on which wildlife tourism depends.
Rio Declaration on Environment and Development and Agenda 21 1992	Soft	The Declaration details the principles that must underpin sustainable development; Agenda 21 provides recommendations for the sustainable conservation and management of natural resources while recognising the social and economic dimensions of such activities.	Provides principles and directives regarding sustainable development relevant to wildlife tourism as an environmentally based industry.

Sources: Meffe and Carroll (1997); Burgman and Lindenmayer (1998); TFS (2003)

Not only are there international policies where there is the opportunity for all nation-states to become signatories, there are also groups of nations involved in supranational policies (Table 5.4). Hall (2000a) notes that the scope of supranational policy has grown substantially in recent years predominantly in response to globalisation and increasing recognition of the value of regional and interest-based alliances. Similarly to global policies, none of these supranational policies are specific to wildlife tourism. Some organisations, such as the Pacific Asia Tourism Association, do focus solely on tourism. Most, however, such as the European Union (EU), the Association of South East Asian Nations (ASEAN) and the Organisation of American States (OAS), have much broader agendas, of which tourism is only one small part. The same comment applies to regional trade alliances such as the North America Free Trade Agreement (NAFTA) and the Asia Pacific Economic Cooperation (APEC).

Table 5.2 Examples of international protected area policies relevant to wildlife tourism

Convention	Form of law	Description	Relevance to wildlife tourism
World Heritage Convention and World Heritage Trust 1972	Hard	Convention provides for the designation of areas of outstanding universal value as World Heritage Sites.	Limited, except wildlife tourism often takes place in world heritage sites (e.g. the Great Barrier Reef, a world heritage site, has 750 licensed tour operators, many focusing on wildlife).
Convention on Wetlands of International Importance 1971 (Ramsar Convention)	Hard	Site must contain representative, rare or unique wetland types and/or be of international importance for conserving biological diversity.	Similarly to world heritage sites and biosphere reserves will provide a focus for wildlife tourism because of tourism opportunities and specifically the diversity of birdlife.
Man and the Biosphere Programme 1968	Soft	Enables designation of international biosphere reserves for a range of reasons including research, monitoring, training, and demonstration as well as conservation.	Many biosphere reserves cater for tourism (e.g. Sian Ka'an in Mexico is beginning to accommodate ecotourism).
IUCN categories of protected areas (defined in a publication by the Smithsonian Institution in 1984 and subsequently revised)	Soft	Categories of protected areas ranging from minimal (strict nature reserve) to intensive human use (managed resource protection area, with sustainable use of natural resources, e.g. forestry).	Potential to protect vulnerable wildlife in strict nature reserves (IUCN Category I); all categories have the potential to be managed in varying ways to cater for sustainable wildlife tourism.

Sources: Agardy (1993); Hall (2000a); Newsome *et al.* (2002); Skeat (2003); TFS (2003)

In reality, much of the policy for many countries in relation to tourism is being determined by the funding priorities set by international and supranational organisations such as the World Trade Organisation, the United Nations Educational, Scientific and Cultural Organisation, the United Nations, the World Conservation Union (IUCN) and the European Union. As Hall (2000a) noted, these

Table 5.3 Examples of international tourism policies relevant to wildlife tourism

Convention	Form of law	Description	Relevance to wildlife tourism
UNEP Tourism Programme	Soft	Promotes and assists with the management of sustainable tourism, especially in relation to protected areas; significant leadership and coordination role.	Relevant especially when wildlife tourism focuses on protected areas.
World Tourism Organisation (part of United Nations system of organisations)	Soft	Leading international policy organisation in the tourism field. Accepted as part of UN in 1969, a number of OECD countries (e.g. Canada, US) still not members.	Limited as the organisation addresses tourism generally, although WTO has an extensive funding programme for regional and local tourism development which could potentially benefit wildlife tourism.
World Travel and Tourism Council	Soft	Private sector organisation providing a forum for global business leaders comprising the presidents, chairs and CEOs of 100 of the world's foremost companies. Their mission is to raise awareness of the full economic impact of travel and tourism.	Currently limited.
The Ecotourism Society	Soft	Surrogate global ecotourism association based in the United States with the objective of making tourism a viable tool for conservation and sustainable development.	Not explicitly addressed, but the Society could potentially focus on issues of sustainability in relation to wildlife tourism.

Sources: Dowling (1996); Hall (2000a); Newsome *et al.* (2002); UNEP (2003); WTTC (2003)

supranationals are having a significant influence, through planning and development activities at a local level, on tourism, including wildlife tourism. These influences extend from Kyrgyzstan (Thompson & Foster, 2003) to the Caribbean (Hall, 2000a).

National and state policies

Similarly to the international domain, there are few policies at the national or state levels that specifically target wildlife tourism. Instead, the implications for wildlife tourism must be gleaned from biodiversity, protected area and sustainability policies (Box 5.1, Table 5.5). The case study of Australian policies is

Table 5.4 Examples of supranational organisations relevant to wildlife tourism

Organisation	Description	Relevance to wildlife tourism
Pacific Asia Tourism Association (PATA), founded in 1951	PATA's mission is to enhance the growth, value and quality of Pacific Asia travel and tourism for the benefit of its membership. Membership includes nearly 100 government, state and city tourism bodies, over 55 airlines and cruise lines, and hundreds of travel industry companies.	Relevant only if wildlife tourism is deemed important by membership.
European Union (EU), proposed and founded in 1950	Europe is still a major force in tourism with the Mediterranean accounting for 35% of all international tourist trade. A central interest has been promoting rural tourism as a key feature of rural development in the poorer countries of the EU. Tourism planning at the local level is embedded in the EU's supranational policies.	Relevant if the rural tourism projects have a wildlife component.
Association of South East Asian Nations (ASEAN), established in 1967	Government membership only, focus is on economic growth, social progress and cultural development, and peace and stability.	Supports annual ASEAN Tourism Forum which may include wildlife tourism.
Organisation of American States (OAS), established 1889–1890, its charter came into force December 1951	Currrently has 35 member states. Purposes are peace and security, democracy and development. Its Intersectoral Unit for Tourism is responsible for tourism matters. Currently supports strategic planning for tourism in developing member countries.	Relevant if the strategic planning includes wildlife tourism components.
International Association of Antarctic Tour Operators (IAATO), founded 1991	Two sets of guidelines exist, one for operators and the other for visitors.	The guidelines for visitors emphasise wildlife protection.

Sources: Hall (2000a); Newsome *et al.* (2002); Bauer and Dowling (2003); IAATO (2003a, 2003b); ASEAN (2004); EU (2004); PATA (2004)

Box 5.1   Australia's policies relevant to wildlife tourism

Australia is world renowned for its biodiversity, with its south-western corner recently recognised as one of 25 biodiversity 'hotspots' in the world (Myers *et al.*, 2000). Wildlife viewing is a principle reason for visiting this country. Australia is a federation of six states and two territories, with a Commonwealth Constitution that leaves the management of most natural resources, including wildlife, to the state and territory governments. The Commonwealth government does, however, have responsibilities in relation to its lands and waters, including military lands and nationally important protected areas such as the Great Barrier Reef and Kakadu National Park, and where wildlife have national importance (e.g. they are endangered).

No single policy explicitly addresses wildlife tourism, however, as in many other countries, management is achieved in the policy interstices through a raft of loosely related legislation and non-statutory policies. As in other domains, these policies address wildlife, biodiversity, protected areas and sustainability. Western Australia's (WA) policies are also explored here to illustrate state level policy influences on wildlife tourism management. This state contains the biodiversity hot spot identified by Myers *et al.* (2000).

At a national level, the legislation most relevant to wildlife tourism is the Environment Protection and Biodiversity Conservation Act 1999 (Cth). This legislation has indirect relevance for wildlife tourism, as do other national-level policies such as the National Ecotourism Strategy and the National Strategy for the Conservation of Australia's Biological Diversity (Table 5.5). Although wildlife tourism is probably within the mandate of non-governmental organisations such as the World Wide Fund for Nature (WWF) and Ecotourism Australia, to-date none of their activities have addressed it.

In Western Australia, wildlife is protected via the Wildlife Conservation Act 1950 (WA). Such protection is independent of who owns the land or waters where the wildlife occurs. Protected areas are managed according to the Conservation and Land Management Act 1984 (WA). Highest levels of protection are afforded to nature reserves (both marine and terrestrial), followed by national parks and conservation parks. At the less protected end of the spectrum are state forests, subject to commercial timber removal, and marine parks where commercial fishing is allowed. This Act also enables the issuing of licences and leases for commercial tourism activities, including those focused on wildlife. The final piece in this state-level legislative puzzle is the Environmental Protection Act 1986 (WA), which provides for the assessment of developments likely to impact on the natural environment. If a proposed wildlife tourism development was of the magnitude and scale that it could potentially impact on wildlife it would be subject to impact assessment. Several state-level non-statutory policies, including the Nature Based Tourism Strategy and the State Sustainability Strategy, are relevant to wildlife tourism although they do not explicitly address it (Table 5.5).

Table 5.5 Selected national and state policies relevant to wildlife tourism in Australia (an illustrative example)

Policy	Policy type	Description	Relevance to wildlife tourism
National (Commonwealth)			
Environment Protection and Biodiversity Conservation Act 1999 (Cth)	Statutory	Enables environmental impact assessment to be conducted on developments and recovery plans prepared for endangered species.	Any developments likely to adversely affect the environment (inc. wildlife) may be subject to impact assessment or recovery planning.
National Ecotourism Strategy 1994	Non-statutory	Provides a framework for the sustainable development of ecotourism in Australia.	Strategy is no longer available or part of government policy.
National Rural Tourism Strategy 1994	Non-statutory	Aims to provide an overall policy framework for developing and marketing rural tourism nationwide.	No explicit mention of wildlife tourism.
National Strategy for the Conservation of Australia's Biological Diversity 1996	Non-statutory	Focused on the conservation of biodiversity Australiawide.	Addresses tourism and sustainable harvesting of wildlife but not wildlife tourism.
State (Western Australia)			
Wildlife Conservation Act 1950 (WA)	Statutory	Wildlife protected from harm independent of the tenure of the land or water where they occur; no provision for habitat protection.	No mention of wildlife tourism, but legislation provides means to protect wildlife both on and off reserves.
Conservation and Land Management Act 1984 (WA)	Statutory	Includes provision for licensing tour operators, inc. wildlife ones, plus leasing facilities and locations to operators.	Ability to manage wildlife tourism industry through permit conditions.
Environmental Protection Act 1986 (WA)	Statutory	Provides means for environmental impact assessment of developments.	Assessment of wildlife tourism development and potential impacts on wildlife.
Nature Based Tourism Strategy 1997	Non-statutory	Provides a framework for growth of nature-based tourism that is sustainable.	Addresses the natural environment but not wildlife tourism explicitly.
State Sustainability Strategy 2003	Non-statutory	Provides a vision and practical means of achieving sustainability in Western Australia.	Includes a section on sustainable tourism, and mentions the importance of protected areas, no explicit mention of wildlife tourism.

Sources: CDT (1994); Charters (1995); Dowling (1996); Wegner (2001); Bates (2002); Government of Western Australia (2003); WATC and CALM (1997)

illustrative in that no policies explicitly address wildlife tourism although a number of both statutory and non-statutory ones facilitate its planning and management. A good case in point is Western Australia's Conservation and Land Management Act 1984 (WA), which provides for the management of protected areas as well as regulating the activities of wildlife tourism operators.

Regional and local policies

Over recent years, tourism has received significant levels of attention at the regional level. It has been identified as a means of progressing development, in disadvantaged rural areas, in both developed and developing countries. The income-generating and employment opportunities offered by tourism, in regions where there are often few other economic opportunities, has contributed to this attention (Dowling, 1996; Hall, 2000a). As such, regional development initiatives and the associated policies will often focus on tourism, which may include a wildlife component. And, as mentioned earlier in this chapter, international and supranational donor organisations are funding tourism as part of their development activities in a number of countries. Such organisations are effectively setting regional and local policy directions through the provision of funding for certain activities but not others. Examples include funding of a tourism development plan for Guyana, a small hotel assistance programme in the Caribbean, and integrated development of the tourism product in Central America by the Organisation of American States (Hall, 2000a). Of these, the last at least has a wildlife tourism component.

Who Makes Wildlife Tourism Policies?

Policies are the outcome of policymaking processes (Hill, 1997). As clarified earlier, in this chapter both public policy (made by government-led processes) and other policies are addressed. Hence in this section government-dominated policymaking is examined through to policy processes from which government representatives are absent or have a minimal role. Those involved in wildlife tourism policymaking can include government agencies, pressure and interest groups, community leaders and members of community groups, international organisations such as the Ecotourism Society and the World Wide Fund For Nature, industry associations, environmental non-government organisations , community members, tourism business owners and operators, and landholders (a detailed description of wildlife tourism stakeholders was provided in the previous chapter). The complexity of policymaking is further increased by the array of jurisdictional scales at which policies can be made, ranging from international to local. Additionally, policy activities at one level influence another, for example, international policies can affect local-level planning and development (Hall, 2003).

Policy networks

Until recently, those studying policymaking focused only on the role of governments in making public policy. Over the last two decades there has been a dramatic change in how policymaking is considered resulting in a far more realistic view and understanding of policy processes. These days, it is widely recognised that policies result from the activities of policy networks, where policy networks are the linkages between state (government) and societal (non-government) actors. Such networks are assumed to be essentially interest-based, with participation directed by each individual furthering their own ends (Howlett & Ramesh, 1995).

Networks persist over time and interactions occur between members on a regular basis. They are differentiated from the policy community, of which they are also part, by their regular interaction. A policy community, as a broader concept, is all those involved in policy formulation and having a specific knowledge base, here a knowledge of wildlife tourism. Policy community members will move in and out of a particular policy network depending on the focus of current policy activities and how these match their individual concerns and interests. Networks may be more or less cohesive, depending on the stability and restrictiveness of their membership, degree of isolation from other networks and the public, and the nature of the resources they control (Howlett & Ramesh, 1995). In terms of wildlife tourism these resources may be money with which the policy may be implemented, the support of other network members, or it may be control over the wildlife itself, for example through land ownership or some other form of property rights.

A network may be dominated by government agencies, usually when there is a public policy focus, or it may have predominantly non-government members in which case the outcome is most likely to be 'private' policy. In Table 5.6 this split is identified and labelled as 'state directed' and 'society dominated' policy making and associated networks. The society-dominated network could include one or more of the following – members of the tourism industry, local residents, and/or environmental non-government organisations. Networks can be further described according to the number of participants. For example, if public policy is the focus, then network possibilities include a network restricted to state agencies (a 'bureaucratic network'), through to a network of three or more groups including state agencies (a 'pluralistic network') (Table 5.6).

Wildlife tourism policy has the potential to be developed by any of the network types given in Table 5.6. This breadth is a function of several factors. First, wildlife tourism is often but not always characterised by government involvement, through responsibilities for either the lands/waters on which tourism occurs or statutory responsibilities for the wildlife itself. It is also characterised by societal interest, especially by the tourism sector, a number of whose members depend on wildlife tourism for their livelihood. As such, both state directed and society dominated

Table 5.6 Types of policy networks

State/societal relations with network	*Number/type of network participants*			
	State agencies	*One major societal group*	*Two major societal groups*	*Three or more groups*
State directed	Bureaucratic network	Clientelistic network	Triadic network	Pluralistic network
Society dominated	Participatory statist network	Captured network	Corporatist network	Issue network

Source: Howlett and Ramesh (1995)

policy networks are part of the wildlife tourism policy landscape (Table 5.6). For example, the Western Australian Nature Based Tourism Strategy (Table 5.5) was initiated and completed by the state government (collaboratively by the Western Australian Tourism Commission and Department of Conservation and Land Management), so was the product of a state directed policy network. The International Association of Antarctic Tour Operators' (IAATO) guidelines for tour operators and visitors, on the other hand, were produced by a society (industry) dominated network (Newsome *et al.*, 2002).

The other related factor is the multiplicity of interests that wildlife tourism policy evokes. Although many natural area tourism policies (and by association wildlife tourism would be expected to be similar) are initiated and completed by government, numerous others are involved. This may include several government departments (as with the Western Australian Nature Based Tourism Strategy), an industry group or groups, community members and non-government conservation organisations. Such broad interest is a function both of the variety of land (and water) tenures, and the juxtaposition of wildlife conservation concerns with commercial, industry-based interests. Given this potential breadth of participants the network type is more likely to be towards the right-hand side of Table 5.6 – with pluralist networks if the policy is being state directed and an issue network if society dominated.

Institutional influences

Policy networks are part of the institutional arrangements within which wildlife tourism is conducted. Institutions are the sets of rules and arrangements that guide the lives of people. They may be formal, such as legislation and regulations, or informal, such as social norms (e.g. no smoking in public places in the United States and Canada, plus many other countries) and the rules guiding professional and personal interactions (e.g. in Malaysia and many other Asian countries, respect shown towards older people). Many of us also refer to formally recognised organisations, such as schools, churches and government departments, as institutions.

Hall (2003) draws attention to the importance of understanding the institutional arrangements associated with ecotourism if the complexity of the industry is to be understood and progress towards sustainable development made. In terms of governmental arrangements, especially with regard to those departments having a role in ecotourism, rather than new departments being created, this policy area has been taken over by existing agencies. This approach explains in part the absence of specific tourism policies. It also means that policies often have to be negotiated between two or more departments.

Another influential feature of these institutional arrangements is the often-close relationships between the government agencies that market tourism products (such as tourism commissions) and the industry itself (Hall, 2003). The industry has an economic interest in supporting these agencies because they lobby and market on their behalf. As a consequence these players may seek to actively exclude other interests, such as those with a 'green' agenda, from policymaking.

Policy Instruments for Wildlife Tourism

Policies are implemented via policy instruments, the tools available to facilitate action (Howlett & Ramesh, 1995; Bridgman & Davis, 2000; Gunningham & Sinclair, 1998). Usually they are included as part of a policy, but may also be part of a suite of complementary but separate actions undertaken by the policy network. For example, a national tourism strategy (= policy) may include instruments such as education, incentives, and opportunities for self-regulation while at the same time the associated policy network may be working at a statutory level, beyond the policy itself, to enact related legislation and regulations. Governments and others who produce policies must decide not only whether or not to produce a policy, they must also determine the 'best' policy instruments for implementation. Very often, the choice of instruments can be as contentious as the policy itself (Howlett & Ramesh, 1995).

As with many parts of this chapter and elsewhere in this book, consideration is given to the policy work of potential relevance to wildlife tourism from biodiversity conservation, protected area management and tourism, because of the limited application and analysis of policy instruments specific to the sustainable management of wildlife tourism. A number of the instruments that are reviewed have yet to be applied in tourism management, but are included because of their successful application elsewhere in environmental management. Table 5.7 indicates which of the instruments are currently used to manage tourism and which are not, but show potential.

Table 5.7 Policy instruments relevant to wildlife tourism

Instrument type	Examples	Currently used to manage wildlife tourism	Currently used to manage tourism	Attribution of ecological damage*
Motivational	Information and education	Yes	Yes	Poor behaviour by people
	Partnerships: Government-community Multi-party (inc. non-government organisations) Industry-community Industry-government Government-government	Yes	Yes	Poor behaviour by people; market/state failure
	Awards and prizes	Not explicitly	Yes	Poor behaviour by people
	Management agreements	Not explicitly	Yes	Poor behaviour by people
Self-regulatory	Codes of practice and guidelines	Yes	Yes	Poor behaviour by people
	Ecolabelling (inc. certification, accreditation)	Not explicitly	Yes	Poor behaviour; market/state failure
	Environmental management systems	No	Yes	Poor behaviour; market/state failure
Economic	Fees and charges	Yes	Yes	Market/state failure
	Licences and leases	Yes	Yes	Market/state failure; uncontrolled human population growth
	Land purchases	No	No	Market/state failure
	Payments: Grants Compensation Subsidies	Yes	Yes	Market/state failure
Regulatory	Legislation and regulation	Not explicitly	Yes	Uncontrolled human population growth
	Direct provision	Yes	Yes	Market/state failure
	Planning: Recovery Management Land use	Yes/Not explicitly	Yes	Uncontrolled human population growth
	Environmental impact assessment	Not explicitly	Yes	Uncontrolled human population growth

* Derived from Mihalic (2003)

Classification of policy instruments

A number of classification systems have been developed for policy instruments. Several systems have also been developed specifically for environmental instruments (e.g. Gunningham & Sinclair, 1998). Such classifications are helpful because of the large number of instruments available and the difficulty in understanding and applying such a large and diverse array. One of the most widely applied classifications is that produced by Howlett and Ramesh (1995), based on a review of numerous previous efforts. They provide a 'spectrum' of policy instruments from those where there is a low level of state involvement in policy implementation through to high levels. Over the last decade, this classification system has assisted in several analyses of sustainable tourism (e.g. Hjalager, 1996; Rivera, 2002). A modified version of their system is used in this book (Figure 5.2).

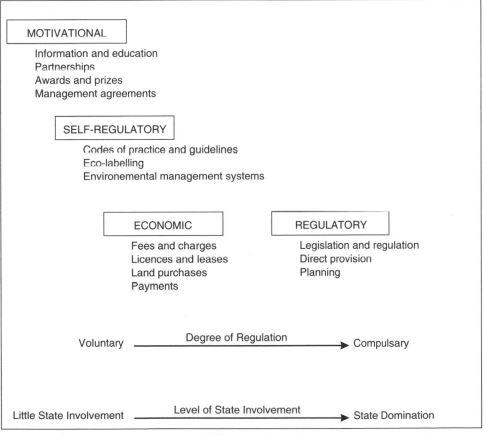

Figure 5.2 Spectrum of policy instruments for wildlife tourism

At the low end of the spectrum, the policy instruments rely on voluntary actions for implementation, while at the high end implementation is made 'compulsory'. Compulsory actions rely on statutory law to obtain the desired outcome or governments may directly implement the policy themselves. An example of the latter is a government agency providing a wildlife-viewing facility as well as associated infrastructure. In the middle are 'mixed instruments', which feature government involvement, while implementation is generally the responsibility of non-government actors (e.g. payments to private landholders used to achieve on-ground conservation outcomes, such as hedgerow restoration in Europe or fencing of bushland in Australia). The majority of policy tools, including self-regulatory and economic approaches, are in this middle area (Figure 5.2, Table 5.7).

Until the 1990s, environmental policy relied on a 'command-and-control' approach (the compulsory end of the spectrum), with governments establishing and seeking to enforce regulations to manage environmental activities (Eckersley, 1995). Regulation of development and polluting activities has resulted in significant progress in improving air and water quality. Criticism has, however, continued to be levelled at such an approach, with concerns including its cost, inefficiency, over-reliance on law, and discouraging improvements in management practices beyond those required by regulation (Kraft & Vig, 1997). Specifically, companies are discouraged from trying innovative and perhaps more effective and efficient environmental protection measures because of the restrictive provisions of regulatory approaches.

In the face of this mounting criticism, voluntary approaches have increasingly been promoted as an alternative. In relation to the tourism industry, these approaches can be divided into three categories based on decreasing levels of government involvement (Rivera, 2002). The first is public voluntary programmes established by government departments to encourage beyond compliance environmental performance. The Eco-Management and Audit Scheme (EMAS) established by the European Union is one such example. The second category includes negotiated agreements between governments and companies, for example, the Costa Rican Certification for Sustainable Tourism. Last are industry-based initiatives such as Ecotourism Australia's Eco-Certification Scheme (EA, 2003).

Tourism as an industry requiring management, and specifically nature-based tourism, has emerged and blossomed over the same decades and has seen the transition from command-and-control to a broader sweep of approaches, including voluntary ones. At the same time, responsibility for environmental policy has extended beyond government to the private sector and again the policy landscape of wildlife tourism reflects this broadening. As such, wildlife tourism not only encompasses the spectrum of compulsory through to voluntary policy instruments, it also illustrates the place of industry and non-government organisations, as well as government, in developing and applying policy instruments.

The classification system used in this book, similarly to the approach taken by Howlett and Ramesh (1995), recognises a spectrum of instruments available for managing wildlife tourism, from voluntary through to government provision (Table 5.7, Figure 5.2). Given the increasing interest in self-regulation and economic instruments, they have been placed in separate categories rather than considering them as part of a pool of mixed instruments. This system is closely aligned to the approach taken by Moore (2001) in her classification of policy instruments in a related environmental field, that of remnant vegetation protection.

A final perspective on classifying worth briefly noting relates to causal attribution. By this it is meant, what are the reason or reasons for a policy response? What is the cause of the problem that the instrument is being used to redress? Mihalic (2003) attributes ecological problems in relation to tourism to three broad sources: poor, ill-informed behaviour by people, failure of the market or the state, and uncontrolled population or economic growth. Each of these has a suite of associated policy instruments (Table 5.7). Her work provides another useful way of thinking about and organising policy instruments.

Motivational instruments

Motivational instruments rely on individuals, and/or the groups of which they are part, being motivated to change their behaviour in desired ways. In relation to environmental management, such instruments include information and education, partnerships, awards and prizes, and management agreements. They have an important complementary role, with people who are positively motivated being more likely to respond constructively to other policy instruments, such as regulation (Young & Gunningham, 1997). Cole (1995) suggested that, in relation to wilderness management and education, that education was best used as a long-term strategy and not expected to solve problems in the short term.

Information and education

These are highly favoured policy instruments in environmental management. They are a 'soft' approach in that compliance is not mandated and the recipient is free to choose the extent to which they adopt the suggested behaviours. This instrument has a long history of use for managing protected areas and by default the associated wildlife. Education also has a valuable role where wildlife move beyond the boundaries of protected areas or occur on land where those concerned about the welfare of the wildlife do not have the authority to act directly but must instead rely on education and other indirect means.

Education may be directed at one or more of the following: tour operators, tourists, wildlife managers and local residents. Most often, it is visitors and tour operators who are the recipients. Many wildlife tour operators, whether they are from the government or private sector, provide environmental education and interpretation as part of their tourism product (Green & Higginbottom, 2000). Non-government conservation organisations, such as the World Wide Fund For Nature (WWF), provide environmental information as part of their core business. Hjalager (1996: 212) commented that providing education, information and inter-pretation services for tourists as well as residents 'might be considered a crucial part of public infrastructure'. Other parts of this book deal with information provision in greater detail – Chapter 3 explored the psychology underpinning educative efforts in relation to wildlife tourism, while Chapter 6 describes education as an essential management strategy.

Partnerships

Partnerships are a favoured policy instrument in the first decade of the 21st century. Partnership approaches to tourism planning are now widely endorsed by governments and their agencies in many developed countries (Bramwell & Lane, 2000a; DITR, 2003). Encouraging partnerships between government and the private sector in sustainable development was one of the major and most controversial themes of the 2002 World Summit on Sustainable Development (Wolmer & Ashley, 2003).

Bramwell and Sharman (1999) define partnerships as regular, cross-sectoral in-teractions between parties based on at least some agreed rules or norms, with the in-tention of addressing a common issue or to achieve a specific goal or goals. Partnerships are particularly pertinent in wildlife tourism because no single stake-holder or stakeholder group is likely to possess all the resources needed for sustain-able management. As with tourism more generally, the complexity of wildlife tourism, encompassing mobile wildlife and a plethora of stakeholders, plus signifi-cant uncertainties around the potential impacts of tourism on the wildlife of inter-est, means partnerships may be essential for sustainability to be achieved.

For wildlife tourism, partnerships are one way of addressing the potential tragedy of the commons associated with wildlife as a fugitive resource. A partner-ship can theoretically allow wildlife to be cooperatively managed as it moves across tenure boundaries, for example, as it moves between protected areas such as national parks and adjacent privately owned land. Here the partnership is between the protected area agency and the adjacent landowners (i.e. predominantly a government-local community partnership, Figure 5.3). There may also be residents within the park relying largely on wildlife for their livelihood who also become part of the partnership. Community conservation in Africa, as pioneered by Zimbabwe's Communal Areas Programme for Indigenous Resource Extraction (CAMPFIRE) (Fabricius *et al.*, 2001), is one such example (Box 5.2).

Another similar type of partnership (and yet responding to a different underly-ing issue) are those formed to prevent a tragedy of the commons in relation to land (or waters) used by wildlife but treated as a common-pool resource. Here, many

Box 5.2   CAMPFIRE – Zimbabwe's Communal Areas Programme for Indigenous Resource Extraction: An example of partnerships

Community-based natural resource management (CBNRM) in Southern Africa in the 1990s was a response to a number of factors (Fabricius *et al.*, 2001). Conservation and tourism were identified as ways of achieving economic growth in rural areas. The embracing of democracy was accompanied by enthusiasm for greater participation by local people in natural resource management. These community conservation projects were also a response to governments realising that rural voters were important. The original motivation was, however, an interest in conserving wildlife outside protected areas, particularly through expanding the number and size of protected areas by incorporating communal lands.

The most widely cited example is Zimbabwe's CAMPFIRE (Communal Area Management Programme for Indigenous Resources) programme. In CAMPFIRE, local communities play an active role in the management of resources, and in the generation and distribution of benefits. Usually local authorities (mostly rural district councils) are responsible for advertising hunting rights, selecting and contracting safari companies, setting quotas, organising anti-poaching, and managing revenues (Campbell *et al.*, 1999). The programme's development has been a partnership between the Department of National Parks, the University of Zimbabwe's Centre for Applied Social Sciences and two non-government organisations, the Zimbabwe Trust and WWF in Harare (Alexander & McGregor, 2000). Since the 1990s, CAMPFIRE programmes have been initiated in a number of other African countries including Botswana, Namibia, Zambia, Tanzania, Uganda and Mozambique.

The central tenet of CAMPFIRE is that communities neighbouring protected areas should receive direct benefits from them and have some say in wildlife management and use. Wolmer and Ashley (2003) concluded from their review of community participation in natural resource management in Southern Africa that although the CAMPFIRE programme has allowed multiple resource use in communal areas (i.e. wildlife, stocks and crops) the driving philosophy is one of conservation not development. The CAMPFIRE areas have become *de facto* buffer zones to take the pressure off the protected areas, enabling the extension of commercial wildlife interests into the communal areas, disguised as public–private partnerships.

As a policy instrument, these community conservation partnerships, of which CAMPFIRE is an example, have been successful in protecting and in some cases increasing wildlife numbers (Fabricius *et al.*, 2001). They have also brought to fruition new partnership models such as land being handed back as leasehold to local communities, collaborative management agreements where communities accept shared management responsibility with the Department of National Parks, and commercial use of a limited part of a protected area.

Recent commentators have become more critical of CAMPFIRE and other CBNRM projects (e.g. Campbell *et al.*, 1999; Alexander & McGregor, 2000; Wynberg, 2002; Virtanen, 2003). They note that there has been a tendency to oversell the programme benefits (Wolmer & Ashley, 2003). For example, the actual benefit per household from CAMPFIRE across Zimbabwe in 1996 was estimated to be US$2.50 (Hasler, 1999 quoting WWF Zimbabwe, cited in Fabricius *et al.*, 2001). The presence of wildlife (a central objective of these projects) can impose costs on local people by interfering with their livelihood, through livestock losses, crop destruction, human injury, and damage to structures (Virtanen, 2003). Also, the financial returns from wildlife tourism may extend no further than the cash-strapped district councils. And, the legacy of conflict and distrust in many districts preceding CBNRM projects makes formation of the partnerships that must underpin these activities extremely difficult, if not impossible (Alexander & McGregor, 2000).

A significant part of the problem relates to the nature of the partnerships between the rural district councils and specialist agencies officially in charge of resources, including wildlife. Local communities do not have a legal place in these partnerships. As a result, many community members continue to see wildlife projects as the responsibility of the government or district councils. Traditional authorities, village development committees and wildlife committees are seldom considered as management partners by state authorities (Virtanen, 2003). As such, there is often strong local opposition to conservation activities. Wynberg (2002) suggested that unless rural communities have secure rights to the land they perceive as their own, and the associated wildlife, then they will be unable to control access to the land, protect its wildlife or raise money from entrance fees to be used for management.

different potential users have access to an area, for example, a richly forested and highly biodiverse region in Indonesia or Malaysia, but none are able to manage it in a sustainable way (McCarthy, in press). This inability may be due to in large part to lack of money, but could also be due to a lack of the required institutional structures and skills needed to derive an income from the area while at the same time protecting its wildlife and other conservation values. Integrated conservation and development projects (ICDPs) are an example of this type of partnering arrangement where partners can include international non-government conservation organisations (e.g. WWF), development donors (e.g. The World Bank), the national

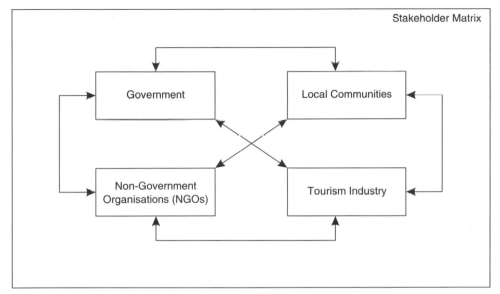

Figure 5.3 Partnerships and wildlife tourism

and state governments of the country concerned, and local people. The aspiration underpinning the ICDP concept is achieving sustainable economic development at a local community level while at the same time conserving the natural environment through legally designated protected areas (Browder, 2002).

Another form of partnership relevant to wildlife tourism is industry-community partnerships (Figure 5.3). This form has an investment and development focus, with governments seeking to facilitate such partnerships as part of stimulating industry investment in tourism. The other part of the focus is drawing industry into development and growth efforts, particularly in developing countries. In South Africa, as the government commercialises state assets, such as tourism concessions, they are requiring concessionaires to address community development. For example, the government is requiring bidders for the commercialisation of a string of hotels along the Eastern Cape, South Africa, to consider land and equity rights for communities while also developing tourism nodes (Wolmer & Ashley, 2003).

Two other types of partnership warranting mention in relation to wildlife tourism are industry-government partnerships and government-government arrangements (Figure 5.3, Table 5.7). In many developed countries, partnerships based on law, between protected area agencies and commercial operations, have been in place for many years. Negotiating and formalising concessions, whereby companies provide accommodation and other services within protected areas, through to guided tours, are part of the daily administrative activities of protected area managers. For example, in 2003 the Great Barrier Reef Marine Park Authority was managing 750 tourist operations in this world heritage area (Skeat, 2003). These legal arrangements are usually formalised through licensing and leasing provisions detailed in the enabling legislation of the protected area agency (see Chapter 6 for more details). Hall (2003) expresses concern that the closeness of this relationship, between government and industry, may exclude other stakeholders from policy making and even from identifying that there is a problem in the first place.

Government-government partnerships are part of the normal machinery of government. The Western Australian Nature Based Tourism Strategy was prepared through such a partnership. These partnerships are increasingly common as government agencies seek to share resources as those available to government decline. Partnerships are also a way of one department preventing another from stymieing their policy initiatives by coopting them early. And, they are also a way of dealing with uncertainty, by sharing collective knowledge.

Awards and prizes

Competitions, awards and prizes are another way of motivating and rewarding changes in practice. Most of the awards, including international (e.g. British Airways Tourism for Tomorrow Awards), national (e.g. New Zealand Tourism Awards) and provincial (e.g. British Columbia Tourism Awards), focus on sustainable tourism rather than ecotourism or wildlife tourism. A smaller number, such as the Scottish Thistle Awards, have a 'tourism and the environment' category. In 2003, this category was won by a wildlife tourism product – the Hebridean Whale and Dolphin Trust (HWDT, 2003).

Management agreements

The management agreements most relevant to wildlife tourism are those where a contract is negotiated between a landholder and a third party regarding the use and management of their land for conservation purposes (Table 5.7). Such agreements are usually voluntary and provide a flexible policy instrument that can be tailored to meet the needs of individuals and the values being managed. A range of levels of commitment from landholders is possible, from non-binding through to binding. They are often used in combination with other instruments, for example, financial incentives may be added to encourage landholders to enter the agreement. Management agreements continue to be a favoured by both government and conservation groups.

They have been most widely applied in relation to the protection of nature conservation values on private lands (Moore, 2001). Such conservation may also provide opportunities for wildlife tourism. Binning and Young (1997) identified three types of agreement involving varying commitments from landholders: non-binding, fixed-term and in-perpetuity. Non-binding agreements depend on the voluntary participation of private landholders. The objectives are to establish networks of like-minded landholders and provide access to management advice. Such agreements formally recognise landholders' conservation efforts without binding them or precluding future land uses. The voluntary Land for Wildlife programme in a number of states of Australia is an example of this approach.

Fixed-term agreements do not bind the landholder in perpetuity. A small financial incentive may be provided to secure landholder participation. Another example from Australia is the Western Australian Remnant Vegetation Protection Scheme, which provided assistance to landholders to fence remnant vegetation. Funding was tied to a 30-year contract deed for the protection and management of the vegetation. Binning and Young (1997) regarded these as 'transition agreements', securing a permanent change in property rights through a one-off incentive payment. Ongoing management then becomes part of the landholder's duty of care and further costs are their responsibility.

In-perpetuity agreements involve placing a covenant on the title of the land, with the entitlements and obligations contained in the management agreement binding on current and future landholders. Such agreements help redefine the duty of care and secure future conservation outcomes; however, their binding nature can discourage landholders from signing up. In Australia, there are active programmes underway in most states to encourage perpetual covenanting of private lands with high nature conservation values. In North America, 'easements' on private lands are acquired either by public agencies such as the US Fish and Wildlife Service or private conservation organisations, to protect fish and wildlife habitats. In many cases, the easements are then used for viewing wildlife. They are generally perpetual, with compensatory payments often made to the landholder. The payment level depends on the extent of rights acquired from the landholder (Johnson *et al.*, 1994).

The strength of management agreements, over other instruments, lies in their focus on management arrangements for an individual site (Binning & Young, 1997). They establish new entitlements and responsibilities for an area of land, individually tailored for a site and its owner. However, because they are site-specific they are more expensive to set up and administer and thus are best targeted to areas of high priority.

Self-regulatory instruments

Both Hjalager (1996) and Rivera (2002), in analysing policy instruments in relation to tourism, emphasised the central role of voluntary instruments, such as the motivational and educational ones just discussed, and those loosely grouped together and described as self-regulatory. Self-regulatory instruments are critical to the management of wildlife tourism for several reasons. The retreat of governments worldwide from policy initiation and a declining regulatory presence, accompanied by an increasing emphasis on industry-led policy and management (Hall,

2000b), means that self-regulatory instruments are currently subject to great inter-est. Self-regulatory means that an industry seeks to 'regulate' itself through codes of practice, industry guidelines and standards (Wearing & Wearing, 1999), eco-labelling, and environmental management systems (Table 5.7). These instruments overlap and a number are complementary.

The other reason self-regulation is critical is that often the only common denomi-nator in relation to a particular wildlife tourism product or setting is the associated tourism industry. The wildlife may be moving across lands and waters under mul-tiple ownership or it may occur in jurisdictions where ownership is contested or absent. Therefore, no one party has clear management responsibilities. Industry self-regulation may be the only means of managing in the face of complexity and uncertainty.

Codes of practice and guidelines

A code is a set of expectations, behaviours or rules written by industry members, government or non-government organisations (Holden, 2000). They aim to influ-ence the behaviour of tourists or the industry itself. Codes may be informal (generally known as codes of ethics) or formally adopted by industry members (known as codes of practice or conduct or guidelines) (Newsome *et al.*, 2002). Codes of ethics are associated with establishing and maintaining professionalism (Jafari, 2000). An example is the Pacific Asia Tourism Association's code for environmen-tally responsible tourism (PATA, 1991). It encourages members and their industry partners to use resources sustainably, conserve wildlife habitat, recognise commu-nity aspirations and values in planning, comply with environmental law and policy, address the environmental impacts of tourism, regularly audit their prac-tices, and provide education and information (Newsome *et al.*, 2002).

Codes of practice and guidelines are more practical and apply to actual practice in specific locations. They may be developed for operators or visitors. Some guide-lines have been developed for specific places and others for nature-based activities such as river rafting. Destination-specific activities detail how tour operators and / or visitors should behave at destinations, while activity-directed codes seek to improve environmental management and reduce the impacts of the activities (Newsome *et al.*, 2002). Guidelines for tour operators and tourists have been in place for a number of years for wildlife tourism in the Antarctic (Box 5.3).

Ecolabelling

Ecolabelling refers to marketing tools that promote good environmental perfor-mance (Font, 2001a). Ecolabels fall into two main categories – environmental quality labels for tourism destinations and environmental performance labels for tourism providers (Buckley, 2001). Both categories could apply to wildlife tourism. In both the applicant is seeking formal recognition of their good environmental per-

Box 5.3   Guidelines for wildlife tourism in the Antarctic: An example of industry self-regulation

Antarctica has become a tourism destination only relatively recently, with the first tourists visiting by air in 1956 and ship in 1958. Much of its appeal rests on its unusual and relatively visible wildlife. Species of interest include whales, seabirds, seals, squid and fish. Tourism to this region is growing rapidly. In the 1999/2000 season about 14,600 tourists visited the continent, up from about 9000 visitors as recently as the 1995/6 season (Newsome *et al.*, 2002; Bauer & Dowling, 2003). Management responsibility for Antarctica is shared by more than 40 countries and is guided by the international Antarctic Treaty, which came into force in 1961, and associated agreements, referred to collectively as the Antarctic Treaty System.

In 1991, the Protocol on Environmental Protection to the Antarctic Treaty was adopted. It designates the Antarctic as a natural reserve and sets out environmental principles, procedures and obligations. The International Association of Antarctic Tour Operators (IAATO), an organisation founded in the same year, has developed guidelines for visitors and those bringing visitors to the Antarctic to ensure all comply with the Treaty and Protocol (IAATO, 2003a, 2003b). The guidelines were adopted at the Antarctic Treaty Meeting in Kyoto in 1994. Both sets of guidelines are voluntary and seek to influence behaviour, there is no recourse to punitive action if they are not followed as is the case with regulations and associated penalties under the law of a country (Mason & Legg, 1999).

The *Guidance for Those Organising and Conducting Tourism and Non-governmental Activities in the Antarctic* (IAATO, 2003a), details key obligations and procedures to be followed pre-, during and post-visit. These guidelines aim to ensure compliance with existing policies such as the Antarctic Treaty System and Protocol, that a sufficient number of experienced, trained staff are hired, environmental impacts are monitored, waste material is disposed of properly, and the activities are conducted safely. Wildlife is not specifically mentioned.

The *Guidance for Visitors to the Antarctic* (IAATO, 2003b) has five parts – protect Antarctic wildlife, respect protected areas, respect scientific research, be safe, and keep Antarctica pristine. The guidance in relation to wildlife is as follows:

'Protect Antarctic Wildlife
Taking or harmful interference with Antarctic wildlife is prohibited except in accordance with a permit issued by a national authority:

- Do not use aircraft, vessels, small boats, or other means of transport in ways that disturb wildlife, either at sea or on land.

- Do not feed, touch, or handle birds or seals, or approach or photograph them in ways that cause them to alter their behavior. Special care is needed when animals are breeding or molting.
- Do not damage plants, for example by walking, driving, or landing on extensive moss beds or lichen-covered scree slopes.
- Do not use guns or explosives. Keep noise to the minimum to avoid frightening wildlife.
- Do not bring non-native plants or animals into the Antarctic such as live poultry, pet dogs and cats or house plants.'

(IAATO, 2003b, part of Recommendation XVIII–1, adopted at the Antarctic Treaty Meeting, Kyoto, 1994)

formance. This recognition is the ecolabel. Companies have various motivations for seeking such recognition. A strong motivation is achieving a competitive advantage over other similar companies that have not achieved ecolabel status. Rivera (2002) notes that the Costa Rican Certification for Sustainable Tourism programme resulted in certified hotels receiving price and sales benefits relative to uncertified ones. Such an advantage relies on tourists recognising ecolabelling and making choices accordingly as a consumer. In their review of wildlife tourism, Green and Higginbottom (2000) noted that the effectiveness of accreditation (namely, eco-labelling) was being hindered by a lack of market recognition.

The language and terms associated with ecolabelling remain confusing. Until recently, many of those involved in ecotourism spoke of 'accrediting' accommodation, tours and attractions. They were actually referring to certification – the testing of individuals and companies to determine their mastery of a specific body of knowledge (Morrison *et al.*, 1992). In contrast, accreditation usually applies to recognition of a programme of study or an institution as meeting certain standards or qualifications (Newsome *et al.*, 2002). Both certification and accreditation are processes that result in an ecolabel being awarded. Much of this confusion has hopefully been resolved by the release in 2003 of a new 'certification' programme by Ecotourism Australia. This organisation has led the way worldwide in terms of ecolabelling, initially with their Nature and Ecotourism Accreditation Programme (NEAP) for certifying tour operators (Font, 2001a), now superseded by their new Eco Certification programme (EA, 2003) (Box 5.4).

In 2001 the number of tourism ecolabels was estimated as exceeding 100, with new labels being created every few months (Kahlenborn & Domine, 2001). They show a concentration in developed countries. Europe has the largest number, mostly around Germany, Austria and Scandinavia (Font, 2001a). As a policy instrument they can provide the information, systems and incentives needed to reduce

---

Box 5.4   Ecotourism Australia's Eco Certification Programme: Another example of industry self-regulation

The Ecotourism Association of Australia was established in 1992 to promote ecotourism and facilitate interaction between all those involved. Membership is drawn from the tourism industry, government and universities. Accreditation has been on the Association's agenda since its formation, with members believing that it would enhance the marketability of ecotourism businesses (Weiler, 1995).

The Australian National Ecotourism Accreditation Programme (NEAP) was launched by the Association and the Australian Tour Operators Network in 1996. Accommodation, tours and attractions could be accredited. In 2000 it was broadened to include nature-based tourism and renamed the Nature and Ecotourism Accreditation Programme and in 2003 it was released as a third edition and re-badged as Ecotourism Australia's Eco Certification Programme. The Programme is still applicable to accommodation, tours and attractions. By 2003 over 400 ecotourism products had been assessed as part of their ecolabelling process (EA, 2003).

The Eco Certification Programme contains revised assessment criteria. These criteria enable companies to self-assess their ecotourism performance against the 'triple bottom line' – economic, environmental and social sustainability. The criteria are grouped under 10 principles: business management and operational planning, business ethics, responsible marketing, customer satisfaction, natural area focus, environmental management, interpretation and education, contribution to conservation, working with local communities, and cultural respect and sensitivity. Under the principle of 'environmental management', a number of criteria specifically address wildlife management: biodiversity conservation, minimal disturbance to wildlife, minimal impact nocturnal wildlife viewing, minimal impact marine mammal and mega fauna viewing, and minimal impact trail riding and animal tours (EA, 2003).

---

environmental impacts and to improve the efficiency of natural resource use. For example, Green Globe 21, an international ecolabelling organisation, addresses efficient natural resource use through reducing energy and water consumption and solid waste production, among other things (STTI, 2002).

Environmental management systems

Environmental management systems (EMS) appeared in the 1990s in the mining and manufacturing sectors to assist in implementing environmental policy. They are described as the organisational structure, responsibilities, practices, procedures, processes, and resources for determining and implementing environmental policy (British Standards Institute, 1994). Today the most widely recognised environmental management system is the International Standard ISO 14001.

To date EMS have not been widely used by the tourism industry; however, practitioners believe they could be (Todd & Williams, 1996; Font *et al.*, 2001). Green Globe 21 requires an EMS as part of certification of a tourism company's operations (Font, 2001b). EMS could also be part of a company's report to shareholders, for example, by the managers of built accommodation such as hotels and resorts. EMS is also beginning to be considered as part of managing protected areas, for example for forest recreation in the United Kingdom (Font *et al.*, 2001). Most recently, the NSW National Parks and Wildlife Service (Australia) has developed, with its industry and not-for-profit partners, an EMS for the Perisher Range Alpine Resorts (Bennett, 2003).

Economic (including market-based) instruments

Many analyses of environmental policy have found that economic instruments can be a better policy option than voluntary approaches, from the point of view of both environmental effectiveness and economic efficiency (OECD, 2003). Many, but not all, economic instruments rely on the existence or development of markets for the environmental attribute of concern (e.g. clean air, reduction in pollution, wildlife for viewing). Much of the policy action in relation to economic instruments is based on the assumption that many of the environmental problems being experienced are due to market failure (Mihalic, 2003). The same assumption has been made in relation to tourism (e.g. Sinclair, 1992). The further assumption is then made that if the market can be corrected by valuing previously unvalued goods, such as wildlife, and by creating markets, then the failure can be corrected and the resources will be properly managed.

For wildlife, it can be extremely problematic to create a market if potential consumers cannot be excluded because of the mobility of the species or lack of ownership or rights to the lands or waters where the species occurs. Market-based instruments that are potentially useful in this regard fall into two groups – those where a price is associated with the wildlife itself (e.g. fees for viewing, licences and leases for tour operators) and those where the land or waters on which the wildlife occurs is afforded a value (e.g. land purchases) (Table 5.7).

Fees and charges

Visitors may be charged a fee to view wildlife by the owners of the lands or waters on which the species occurs. Such an approach relies on the 'owner' being able to prevent those who do not pay from accessing the wildlife. Tourists may also pay to participate in research expeditions involving wildlife, such as the Landscope Expeditions in Western Australia and Earthwatch worldwide (Green & Higginbottom, 2000).

Licences and leases

These are a less direct way of collecting money from wildlife tourism. In many countries, tour operators and other providers are required to pay protected area agencies, usually through licensing and leasing arrangements, to access these areas and the wildlife they contain. These payments are made indirectly by tourists through the increased fees collected from them by licensees and leasees to cover permitting expenses (see Chapter 6 for more details). These permits generally have associated environmental conditions. For high value and potentially vulnerable resources, such as whale sharks off the Western Australian coast, the issuing of licences is a competitive process enabling protected area managers to select the 'best' operators. In Zaire and Rwanda the income received from tourists visiting mountain gorillas has been sufficient to pay for habitat conservation and anti-poaching measures (Green & Higginbottom, 2000).

Land purchases

The other group of market-based economic instruments involves creating a market for the land or water on which the wildlife occurs. Such an approach is becoming increasingly widespread in relation to lands with nature conservation values but has yet to make its way into the policy processes for managing wildlife tourism. The intention behind this group of instruments, which includes land purchases and revolving funds, is to create a viable functional market for land (and waters) with nature conservation values (Moore, 2001). Increasingly, lands are being purchased for their nature conservation values. Some of these are then being developed for the wildlife tourism opportunities they offer (e.g. Warrawong Earth Sanctuary, South Australia). Revolving funds involve purchasing land, placing that land under covenant and then re-selling (Cripps *et al.*, 1999). This enables the land to be purchased, through the market place, by someone who values it, for nature conservation or potentially for wildlife tourism.

Payments

A final group of economic instruments need mention here – grants, compensation and subsidies. Although many commentators regard them as market-based instruments, they are not part of general 'free market' activities. Rather, the application of these instruments generally hinges on governments and non-government conservation organisations paying landholders to protect wildlife and other conservation values on their lands by changing or modifying their resource management practices. A number of commentators have noted that because environmental values, such as wildlife, tourism, recreation and the landscape, have obvious public good characteristics (they have benefits for the broader public while no one person can be excluded from enjoying them) public intervention is required for their protection (Feinerman & Komen, 2003). This is the rationale for payments by governments to private individuals and groups to maintain or enhance these values.

Management agreements, as described previously under motivational instruments, are often accompanied by payments. A suite of possible payment mechanisms exists for landholders with nature conservation values on their lands (Binning & Young, 1997). Wildlife tourism may be a motivator and by-product of such management. Grants are generally one-off payments to landholders to encourage them to change their land use practices to protect nature conservation values. For example, the Commonwealth Government of Australia pays agricultural landholders to protect existing vegetation from livestock grazing using grants from the Natural Heritage Trust. Compensation is also usually a one-off payment for landholders precluded from pursuing an existing land use practice. For example, a landholder may be paid compensation for the loss of rights to clear an area for cropping. Subsidies are ongoing payments. Trusts and discretionary funds can be set up to provide these.

In relation to rural areas in the European Union, Feinerman and Komen (2003) suggested that direct compensation payments to farmers combined with direct government assistance (including government investment in basic infrastructure such as roads through to assisting landholders with tourism marketing) seems promising for rural development. Farmers would receive a per-hectare compensation payment for less-profitable, environmentally beneficial farming practices to meet increasing demands for outdoor recreation and tourism, nature and wildlife conservation, and landscape. Such an approach is already widespread in the European Union, to reduce agricultural 'over-production' as well as maintain the rural landscapes that are desired by so many. In the United States, about US$1.5 billion is spent annually on contracts for 12–15 million ha of land (Ferraro, 2001).

Although rare outside high-income countries, direct-payment systems can also be found in the tropics (e.g. Costa Rica's environmental services payment programme) (Ferraro, 2001). In developing countries the most serious challenge to direct-payment systems working may be difficulties in allocating property rights. For such an approach to work, rights must be allocated to those who can control the use of the resource (Ferraro, 2001). With wildlife tourism, this can be difficult both in terms of excluding those who are not willing to pay for the experience and even more vexing, preventing the wildlife itself being removed by poaching or out-competed for habitat and other resources by domestic animals.

Regulatory instruments

This group of instruments has the greatest level of government involvement and includes statutory means such as legislation and regulation, direct provision of services by governments, and then a raft of planning measures, plus environmental impact assessment (Table 5.7). Planning is only addressed in sufficient detail here to illustrate its place in wildlife tourism policy. Interestingly, all the forms of planning discussed below can be identified not only as policies but also as policy instruments (hence their inclusion in this section of the chapter) (Figure 5.1). To make matters even more confusing, these plans also rely on a number of individual policy instruments for implementation, including education and partnerships. Planning has been well treated in other tourism-related textbooks (e.g. Hall, 2000a; Newsome *et al.*, 2002) hence the focus here on policy.

Legislation and regulation

Legislation is the laws, usually described and written as 'Acts', that guide the activities of governments. In democracies, legislation can only be changed if the parliament of the day agrees. Such Acts are often accompanied by regulations that provide more details on implementation of the legislation and can also be more easily amended as circumstances change. Very little legislation or regulation refers specifically to wildlife tourism (as reviewed in Tables 5.1–5.3). There is, however, mention of tourism in legislation and regulations guiding the management of protected areas and of wildlife independent of land tenure. Thus, wildlife tourism can be directed using these policy instruments.

Young and Gunningham (1997) cautioned against relying on regulation (and hence legislation) alone, in relation to nature conservation management. Regulations can 'fail' especially if there are not the resources to implement and enforce them. They should be regarded as a safety net to direct those who do not respond to other incentives, if all else fails. Often too, regulations address the symptoms of the problem, not the underlying causes. It is more efficient and effective to address the underlying causes rather than regulate once the symptoms have appeared. For example, if a landholder has to pay similar taxes on his productive agricultural lands and on uncleared lands, which produce only a small income from wildlife tourism, it is more efficient to change the taxation system than to regulate to prevent clearing.

Direct provision

Direct provision of services has always been a central function of governments. Even with downsizing of the public sector and privatisation of many of its functions, governments still have a major influence on the tourism industry, including wildlife tourism. Tourism continues be the focus of government interest because of its employment and income producing possibilities (Hall, 2000a), particularly in rural areas where economic development opportunities are often very limited. Direct provision may be basic infrastructure such as roads, domestic water supplies and marinas. It may also include marketing of destinations and tours, legal assistance in privatising access rights, and information provision (Feinerman & Komen, 2003). Providing and managing facilities on public lands, such as national parks, and provision of interpretation and education are also examples of direct provision (see Chapter 6 for a detailed review of these approaches).

Planning

Three types of planning are directly relevant to wildlife tourism, remembering that this form of tourism may focus on protected areas but also occurs across a multitude of land tenures – recovery planning for endangered species, management planning of protected areas and land use planning. Over the last two decades, recovery plans have been prepared for many endangered species in countries such as the United States and Australia (Moore & Wooller, 2003). In both these countries there is legislation directing such planning. Plans may be prepared for individual species, groups of similar species or for whole ecosystems covering thousands of square kilometres (Jewell, 2000). Although a number of recovery plans note the impacts of visitors on endangered wildlife, no plans seem to identify wildlife tourism as a threat or discuss tourism as part of the recovery management of the species.

Similarly to recovery planning, a number of countries have legislation requiring the preparation of management plans for protected areas. Usually management entails conserving an area's natural values while at the same time providing for recreation and tourism to the extent that it does not damage these values. Providing for wildlife tourism and the associated experiences while protecting the wildlife is part of this balancing act. Similarly to recovery plans, management plans can be regarded as policy instruments themselves while at the same time containing a number of instruments to effect management change. Very often such plans also include detailed management strategies such as construction of facilities, regulation of visitor numbers and interpretive requirements (as described in Chapter 6).

Land use planning is a much more broad-scale undertaking than management or recovery planning. It is often the responsibility of local shire or provincial governments who may have the option of zoning areas for nature conservation (Binning *et al.*, 1999) and hence implicitly for wildlife tourism. At a larger scale, regional tourism development across a number of shires/provinces/counties may be co-ordinated via land use planning. Approaches such as Dowling's (1993) environmentally based planning model enable values of the natural environment of relevance to tourism, such as wildlife, to be clearly recognised and considered.

Environmental impact assessment

Legislative and regulatory requirements exist in many countries for environmental impact assessment (EIA) to precede developments likely to impact on the environment. Tourism developments are often subject to EIA because of their proximity to protected areas and in the case of wildlife tourism their reliance on wildlife as the reason for the development. Wildlife tours would be unlikely to require formal environmental assessment; however, accommodation or viewing facilities such as floating pontoons in marine parks, would usually be assessed. Warnken and Buckley (2000) noted that 175 tourism developments in Australia were subject to EIA from 1980 to 1993.

Factors Influencing the Choice of Policy Instruments for Wildlife Tourism

A number of factors influence the choice of policy instruments. The most critical are covered – how the problem to which the policy is responding is defined, the policy context, and working with uncertainty. Mihalic's (2003) three 'theories' of the causes of environmental problems reviewed earlier in the chapter – poor behaviour through ignorance or lack of morality, failure of the market or the state (i.e. system failure), and uncontrolled growth – assist in determining instrument preferences. If a policymaker views environmental problems as the result of poor behaviour, then motivational and self-regulatory instruments will be preferred. If the problem is identified as a market or state failure, then economic, self-regulatory and perhaps some regulatory approaches will be seriously considered. And, if uncontrolled growth is the culprit, then regulatory instruments will be favourably viewed. As indicated in Table 5.7, often a policy instrument reflects a response to more than one perceived cause of an environmental problem. For example, partnerships are a policy response to both behavioural and system failure concerns.

The policy landscape, including the political, cultural, economic and biophysical context within which policymaking occurs, clearly influences the choice of policy instruments. This context also includes what is happening internationally, nationally, regionally and locally (Edwards & Steins, 1999). Political and social unrest internationally and nationally, for example, may dramatically affect tourist numbers (Briassoulis, 2002). National and regional development policies can directly affect the choice of policy instruments. How these broader policies consider and advocate subsidies, incentives, taxation, and the provision of infrastructure all influence how wildlife tourism is managed. In the European Union for example, subsidies to agricultural landholders as part of rural development initiatives mean that payments are appearing as a preferred policy instrument for the provision of wildlife tourism.

The choice of policy instruments is also culturally influenced. For example, Hjalager (1996) noted the Nordic preference for bureaucratic instruments while self-regulatory approaches are manifested in Anglo-Saxon countries. There are also other persistent national differences – in The Netherlands, for example, environmental groups prefer charges while in the United States they prefer regulation (Eckersley, 1995). In liberal democracies citizens and policymakers may prefer instruments that are less coercive rather than equally effective or efficient alternatives (Howlett & Ramesh, 1995).

As noted in several places throughout this chapter and elsewhere in the book, wildlife tourism is accompanied by uncertainty. This uncertainty derives from a lack of scientific knowledge regarding the impacts of tourism on wildlife, uncertainty about the efficacy of potential policy and management responses, and uncertainties associated with the tourism industry itself. Adaptive management, based on the premise that everything is not known about the natural resources that are being managed and as such an experimental approach should be taken, seems a sensible approach. Although adaptive management means different things to different people (McLain & Lee, 1996), key characteristics are including the natural and social sciences; recognising uncertainty, complexity and long time-scales; regarding policy and management interventions as objective-driven and experimental, with monitoring an integral part; including stakeholders; and using feedback (Dovers, 2003; Ewing, 2003).

If this paradigm is adopted for wildlife tourism it means selecting policy instruments that allow experimentation, can cope with uncertainty, facilitate participation, and allow frequent review of management practices (Briassoulis, 2002). Motivational and self-regulatory instruments would seem better than regulation, or direct provision and payments. Market-based instruments would also seem to be desirable within this paradigm.

Evaluating these choices

There are clearly many, many policy instruments. What then determines which one or ones to use? And, how can the success or otherwise of policy activities be judged? In public policy, authority, justice and efficiency have been identified as fundamental principles that must be considered (Anderson, 1979). The individuals or organisations responsible for implementing the policy must have the authority to do so, otherwise they will fail or the process may become coercive. There is an intimate connection between the principles of authority and justice, and the associated concepts of freedom and rights (Anderson, 1979). Justice is important because most policies have distributional consequences. For example, in the case of wildlife someone may gain rights in relation to a species and others might lose them. Efficiency is using the most efficient means to achieve the ends. All three principles are important, meaning that the temptation to judge policies based on the efficiency alone should be resisted.

Little attention has been given in tourism to-date to analysing policy activities. This lack of attention includes ecotourism and wildlife tourism. There has, however, been some recent work in relation to identifying the attributes of 'good' biodiversity policy instruments (e.g. Young & Gunningham, 1997; Moore, 2001). This work provides a starting point for developing an understanding of what might

Table 5.8 Attributes of 'good' policy instruments for wildlife tourism

Criteria	Explanation
1. Economic efficiency	Any trade-offs created by the instrument are achieved at least cost and the reassignment of property rights makes at least some one better off and no one worse off
2. Administrative feasibility and cost	Instrument creates minimal enforcement and monitoring costs, and its requirements and associated decision-making processes are easy to understand
3. Political acceptability	Instrument motivates people, and is regarded as legitimate, consistent with government policy and has bipartisan support
4. Equity	No individual or group, now or in the future, is disadvantaged by the instrument
5. Flexibility	Instrument can cope with changing technology, prices and climate, as well as encouraging innovation and going 'beyond compliance'
6. Biodiversity robustness	Instrument will deliver the desired biodiversity target even when knowledge about the social and economic consequences of the instrument are uncertain
7. Precaution	Instrument avoids the chance of serious, irreversible consequences, especially where there is scientific uncertainty

Source: Young and Gunningham (1997)

be 'good' wildlife tourism policy instruments. Young and Gunningham (1997) began their list with the widely recognised attributes of good public policy – economic efficiency, administrative feasibility and cost, political acceptability and equity considerations (Table 5.8). These five criteria are anthropocentric, that is, they are human-focused and address human concerns. They are concerned with whether the instrument is economically sensible, administratively possible and ensuring that no one is unduly disadvantaged by the policy being implemented.

Young and Gunningham (1997) suggested two criteria additional to the usual public policy considerations, both grounded in a fundamental concern with protecting biodiversity. This concern is also very relevant to wildlife tourism, which relies on elements of biodiversity for its sustainability as an industry. The criteria are dependability (which has been relabelled as biodiversity robustness) and precaution (Table 5.8). They argue that because biodiversity is recognised, through international and national treaties, as the cornerstone of sustainability then a policy instrument must deliver the desired biodiversity outcome even if there is uncertainty associated with the social and economic outcomes. This means that wildlife tourism policy must be explicitly judged in terms of whether it protects wildlife. Ferraro (2001) noted several other policy features important for achieving such robustness – ideally policy instruments should achieve conservation objectives in the short and long term and at the scale of ecosystems, and provide clear, direct incentives for local people to actively protect habitat.

The other additional criterion is precaution, a desired attribute across environmental policy. Lack of knowledge, plus the prospect of irreversible loss (especially with species becoming extinct), means that precaution must underpin the design and consideration of any wildlife tourism policies. This lack of knowledge extends beyond lack of knowledge about wildlife, to the lack of information and uncertainty that may surround ownership of the wildlife and the land or waters on which it occurs, who might be the relevant stakeholders as well as the ongoing uncertainties associated with tourism as an industry.

Conclusions

This chapter has described wildlife tourism policies, in many cases relying on practices in relation to tourism more generally, sustainability and biodiversity conservation because of the lack of policies specifically addressing wildlife tourism. These policies sit within a policy landscape, here characterised by the fugitive, common-pool nature of wildlife tourism. This means that where ownership is poorly defined, there is the potential for open access and a tragedy of the commons can result. Policies, therefore, need to address these features before sustainability can become a possibility.

As part of describing this landscape, policies affecting wildlife tourism are described internationally, supranationally and nationally, and at regional and local levels. Also covered are the policy networks that identify problems that need policy attention and then assume responsibility for policy preparation. The discussion here is broadened to include not only government (i.e. public policy) but also industry and other stakeholders, in recognition of wildlife tourism as an interface between public and private interests.

The second half of the chapter covers policy instruments, moving from voluntary instruments where there is minimal coercion by governments through to regulatory instruments, such as legislation and regulation. The wealth of instruments in between (Howlett & Ramesh's (1995) so-called mixed instruments) includes self-regulation and economic instruments. The chapter concludes with a brief discussion of the factors influencing the choice of policy instruments, plus a simple set of criteria for evaluating these choices.

The next chapter moves onto providing a wealth of detail on how wildlife can be managed in the quest for sustainability. Much of this detail focuses on site management and relies on an individual or organisation being able to control visitor use through having property rights, usually over the lands or waters where the wildlife occurs. Similarly to this chapter, much of the discussion is drawn from protected area management and then related either explicitly or implicitly to the management of wildlife tourism.

Further reading

As mentioned previously, little material exists that deals specifically with wildlife tourism policies. As such, much of this chapter has transferred practice across from other areas of tourism or from even further afield, for example, from conservation biology (e.g. Ferraro, 2001). The following readings are similarly drawn from outside wildlife tourism but all provide insights to this important tourism sector.

Howlett and Ramesh (1995) provide an excellent introduction to public policy. They bring together the wealth of research and practice in this area and synthesise it in an accessible and topical way. An easy-to-access overview of public policy is provided by Bridgman and Davis (2000). This short book includes chapters on institutions, policy instruments and policy evaluation, plus other stages in the policy cycle. In terms of policies and tourism, the edited book by Fennell and Dowling (2003) is one of the few books to deal with tourism policy in a comprehensive way. It includes theoretical material complemented by case studies at regional, country and continental levels.

This chapter necessarily focuses on policies, with limited mention made of planning. Further information on planning as it relates to tourism is available from Hall (2000a). This book provides an excellent overview of policies, processes and relationships, from a planning perspective. Particularly useful is Hall's analysis of planning at international, supranational, national and sub-national levels. Newsome *et al.* (2002) provides detailed, current information on the state-of-play with regard to planning for natural area tourism. This book is very relevant to wildlife tourism given the enormous dependence of this form of tourism on protected areas.

Much of this chapter focuses on policy instruments. Two books in particular provide excellent, detailed information on specific sub-sets of instruments. Font and Buckley (2001) provide a comprehensive coverage of ecolabelling, which includes the potentially confounding and confusing instruments of certification and accreditation. Bramwell and Lane's (2000b) book on collaboration and partnerships, another edited collection, provides current information on the plethora of partnering opportunities being pursued and realised.

For those interested in the more theoretical frontiers of tourism policy, several articles in particular make for interesting reading. Briassoulis (2002) begins an important examination of the implications for tourism of its common-pool characteristics. As explored in this chapter, this character fundamentally influences the choice of policy instruments and what types of management are likely to succeed or fail. Mihalic (2003) groups and considers policy instruments for tourism according to whether the policy is a response to bad behaviour, some sort of system failure or uncontrolled growth (Table 5.7). An important implication of her work is that the choice of instrument will be very much influenced by people's perceptions of the 'causes' of the problem. Last but not least, Hall (2000a, 2000b, 2003) continues to explore the complexities created for tourism management by the declining role of government, tourism as an interface between the public and private sectors, and influential industry groups with close relationships with governments potentially seeking to exclude other stakeholders.

Chapter 6

Managing Potential Impacts

Introduction

The purpose of this chapter is to provide a general account of the various approaches that can be used in managing wildlife tourist interactions. In accordance with the interrelationship between impacts and management and the interdependent array of wildlife management strategies there will be some overlap, both within this chapter and between this chapter and Chapters 2 and 5.

Pathways in wildlife tourism management

In most parts of the world national government strategy is to reserve areas of high conservation significance and wildlife tourism importance as national parks, nature reserves and special natural areas. Such reservation will normally have legislative backing and will be subject to a management planning process. Specific policies (Chapter 5) can be formulated which are subordinate to an overall national conservation strategy but nevertheless are very important in relation to the use of reserved areas. For example, in Western Australia the Nature Based Tourism Strategy (1997) helps to set the focus and direction for the recreational use of protected areas in Western Australia. Commensurate with this approach is the development of management plans that specify the direction of policies and all planning priorities for a specific protected area.

Such planning processes may include details of tourism planning frameworks such as Limits of Acceptable Change (LAC) and the Recreation Opportunity Spectrum (ROS). Planning frameworks allow managers to define visitor expectations and attractions, exercise controls over the tourism experience, aid in the definition of acceptable conditions and set the course of implementation of various management actions. A range of planning frameworks currently exists and these are fully described in Newsome *et al.* (2002). A recovery/reintroduction plan may also be a component of the planning process in which a specific plan will have been devised in order to conserve and rehabilitate a particular species that is rare or endangered and otherwise under threat from various factors. Tourism may be an explicit part of such recovery plans.

Specific tourism management plans are not widespread and, where manage-

- Statement of policies and guidelines as they relate to tourism.
- Identification and involvement of stakeholder interests.
- Audits of recreation and tourism facilities (e.g. campgrounds).
- Assessment of access through protected area.
- Assement of nature conservation valuse and threats.
- Identification of recreational and tourism usage.
- Joint management arrangements with indigenous peoples.
- Determination of suitable areas for the development of recreational and tourist sites.
- Establishment of key performance indicators.

Figure 6.1 Aspects of tourism that may be incorporated in the management planning process in Western Australia

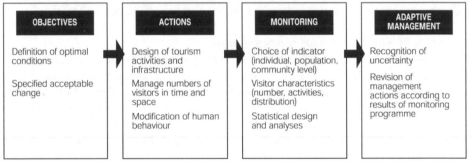

Figure 6.2 Framework for the management of wildlife tourism
(Derived from Higginbottom *et al.*, 2003)

ment plans exist, aspects of tourism management tend to be incorporated within the general management planning process (Figure 6.1). Management plans will specify management objectives, strategies and management actions. The plan can specify zoning of natural areas into general use, recreation, sanctuary and special purpose zones. The purpose of zoning is to prohibit access, ration use and restrict activities. Zoning, for example, may be used to temporarily restrict access to colonies of breeding seabirds. Those zones that allow temporary or unrestricted access are subject to more indirect management techniques depending on the situation.

Indirect techniques are concerned with influencing and modifying human behaviour and include various site and visitor management techniques (see Figures 6.2 and 6.3). Site management includes the physical design of the setting such as the use of walkways, barriers and hides. Such features help to influence where people go and what they do. Visitor management involves the use of fees and permits, reg-

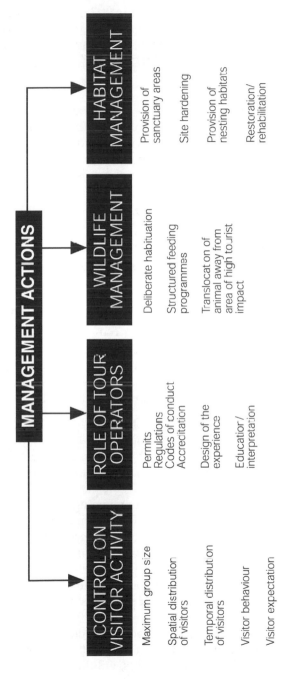

MANAGEMENT ACTIONS

CONTROL ON VISITOR ACTIVITY

Maximum group size

Spatial distribution of visitors

Temporal distribution of visitors

Visitor behaviour

Visitor expectation

ROLE OF TOUR OPERATORS

Permits
Regulations
Codes of conduct
Accreditation

Design of the experience

Education/
interpretation

WILDLIFE MANAGEMENT

Deliberate habituation

Structured feeding programmes

Translocation of animal away from area of high tourist impact

HABITAT MANAGEMENT

Provision of sanctuary areas

Site hardening

Provision of nesting habitats

Restoration/
rehabilitation

Figure 6.3 The management action component of a wildlife toursim management framework
(Derived from Higginbottom *et al.*, 2003)

ulation of numbers accessing a site, the use of staff to enforce regulations, supervise and educate the public. In addition to this tour operators can be managed via the use of leases and licences. Their businesses are also increasingly subject to being validated through systems of certification and accreditation.

Management frameworks

In exploring a framework for the management of wildlife tourism Duffus and Dearden (1990) linked the academic wildlife disciplines with non-consumptive uses of wildlife, including tourism, through the three foundations of the ecology of the wildlife species, the attitudes and practices of the recreational user and the historical/social/cultural context of the interaction between people and wildlife. Higham (1998) noted four important consequences of an application of Duffus and Dearden's model to wildlife tourism at the North Royal Albatross Colony, Taiaroa Head, New Zealand:

- Without management of the wildlife tourism experience, changes to the habitat, the wildlife species or the nature of the interaction between species and visitor occur to the overall detriment of both the wildlife species and the tourism experience.
- Although a wildlife species may appear to tolerate engagement with tourists, sigificant harmful changes to the species may be occurring.
- The results of studies of putative impacts of wildlife tourism are site and species specific, with limited opportunity for transfer to other sites and other species.
- Many putative impacts may only be revealed by long-term data sets, highlighting a need for extensive monitoring and use of time-series analyses.

However, the situation need not be overly discouraging. Higginbottom *et al.* (2001b) claimed that the above costs may be offset by benefits such as delivering extra funds for conservation and providing incentives to manage wildlife and wildlife habitat sustainably.

Higginbottom *et al.* (2003) present a framework for managing negative impacts. Its main elements are summarised in Figures 6.2 and 6.3. The main framework can be divided into four components that entail specified objectives and clearly defined actions designed to meet the objectives of the framework. Monitoring is a critical component providing the scope for any negative changes to be detected. Lastly, and especially because of uncertainty, there needs to be room for the results of monitoring programmes to be fed back into the management process so that actions can be further adjusted in order to meet objectives.

Figure 6.3 indicates the management actions aspect of a wildlife tourism management framework. Management can be defined as consisting of four distinct areas: controls on visitor activity, role of tour operators, wildlife and habitat management. In terms of visitor activity group sizes can be restricted to a maximum number of individuals and tourism can be concentrated in site hardened specific areas. Tourism activity can be reduced or restricted during sensitive phases of an animal's lifecycle. Visitor behaviour can be modified through direct instruction and supervision and expectations can be altered by education and interpretation programmes.

As already stated tour operators can be regulated or left to self-regulate. Higginbottom *et al.* (2003) identify that both tourists and operators sometimes do not comply with regulations and that visitor satisfaction may be reduced where feeding/close contact with wildlife is not allowed. With industry self-regulated tour operators the likelihood of compliance is considered to be high but, as noted by Higginbottom *et al.* (2003), the effectiveness of this approach remains to be demonstrated.

The remainder of this chapter explores important aspects (controls on visitor activity, role of tour operators) of the wildlife tourism management framework described by Higginbottom *et al.* (2003) in more detail. Its focus is on various management actions as applied to a range of wildlife tourism situations and in accordance with the wildlife tourism paradigm (Table 2.1) described in Chapter 2.

Managing Access to Wildlife

Road access

Because of the potential problems associated with the construction and use of roads in natural areas it is important that the actual need for road access is determined along with restricting road development to only what is deemed essential. Roads need to be planned so that location and design allow them to be permeable to wildlife and that the risk of road kill is minimised (Table 6.1). The use of fencing to reduce road kill in Banff National Park (Figure 6.4) has been evaluated by Clevenger *et al.* (2001). They found that ungulate vehicle collisions declined by 80% when a section of the Trans-Canada Highway was fenced to reduce the road kill problem. Their study also demonstrates the problems of road kill associated with unfenced high-speed busy roads that traverse natural areas.

Fences may reduce the road kill problem but they also act as barriers and reduce connectivity between populations and habitats. This problem can be overcome by the provision of underpasses. Animals can be directed to underpasses by the use of drift fencing, earth berms and lines of vegetation that provide cover (Huijser & Bergers, 2000). Clevenger *et al.* (2003) recommend that underpasses should be located close together so that wildlife do not choose to cross a road as in the case when underpasses are located far apart from one another. Ng *et al.* (2004) have found that underpasses, tunnels and culverts in California were used by ground squirrels (*Spermophilus beecheyi*), skunks (e.g. *Mephitis mephitis*), raccoons (*Procyon lotor*), bobcats (*Lynx rufus*), mountain lions (*Puma concolor*) and mule deer

Table 6.1 Managing the use of roads and reducing impacts on wildlife

Management feature	Function
Suitable road planning framework	Avoids construction of roads in sensitive areas. Avoidance of heavy use, fast roads
Road desien that discourages fast driving Sinuous sections Rumble bars Speed arrestor bumps	Reduce speed
Use of light-coloured road aggregate	Produces a light road surface colour making animals more visible against the pale road surface
Use of wide road verges on bends where visibility is reduced	Discourages the crossing of wildlife at that point
Overpasses	Allows wildlife to pass over the road
Earthen escape ramps	Allows animals to escape from road
Underpasses Culverts Pipes Amphibian and reptile tunnels	Allows a range of wildlife to pass under the road
Fish ladders	Allows migrating fish access upstream where road engineering has created stream barriers
Fencing	Prevents wildlife accessing the road
Wildlife reflectors	Deflect red light from vehicle headlights scattering light into the surrounding vegetation
Electronic wildlife protection systems	Camera detects wildlife. A computer is then activated which in turn activates a flashing warning sign. The flashing sign warns drivers that wildlife is on the road ahead of them
Features dependent on driver compliance	*Purpose*
Driver awareness resulting from educative materials and guides	To raise awareness
Wildlife crossing signs	To raise awareness
Reduced speed zones	Reduce speed and reduce road kill

(*Odocoilleus hemionus*) and various reptiles. A factor in predicting use by wildlife, however, was the presence of suitable habitat at either end of the underpass.

In Cradle Mountain National Park, Tasmania (Figure 6.4) Jones (2000) found that 80% of road-killed wildlife were located in the vicinity of tourist facilities such as the tourist accommodation zone. Road conditions in these areas consisted of straight and fast segments. Wildlife were also attracted to these areas because of

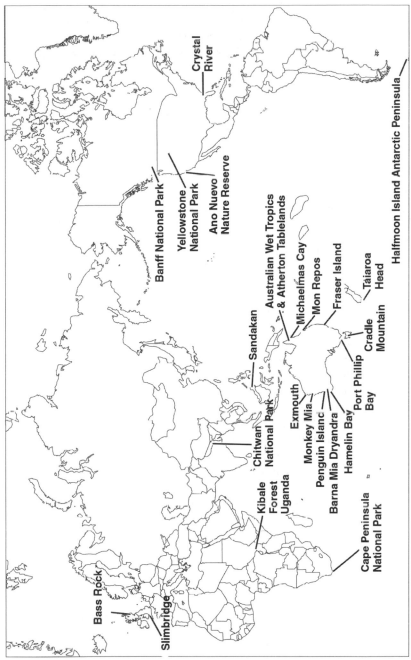

Figure 6.4 Map of sites referred to in this chapter

food provisioning and the presence of palatable exotic vegetation. Jones (2000) also noticed that it was possible for crossing animals to be trapped on roads when steep banks and deep gutters occurred on the other side of the road.

Management to reduce the road-kill problem in Cradle Mountain National Park consisted of three groups of actions:

- Physically reducing traffic speed in conjunction with signage and education.
- Provision of ramps so that wildlife could escape from the road and installation of pipes as refuge and escape areas.
- Use of wildlife reflectors that deflect red light from vehicle headlights into the surrounding vegetation.

The implemented management reduced vehicle speeds by as much as 20 km/hr, and wildlife was observed to use the ramps and pipes as escape routes. The populations of eastern quoll (*Dasyurus viverrinus*) and Tasmanian devils (*Sarcophilus harrisii*) that had been depressed as a result of road death were in the process of recovery as a result of these actions.

Zoning, sanctuary areas and the restriction of access

Important and effective management tools involve the use of zoning, provision of sanctuary areas that restrict access and the control of visitor numbers (Table 6.2). With the choice of any strategy it is important that it is consistent with management objectives and its difficulty to implement is assessed. Further to this it is also valid to calculate the probability of achieving desired outcomes and its effects on visitor freedom (Vaske *et al.*, 1995).

Some natural areas are temporarily closed for three or four months during sensitive animal breeding seasons, while others may have permanent no public access zones. Zoned areas can be marked or fenced off or if a lake or offshore waters can be delineated by marker buoys. Islands are particularly sensitive to human disturbance (Newsome *et al.*, 2002) and in response to increasing visitation to off-shore

Table 6.2 Zoning and restriction of access as management strategies

Zoning	*Rationing use intensity*	*Restricting activities*
Separate users by level of experience	Limit use via access point	Restrict type of use
Separate incompatible uses	Limit use via campsite	Limit size of group
	Rotate use	Limit length of stay
	Require reservations	Restrict camping practices
		Prohibit use at certain times

Source: Derived from Vaske *et al.* (1995)

islands in Australia the Great Barrier Reef Marine Park Authority has developed a number of guidelines (Table 6.3) for the management of human visitation to seabird breeding islands (GBRMPA, 1997).

Work carried out by Anderson and Keith (1980) demonstrates the potential for negative impact if ill-informed and uncontrolled tourist activity occurs in island settings (see Box 2.3 in Chapter 2). Moreover, Anderson and Keith (1980) note that tourists often perceive that they have a right for close access and entry into seabird colonies. Such access can be controlled under the supervision of interpretive guiding at selected viewing sites such as in the case of seabird breeding colonies on the Galapagos Islands. This approach of allowing viewing in selected areas while prohibiting widespread access is now employed in many situations and was born out of seabird disturbance and impact studies (see Chapter 2, p. 52).

Anderson and Keith (1980) recommend:

- the total number of people, frequency and duration of visits should be controlled;
- sanctuary areas that are free of people should be provided;
- visitors should be supervised by a reserve warden.

Buffer zone distances, the use of cars, restricted access during peak tourist periods and education are also recommended by a number of authors as planned strategies to protect birds from tourism related impacts (e.g. Klein *et al.*, 1995; Rodgers & Smith, 1995, 1997). Disturbance to birds is likely to be reduced in situations where guiding, interpretation and nature trails are in place. Some species, however, are more tolerant of human intrusion and can be readily viewed at a breeding site. Management of regular visitation to colonies of breeding birds can be planned via the establishment of critical approach distances.

The Ano Nuevo State Reserve in California (Figure 6.4) is a wildlife visitor attraction where elephant seals (*Mirounga leonina*), which utilise the beaches for moulting and breeding purposes, can be viewed. The reserve is zoned as 'wildlife protection area' in which permits are required. There is also a sensitive area of dunes that is closed to public access. A visitor centre and signage along nature trails provide interpretive material about the reserve as well as preparing visitors for the seals. Reserve staff and docents, who have undergone interpretive training, patrol the beach and are stationed at a distance of eight metres from the resting seals. During the period when the seals are in moult visitors are allowed to approach up to the eight metre line where staff and docents interact with the public providing facts about the seals and other wildlife in the area. There are no specifically constructed viewing structures and the presence of docents aid in avoiding close encounters between elephant seals and patrons (see, e.g. Plate 2.4 in Chapter 2, p. 60). Breeding activity takes place from December to March. During this time the reserve can only

Table 6.3 Importance of zoning and restriction of access in managing human visitation to seabird breeding islands

Management action that can be applied	*Burrow nesting species (colonies can cover an entire island)*	*Surface nesting species (nesting tends to occur in localised dense colonies)*	*Tree nesting species (generally require a long period to complete the breeding cycle)*
Construct hard surface pathways	Prevents trampling of burrows	Reduces potential impact on breeding seabirds	Reduces potential impact on breeding seabirds
Construct boardwalk through colony area	Prevents trampling of burrows. Prevents human injury from collapsing burrows	Reduces potential impact on breeding seabirds	Reduces potential impact on breeding seabirds
Visitor education and signage	Keep to pathways, avoid disturbance	Keep to pathways, avoid disturbance	Keep to pathways, avoid disturbance
Clearly designated camping areas	Avoids disturbance and prevents obstruction of bird 'runways'	Avoids disturbance	Avoids disturbance
Limit number of visitors (especially at night)	Reduces disturbance	Reduces disturbance	Reduces disturbance
Limitation on types of human activity in areas where breeding colonies have been established	Limit human activity to less vulnerable areas	Limit human activity to less vulnerable areas	Limit human activity to less vulnerable areas
Close sections of islands that are occupied by sensitive species		Where closure is discontinued during the non-breeding season re-establish closure one month before arrival of birds for next breeding season	Where closure is discontinued during the non-breeding season re-establish closure one month before arrival of birds for next breeding season
Close smallest islands to visitation		Avoids disturbance	Avoids disturbance

Source: GBRMPA (1997)

be visited as part of a guided walk, a strategy designed to reduce any potential impact to an absolute minimum.

The significance of sanctuary areas is highlighted by the case of the endangered Florida manatee (*Trichechus manatus latirostris*) at Crystal River National Wildlife Refuge, Florida (Figure 6.4). King and Heinen (2004) describe the importance of sanctuary areas to manatees. They have shown that when boating activity and swimmers increased, the use of sanctuaries by manatees increased emphasising that such areas are effective in reducing human impacts on the animals. The problems associated with increasing tourism interest in manatees include: harassment, the displacement of manatees into less favourable feeding areas and reduced resting, nursing and feeding behaviour. Given that tourism is still expanding King and Heinen (2004) propose that additional sanctuary areas be created so that existing areas do not become crowded or depleted of food.

In many cases the designation of sanctuary areas is not enough to minimise potential impacts. For example, Michaelmas Cay in north-east Australia (Figure 6.4) is an important seabird-breeding island with an annual visitation of at least 90,000 people (Muir & Chester, 1993). Despite limits of not more than 100 persons on the beach at any one time it was found that this figure was frequently exceeded and people entered a restricted vegetated area that is important for breeding birds. In response to increasing tourism demand Muir and Chester (1993) suggested that without controls there would have to be a significant increase in on-site management including the possible provision of fences (a potential hazard to seabirds on islands) to separate visitors from the birds. They also proposed a gradual reduction in the numbers of tourist operators and levels of visitation, with permit conditions that limited the number of persons taken on to the cay at any one time.

Management of Wildlife Viewing

Approaches to managing various types of viewing activities

The bulk of wildlife tourism normally involves various combinations of visitor activity as indicated in Figure 6.5. People can view wildlife on their own or under supervised conditions. Reducing disturbance is, however, strongly dependent on the application of wildlife watching etiquette and adherence to codes of conduct (Figure 6.6). Because etiquette and codes of conduct rely on voluntary actions some form of direct or indirect management may also be in place. The function of management is to protect resources and provide desirable social conditions and this can be achieved in a number of ways (see Figures 6.2 and 6.3). Techniques that focus on regulating human behaviour include limiting group size and length of stay and restricting/prohibiting certain activities. Techniques designed to influence or modify human behaviour include road designs to reduce speed, the redistribution of visitor use, education and interpretation. For example, birdwatchers are often directed to visitor centres, observation hides and designated pathways. Specific

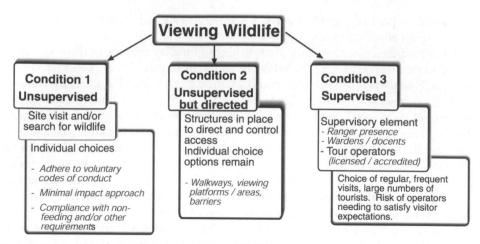

Figure 6.5 Various conditions in which wildlife can be viewed

reserves and birdwatching sites in many parts of the world usually have some form of controlled access, a range of the above facilities and an on site guide or warden. Furthermore, clubs, organisations and the birdwatching literature promote codes of conduct and strongly encourage members and readers to support conservation

The type of management actions required differs according to the various conditions that wildlife tourism takes place in. In the case of popular high visitation sites such as at Taiaroa Head in New Zealand (Figure 6.4) there can be many tours, a visitor centre, a specific viewing area and the development of infrastructure (see Box 2.1 in Chapter 2). In other cases the visitor becomes much more part of the animals' environment. This is achieved by walking instead of travelling in a vehicle or using various animals themselves in order to view other animals. This closer 'less separated contact' is seen as being more authentic and has the potential to be a much deeper and substantial wildlife experience. In Chitwan National Park in Nepal (Figure 6.4), for example, tourists are taken out on elephants to search for and view the Indian rhinoceros (*Rhinoceros unicornis*). This is also undoubtedly less damaging to the environment than a vehicle ride. Secondly it is arguably less stressful for the target species and provides for a greater degree of authenticity to the visitor experience.

In Australia a client may undertake a guided tour in order to view birds or observe nocturnal species at night. Such activities that are conducted by tour operators can be managed and monitored through licences and / or leases. Licences can be issued that allow access to various natural areas or be designated for a particular tour use. In Western Australia they are either issued on an annual basis or for specified longer periods and indicate access conditions and regulations concerned with

- Adhere to management actions and stay out of sanctuary areas (e.g. keep to marked trails).
- Avoid areas that are important for wildlife in terms of resting, feeding and parental care.
- Observe animals from a safe distance.
- In the case of birds remain well back from nests, roosts and display areas.
- View wildlife from observation areas.
- Use binoculars and telescopes for close-up views.
- Move slowly in the presence of wildlife.
- Do not block an animal's line of travel or escape route
- Do not attempt to make the animal do something (let the animal be itself).
- Never chase or harass wildlife.
- Do not use calls or food to attract animals.
- Do not feed wild animals.
- Educate and control children.
- Leave pets at home.
- Limit the time you spend watching an animal (use the animal's behaviour as a guide).
- Respect others who are viewing.
- Be aware of the cumulative effects of human presence (reduce group size and excessive noise).
- Avoid animals that behave aggressively.
- Document and report unethical behaviour by other visitors.
- Learn as much as you can about the wildlife that you are observing and/or photographing.

Figure 6.6 Core aspects of watching wildlife etiquette

minimal impact conduct. Leases, on the other hand, specify exclusive use of an area and are site dependent. The leased area may be managed as a visitor centre or viewing area. Leases can be granted for periods of up to 21 years in Western Australia.

An interesting strategy in managing visitor expectations of close contact with wildlife is the participatory approach described by Shackley (1996). Participation is where the public can directly participate in wildlife conservation progammes. She includes the example of the Sandakan Turtle Nesting Sanctuary in Sabah (Figure 6.4) where visitors can watch turtles lay eggs and then help staff collect eggs that will be reared separately in order to increase their chances of survival. Future visitors can then watch young turtles hatching and assist in returning them to the sea. In this way tourists are directly involved in helping to protect the turtles.

The public can also participate in conservation and help foster an environmental protection ethic in other ways by assisting in scientific research programmes. One example of this type of approach is the Landscope Expedition programme that operates annually in Western Australia. Expeditions are organised and run by the Department of Conservation and Land Management, which is responsible for national park management and wildlife protection in Western Australia, and the University of Western Australia. Landscope expedition clients provide a financial contribution and assist in the collection of scientific information. Destinations frequently include the remote and arid interior of Western Australia in order to trap native mammals and reptiles, carry out bird censuses, collate records of breeding birds and conduct flora surveys. Expedition members work closely with scientists and gain knowledge of nature conservation, natural history and scientific methods.

Wildlife tourism, however, involves an array of species and situations ranging from 'developed' (e.g. Monkey Mia dolphin feeding), participatory (Earthwatch – http://www.earthwatch.org/expedselect.html and Landscope Expeditions – http://www.calm.wa.gov.au/tourism/expedition.html) through to 'pristine/ authentic' (viewing wildlife with minimal disturbance in their natural habitats). The following sections further consider various aspects of management and the role of tour operators in a number of different wildlife tourism situations.

Management of wildlife tourism in the marine environment

Wildlife tourism in the marine environment embraces fish viewing and feeding, interactions with stingrays, birdwatching and visits to seabird breeding islands and the viewing of, and interaction with, marine mammals. Marine mammal tourism can involve visiting seal colonies and haul out sites, swimming with sealions, swimming with whales and dolphins, and dolphin feeding programmes.

In Western Australia it is possible to interact with wild dolphins and view dugong at Monkey Mia (Figure 6.4) and swim with whales, whale sharks (*Rhincodon typus*) and manta rays (*Manta birostris*) in the Ningaloo Marine Park (Figure 6.4). All of these Australian tourist programmes have rules associated with them that are specified in wildlife interaction licences provided for by legislation (e.g. see Box 6.1). These rules always specify contact zones for boats, minimum approach distances and requests to respect the wild nature of the animals concerned. Educational material is often available in the form of brochures that describe aspects of biology, ecology and specific aspects of visitor management.

Where food provisioning is a formal aspect of a tourist attraction specific management is put in place to reduce impacts. Food provisioning provides for shore-based shallow water close interactions with fish and dolphins. Dolphin

---

Box 6.1   Licensing tourism associated with pinnipeds in Western Australia

A prospective tour operator would need to supply an application that indicated the operator's knowledge and experience of pinniped behaviour. In addition the documentation would have to contain an environmental impact and risk assessment of the proposed operation. Annual licences are granted under the Wildlife Conservation Act (1950). The Wildlife Conservation (close season for Marine Mammals) Notice (1998) stipulates that vessels must not restrict the normal behaviour of marine mammals. Close approach, herding or chasing is not allowed. Licence conditions cover the species concerned, location, method of approach and approach distances. The licence may specify the need to gather and provide data to the management agency. It should be noted that such licensing guidelines are not in place at some important pinniped tourism sites around the world.

(*Source*: Kirkwood *et al.*, 2003)

---

feeding takes place at three locations in Australia and is subject to management control (Figure 6.7). Management is designed to reduce any altered natural foraging patterns, negate alterations in natural behaviour, control the quality of food supplied and interpret dolphin behaviour so that dolphin harassment is reduced and any risk of aggression towards humans is mitigated (Mann & Kemps, 2003).

Whale watching can take place from shoreline lookouts or platforms or from tour vessels. Some boats work in conjunction with spotter planes and/or use hydrophones to detect whales underwater. Tour guides are often on board to deliver interpretive material to patrons. Many countries have regulations in place to control the potential effects of whale watching but according to Rice (1996) their adequacy in many situations remains to be proven. Having noted the concerns of Rice (1996) it is likely that regulations, such as 100 m buffer zones between whales and boats, are of benefit as indicated by the work of Williams *et al.* (2002) who concluded that non-compliance was likely to result in greater levels of disturbance. Garrod and Fennell (2004) report on the variable nature and content of whale watching codes of conduct and stress that there are very few really successful codes.

The Whale and Dolphin Conservation Society (2004) and Johnstone Strait Killer Whale Interpretive Society (2004) have developed guidelines that are designed to allow minimal impact whale watching to take place. The main elements of these guidelines are:

- minimise boat speed and avoid sudden changes in boat direction;
- use specified approach distances;

- Human-dolphin interactions are supervised by rangers in order to prevent touching of dolphins by the public.
- An exclusive dolphin interaction area has been designated in which boating and swimming are prohibited.
- The feeding of dolphins is prohibited outside the designated interaction area.
- Fish used to feed the dolphins is caught in the local area, frozen and stored for no longer than three months. In order to minimise the risk of disease it is thawed immediately prior to being fed to the dolphins.
- Dolphins are only offered fish in the mornings (between 8 am and 1 pm) and there is no fixed feeding time. This is to ensure that dolphins spend time foraging naturally and engage in natural social behaviour.
- There is a maximum of three feeds per day. Only a few members of the public can be chosen to feed a dolphin at any one time. No members of the public are allowed in the water when a calf is present.
- Only female dolphins are offered fish. This is to prevent male dolphins becoming aggressive and using the situation to herd females.
- In order to prevent dependency the dolphins are only offered one-third of their daily requirement of fish.

Figure 6.7 Main elements of the management strategy in place at Monkey Mia, Western Australia
Source: CALM (1993); Wilson (1994)

- utilise minimal disturbance approach direction and angle of approach;
- reduce noise levels;
- avoid the pursuit, encirclement or separation of whales;
- allow whales to control the duration and nature of the experience;
- consider the cumulative effects of time spent with whales and the number of boats that visit whales.

Virtually all-commercial cetacean tourism around the world today is subject to licensing and regulation. Whale watching tourism has been in operation in Western Australia since 1989 and licensing and guidelines for whale watching were introduced early (Box 6.2, Figure 6.8). In conjunction with this there is an ongoing monitoring programme designed to determine whether tourism is causing any shifts in the distribution of whales or any changes in migratory habits. The challenge for managers in the future will be in determining how many licences can be issued in the face of increasing demand from tour operators and in determining acceptable levels of disturbance to the whales.

Box 6.2   Whale watching rules in Western Australia

1.   Aircraft are not permitted to fly within 300 metres of a whale.
2.   Swimming with and feeding or touching whales is not permitted. If you are in the water and a whale approaches you must endeavour to keep a minimum of 30 metres distance between you and the whale.
3.   Any marine vessel that is within a distance of 300 metres from a whale and within the whale contact zone:
     (a) A vessel must not cause a whale to alter its direction of speed of travel.
     (b) A vessel must not disperse or separate a group of whales.
     (c) A vessel must not approach a whale from a direction within an arc of sixty degrees of the whale's direction of travel or an arc of sixty degrees of the whale's opposite direction of travel.
4.   A vessel must not approach a whale within a distance of 100 metres.
5.   Where a whale approaches a vessel and the distance between the whale and the vessel becomes less than 100 metres, the vessel master must place its motor or motors in neutral or move the vessel at less than five knots away from the whale until the vessel is outside the contact zone.
6.   A vessel must not block the direction of travel of a whale, or any passage of escape available to a whale, from an area where escape is otherwise prevented by a barrier, shallow water, vessel or some other obstacle to the whale's free passage.
7.   A vessel master must abandon any interactions with a whale at any sign of the whale becoming disturbed or alarmed.

(Adapted from CALM, 1999)

Some tourism operations focus their attention on a swimming experience with whales or dolphins. Some of the impacts associated with this activity include: avoidance behaviour, an increased risk of disease, boat collision injuries, harassment and injury to cetaceans and aggression directed at humans (Samuels *et al.*, 2003). As already stated, licences and regulations are aimed at minimising impacts and ensuring visitor safety but Samuels *et al.* (2003) note that protection will be best afforded when the number of licensed operators is also controlled. Such a control is aimed at reducing the number of boats and swimmers and therefore the time spent with the animals (e.g. Constantine *et al.*, 2004). It would also seem that if regulations are in place they are not always adhered to. Scarpaci *et al.* (2003) report on non-compliance in the case of swim with dolphin tour operations in Port Phillip Bay, Australia (Figure 6.4). They found that the following conditions had been disregarded:

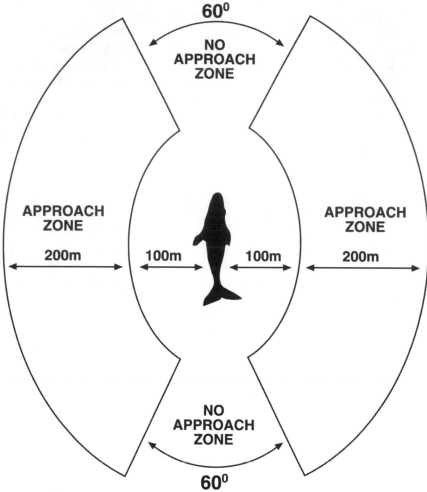

Figure 6.8 Specified approach distances for vessels involved in whale watching activities in Western Australia

- Not to approach dolphins head-on (36% non-compliance).
- Dolphin swim time a maximum of 20 minutes (61% non-compliance).
- Tour vessel not to remain within 100m for more than 20 minutes (61% non-compliance).
- Swim not to proceed if a foetal fold calf is present (30% non-compliance).

Given that regulations are designed to reduce impacts and protect the dolphins these data confirm the view of Samuels *et al.* (2003) that there is a need to control actual numbers of operators. Scarpaci *et al.* (2003) suggest that compliance may be improved with tour operator education, client education and the enforcement of regulations. The importance of tour operator education has already been recognised by Sirakaya and Uysal (1997). In a survey of tour operators in Ecuador, USA and Canada Sirakaya and Uysal (1997) investigated compliance with ecotourism guidelines. Their results showed that educating tour operators about desired practices and in the benefits of compliance was more likely to result in conformance behaviour.

Management of spotlighting activities

Viewing wildlife at night involves scanning wildlife habitat from a vehicle or on foot (see Chapter 2, p. 71). The activity can involve the use of a 30-watt spotlight, headlights and/or powerful torches. People search for a nocturnal animal's eye shine and use that to detect a range of mammals, birds, reptiles and some invertebrates, particularly spiders. Recent work by Wilson (2000) in the wet tropics of north-east Australia (Figure 6.4) encapsulates the issues that need to be taken into consideration when viewing nocturnal wildlife. She identifies a range of management strategies that are geared to ensure visitor satisfaction and helps reduce impacts on target species (Table 6.4). A practical example as to how a range of management techniques can be employed in order to manage a walk-based nocturnal guided tour is presented in Box 6.3.

Arguably one of the most important aspects of nocturnal wildlife viewing is observing turtles come ashore to lay their eggs or to watch hatchings emerge from a nest. Tourism has developed around viewing turtles in Florida, Brazil, Sabah, Costa Rica, South Africa and Australia.

It is generally considered that repeated disturbance would result in a decline in nesting activity and success on beaches preferred by sea turtles (e.g. Wilson &Tisdell, 2001; Tisdell & Wilson, 2002). Problems are likely to arise when vehicles use beaches as the resultant tyre marks can increase the time it takes for a hatchling to reach the sea by 35% (Hosier *et al.*, 1981). Situations where many people randomly search the beach with torchlight are likely to disrupt turtle emergence from the sea and subsequent nest excavation causing turtles to return to the sea without laying their eggs.

Because of these risks and the increasing popularity of turtle tourism the ongoing viewing of turtles needs to come under management control, such as limited access and visitor numbers and an interpretive presence such as at Mon Repos in north-east Australia (Figure 6.4). At Mon Repos the beach is under management control and adjacent waters have been designated marine park status. The aim is to reduce disturbance to a minimum so that successful nesting

Table 6.4 Management of spotlighting activities centred on possums in the Australian wet tropics

Management strategy	Rationale	Benefits
Rotate use across a range of selected sites	Spreads any impact across more than one site	Reduces disturbance on specific populations of wildlife
Use a range of pre-determined areas but at the same time leaving many areas free of spotlighting disturbance	Leaves some wildlife populations free of spotlighting related disturbances	Impact affects fewer populations of wildlife
Control group size	Reduces risk of noise and inappropriate behaviour and reduces stress on wildlife	Less disturbance and greater chance of seeing wildlife
Reduce noise and disturbance via guiding and interpretation	Less disturbance and greater chance of seeing wildlife	Increased visitor satisfaction
Avoid close approach via use of binoculars and telescopes	Less disturbance and greater chance of seeing wildlife. More people likely to see animals	Increased visitor satisfaction
Reduce use of light	Reduces disorientation and stress on target animal	Increases chance of seeing target species in the longer term
Reduce intensity of light by application of filters	Reduces disorientation and stress on target animal	Increases chance of seeing target species for a longer period of time

Source: Derived from Wilson (2000)

takes place and to avoid the disorientation of hatchlings. Although there is no restriction of access during the day dogs are not allowed and visitors are requested to only use beach umbrellas below the high tide mark so as to avoid disturbing nests. Jet-skis and similar craft are not permitted during the nesting season so as to avoid the disturbance of turtles that are congregating offshore. At night access is regulated and under the control of park staff. A 1.5 km radius darkness zone has been established to reduce disturbance from light. The height of buildings in the area is regulated and there is no street lighting during the nesting season. Screens of vegetation have also been established to reduce light glow and help darken the landward horizon.

Visitors enter the site via a visitor centre that is also rear lighted to avoid light pollution. Clients wait in the visitor centre until a staff member sights a turtle. This practice avoids the need for large numbers of people to search the beach with torch-

---

Box 6.3   Wait-a-while Tours: Best practice viewing of nocturnal wildlife in north-east Australia

The guide in charge of the tour (maximum of 8–10 people) provides some pre-visit information which is particularly focused on visitor expectations. It is pointed out that visiting a natural environment is not like visiting a zoo and that some animals may not be seen. Clients are instructed in the use of torches and in the detection of eye shine. If clients find an animal they are to inform the guide who will request all torches issued to clients to be switched off. The guide then controls the viewing activity.

A maximum of two spotlights are used and the group, using low intensity hand-held torches, is instructed to walk in a straight line. This avoids the need for indiscriminate use of torches and helps to reduce noise levels. Once an animal is spotted a request is made for all light to be extinguished. The guide uses a 50 watt spotlight fitted with a red filter. The time taken for a nocturnal animal to recover its night vision from red light torch beam is approximately 2–5 minutes whereas recovery from a high intensity white light can take as much as 30 minutes. Only red filtered light is used for observation and the animal is observed for 1 minute only. The guide is constantly observing for signs of stress. For example possums can give a nervous reaction in the form of moving off, alert/freeze behaviours and scratching. No flash photography is allowed.

The guide interprets each species seen providing details on arboreal adaptations, behaviour, diet and breeding. Species such as pythons that are frequently located on tours are never handled and explanation is given as to why. In terms of site access only site-specific licenses are given to operators. Permits are available for three areas of the Atherton Tableland (Figure 6.4). The frequency of site usage is four nights per week for a period of 1 hour. Tour operators are required to provide monitoring data on weather conditions, number of people on the tours, duration of visit and on species seen.

---

light. During the wait in the visitor centre interpretive material is supplied which is designed to increase public awareness and provide information to the public as to how they can help conserve sea turtles. Up to 70 people at a time may be taken to see a turtle. Large group sizes such as this are sat in concentric semi-circles with children at the front. The public is instructed as to when they can put on lights and take photographs (see Figure 6.9). At the same time Wilson and Tisdell (2001) maintain that other approaches can be utilised to give public access to turtle nesting behaviour. These include the use of noise and lightproof hides, use of night vision

Emerging from the water
(1) To avoid disturbing turtles entering the beach, be sure to walk along the shoreline looking for tracks leading up the beach from the water.
(2) If a turtle can see you, it will return to the water. So, if you see a turtle, stay down and wait until she is out of your sight before following her track to the body pit site.

Digging the body pit
(3) No torches should be used at this stage. If you use your torch on the beach, you are less likely to see a turtle.
(4) Look for turtle tracks leading form the water up the beach. Their tracks look like tracks left by a large truck.
(5) Once you can see the turtle, stay low and do not move closer than 5 metres. Position yourself/group behind the turtle, so she cannot see you. If the sand is being pushed towards you, then you are in a suitable position behind the turtle.

Excavating the egg chamber
(6) Once she has stopped throwing sand behind her, she will start digging an egg chamber. You can get closer.
(7) Marine turtles use their back flippers to dig the egg chamber. She will choose whether this is a good place to nest at this stage, so be very still and do not get too close.

The egg laying process
(8) After about 20 minutes, check to see whether she has stopped digging the egg chamber by peering into the body pit.
(9) If she has stopped, you can get within half a metre from the turtle and observe the egg laying process by shining your torch into the body pit from behind the turtle.

Covering and camouflage
(10) Once she has stopped laying her eggs, she will start filling in the egg chamber with her back flippers.
(11) After she has done this, she will start throwing sand over the body pit. Unless you want to be covered in sand, it is best to move at least 5 metres from the turtle, continuing to stay behind at all times.

Returning to the sea
(12) After a considerable amount of time spent covering her nest, she will return to the water to recover from this exhausting nesting process.

(Derived from Waayers & Newsome, 2003)

Figure 6.9 Watching nesting marine turtles: A code of conduct for turtle observation

equipment and, while in the hide, presentations of live video footage of the egg laying process.

Not all sea turtle tourism, however, takes place in this way. In some cases, such as at Exmouth in north-west central Western Australia (Figure 6.4) a less controlled approach currently exists where free independent travellers and licensed tour operators view turtles in a more informal fashion. Brochures are available and there are plans for the development of a visitor centre. Recent work has focused on the development of a community-monitoring programme with an emphasis on the training of volunteers to monitor nesting success and develop a code of conduct (Figure 6.9) for the watching of sea turtles (Cape Conservation Group, 2003; Waayers & Newsome, 2003).

Physical separation of visitors from wildlife

This is commonly achieved through a combination of zoning and the control of visitor access. Site hardening is an integral component of physical separation and involves the provision of infrastructures such as fencing, structures that facilitate

Plate 6.1 Bird observation hide at Otmoor Nature Reserve, Oxfordshire, England. The hide is accessed from a walkway that is set lower in the landscape so that visitors can enter the hide without being seen by the birds. The hide itself provides an effective screen and reduces disturbance, allowing observers to watch birds for a longer period of time.
Source: David Newsome

the flow of tourists, (e.g. fenced walkways/boardwalks), hides (Plate 6.1), viewing platforms/barriers, feeding stations and observation towers. Such features serve to contain the public while allowing access and observation of wildlife at the same time.

Fences, especially those that contain explanatory signage, provide an effective barrier between wildlife and tourists. It is also desirable that fencing does not significantly protrude above the height of surrounding vegetation. GBRMPA (1997) caution that wire and barbed wire fencing is a hazard to birds particularly at night. On seabird breeding islands it is desirable to use rope fencing that allows movement if struck by a bird (GBRMPA, 1997). Various forms of fencing (e.g. roped off trails) can be used in conjunction with pathways in order to contain the movement of people. Evidence of the effectiveness of fencing is provided by Ikuta and Blumstein (2003). They found fencing to be an effective barrier in restricting human access in wetland reserves in California, in that the fence allowed the birds to behave as if they were in undisturbed conditions.

Boardwalks can be utilised to direct people to hides and observation platforms. The major wildlife attraction at The Boulders in the Cape Peninsula National Park in South Africa (Figure 6.4) is a breeding colony of African penguins (*Spheniscus demersus*). Until the last few years the general public could gain access to the penguins on the beach. There was a sign and rope lying along the ground that served as a token but psychological barrier that many people still ignored. The lack of a well-defined physical barrier meant that many people would still cross the rope in order to take photographs. Such desired close contact with many species remains a problem for natural area managers (e.g. Plates 2.4 and 2.5 in Chapter 2). Since that time a number of elevated boardwalks and viewing stations have been constructed. The penguins are now physically separated from visitors and the boardwalks prevent damage to the sensitive coastal vegetation (Plate 6.2). The separation approach is supported with interpretive signage and staff are on site and available to interact with the public.

The essence of physical separation is that it involves viewing animals from a distance. Another technique used to achieve this is through viewing hides that are designed to enable people to see wildlife while minimising disturbance. GBRMPA (1997) note that hides on seabird breeding islands should enable adequate viewing of the breeding areas given that there is a suitable buffer zone, be positioned so that favourable light conditions, necessary for observation, exist throughout the day and contain information on codes of conduct, bird ecology, management and protection of the birds. Some hides provide fixed binoculars to assist in people viewing the wildlife. Furthermore, wildlife can be increasingly viewed from inside a visitor centre via remote video camera linkages such as in the case of the gannet (*Sula bassana*) colony at Bass Rock in south-east Scotland (Fig.6.4).

Plate 6.2 Viewing of African penguins at The Boulders, Cape Peninsula National Park, South Africa. Boardwalks prevent trampling of coastal vegetation and fencing/observation decks provide a barrier between the penguins and visitors. Information boards describe penguin ecology and the rationale behind management is explained. Volunteers are available to provide face-to-face interpretation and facilitate appropriate use of the infrastructure.
Source: David Newsome

Buffer zone/setback distance separation of visitors from wildlife

Because of the attraction and importance of birdwatching in natural area tourism much work has been directed at understanding and managing the impacts of human visitation on colonies of breeding birds (e.g. Stokes *et al.*, 1996; Rodgers & Smith, 1995; Burger *et al.*, 1995; Carney & Sydeman, 1999; Nisbet, 2000; Sekercioglu, 2002; Blumstein *et al.*, 2003). An important aspect of management that has emerged is the use of critical approach distances. Dunlop (1996) defines the critical approach distance as the distance at which a bird can be approached without causing it to show anti-predator or escape behaviour (Box 6.4). Critical approach distances can thus be used to manage visitation to seabird breeding islands and colonies of water and other birds. Accordingly the critical approach distance is then used to deter-

---

Box 6.4   Identifying the responses of birds to human disturbance and implications for management

Burger *et al.* (1995) suggest that four measurements can be made that represent the responses of birds to human intrusion:

(1) Approach distance. Distance at which a bird can be approached head-on without disturbance.
(2) Tolerance distance. Distance at which a human can pass a bird in a tangential fashion without causing disturbance.
(3) Response distance. Distance between a bird and human at which a response can be detected (e.g. interruption of normal behaviour, increased alertness). Fernández-Juricic *et al.* (2001) consider alert distance as an indicator of tolerance. They define it as 'the distance between an animal and an approaching human at which point the animal begins to exhibit alert behaviours to the human'.
(4) Flushing distance. Distance at which a bird will leave its nest or feeding site. Also termed flight initiation distance (e.g. Blumstein *et al.*, 2003).

---

mine buffer zones that are designed to provide space between birds and birdwatchers and allow the birds to go about their activities of daily living. Critical approach distances, however, do vary between species and their breeding seasons, across different geographic areas and according to varying levels of habituation (e.g. Nisbet, 2000; Gill *et al.*, 2001).

Insight into the complexity surrounding critical approach distance determinations is provided by Rodgers and Smith (1997) who investigated the response of 16 species of waterbird to various types of disturbance. They found that species varied in their response to the same type of disturbance, for example walking or boat traffic. Mean flushing distance, which is the average distance to which an animal will tolerate the approach of a human before escaping, differed between species. Brown pelicans (*Pelecanus occidentalis*) would flush at about 27 m when approached by a walker. Ring-billed gulls (*Larus delawarensis*) flushed at 33 m while sanderling (*Calidris alba*) flushed at around 13m. These data, and determinations carried out on other species, were used as a basis for recommending buffer zones between visitors and waterbird areas. Repeated and frequent disturbance could result in increased energy expenditure, loss of time obtaining food and increase the chance of eggs and young being exposed to predation. Because of this Rodgers and Smith (1997) suggested that buffer zones should be determined according to the flushing response of the most sensitive species in mixed species situations. A buffer zone distance of around 100m (mean of flushing distances plus a 40m buffer distance) was recommended in order to ensure a disturbance free zone for the birds.

Fernández-Juricic *et al.* (2001) provides further evidence of variability among birds in the form of alert distances (Box 6.4). They also state that alert distances are a more conservative indicator of tolerance to humans than flushing distances because alert distance provides a 'buffer zone' between alert and flushing distance. Blumstein *et al.* (2003) confirm the species-specific nature of flushing distances and confirm the need for a conservative approach in setting the boundaries of buffer zones. Negative impacts on birds can be further reduced if birdwatchers apply a suitable code of conduct in combination with adhering to critical approach distance recommendations (Table 6.5).

Table 6.5 Voluntary guidelines for birdwatching activities

Guidelines for visitors	*What the visitor can do*
Establish low impact philosophy	Maintain ethical birdwatching conduct
Avoid close approach, especially if noticed by the bird	Adhere to critical approach distance regulations
Be aware that birds can be intimidated by direct observation (humans looking directly at them) and camera lenses/photography	Use binoculars, telescopes and reduce time spent watching
Minimise being seen	Use hides
Avoid use of tapes	Exercise patience in searching for elusive species
Avoid nesting birds and birds caring for young as much as possible	Use binoculars/telescopes from hides and reduce the time spent watching
Show special consideration in case of rare and endangered species	Use binoculars/telescopes from hides and reduce the time spent watching Adhere to critical approach distance regulations

Managing the Desire to Feed Wildlife

Managing the expectation of visitors to feed wildlife

As stated in Chapters 2 and 3 people can have a strong desire to feed wildlife as it helps to satisfy nurturing behaviour and allows close contact with wildlife. On the other hand it can result in many problems such as those considered in Chapter 2. The feeding of wildlife is also used to attract species to particular sites, as in the case of feeding birds, so that visitors can obtain prolonged and even close views of various species. In attempting to understand and manage the feeding of wildlife it is important to make the distinction between unstructured and structured feeding situations. In unstructured feeding situations the public may have little knowledge, be free to behave as they wish and give little thought to how and what they feed to wildlife (e.g. Newsome *et al.*, in press; Box 2.4). Informal feeding such as this that takes place in protected areas can either be tolerated but discouraged or entirely prohibited, depending on the situation – lthough policing such activities can be difficult. The situation can be complicated further by the fact that a species may be fed in one situation, for example on private land, while feeding of the same species is not allowed in nearby protected areas.

With a structured feeding programme, which can be under direct management control, supervised by a tour operator or conducted on private property, information can be delivered, patrons supervised and the amount and type of food can be controlled. Such programmes, however, may not be entirely problem free. Table 6.6 summarises some of the main advantages and disadvantages associated with various structured feeding scenarios. One advantage of supervised feeding is that in bringing people closer to wildlife a greater understanding can be fostered which in turn can lead to increased conservation supporting behaviour. Feeding situations can go even further in relation to conservation programmes. Orams (2002) cites several cases where supplemented feeding can be used to help increase animal populations. Feeding wildlife during periods of environmental stress such as drought or during freezing conditions can help to prevent losses.

Structured feeding of wildlife: The role of operators

The feeding situation at Kingfisher Park, Julatten, Australia (Figure 6.4), besides providing viewing and photography opportunities for the visitor, appears to favour the birds. The park consists of 12 acres of privately owned rain forest and provides accommodation for birdwatchers. The park owners offer high quality interpretive guiding and 150 species can be seen in and around the park. A structured feeding programme is employed in order to attract birds to the park. This involves the provision of seven water dishes, two nectar feeders, one fruit feeder, one seed feeder and plantings of bird attracting plants such as *Grevillea sp*. This combination of feeding attracts many species to the park and rather than 'manipulating' the birds provides an opportunity for the birds to exercise their natural foraging behaviour. In times of drought and during very hot weather the water and food provide benefits to local populations of birds.

Potential negative impacts are managed in that predators, such as the laughing kookaburra (*Dacelo novaeguineae*) and black butcherbird (*Cracticus quoyi*), are not part of the feeding programme. The nectar feeders contain sugar, water and nectarvite (vitamins) and 60% of the water dishes are placed > 1.5 m. high so that non-ground dwelling species can feel safe. The fruit feeder is supplied with fruit that is not grown locally (see Table 6.6) and the seed feeder is supplied with a special

Table 6.6 Advantages and disadvantages associated with structured feeding of wildlife in tourism situations

Tourism situation	Advantages	Potential disadvantages
Fish feeding, Great Barrier Reef, Australia	Close viewing and contact for visitor. Interpretation can be delivered. Management can control the amount and quality of food. Situation can be monitored.	Risk of visitors being bitten. Larger and more aggressive fish become dominant. Fish may ignore natural food sources. *No evidence of problems has been reported*
Feeding Komodo dragons, Indonesia	Close viewing and contact for visitor. Interpretation can be delivered. Management can control the amount and quality of food. Situation can be monitored.	High concentration of dragons at feeding site. *Practices have been altered in order to discourage unnatural concentrations of dragons*
Feeding hummingbirds, Monteverde, Costa Rica	Close viewing and contact for visitor. Interpretation can be delivered. Enables photography. Management can control the amount and quality of food. Situation can be monitored.	Risk of aggression between same and different species at feeders. *No evidence of problems reported*
Bird feeding, Kingfisher Park, Julatten, Australia	Close viewing and contact for visitor. Interpretation can be delivered. Management can control the amount and quality of food. Situation can be monitored.	Attraction of predators. Fruit eating birds acquiring a taste for commercial orchard crops.
Feeding Tasmanian devils, Australia	Close viewing and contact for visitor. Interpretation can be delivered. Management can control the amount and quality of food. Situation can be monitored.	Aggression towards visitors.
Dolphin feeding, Monkey Mia, Australia	Close viewing and contact. Interpretation can be delivered. Management can control the amount and quality of food. Situation can be monitored.	Aggression towards visitors. Alteration of foraging behaviour. Increased risk of disease in dolphins and risk of accidents with boats. *Controversy surrounds the argument for continued habituation of dolphins*

finch mix. Given that rain forest in the area continues to be cleared stations such as this provide benefits for the birds.

Structured feeding of wildlife: The role of managers

Economic and political pressures may dictate that managers have to provide for and structure the feeding of wildlife. Management control reduces the risk of negative impacts and helps to mitigate the aggressive behaviour of habituated species being positively reinforced by visitors giving up food to pushy animals. Structured feeding takes place in many situations and is designed to allow safe observation and/or close contact and provide an opportunity to educate the visitor and foster appropriate behaviour towards wildlife. In Australia examples include dolphin feeding at Monkey Mia (Figure 6.7) and devil kitchens where Tasmanian devils can be observed at night feeding on a carcass.

Combining feeding with a natural experience: Barna Mia, Dryandra Woodland, Western Australia

Barna Mia is a 2.5 ha enclosure situated in Dryandra Woodland in south-west Western Australia (Figure 6.4). The woodland itself, an extensive *Eucalyptus wandoo* remnant, is noted for wild populations of rare and endangered marsupials such as the numbat (*Myrmecobius fasciatus*), tammar wallaby (*Macropus eugenii*) and woylie (*Bettongia penicillata*). Dryandra is an established wildlife tourism destination with independent travellers and tour operators visiting the site for birdwatching, rare mammal sightings, spotlighting activities and wildflowers. Successful rare mammal recovery programmes conducted by the Department of Conservation and Land Management have resulted in the recovery of the numbat and woylie in particular.

Following on from these successes a 20 ha enclosure has been constructed within Dryandra in which additional rare species that once occurred in the area are captive bred. Barna Mia is located close to this facility and is designed to provide the opportunity for visitors to see and interact closely with rare and elusive nocturnal mammals. Barna Mia thus adds to the wildlife tourism experience already being offered at Dryandra in enabling visitors to view bilbie (*Macrotis lagotis*), banded hare-wallaby (*Lagorchestes fasciatus*) and boodie (*Bettongia lesueur*) at close quarters while receiving an educational component at the same time.

Visitors are taken to Barna Mia from a predetermined meeting point. The facility is introduced and regulations regarding nocturnal viewing of wildlife are presented to the group e.g. need to be quiet, no torches or flash photography. This is followed by a 30 minute presentation which provides information on Dryandra Woodland, feral predator controls, rare species breeding and reintroduction programmes. The species contained in the Barna Mia enclosure are introduced and illustrated. Preprepared feed trays (up to eight) are given out and the guide, using a red filtered light, leads the group into the enclosure. The group then stops at various permanent feeding stations comprising a clearing and logs for people to sit on. A member of the group with a feeding tray then places it in position as indicated by the guide and the group waits for animals to appear. Visitors are able to see rare species at close hand. Studies indicate high levels of visitor satisfaction with the public being excited by the close contact, the movement of animals around them and the feeding behaviour of the animals (Hughes *et al.*, in press). Other aspects identified as contributing to high levels of satisfaction were the natural appearance of the enclosure and the clear evidence for wildlife conservation.

The Barna Mia experience provides another example of how visitors can become involved in a controlled wildlife feeding situation. It also demonstrates tourism input into a species recovery programme especially via raising awareness in support of such programmes. Such activities, however, are not problem-free. Although sufficient quality and quantity of food is provided there appears to be some aggression among the feeding animals that are attracted to humans and the feeding stations as they compete for food (M. Hughes, Pers. Comm.).

Role of feeding captive species: The case of Slimbridge, England

The Slimbridge Wildfowl and Wetlands Centre in southern England is part of the UK Wildfowl and Wetlands Trust and contains the world's largest captive collection of wildfowl including many rare species. Slimbridge is also an important nature reserve where wild birds can be seen on a series of lakes, ponds, on adjacent farmland and on the nearby Severn Estuary. There are 16 hides that overlook the wetland areas and the public is encouraged to also take an interest in and identify wild birds of which more than 250 species have been identified. The site contains a visitor and discovery centre but a focus of activity for the public is the feeding of birds which is a popular practice in Britain especially during winter when birds are under stress because of cold conditions.

Formulated mixes can be purchased at Slimbridge and patrons are allowed to feed captive birds throughout the year. During winter wild birds are fed at scheduled times at one of the hides. In addition to this, evening floodlit feeds with commentary are organised for groups of visitors. A number of perspectives can be derived in relation to the feeding programme at Slimbridge. On the negative side it could be argued that allowing feeding of this nature encourages people to feed wild animals resulting in the possible consequences discussed in Chapter 2. On the other hand, if patrons are allowed to feed captive species under controlled conditions (e.g. appropriate foods supplied) they have the opportunity to readily satisfy their desire to feed and obtain close contact without any negative consequences. At the same time an interest in wild species is fostered through education and activities at the centre. The feeding of wild birds is supervised and a winter phenomenon. Indeed the feeding of wild birds during the northern winter can prevent death from starvation during severe weather. Supervised feeding educates the public as to what to feed and clarifies why birds are being fed. Feeding of this nature also helps to reduce stress that birds are under from other environmental influences.

Feeding of wildlife needs to be managed with caution

Some structured feeding operations appear to be working well and it can be concluded that feeding under the contexts described (Julatten, Monkey Mia, Barna Mia and Slimbridge) are largely benign and mostly beneficial and foster an interest that can lead to conservation supporting behaviour. Moreover these examples serve to illustrate that a structured programme of feeding wildlife is a possible option, depending on the situation.

Although there are social and economic benefits to be derived from structured feeding operations it is important to gauge the real need for such activities. Lewis and Newsome (2003) explored stakeholder interests in relation to existing unmanaged and potential managed stingray tourism at Hamelin Bay in Western Australia (Figure 6.4). Their survey revealed that seeing animals in the natural state was the most important aspect of wildlife tourism to visitors and feeding wildlife was ranked sixth out of a possible total of seven items of ascending order of importance. Croft and Leiper (2001) found that in terms of tourist interaction the visitors they surveyed ranked touching and feeding wildlife to be of low importance. It is however probable that, depending on the situation, where the owner/operator or manager enhances the chance of viewing species through a management controlled structured feeding programme (e.g. Julatten) a much larger percentage of visitors will rank structured feeding as an important component of the experience. It is likely that the results presented above reflect the case when the public feeds wildlife rather than management, especially in un-supervised situations. Such results may also reflect a changing attitude of client interest from manipulative (touching and feeding) to the more appreciative/respectful end of the visitor expectation/attitude spectrum (see Figure 2.5 in Chapter 2).

The summary of issues presented in Chapter 2 (Table 2.7), however, demonstrates that any proposal to allow the feeding wildlife should be examined on a case-by-case basis as some species and situations are much more conducive to safe feeding than others. The experience gained from impact studies (Chapter 2) shows that if feeding is planned to be part of a wildlife tourism experience it needs to be supervised, interpretive and responsive to both visitor monitoring and the monitoring of wildlife.

At all times an educative approach should be taken. Evidence that even simple signage is an important tool in raising awareness of management preferences is supplied by Mallick and Driessen (2003) who found that the majority of people they surveyed in Tasmanian national parks had noticed and read signage that indicated that feeding is not good for wildlife. Nevertheless, and most important of all, management should aim to restrict formal feeding activities and concentrate more on natural authentic wildlife experiences. There is strong evidence for such a trend in Australia (e.g. Lewis & Newsome, 2003; Mallick & Driessen, 2003). The surveys conducted by Mallick and Driessen (2003) showed that 92% of respondents were against the feeding of wildlife. Furthermore, and as exemplified by the tragic death of a child on Fraser Island (see Chapter 2, Tables 2.6 and 2.7; Figure 6.4), informal, unsupervised feeding of wildlife should be prohibited in all natural areas.

The Importance of Education and Interpretation

Modification of visitor expectation and increasing visitor satisfaction

Alcock (1991) states that education is the most important wildlife management strategy. This is because, as has been pointed by various writers, undesirable and damaging behaviour is more the product of ignorance than deliberate destructive behaviour. Education aims to increase visitor knowledge and understanding while interpretation is more of an emotionally stimulating experience. Orams (1996) thus defines interpretation as an educational approach that invokes meaning and explains relationships and which take place in natural settings. As a result there is an increased probability that tourists will take a much more active role in minimising their impact and move towards protecting wildlife even long after their visit to a natural area is over. Nonetheless, Orams (1996) highlights education and interpretation as underutilised strategies in managing tourist–wildlife interactions. He stated that in many cases a lack of trained and knowledgeable guides remains an obstacle to the wide implementation of educational strategies. However, where education and interpretation are skilfully and comprehensively applied it does work in modifying visitor attitudes and reducing impacts (e.g. Medio *et al.*, 1997). This is particularly the case where young people are involved as interpretation is crucial to establishing longer-term desired attitudes to wildlife and nature and there is much scope to do this by working with children. Best practice consists of involving the client in the interpretive process. By working with children a guide can more readily engage adults and involve them in the interpretive process at the same time.

When implemented, the management of wildlife tourism through education and interpretation usually takes place by the public being made aware of species ecology and biology along with guidelines for observation and visitor codes of conduct (e.g. see Figure 6.9 and Table 6.5). In many cases this is carried out by management and achieved through publications, signage, the presence of a ranger and/or a visitor centre. An example of this is the interpretation and public information focusing on the winter ecology of wildlife, potential problems of attraction and habituation and knowledge of approach distances to wildlife that form part of the wildlife disturbance management strategy at Yellowstone National Park (Figure 6.4). Olliff *et al.* (1999), nevertheless, maintain that such a strategy would be more effective if the number of face-to-face interpretive contacts with the public were increased.

Higginbottom *et al.* (2003) note that education works best with small group sizes and on guided tours. Reducing tourist group size makes good tourism management sense, as smaller groups are more likely to achieve greater visitor satisfaction through reduced crowding and more effective interpretation. This is a recommendation forwarded by Johns (1996) who examined the effects of tourism on wild chimpanzees (*Pan troglodytes*) in the Kibale Forest, Uganda (Figure 6.4). Johns (1996) concluded that small groups of tourists had no impact on the chimpanzees but larger groups of up to 15 people caused an increase in vocalisation response. Larger tourist groups are also implicated in causing more stress and agitation to the crested black macaque (*Macaca nigra*) in Sulawesi (Kinnaird & O'Brien, 1996). By enforcing small visitor group size tourism operators and guides can help reduce stress on target species and foster a greater degree of visitor satisfaction.

In many situations a tour operator will deliver the 'wildlife experience' particularly if transport is required for closer observation. Recent surveys of visitors engaging in swim with dolphin tours in New Zealand support the view that visitors wish to be educated while on a tour (Luck, 2003). In many parts of the world tour boats are regularly used to gain access to sites supporting waterbirds (e.g. Galicia & Baldassarre, 1997; Rodgers & Smith, 1997). Galicia and Baldassarre (1997) report on the impact of tourboats on American flamingos (*Phoenicopterus ruber ruber*) and the authors recommend that disturbance would be greatly reduced through interpretive techniques such as tourist education, publications and a visitor centre. Such work emphasises the role of trained guides and interpretation in reducing impacts in these circumstances. As exemplified by Newsome *et al.* (2002) tourist operators have a very important role to play in providing interpretive experiences that foster appropriate attitudes and a sensitive approach towards viewing wildlife.

The importance of visitor centres can be illustrated by the situation on Penguin Island, Western Australia (Figure 6.4). The island is a very popular day visit recreational site and important breeding area for the little penguin (*Eudytula minor*). Many visitors wish to view penguins and this desire has been catered for by the construction of a visitor centre which houses injured and wild penguins. The captive birds provide the opportunity for close contact and this is supported by regular interpretive talks on penguin biology, consequences of adverse impact and conservation (Plate 6.3). This strategy, combined with physical approaches such as boardwalks and footpaths, has effectively managed increased visitation and substantially reduced tourism pressure on Penguin Island since its implementation.

Tour operator's role in educating clients

Tour operators have to be knowledgeable in order to conduct a good business in terms of customer satisfaction and environmental management. There is a plethora of tour operator situations but many focus on birds either as part of a general wildlife experience or as a specialist birdwatching operation. A number of tours operate

Plate 6.4 Captive penguin exhibit and visitor centre at Penguin Island, Western Australia. Such exhibits enable visitors to see and learn more about wildlife. The visitor centre satisfies a number of visitor expectations while at the same time providing interpretive content. The captive penguin display, consisting of injured and rehabilitated captive birds, satisfies the visitor who desires to see and have close contact with the animals that use the island for breeding purposes. Adult fairy penguins spend the day foraging at sea and come ashore at night and many visitors may otherwise feel disappointed about not seeing a penguin. It also negates the need to search for a wild penguin therefore reducing the risk of habitat damage. Those people who have a desire to see wildlife being fed can also be accommodated via a structured feeding programme where visitors also learn about the natural diet of penguins.
Source: David Newsome)

in north-east Queensland in the vicinity of Port Douglas, Cairns and the Atherton Tablelands (Figure 6.4). Interpretive material is delivered in relation to the distribution and ecology of local birds. This is an important process in engaging the client and is dependent upon knowledge and the experience of the operator. In terms of visitor satisfaction clients are made aware of what the potential is in regard to the places they will visit. Expectations may vary from group to group and within groups of people on the tour and clients are directed accordingly. Disturbance of birds is reduced through the use of hides and telescopes. Access along already established road corridors enables the transporting vehicle to be used as a moving hide. Because the operator understands the bird he is aware of different approach margins for different species. Tactful birdwatching is to know how close the group can get to a bird before it takes flight. This can be explained to clients and a comprehensive and successful view of a bird can be achieved with the use of binoculars and telescopes. As some birds will stay and others leave, a patient temperament needs to be encouraged. In some cases the time spent viewing has to be controlled. Impacts such as excessive disturbance and damage to vegetation/habitats can be avoided if there is a willingness on behalf of the client to understand wildlife and the beforementioned direction from the tour operator is maintained.

The Role of Monitoring

Monitoring is a vital aspect of wildlife tourism management and involves the systematic gathering and analysis of data over time (Newsome *et al.*, 2002). It is crucial in obtaining data pertaining to impacts and in formulating management response. In particular Duffus and Dearden (1990) emphasised the need for 'establishment of behavioural and reproduction benchmarks that will allow managers to recognise when focal species are being disturbed, and if that disturbance has potential to harm the individual or the population.' Higginbottom *et al.* (2003) provide some examples of wildlife attributes and habitat factors that could be monitored (Table 6.7). Aspects of science relevant to the design of monitoring programmes are considered further in Chapter 8.

In addition to this it is also important to collect data on visitor use so that indicators can be formulated that address the social environment. Such visitor use data is important for management and planning for interpretation. Visitor monitoring can involve counting visitors, aerial surveys, questionnaires, interviews and the observation of visitors (Newsome *et al.*, 2002).

In order to accurately detect visitor related impacts any monitoring system must be capable of accounting for natural variation (see Chapters 7 and 8). Acero and Aguirre (1994) devised a monitoring programme to detect tourism impacts on penguins on Halfmoon Island in Antarctica (Figure 6.4). The monitoring plan included collecting data on assemblages of species, their distribution, population estimates, population ecology, reproductive status and spatial and temporal use of occupied areas. Any changes in breeding and nesting behaviour were also recorded. The behaviour of each species in response to disturbances was analysed from fixed observation points with continuous video recording before, during and after the visits of tourist groups. Control sites, where no tourism occurred, were also monitored so that any background changes in the absence of tourism could be detected.

This information is then used to develop hypotheses and experimental testing in order to explain the dynamics and interrelationship of tourism and the environment (see Chapter 8). Preliminary results indicated a 5–10% reduction in breeding success over one year at a site visited by some 2300 tourists. Establishing causal

Table 6.7 Ecological, behavioural and physiological attributes and habitat factors that can be monitored as part of a wildlife tourism management strategy

General indicator	*Example*	*Issues*
Presence or absence of a species	Target species avoiding humans Attraction to tourist sitesIncrease in habituated and/or scavenging species	Need adequate baseline data Data must be sufficiently long term to allow for seasonal change
Relative abundance of a species	Decline in breeding success Avoidance	Need adequate baseline data Data must be sufficiently long term to allow for seasonal change Long-lived animals may persist for years without breeding leading to sudden declines when they die of old age. Thus recruitment should be measured
Measurements of species diversity	Changes occurring at the community level	Need adequate baseline data Data must be sufficiently long term to allow for seasonal change Difficulty in relating to tourism impact
Behavioural measurements	Records of pushy and aggressive behaviour towards visitors Behavioural indicators of stress and avoidance Aggressive interactions between members of same species Altered foraging patterns Changes in breeding success	Patience, skill and observer training are essential to reliable data Data must be sufficiently long term to allow for seasonal change Long-term impact difficult to establish. Uncertainty regarding significance over longer periods of time Apply precautionary principle when uncertainty is high Some habituation may be an essential part of tourism
Physiological measurements	Altered heart rate Changes in body temperature Levels of stress hormones	Often complex and expensive to undertake Measures are often high during habituation Obtaining data may stress animals Requires specialist input Uncertainty regarding significance over longer periods of time Apply precautionary principle when uncertainty is high
Quality of habitat	Reduced cover and resting areas Change in quality of breeding habitat Weed invasion Incursions of exotic animals Increased pressure on sources of food	In the absence of long-term studies the effects on wildlife can be difficult to establish Detailed preliminary studies to establish elements of quality habitat that are essential Different types of habitat are sometimes needed at different times of the year

Source: Adapted from Higginbottom *et al.* (2003)

effect between tourism activity and a decline in reproductive success will clearly depend upon data collection over a number of years. Although it may take 6–10 years to collect viable monitoring data, Acero and Aguirre (1994) stress that such information is vital in the sustainable management of wildlife tourism in the future.

Higham (2001) reports on how detailed monitoring of nest site positioning and chick behaviour allowed the detection of a change in the distribution of nests and recorded alterations in chick behaviour that constitute risks to the long term viability of the colony. Higham (2001) also notes that the original nesting area is now a car park and that in 1999 only one nest was visible from the observatory. There are implications for visitor satisfaction and even in the possible redesign of infrastructure to accommodate these changes

Tour operators are normally required to provide monitoring data as part of their licence conditions (e.g. Box 6.3) and managers are increasingly required to devise monitoring systems that enable the detection of changes in conditions. The development of indicators and standards (see Figure 6.10) such as in the Limits of Acceptable Change or Visitor Impact Management Planning Frameworks allows changes to be detected with management being able to respond accordingly (Newsome *et al.*, 2002; Moore *et al.*, 2003). Such measures can be used to audit management performance and detect whether certain management strategies are working or not. An example of this might be the case of visitors being allowed to feed wildlife within a specific designated area that has an interpretive programme geared to assist in managing the activity. Monitoring visitor activity could show whether less feeding of wildlife outside the designated area was occurring, it could detect the results of interpretation geared to reduce wider informal feeding activity, detect the use of correct food items and provide information on any change in visitor expectations.

Conclusions

Many authors agree that the impacts surrounding wildlife tourism are difficult to study because our knowledge of target species biology and ecology is lacking and because of the wide range of tourism situations (e.g. Shackley, 1996; Birtles *et al.*, 2001; Green & Higginbottom, 2001). Natural variation, in particular, makes it is difficult to accurately detect the effects of tourism on wildlife. Given this situation it would seem prudent to employ the precautionary principle until management understands the conditions surrounding a particular wildlife tourism attraction better. Management of wildlife tourism involves various approaches and facilities, can be basic to complex and manifest as minimally intrusive for the visitor to being very controlled and restrictive for the visitor. All these approaches have their place with education and interpretation being universally applicable and essential components of best practice.

The intentional feeding of wildlife remains controversial. Samuels *et al.* (2003) point out that very few studies have confirmed the view that close interaction that

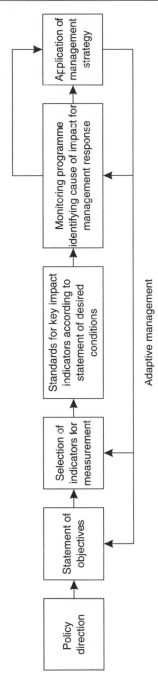

Figure 6.10 Possible steps in monitoring for adaptive management
(Adapted from *Vaske et al.*, 1995)

involves touching and feeding is absolutely necessary for the initiation of conservation supporting behaviour. It would also appear that the desire for close contact is changing, as more people appear to desire natural, more authentic experiences. This in itself, however, may bring new challenges in terms of visitor satisfaction and impacts in providing for such experiences.

Effective management in the future will therefore depend on increased knowledge and monitoring of behavioural reactions of wildlife to tourism and knowledge of the implications of such behavioural responses for the population as a whole. Tour operators need to be well informed about the environment and wildlife and develop the necessary skills in interpretive guiding. Moreover, interpretation should also be used to help the public understand and accept management strategies aimed to protect wildlife.

Additional relevant texts

Shackley (1996) remains a useful text that explores education, separation, integration and participation as visitor management strategies. A number of reports produced by the Australian Cooperative Research Centre for Sustainable Tourism provide further details on Australian and general aspects of wildlife tourism management (e.g. Green & Higginbottom, 2001; Lawrance & Higginbottom, 2002). Knight & Gutzwiller (1995) explore a number of management scenarios. Newsome *et al.* (2002) provide a comprehensive introduction to planning frameworks and monitoring in natural area tourism. Manfredo (2002) provides an account of the application of planning in wildlife tourism in North America. Further details on the use and application of indicators and standards are contained in Moore *et al.* (2003). It is recommended readers consult Thompson *et al.* (1998) for details of monitoring and Burgman and Lindenmayer (1998) and Lindenmayer and Franklin (2002) for an account of monitoring programmes and adaptive management.

Chapter 7

Natural Science and Wildlife Tourism

Contributed by KATE RODGER and MIKE CALVER

Introduction

Managing human–wildlife tourism activities requires an understanding of the interaction between humans and wildlife drawing primarily on the basic scientific discipline of wildlife biology and the action of wildlife management. Wildlife biology explains the actions of the animals themselves through studies of their ecology and behaviour. Wildlife management is concerned with the application of the findings of wildlife biology to manipulate or conserve wildlife populations and with the social, legal and political contexts which contribute to the decisions (Caughley & Sinclair, 1994; Taber & Saharia, 1995). Together, science and management recommend how interactions between people and wildlife can be arranged to maximise the benefits and minimise the problems for all parties. Furthering a basic understanding of the concerns and practices of wildlife biology enhances pleasure in the wildlife tourism experience by explaining why animals behave as they do, while an understanding of wildlife management is essential for people seeking to introduce a tourism perspective into management decision making (Braithwaite & Reynolds, 2002).

Scope of this chapter

This chapter examines the current contribution of science, in particular wildlife biology, to the sustainable management of wildlife tourism. To begin we briefly examine the concept of science, discussing how science is currently defined and practised. The popular view of science is that it is objective, value-free and concerned with indisputable, established facts. However, in practice science is steeped with values, objectivity is an illusion, and scientists often disagree about the interpretation of specific phenomena (Merton, 1973; Chalmers, 2000). Therefore, before calling for 'science' in managing wildlife tourism, it is necessary to understand its potential and limitations. Following on from this we look at the different ways science currently contributes to the management of wildlife tourism. Finally, we examine barriers that impede the involvement of wildlife biologists in conducting research into the impacts of tourism on wildlife.

Nature of Science

In today's society it is difficult to find a consensus on a definition of science or what constitutes science. Science and knowledge are often used interchangeably as *scientia*, the Latin from which science derives, means knowledge. The Australian Concise Oxford Dictionary defines science as 'knowledge; systematic and formulated knowledge, the pursuit of this, an organised body of knowledge'. Differing viewpoints on science have been suggested over the years including Aronowitz (1988) who argued that science has established itself as the only legitimate form of human knowledge or Chalmers' (2000) view of science as knowledge that has been derived from the facts of observational and experimental results. Jarman and Brock (1996) suggested that science is fundamentally concerned with answering questions that advance knowledge while Neuman (2000) remarked that science refers to both a system that produces knowledge as well as the knowledge produced from that system. This idea is compounded by Simmons (1993) who noted that for the most part science is commonly taken to mean 'western science' and often has the reputation of producing knowledge that has been elevated by some of its practitioners to the level of being the only knowledge worth having.

Characteristics of science

The traditionalist viewpoint of Western science considers the scientific research community to be predominantly impartial, objective and open-minded (Mulkay, 1991). The primary reason for this is that most sciences are firmly founded on a positivist ontology (the belief that there is a single set of rules for distinguishing science from non-science and truth from non-truth) that has guided the ways of science since Aristotle developed the formulation of both deductive and inductive methods of enquiring about natural phenomena (Richards, 1983; Chalmers, 2000). Needham (1969) noted that this dominant ontology has endured because of its European philosophical origins coinciding with the propensity of Eurocentric views to dominate global scientific and philosophical discourse. This has resulted in most practitioners of the natural sciences and many in the social sciences reflecting a positivist ontology. Although there has been criticism over the positivistic approach to science most scientific disciplines were founded on this ontology (Chalmers, 2000; Neuman, 2000). Therefore, for this book we take primarily a positivist approach because of its strong influence in the natural sciences and in particular environmental science.

The ideas of positivism were taken up in Vienna in the 1920s by a school of philosophy which attempted to formalise the ideas that Auguste Comte had introduced in the 19th century. Positivist science is based on the realist position and its studies generally attempt to test theory to increase understanding of a particular phenomenon believing that knowledge is derived from the facts of experiences (Chalmers, 2000). Neuman (2000) commented that science is given a life through the operation of the scientific community which sustains the assumptions, attitudes and techniques of science. This then determines the norms of the scientific community as well as defines the ethos of science to which most scientists generally conform as a part of their profession (Richards, 1983; Mulkay, 1991). Positivistic science has three main characteristics which should not be thought of as mutually exclusive: (1) the scientific method; (2) the norms of science; (3) the validity of science.

Scientific method

Science is thought to be demarcated from other modes of acquiring knowledge by the assumptions on which it is based and its methodology (Frankfort-Nachmias & Nachmias, 1996). It is the process or method which science follows that ensures the findings are robust. The scientific method systematically uses theory, observation, measurement and logic. Empirical validity, sampling validity and repeatability are essential to the scientific method (Caldwell, 1982). It was Karl Popper in the early 20th century who added the important element to scientific thinking of hypothesis testing. This allowed for theories or observations to be tested. If they could not be refuted then they were conceded as scientific knowledge until proven otherwise (Richards, 1983).

The scientific method that most natural scientists would be familiar with can be seen in Figure 7.1. This illustrates how the scientific research process requires a number of steps. The steps are followed for every research project on a particular study or topic. Each project builds upon prior research and contributes to the overall body of knowledge. Related hypotheses that stand the test of time are sometimes bound together to be known as theories. However, even with the scientific method to ensure reliability there is no absolute truth in science and a scientist's acceptance of a theory is always provisional (Raven & Johnson, 1991).

The scientific method is considered to be by many scientists as what science is all about. Chalmers (1982) noted that most self-avowed scientists mainly see themselves as following the 'empirical method'. Yet, this is a mistaken view of science as there is no method that enables scientific theories to be proven as true (Chalmers, 2000). Patterson and Williams (1998) support this idea noting that although there is a general belief that science equals methodology in reality science is much more.

The scientific community

Behaviour in any human community is regulated by social norms. Kuhn's (1970) view of science is one of communities of scientists rather than individuals and the paradigm of science is developed through background information, laws and theo-

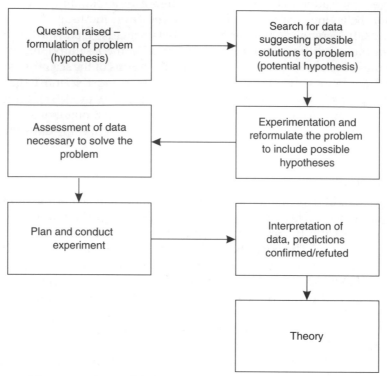

Figure 7.1 The scientific method
(Raven & Johnson, 1991; Neuman, 2000)

ries. Research activities of a community are guided by the ideology of science at any given time. If one wishes to be included into the scientific community then one must believe that what is being taught by scientists is deemed true (Richards, 1983). In 1952 Robert Merton (1973) first discussed the idea of the scientific community having its own set of norms by which it abides believing these were responsible for the rise of modern science (Ziman, 1984). He described the professional norms and values that scientists and researchers learn and internalise through their years of schooling. The norms are reinforced by the settings in which scientists operate and contribute to the unique role of the scientist. They are believed to be what set scientists apart from other people in other social institutions (Neuman, 2000).

Merton alleged that there are four basic norms of the scientific community; *universalism, communalism, disinterestedness* and *organised skepticism. Universalism* is where acceptance of one's research is based on its scientific merit and not a person's race, gender, age or nationality. It has the intention of guaranteeing that all new knowledge is appropriately archived so that those following later can access it. *Communalism* is intended to ensure that all scientific findings are shared with the larger community so that the knowledge of science can grow. Scientific secrecy is frowned upon. *Disinterestedness* is where science is done merely for its own sake. Scientists only undertake research and present their results so that knowledge can advance rather than for personal motives. As scientists are not committed to any ideology therefore they can follow the truth wherever it may lead them. Last is *Organised Skepticism*, this norm is intended to differentiate science from other institutions. Scientists should take nothing on trust, they need to challenge and question all evidence that is presented to ensure that the methods used in the research can stand close examination (Chalmers, 1982; Charlesworth, 1982; Merton, 1973; Mulkay, 1991; Neuman, 2000).

Additionally Cullen (1990) noted that there are several common themes that are present in the 'culture' of the modern scientific community. These include sharing and openness through publication, honesty about limitations of data and evidence, emphasis on peer review, peer rewards from quality of work and selection of problems addressed, low status of data unless collected to test a hypothesis, applied science and independence over the areas studied by scientists. Furthermore, Horwitz and Calver (1998) observed that scientists are nestled within a range of peer groups including scientists in laboratories, those involved in research projects, those involved in broader disciplines, and those involved in the scientific community. Each scientist also has an institutional affiliation or allegiance. With this allegiance comes obligations, duties and constraints on what is funded, how experiments are conducted and what conclusions are reached (Horwitz & Calver, 1998). Some authors are especially concerned at the possibility that scientists may be biased to support the individuals/organisations that fund their work (e.g. Theodoropolous, 2003).

Validity

Science is often thought of as being value-free. However, this view is now considered to be out of date as science is open to values and bias just like any other area of human inquiry. All disciplines are value laden and values are an important component of the scientific process (Calver *et al.*, 1998).

Having understood that science is not value-free one can examine how the validity of scientists' work, including their methods and results, needs to be guaranteed. Publication, peer review, conferences and forums of knowledge enhance credibility and expose fraud in the scientific community. These measures allow for the methodology to be examined and validated, which determines whether the results are justifiable (Merton, 1973; Cullen, 1990; Horwitz & Calver, 1998). This idea fits with Merton's norm of communalism.

Publication is the main technique for communicating findings and some authors argue that work not published in the peer-reviewed literature is unfinished or even undone. Peer review involves critical appraisal of the quality of the work and the presentation of the results, while formal publication increases the accessibility of the work to a wide readership and makes a lasting contribution (Ratti & Garton, 1996; Calver & King, 2000).

Revolution vs. evolution

Science can no longer be thought of as one subject or area of research. Today there are countless different scientific disciplines researching into many different areas. There are numerous science disciplines that study nature including biology, ecology, animal behaviour and environmental science to name a few. In 1950 Singer (1950) suggested that as knowledge advances it must become more divided, which has been made necessary by the vast and rapid increase of knowledge. In today's society there are numerous scientific disciplines with each having its own beliefs and norms, and methods that it abides by. Each scientific paradigm or discipline has its own philosophical assumptions (ontology) that justify the methods that they use for their research (epistemology) which then in turn sets the boundaries of the goals that will be achieved (axiology) (Patterson & Williams, 1998).

Kuhn (1970) believed that science is what the scientific community accepts at the given time. New knowledge can replace existing scientific thought at any juncture. Therefore, scientific methods continuously change over time depending on the current view of science at any given period (Charlesworth, 1982; Chalmers, 2000). There are differing viewpoints on how science advances. In 1962 Kuhn (1970) published his theory on the progression of science which can be summarised by 'Pre-science – normal science – crisis revolution – new normal science – new crisis' (Chalmers, 2000: 108). Normal science is where scientists spend most of their time and it is from this stage that the crisis revolution develops. The crisis revolution results from the rising number of anomalies that challenge the existing practice of science. Eventually the crisis revolution becomes structured when a scientific community conforms to a single paradigm and reverts to new normal science (Kuhn, 1970). Therefore knowledge comes about in spurts and revolutions (Campbell, 1953; Richards, 1983; Chalmers, 2000).

Another view on how new scientific disciplines develop is the idea of knowledge advancing in incremental steps. Mulkay (1991) suggested that with science new problem areas are regularly created and therefore the associated social networks are formed. Scientists are at work in an existing area when unresolved problems or unexpected observation arise that are outside of their domain. This leads to migration of scientists to this new field. Scientists tend to migrate from research networks that have definite characteristics including networks where there has been a decline in significant results and networks where members have few avenues of research available (Mulkay, 1991). Disciplines can fragment, however there is also the trend to interdisciplinary research that builds bridges between different disciplines. Environmental science is a clear example of this, because it blends the physical and the life sciences.

In summary, science can collect and analyse data through the scientific process that is relevant to the management of wildlife tourism. At its best, it can predict the most likely consequences of different management actions. However, science rarely deals in certainties and the questions researched and conclusions drawn are subject to values and possibly bias. With that in mind, it is possible to now closely examine the contributions of wildlife biology, the discipline closest to wildlife tourism, can and does make to the sustainable management of wildlife tourism and the wildlife tourism experience itself.

Wildlife Biology

People have always been captivated by animals. Their behaviour, interaction with the environment and needs for survival have interested humans for centuries (Shackley, 1996; Orams, 1999; Higginbottom *et al.*, 2001c; Reynolds & Braithwaite, 2001). This interest has led to the development of scientific disciplines to understand and investigate the four common problems that all animal life confronts:

- obtaining the water and nutrients needed for metabolism;
- removing metabolic wastes from the body;
- surviving in the face of threats from predators, parasites and disease; and
- reproducing the species.

Wildlife biology is concerned with how animals behave in their natural environment to solve these four problems and how these behavioural solutions contribute to the distribution and abundance of particular species. An understanding of these issues can then be applied in the management and / or conservation of wildlife populations. In particular, wildlife biology is concerned with one or more of the questions:

- *How does a particular behaviour pattern contribute to solving one of the major problems of life?* For example, courtship behaviour is related to identifying a suitable mate of the same species to increase the chance of reproducing successfully. Such studies often involve a consideration of how the behaviour evolved and how it adapts the animal to its environment.
- *What are the immediate causes of an animal behaving as it does?* At any time, an animal is confronted with a range of stimuli. How does it prioritise these to give rise to the behaviour it expresses? Answering this question often involves determining whether the behaviour is learned, an innate response to particular stimuli, or a complex of both.

- *How do individuals interact with others of their kind in populations?* This question is addressed by considering the dynamics of wildlife populations and the underlying causes of population change.
- *How do animals interact with other species in their environment?* Interspecific interactions such as predation, competition and facilitation (where the actions of one species benefit another) are important in the survival of both individuals and populations.
- *How can an understanding of the behaviour of wildlife be used to achieve desired management outcomes?* Examples include reversing the population decline of an endangered species, reducing damage to crops from pests, or minimising dangerous interactions between wildlife and tourists.

Answers to these questions are explored at the level of the behaviour of individual animals, the interrelationships of individual behaviour and complex social patterns, and the consequences of individual and social behaviour for the distribution and abundance of animal species. Therefore, wildlife biology ensures managers have knowledge to answer these questions and furthermore contribute to the management and survival of wildlife populations.

Wildlife Biology and Wildlife Tourism

Throughout the world the wildlife tourism industry is growing. All tourism will have some impact (be it positive or negative) on wildlife. With the increase in wildlife tourism there is also a growing number of tourists wanting close interaction with wildlife and their habitats (Duffus & Dearden, 1990; Reynolds & Braithwaite, 2001). This rapid growth has led to increasing concern about the impacts on wildlife and their habitats as well as the sustainability of the industry itself (Knight & Gutzwiller, 1995; Green & Higginbottom, 2001; Higginbottom *et al.*, 2001c; Reynolds & Braithwaite, 2001). Researching human–wildlife interactions requires baseline knowledge of species including their habitat requirements, their behaviour and natural movements as well as their response to tourism activities.

Gilbert and Dodds (1992) noted that trying to manage wildlife without first gaining adequate knowledge of the ecological interactions, environmental constraints and the zoological realities of the situation could cause more harm than good. A good example of this are whale sharks (*Rhincodon typus),* where concern has grown over the lack of information on basic biology which could lead to serious conservation problems as this species becomes increasingly used for wildlife tourism purposes (Colman, 1998). Currently wildlife management uses a multidisciplinary approach drawing knowledge primarily from wildlife biology which subsumes scientific disciplines such as ecology, animal behaviour, and conservation biology. For ecological tourism activities (including wildlife viewing) to be sustainable managers need scientific knowledge on which they can base their decisions (Gilbert & Dodds, 1992).

There are four main reasons why wildlife biologists need to become involved in studies of wildlife tourism: (1) impacts from tourism on wildlife and their environment can be identified and minimised; (2) the methods of wildlife biology are appropriate to determine the presence and extent of any problems and the success of ameliorative strategies; (3) education and conservation; and (4) anticipation of future problems. Each of these points is considered in more detail below.

Impact management

Past research in wildlife tourism has focused on the tourism experience including visitor satisfaction, visitor characteristics, visitor behaviour, and carrying capacity (Reynolds & Braithwaite, 2001; Rodger & Moore, 2004). In the past the effects of tourism on wildlife has received little systematic attention which has resulted in a knowledge base that could be regarded as disparate (Boyle & Samson, 1985; Knight & Gutzwiller, 1995; Hammitt & Cole, 1998). Knight and Cole (1995) noted that studies that have investigated the effect of tourism on wildlife have shown that human disturbance can result in changes in a variety of ways (Table 7.1). Nevertheless even with the awareness of negative impacts Hodge (2002: 40) still recently noted 'There is scant scientific research into the direct impacts of tourism on wildlife'.

Currently managers are juggling conservation with the provision of an authentic viewing experience (Schanzel & McIntosh, 2000). An understanding of wildlife's biology also allows managers to anticipate possible negative consequences of wild-

Table 7.1 Different types of impacts from tourism–wildlife interactions

Tourism impact	*Example of species*
Wildlife physiology	Magellanic penguins (*Speniscus magellanicus*) colony at Punta Tombo, Chubut, Argentina (Fowler, 1999)
Behavioural changes	Humpback whales (*Megaptera novaeangliae*) in Hervey Bay, Queensland, Australia (Corkeron, 1995); southern stingray (*Dasyatis Americana*) in Cayman Islands (Shackley, 1998)
Population levels	West Indian manatee (*Trichechus manatus*) in Southern Florida (Shackley, 1992)
Reproduction	Little penguins (*Eudyptula minor*) on Penguin Island, Western Australia (Weinecke *et al.*, 1995); greensea turtles (*Chelnia mydas*) nesting in Tortuguero National Park, Costa Rica (Jacobson & Lopez, 1994)
Species composition and diversity	Habitat of breeding seabirds on Penguin Island, Western Australia trampled by visitors observing birds (Weinecke *et al.*, 1995).

Box 7.1   Glow-worms and tourism

Glow-worms (*Arachnocampa flava*) are an increasingly popular wildlife tourism attraction in Australia with both domestic and international travellers including 'glow-worm tours' in their itinerary. However, very little is known about the effects of tourism on glow-worms (Pugsley, 1984; Merritt & Baker, 2001). Natural Bridge, in Springbrook National Park, located in south-east Queensland, is a popular glow-worm destination. Due to the increasing tourism market and potential there is a need to establish management practices to ensure impacts to the glow-worms are minimal but keeping tourism satisfaction high. However, management of the glow-worm populations at Natural Bridge is limited due to the lack of knowledge of the biology of these animals. Merritt and Baker (2001) noted that an increase in educating tourists on glow-worms could only be achieved through scientific research. Negative impacts of tourism on glow-worm colonies would also be reduced if information on their biology is obtained and shared. Consequently, more impact studies are needed to ensure sustainable glow-worm populations for tourism viewing.

---

life tourism ventures. Wildlife tourism as an industry is expected to grow over the coming years. There are numerous claims that tourists are demanding greater opportunities to see and interact with wildlife (Roe *et al.*, 1997; Shackley, 2001). Coinciding with this is the trend for wildlife tourists to become more specialised, seeking out specific species (often unique and endemic species e.g. wildlife tourism in rain forests) that can be found only in remote places (see Box 7.1). Care is needed to ensure that this increase in wildlife tourism does not have disastrous consequences.

In Australia Green and Higginbottom (2001) noted that when conservation agencies were asked what research would be most useful the answer was a better understanding of the effects of wildlife tourism on wildlife and ways to manage those effects. Wildlife biologists can provide this information through carefully structured research. However, it also needs to be recognised that wildlife scientists' activities in studying wildlife may have deleterious consequences for the animals themselves. Some of these problems are documented carefully in research papers so that mistakes are not repeated (e.g. Recher *et al.*, 1985; Williams *et al.*, 1993; Saunders & Ingram, 1998) while others form the basis of regulatory codes that govern the conduct of wildlife research (e.g. NHMRC, 1997, see also discussion in Dyson & Calver, 2003). Furthermore, Braithwaite and Reynolds' (2002) data show that the absence of deleterious impacts is an important part of the wildlife experience of many professionals.

Appropriate methodologies

Wildlife biology also provides the methods needed to determine with confidence that wildlife tourism is not damaging wildlife or wildlife habitat. Long-standing experience has perfected methods suitable for describing and quantifying behaviour, population dynamics and wildlife habitat (e.g. Berwick & Saharia, 1995; Bookhout, 1996). Thus students of the putative impacts of wildlife tourism need not develop new methods of their own, but can draw on a wide range of tested techniques. A very important perspective provided by these methods is a caution against anthropomorphism, which is the attribution of human perception and motives to animals when describing their behaviour. Avoiding anthropomorphism is not helped by the inevitable connotations of language (e.g. the expression 'begging behaviour'), but even the effort to do so is a constant reminder that animals are not humans in a different body (Krebs & Davies, 1997). Furthermore, wildlife biology cautions that results are often stated as probabilities of outcomes, not certainties.

Education and conservation

Late in August, on our final day at Monkey Mia for the year, Janet and Julie and I watched Cookie and Smoky chasing tiny fish together. Both turned belly up just under the water and zoomed around, buzzing like a pair of electric shaving devices gone haywire, twisting and turning as the fish evaded them. On a few occasions they almost collided with each other as they both pursued the same fish. Later they both went down to the bottom in shallow water over a seagrass bed. Both poked their beaks into the seagrass and made the peculiar sounds we had often heard other dolphins make when they were doing the same thing. Smoky suddenly darted off and poked his beak into another clump, and Cookie followed. They were bottom grubbing together for fish that hide in the seagrass. They broke off occasionally to tumble around, charging gleefully together into a swirl of churning and splashing. Several times they returned to their mothers for some 'R&R', whistling as they went. (Smolker, 2001: 200)

Those words were written by a scientist, not a tourist, and reflect the fascination and enthusiasm wildlife scientists have for the subjects of their study. Braithwaite and Reynolds (2002) found that these feelings are widespread, with a sample of wildlife biologists indicating uniqueness (the unusual nature of the experience), exhilaration (the level of excitement felt), environmental ethicality (the observer was satisfied that there were no negative impacts to the animals or their habitat) and information content (understanding what was happening) as the major factors contributing to their most satisfying wildlife experiences.

Scientific knowledge can be used for management purposes (to help achieve sustainability) and also to enrich the wildlife tourism experience with information.

Box 7.2   Sea turtles

Non-consumptive wildlife has the potential to ensure the conservation of wild-life resources in the long term. The economic possibilities for using wildlife resources in a non-consumptive manner have been shown to be large. Prime examples of this are dolphins, penguins, along with a large variety of bird species (Davis *et al.*, 2000; Hoyt, 2000). Currently sea turtles are under threat from direct consumptive activities such as harvesting of eggs and turtles for their meat as well as indirect impacts, e.g. boat strikes, entanglement in crab pots. However, in the last 10 years sea turtles have begun to show their economic importance as a non-consumptive wildlife tourism attraction.

Sea turtles have been described as living fossils that have navigated the world's ocean since the time of dinosaurs (Wilson & Tisdell, 2001). Sea turtles are an excellent species for wildlife tourism because they can easily be viewed when they come ashore to nest. Their distinctive attributes make them a valuable wild-life resource, attracting large crowds especially during the nesting season. Wilson and Tisdell (2001) suggest that non-consumptive wildlife-oriented recreation tourism, such as turtle-based ecotourism, can result in the long-term conservation of turtles. Sea turtle based tourism viewing can generate income, provide employment and at the same time support the conservation of the turtle. Public education and awareness through sea turtle tourism can also assist in the preserving and conservation of these animals. In Sri Lanka turtle viewing has increased public awareness through educating the people on the threats facing sea turtles and their habitats (Gampell, 1999). However, a balance is needed to ensure conservation and education are growing but in a way that minimises impacts on the sea turtles. To achieve this, guidelines and criteria for evaluation are needed that encompass science, in particular biological knowledge of the turtles, to ensure a sustainable future.

Many seeking an interaction with wildlife prefer to gain some learning from the experience. Wildlife tourists share the fascination that comes from watching animals hunting, mating and interacting in their own environment. Excitement may come simply from observing or being close to large animals such as whales or from watching a real-life drama such as a birth, a courtship ritual or an escape from a predator (e.g. Findlay, 1997; Orams, 2000b).

Wildlife viewing can increase public awareness of the threats faced by many species and their habitat, can raise money for conservation (see Box 7.2). Many wildlife tourists are also concerned that their activities have no negative effects on the animals they observe (Green & Higginbottom, 2000). Visitor centres and museums can enhance the knowledge of tourists and their need for protection. Shared interests between wildlife scientists and wildlife tourists should encourage mutually rewarding co-operation. Tourists can find their experience enriched by the special understanding of behaviour that wildlife biologists provide (Coates, 2001), while the scientists in turn enjoy the excitement of discussing their subject with a receptive audience (Recher, 1992, 1998; Hobbs, 1998). There is also a common purpose in safeguarding the welfare of the animals, while some wildlife tourists want to participate actively in research into the behavioural ecology or conservation of wildlife as part of their tourism experience (Coates, 2001).

Anticipate problems

If wildlife biologists investigate and monitor human–wildlife interactions then negative changes can be identified immediately. Nowhere is this clearer than cases that involve simple observation of animals in the wild, which are often perceived as non-intrusive. However, there is ample evidence that animals may be distressed by observers approaching too close, leading to problems such as disruptions to feeding behaviour (Kerley *et al.*, 2002) and nest desertion (see Box 7.3). Subtler possibilities are that large numbers of observers may damage habitat, create trails that predators may later follow to attack the animals observed or transmit diseases to

---

Box 7.3   Penguin Island, Western Australia

Penguin Island off the coast of Western Australia is an important nesting ground for Little Penguins (*Eudytula minor*) and several other seabirds (Dunlop *et al.*, 1988). Visitors to the island often trampled vegetation and sand dunes in their quest to see penguins and the habitat alteration plus the high level of disturbance lowered the breeding success of the penguins and other seabirds (Wienecke *et al.*, 1995). The management solution involved constructing boardwalks above the sensitive habitat, restricting walk areas (Plate 7.1), banning any form of overnight stay on the island so that 24 hour supervision was unnecessary and building a penguin viewing centre where tourists could see captive penguins (including penguins that have been injured) and attend talks on penguin biology and the island's ecology, as well as the need for conservation (http://www.calm.wa.gov.au/tourism/penguin_island.html). This action is preventive and, in the long term, saves funds because it is almost certainly cheaper than the cost of restoring degraded habitat and re-establishing breeding seabird colonies. Prevention also works well in public education because people are often more inclined to abide by restrictions if they understand why they are needed (see further examples in Higham, 1998 and Calver, 2000).

Plate 7.1 Walking trails on Penguin Island, Western Australia (*photo:* Courtesy of Michael Hughes)

the wildlife (NHMRC, 1997; Butynski & Kalina, 1998). Even when problems such as this have not been demonstrated, precautions such as setting minimum approach distances, limiting visitor numbers to reduce habitat damage and barring people with obvious respiratory infections from participating can be enforced (e.g. Adams *et al.*, 2001).

Barriers that Impede Research into Wildlife Tourism

Roe *et al.* (1997) noted that there have been few quantitative studies of actual impacts or of their importance. Even with wildlife biology contributing to wildlife management it appears that more is needed to ensure a sustainable wildlife tourism industry. Undeniably the further development of wildlife biology could help maintain wildlife and ensure visitor satisfaction. Yet for all of its importance there is a dearth of information and research on the current impacts of tourism on wildlife. There appear to be two main barriers that prevent research into wildlife tourism: (1) scientists are more concerned with conservation rather than impacts from tourism; and (2) the complexity and the cost of research into tourism impacts is high.

Conservation not tourism

Involvement of scientists into research on impacts of wildlife–tourism interactions is still limited. There is a need for research to move beyond wildlife biology,

---

Box 7.4   Gorilla tourism

For over a hundred years man has hunted, studied, eaten, captured and observed the mountain gorilla (*Gorilla gorilla berengei*) making the chances of its
survival for another hundred years questionable (Lanjouw, 2002). Tourism to
view the gorillas (gorilla tourism) has often been seen as the best way to conserve
these animals and their habitat (Woodford *et al.*, 2002). Yet the conflict of conservation versus impact research is illustrated by the critique of gorilla tourism
given by Butynski and Kalina (1998) who highlighted potential biological
impacts from tourism. Gorillas must be habituated for at least a year to permit
tourists to approach them closely and the authors noted: 'The habituation
process is obviously a stressful one for the gorillas but the impact of this stress on
the fitness of the gorillas [their ability to survive and reproduce] has never been
studied' (Butynski & Kalina, 1998: 306). Furthermore, gorillas are susceptible to
many human diseases and well-documented fatal outbreaks of measles and respiratory diseases such as bronchopneumonia have occurred (Woodford *et al.*,
2002; Guerrera *et al.*, 2003). These may cause very high mortality and significant
population declines could further threaten the viability of small populations.
Tourists are a strong risk factor because they are stressed by travel and exposed
to a wide range of pathogens, which can facilitate the spread of disease. Therefore it can be argued that gorilla tourism and gorilla conservation are in conflict
and although tourism does help conserve wildlife populations it is now time to
investigate conservation implications (see McNeilage *et al.*, 1997; Wilkie &
Carpenter, 1999) and in particular the long-term impacts of tourism on gorilla
populations.

---

gathering baseline information of wildlife for conservation purposes, to investigating the long-term effects of human–wildlife interactions on wildlife and their
environments. Yet this is not transpiring. Rodger and Moore (2004) note that
research into the impacts of tourism on wildlife and their environments is not currently regarded as important by many wildlife scientists. Scientists are more
concerned with the survival and conservation of wildlife populations rather than
the effect of tourism on wildlife. Gorilla tourism is often seen as a way of conserving
this endangered species (Newsome *et al.*, 2002) but allowing people to visit gorillas
is risky and research into the impacts and long-term effect of tourism on these
animals is limited (See Box 7.4).

Many species worldwide have become extinct or so low in numbers that they are
considered 'ecologically extinct' (Primack, 1998). The 2000 IUCN Species Extinction
Brief states that one in every four mammal species and one in every eight bird

species face a high risk of extinction in the near future. Conservation Biology, a newer multi-disciplinary crisis science, has developed in response to the depletion of many animal species. This discipline has two goals: (1) to investigate human impacts on species, communities and ecosystems, and (2) to develop practical approaches to prevent the extinction of species and if possible to reintegrate them into properly functioning ecosystems (Burgman & Lindenmayer, 1988). What needs to be recognised is that wildlife tourism in many cases is based on those threatened or endangered species that biologists are trying to conserve (Higginbottom *et al.*, 2001c).

Within the scientific community how science is practised is often influenced by institutional affiliations, allegiances and obligations, which in turn creates constraints on where funding goes, how experiments are conducted and what conclusions are reached (Horwitz & Calver, 1998). Therefore a scientist's behaviour and way of conducting research often depends on their present institutional allegiances as well as past allegiances, including where and in what disciplines they have trained. This concept implies that present day wildlife biologists do not see wildlife tourism research as an imperative area of research. Conservation of wildlife instead of impact studies is the focus because of the current normative beliefs of wildlife biologists.

Complexity and cost of research

Research into the putative impacts from tourism on wildlife is not easy as impacts can be hard to identify and measure. Wildlife species are not stationary and thus the impacts can be difficult to recognise as they are not always obvious, direct or easily measured. The size and nature of impacts will vary according to the type of activity, the characteristics of the species, the ecology of the area, as well as the differences between individuals within a species (Roe *et al.*, 1997). To add to this many studies are examining the short-term effects and there is little research on the long-term effects of wildlife disturbance by tourists. Higham (2001) commented that the impacts of tourism on wildlife have the potential to be severe and difficult to recognise in the absence of long-term research. All of this makes it extremely difficult to determine whether tourism is actually having a negative impact on wildlife.

These difficulties in wildlife tourism research are highlighted by Frohoff's (2000) work which examined the response of free ranging dolphins to interactions with humans. Research into dolphins has been mainly restricted to short-term studies due to the difficulties in observing behavioural impacts. This review highlighted the importance of long-term quantitative studies and that 'Management appeared to be most effective when it was based on research, was site- and animal specific and was implemented early in the development of the interaction' (Frohoff, 2000: 1).

Scientists involved in such work need to be multidisciplinary and yet science today is becoming more and more specialised rather than generalised (Caldwell, 1982). With research into wildlife tourism interactions being so multifaceted often scientists do not have the necessary skills to undertake such complex work. Coinciding with this is the expensive costs of researching, monitoring and managing the impacts of tourism on wildlife (Green & Higginbottom, 2001). Buckley (2000) noted that the current research funding mechanisms do not support research on the impacts of tourism.

Conclusions

The purpose of this chapter has been to outline the important, although somewhat limited role that science currently plays in the sustainable management of wildlife tourism and suggest how this might expand in the future. Research into the nature of science shows that it is subject to values and bias just the same way as other human enterprises. Nevertheless, it can still contribute to the sustainable management of wildlife tourism by predicting the likely consequences of specific actions as well as offering standards for ongoing monitoring to prevent serious impacts. At this time wildlife biology provides managers of wildlife with knowledge to conserve animal populations. However, human–wildlife interactions are increasing world wide and an understanding of how these interactions impact on wildlife and their environment is now needed. This would provide not only knowledge for management purposes to ensure a sustainable wildlife tourism industry but also enrich the tourist experience through education and interpretation. Wildlife biologists need to become involved and to begin examining what short- and long-term effect tourism is having on wildlife and their environment. Barriers that impede research into wildlife tourism impacts need to be overcome to ensure a sustainable wildlife tourism industry for the years to come.

Further reading

A more detailed understanding of the philosophy of science can be obtained from several sources including Aronowitz (1988) and Mulkay (1991). Chalmers (2000) is an excellent introductory textbook on contemporary trends in the philosophy of science whereas Merton (1973) and Charlesworth (1982) both provide a useful introduction to the norms of the scientific community.

Duffus and Dearden (1990) and Reynolds and Braithwaite (2001) provide a comprehensive view on the increase in wildlife tourism and the growing number of tourists wanting close interaction with wildlife and their habitats; while Higginbottom *et al.* (2001c) and Knight and Gutzwiller (1995) give a thorough overview of the current status of wildlife tourism illustrating what it involves, how it developed along with negative impacts that can occur.

Roe *et al.* (1997) discuss the concerns about the minimal quantitative studies of actual impacts or of their importance. Further information on past studies investigating negative impacts of tourism on wildlife can be found in Knight and Cole (1995) and Green and Higginbottom (2001).

Chapter 8

Researching Ecological Impacts

Contributed by MIKE CALVER

Introduction

Wildlife tourism seeks to increase people's chances of exhilarating close encounters with wildlife in a context that also protects the animals. The methodologies developed by wildlife biologists to study the behaviour, ecology and management of wildlife are integral in achieving this aim and informing management of the best options to ensure the sustainability of wildlife tourism operations.

An emphasis on testing predictions derived from hypotheses may be the most important approach wildlife biology can give to applied studies of the impacts of wildlife tourism. The experience of over 50 years of wildlife biology crystallised in the 1980s and 1990s into the view that research should collect experimental or observational data to test explicit predictions about the system under study. A concise formulation of this position is:

> ... specific questions about nature ... ordinarily are stated as hypotheses, which are statements about how someone thinks that nature works. In other words, they contain implied predictions, and confirmation of those predictions is the most powerful means available to demonstrate their accuracy of our understanding of the world around us. (Hairston, 1989: 12)

Hypotheses that do not yield testable predictions only describe events rather than explain them, so an emphasis on predictions links cause and effect explicitly and offers unambiguous advice to management (e.g. Bergerud, 1974; Romesberg, 1985; Caughley & Gunn, 1996; Ratti & Garton, 1996; Ford, 2000).

In keeping with this philosophy, this chapter has five aims:

- to outline a hypothesis-testing framework for answering questions about the impacts of wildlife tourism;
- to demonstrate how testable predictions can be developed for assessing putative impacts of wildlife tourism;
- to facilitate choice of study techniques by providing concise descriptions of

the major research approaches and field techniques relevant to elucidating the impacts of wildlife tourism, with an indication of key references which expand these points more fully;

- to outline key issues in data analysis, drawing conclusions and publishing the results of studies of the impacts of wildlife tourism;
- to show how the hypothesis-testing framework can be integrated into adaptive management of wildlife tourism.

Each of these is now covered in turn.

A Framework for Planning Studies

Wildlife biologists were driven to their focus on testing predictions by the legal challenges often arising over their methods and conclusions, especially in cases where conservation aims clashed with resource exploitation (e.g. Shrader-Frechette & McCoy, 1995). Similarly, studies of the putative impacts of wildlife tourism may also recommend management initiatives that are contentious because their implementation will cost somebody money. If contention is pushed to legal challenge, methods and data will receive intense scrutiny and, in the words of Caughley and Gunn (1996: 4–5): 'In courts, as elsewhere, weak inferences tumble before the evidence rigorously arrived at through sound experimental design.'

Figure 8.1 shows a framework based on deductive reasoning to assist in arriving at such a design. A common starting point may be a change or pattern observed, such as a tourism operator reporting that whales no longer approach as close to the coast as they did before whale watching cruises in the area began. It is then possible to propose explanations (sometimes grandly called theories) for the observation, framing them as predictions which should be true if the explanations are correct. Other outcomes, known collectively as counter-hypotheses or null hypotheses, cover all possibilities if the predictions are incorrect. Methodologies are then chosen and applied to test the predictions. Should the predictions be verified the explanation is supported; while if they are not, further explanations are proposed. Predictions are tested commonly using statistical techniques, determining whether the null hypothesis (H_o) of no change or the alternative hypothesis (H_a) is most likely. The ability to put predictions to such rigorous testing is sometimes termed 'falsification', meaning that the prediction has been put to a test which it would have failed if it was wrong. Predictions which cannot be tested in this way are termed 'unfalsifiable' and not accepted as legitimate explanations.

Avoiding this framework risks poor planning and inconclusive results at the end of the study. Thus this chapter now deals with the issues involved in applying each step of the framework and drawing the strongest possible inferences from research.

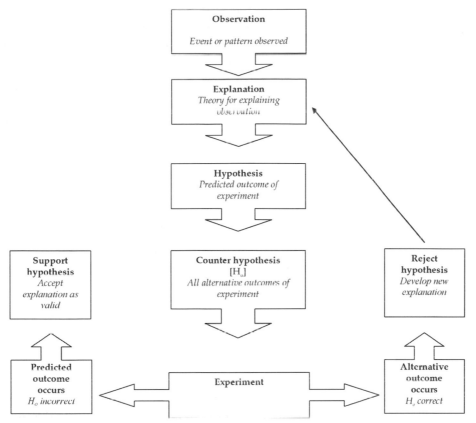

Figure 8.1 A flowchart of steps in testing a putative impact of wildlife tourism on wildlife © Mike Calver *J. Biol. Education,* UK

Reproduced from Finn *et al.* (2002)

Formulating and Testing Predictions

What is a testable prediction?

Data collection on issues relating to wildlife tourism is most useful if it moves beyond description to explanation. This involves proposing explanations of the phenomenon observed and testing predictions that should be true if the explanation is correct. As an example, consider a hypothetical case of wildlife tourism where tourists watch breeding colonies of albatrosses (a large seabird) from specially designed observatories. Biologists observe that albatross chicks hatching near the observatories leave their natal nests earlier than chicks hatched elsewhere in the colonies, interfering with feeding from their parents. One possible explanation is that the birds are disturbed by reflections from observatory windows. A prediction arising from this explanation is that if the windows of some observatories are fitted with non-reflective film, then the chicks hatching near those observatories will stay in their nests longer than chicks hatching near observatories without tinted windows. Such explicit statements of possible explanations and of tests of predictions arising from them are an essential first step in planning a study. If the test proposed is carried out, it should be clear whether or not the explanation is correct or whether a new explanation must be sought. Without testing predictions arising from proposed explanations, the research lacks focus and is unlikely to yield valuable conclusions.

Tests of proposed explanations may occur via manipulative experiments, in which events are controlled by the observer, or via non-experimental approaches which do not involve controlled manipulation of variables (Eberhardt & Thomas, 1991). In some cases, careful observation may be needed before explanations and predictions can be proposed.

Testing predictions via manipulative experiments

Studies of the potential impacts of wildlife tourism on coral reef communities provide an excellent example of the use of predictions and manipulative experiments. The spectacular aggregations of marine fauna on coral reefs are extremely attractive for wildlife tourism activities such as diving and sight-seeing with glass-bottomed boats, as well as more general tourism activities to enjoy the scenery, beaches, climate and fishing opportunities (e.g. Shafer & Inglis, 2000; Williams & Polunin, 2000). However, the anchors of boats positioned for viewing the reefs through glass bottoms or for diving platforms may shatter areas of coral, destroying habitat for marine animals and altering their abundance and distribution. Lewis (1997, 1998) considered the possibility of such impacts on the Great Barrier Reef, off the coast of eastern Australia. He predicted that, relative to undamaged reef, damaged reef will show:

- reductions in the total number of individual fish of all species present;
- reductions in species richness (the total number of species present); and
- a decline in the abundances of individual fish species.

To test these predictions, two hypotheses were created for each one: the null hypothesis (H_o) which proposed that there is no change in the variable being measured, and the alternative hypothesis (H_a) which proposed that damaged reef will decline relative to undamaged reef in the variable being measured. The hypotheses were tested by deliberately damaging some areas of the reef (treatments) to compare to undamaged areas (controls).

Ten bommies (small, discrete patches of reef within a lagoon) were selected and five allocated to the experimental treatment (damage) and five to the control treatment (undamaged). The control bommies served as a yardstick to determine the extent of change in the damaged bommies. The spatial allocation of control and treatment bommies was important, because if all the control bommies were aggregated at one part of the study site and all the experimental bommies elsewhere, then there would be a greater chance that some environmental features would apply to one group and not the other. To overcome this problem, Lewis (1998) interspersed the treatment and control bommies (see Krebs, 1999: 344–6 for a detailed discussion of this issue in experimentation).

Fish were censused at the bommies every 30 days between October and February and every 60 days between March and September for the first year of the study, with data on abundance, location and size distribution of a wide range of species recorded. After that year, half of the bommies were disturbed by breaking bushy, tree-like corals into small pieces with a mallet and leaving the remains where they fell. Other coral types were not disturbed. Censuses resumed at all bommies after the treatment. Statistical analyses of the census data were used to determine difference between the control and treatment groups over the period of the experiment. Total numbers of fish and species richness of fish declined on the treated bommies relative to the controls, accompanied by declines in the abundance of five individual species of fish. In relation to his three predictions, Lewis (1998) found:

- total numbers of fish were reduced on the damaged bommies;
- species richness on the damaged bommies was reduced; and
- five individual fish species declined in abundance.

On the basis of these results, he rejected his null hypotheses and concluded that physical damage similar to that caused by anchor drag reduced total fish numbers, the species richness of fish and the abundance of some, but not all, fish species.

The approach described is that of a manipulative, replicated experiment, in which the researcher controls exactly what happens to control and experimental groups and there are multiple replicates of each group. Many authors argue that this leads to the strongest inferences about cause and effect (e.g. Caughley & Gunn, 1996).

Overall, field experiments such as this one have clear advantages and limitations:

> Field experiments are inherently attractive and impossibly messy. They are attractive because they include a 'control' which becomes the yardstick by which the experimental treatment can be judged. . . . Field experiments are messy because it is difficult to match sites so that all relevant conditions are equal at the start of the manipulation, and replication is rarely as frequent as anyone would like. (Krebs, 1988: 145)

In this case, the major advantage is the clear determination of changes in abundance and species richness of reef fish on bommies in response to the kind of structural damage that anchor drag can cause. However, achieving this required great care in experimental design, including resolving questions of the comparability of control and experimental plots and their relative placements, the sample sizes and the choice of statistical analysis. Although the final experimental results were clear, their implications for management could be contentious because they may be representative for only a limited range of reef ecosystems; nor is it certain that further impacts would not develop after more time. All these issues are likely to arise in planning experiments testing putative impacts of wildlife tourism, and the value of the work will depend on the thoroughness with which they are addressed.

Testing predictions via non-experimental approaches

However, not all problems arising in wildlife tourism are likely to be amenable to manipulative experiments. For instance, ethical issues may prevent the application of certain experimental treatments, especially those which require habitat alteration, culling of animals or introduction of exotic species (e.g. Cuthill, 1991; Putman, 1996; Fulton & Ford, 2001). A further problem is that there may not be opportunities to replicate a study because the wildlife tourism occurs at only a single location, or the stimulus for the study may be a sudden unforeseen event such as a sewerage leak. In recognition of these issues, a full survey of approaches available for studies of the impacts of wildlife tourism is given in Table 8.1.

The non-experimental approaches are sometimes criticised because they may not make specific, falsifiable predictions, but this need not be the case. As an example, consider a situation where the numbers of breeding penguins on a sub-Antarctic island have been monitored annually for 40 years. The researchers note the number and sex ratio of the penguins in a single census month each year. At the end of the 40th year a wildlife tourism venture is planned for the island, in which parties of tourists will visit for a day each month. Given the long series of observations prior to the proposed intervention, an intervention analysis (Table 8.1) can detect any marked change in the sequence of observations at the time of the intervention (the beginning of the wildlife tourism) (see Rasmussen *et al.*, 2001 and included references for worked examples and practical applications). The falsifiable prediction in this case is that the time series will reveal a change after the instigation of wildlife tourism. The null hypothesis is that the time series will not reveal any appreciable change dating from the beginning of the wildlife tourism.

The attraction of such an approach is that it uses existing data sets to enable detection of effects in an unreplicated system, but the test of the hypothesis is weaker than that arising in a conventional controlled and replicated experiment. The intervention analysis can identify a change that occurred when the tourism visits began, but it cannot establish cause and effect – the change might have occurred irrespective of the tourism. In this case, detailed supporting data might be collected to support the case that tourism was the cause. The time budgets of the

Table 8.1 Broad approaches to the design of environmental studies, as classified by Eberhardt and Thomas (1991). All approaches are also applicable to the study of the impacts of wildlife tourism

Study type	When to use it	Features/issues	References
Replicated experiments – events controlled by observer	When a change or impact is planned for one or more areas (treatment) and will be compared against one or more other areas where no change or impact will occur (control). Replicated experiments have the further requirement that the control and each experimental treatment are replicated at least once, so that natural variability within treatments can be accounted for in making comparisons between treatments.	Replicated experiments may produce very strong evidence for or against a particular impact. However, it can be difficult to find matching control and treatment sites and high variability in responses between sites may require very high levels of replication. Statistical analysis is often required.	Krebs (1999) Bookhout (1996) Mead (1990)
Unreplicated experiments – events controlled by observer	Although it is always preferable to use replicated experiments, logistics, cost or ethical considerations may prevent this. In these cases, legitimate conclusions may still be drawn from carefully designed unreplicated studies in which there is no replication of the treatment and the control.	Interpretation of unreplicated experiments is often problematic. Careful attention to experimental design is required, as well as special techniques of statistical analysis.	Milliken and Johnson (1992, 2001)
Sampling for modelling – events controlled by observer	Data are collected for fitting to specific statistical models, with a view to estimating parameters in those models. An example might be modelling the spread of effluent from septic tanks serving a tourist facility.	There is usually a response variable (responding to other variables in the model), predictor variables which are measured inputs to the model and one or more constants or parameters that determine the relationships between the variables.	Eberhardt and Thomas (1991)

Table 8.1 Broad approaches to the design of environmental studies, as classified by Eberhardt and Thomas (1991). All approaches are also applicable to the study of the impacts of wildlife tourism

Study type	When to use it	Features/issues	References
Intervention analysis	Intervention analysis arises where a long-term, ongoing data set for a wildlife population is interrupted by a single event and monitoring continues after the event. The existence of a control area which is undisturbed by the event permits comparisons.	Intervention analysis may be a response to an event over which the investigator has no control, such as an oil spill, implying that it is a non-experimental approach. However, intervention analysis may be regarded as a large-scale unreplicated experiment if the intervention is planned, such as the building of a tourist resort. Irrespective of whether or not the intervention is planned, the broad characteristics of the approach to such studies are the same. The statistical analysis is a derivation of the methods of time-series analysis.	Rasmussen *et al.* (2001) Eberhardt and Thomas (1991)
Observational studies	Observational studies involve assessing the effect of a particular event or process by contrasting individuals or groups experiencing differing levels of the event or process. Thus the researcher observes natural groups rather than constructing specific groups via an experimental manipulation.	The presence of unrecognised and uncontrolled bias is the greatest threat to reliable observational studies. Nevertheless, they are a promising option for non-experimental studies of wildlife tourism.	Cochran (1983)
Descriptive sampling	In descriptive sampling, the aim is to assess the abundance and distribution of the animal(s) of interest over a large area, possibly a reserve or national park. Such data are very valuable as a baseline against which to assess changes in management or tourism approaches.	Descriptive sampling gives the background essential for answering questions such as: • is a particular species likely to leave an area if a camping ground is constructed there? • are there locations used extensively by females with young which should be kept as free of disturbance as possible?	Sutherland (1996) Krebs (1999) Southwood and Henderson (2000)
Analytical sampling	Analytical sampling aims to explain any differences in local abundance, using the same survey techniques as descriptive sampling.	The sampling is directed towards testing specific, falsifiable hypotheses.	Sutherland (1996) Krebs (1999) Southwood and Henderson (2000)
Sampling for pattern	In such studies, the aim is to describe a spatial pattern in the distribution of organisms.	These studies may be of value in planning wildlife tourism excursions to encounter (or sometimes avoid) certain organisms.	Sutherland (1996) Krebs (1999) Southwood and Henderson (2000)

penguins (the amount of time devoted to different activities) could be recorded in the presence or absence of tourists, for instance, to demonstrate changes in penguin behaviour in response to tourists.

Jones (2000) used such a combination of before/after data and corollary evidence to demonstrate that upgrading of a tourist road in a National Park decreased local wildlife populations markedly through road kills, but that ameliorative road design and public education strategies reversed the trends. Acceptance of cause and effect in unreplicated intervention analyses often rests on such corollary evidence. Despite these weaknesses, the example still illustrates the important precept that testable predictions can be framed and evaluated using approaches other than experimentation.

Using structured observations to develop predictions

In some instances of wildlife tourism the initial data are limited and there is a crucial need for more background information before explanations and testable predictions can be formulated. Indeed, some authors have cautioned against formulating and testing predictions too early, because they may turn out to be irrelevant (Erskine, 1994). However, if the initial descriptive work is well designed, testable predictions should arise after its completion.

Wrangham's (1974) detailed observational study of the behavioural consequences of a decade of artificial feeding of the chimpanzees (*Pan troglodytes*) and baboons (*Papio anubis*) in Gombe National Park, Tanzania, is a case in point. The work began with the modest aim of describing the behaviour of the animals during artificial feeding, but aggression among the animals was perceived as a problem and attention turned to ways of reducing the aggression. The large number of observations over many years suggested that aggression was highest when access to available food was restricted.

However, Wrangham (1974) admitted that the interpretation suffered from lack of a suitable control. Thus one cannot be sure that the decline in aggression in some feeding systems used was definitely a result of the feeding system rather than some external factor such as an increase in food availability overall. Nevertheless, the results do give rise to the prediction that maximising food access to individuals during artificial feeding should produce fewer aggressive interactions than when access is restricted. Experimental tests of that prediction could confirm its validity as a guideline for practice. This shift from description to prediction can be one of the most useful outcomes of observational research.

Choosing a Technique for Data Collection

Once an explanation for a problem has been proposed and a prediction drawn from it for testing, the next step is to choose the actual techniques for collecting the data. The possible choices are wide (see Table 8.2 and included references) and it may be possible to use more than one method in any study (e.g. the combination of

Table 8.2 A classification of major ecological, behavioural and veterinary techniques available for assessing the impacts of wildlife tourism. It is not exhaustive and examples of further specialised techniques are given in the major references

Technique	Description	Features/issues	References
Census - Population dynamics, distribution and habitat use	These methods estimate population parameters such as size, trend, birth rates and mortality rates, or describe the distribution of populations. Aims may be descriptive, or to determine if these values change under wildlife tourism impacts.	Many of the methods require capture, handling and marking of animals. Techniques for this should be chosen after considering animal welfare, cost and investigator convenience.	Schemnitz (1996) Nietfeld *et al.* (1996) Thompson *et al.* (1998) Sutherland (1996)
Capture/recapture	In this method animals are tagged, released and potentially recaptured, with data on the capture history of individuals used to estimate a wide range of population parameters. Several models are available.	Each model available makes explicit assumptions which, if violated without correction in analysis, may invalidate results. Furthermore, repeated capture and handling may harm animals so ethical issues may be important in planning studies.	Krebs (1999) Southwood and Henderson (2000) Begon (1979) Boyce (1995a) Skalski and Robson (1992)
Quadrat and transect counts	These involve counting animals captured, seen, or known to be present from signs (e.g. droppings, tracks), using quadrats of known size or along transects. Scales are variable, from small 1m² plots for some invertebrates through to areas of many square kilometres in aerial surveys for large vertebrates.	Location and size of quadrats and length of transects are significant issues in determining the representativeness of data. Repeated observations of the same animals may bias population estimates.	Krebs (1999) Southwood and Henderson (2000) Sutherland (1996) Lancia *et al.* (1996) Litvaitus *et al.* (1996)
Life tables	Life tables represent age-specific mortality for a population. They can demonstrate shifts in mortality patterns under an external impact such as wildlife tourism activity.	Life tables require detailed population census data obtained using other techniques.	Krebs (1999) Southwood and Henderson (2000) Johnson (1996) Boyce (1995b)
Key factor analysis	Predicts the 'key factor', the cause of mortality which is the best predictor of future population sizes. Thus it can assess the importance of mortalities from wildlife tourism relative to those caused by other factors.	The technique was developed for insect populations with discrete generations where causes of death operated sequentially on different stages. The assumptions and approaches may only be indicative for vertebrates.	Krebs (1999) Southwood and Henderson (2000) Sibley and Smith (1998)

Table 8.2 (*cont.*) A classification of major ecological, behavioural and veterinary techniques available for assessing the impacts of wildlife tourism. It is not exhaustive and examples of further specialised techniques are given in the major references

Technique	Description	Features/issues	References
Radiotelemetry	Animals are followed from day-to-day using radiotransmitters. Data on movement, territories and habitat use are collected.	The technique can be expensive and substantial field time is required.	Samuel and Fuller (1996) Knowlton (1995) Brewer and Fagerstone (1998)
Sampling for population studies	Few studies permit counting or observing of all the target animals, so sampling is required. The type and frequency of sampling influences subsequent analysis and the conclusions that can be drawn from the data. Sampling may occur in space or time and is an essential part of many research designs.	Statistical analysis often needs random, independent replicates for each combination of treatment effects (the major controlled variables in the study). A common fault is not to replicate samples, or to confuse subsamples (repeated samples on the same unit) with independent replication.	Krebs (1999) Green (1979) Ratti and Garton (1996)
Random sampling	Samples are drawn at random from a larger population and inferences on the characteristics of the population are drawn from the sample. For example, blood samples may be drawn from randomly selected animals to determine if they were exposed to human pathogens during interactions with wildlife tourists.	True randomness requires that each unit in the population has an equal chance of being chosen. Many 'random' samples are incorrectly based on investigator selection of 'appropriate' or 'typical' units. If samples are not truly random, inferences are invalid.	Krebs (1999) Southwood and Henderson (2000) Green (1979) Cormack et al. (1979) Bart et al. (1998) Thompson et al. (1998) Ratti and Garton (1996)
Stratified random sampling	The study population is divided into discrete groups, each of which is then sampled randomly. This can help if sampling problems vary between different study sites, or if collaborating researchers are assigned different parts of a larger sampling design.	Sampling within each stratum must be truly random.	Krebs (1999) Southwood and Henderson (2000) Green (1979) Cormack et al. (1979) Bart et al. (1998) Thompson et al. (1998)
Systematic sampling	Systematic sampling occurs when samples are spaced at regular intervals or otherwise distributed evenly across a study area. It is common where the aim is to sample evenly across a habitat, or to avoid the effort of positioning samples randomly.	Systematic sampling is convenient, but may introduce bias. Sound advice is: '…if you have a choice of taking a random sample or a systematic one, always choose random sampling. But if the cost and inconvenience of randomisation is too great, you may lose little by sampling a systematic way' (Krebs, 1999: 293).	Krebs (1999) Southwood and Henderson (2000) Green (1979) Cormack et al. (1979) Bart et al. (1998) Thompson et al. (1998)

Table 8.2 (*cont.*) A classification of major ecological, behavioural and veterinary techniques available for assessing the impacts of wildlife tourism. It is not exhaustive and examples of further specialised techniques are given in the major references

Technique	Description	Features/issues	References
Sampling for behavioural studies	These are concerned with the behaviour of individual animals. Possible study questions may include how behaviour is altered by wildlife tourists, or how it can be regulated to minimise harmful interactions between people and wildlife. It is also possible to create a complete description (ethogram) of the behaviour of a species during wildlife tourism encounters.	All behavioural studies are potentially highly sensitive to observer effects. Of particular concern are discrepancies between repeated measurements from the same observer and discrepancies between different observers. Calibration of these biases, or eliminating them by training, is essential.	Lehner (1996)
Focal-animal sampling (focal follows)	This technique generates detailed data on many behaviours for a single animal or occasionally a small group. It may incidentally involve the behaviour of other animals as the focal animal interacts with them. For example, all behaviours of a single animal may be monitored for the duration of wildlife tourism encounter. Data may be collected by continuous sampling (the frequency of occurrence, the duration and the sequence of all relevant behaviours) or time sampling (recording behaviours occurring at specified time intervals).	Focal animal follows is excellent for detailed study of the behaviour of individuals, but significant issues to be resolved in each study include: • how periods when the focal animal is 'out of sight' will be treated in the overall activity budget; • it may be difficult for the observer to record all relevant behaviour, especially when the animal reacts speedily or many behaviours follow in rapid succession; • sequential observations on the same animal are dependent and hence violate the assumptions of independence required in many statistical tests.	Lehner (1996) Bakeman and Gottman (1997)
All-animals sampling	If few behaviours are to be recorded for a large group of animals, all-animals sampling is appropriate. For example, the researcher may be interested solely in aggressive interactions between monkeys drawn to a feeder where they are observed by tourists. Data may be collected by continuous sampling or time sampling (see above).	Individual animals may still have periods 'out of sight' and all individuals are seldom equally visible. Recording problems may be compounded and sequential observations on the same animal still raise issues of statistical independence.	Lehner (1996) Bakeman and Gottman (1997)

Table 8.2 (*cont.*) A classification of major ecological, behavioural and veterinary techniques available for assessing the impacts of wildlife tourism. It is not exhaustive and examples of further specialised techniques are given in the major references

Technique	Description	Features/issues	References
Assessing diets	Wildlife tourism may lead to changes in animal diets, through supplementary feeding, changes in distribution or habits, or raiding of refuse. Assessing these impacts may require detailed studies of the diets of target animals.	As indicated for specific techniques below.	As indicated for specific techniques below.
Observations	Animals may be observed eating particular foods.	Observations may be biased towards conspicuous feeding behaviours.	Calver and Porter (1986) Morrison *et al.* (1990) Blankenship and Satakopan (1995)
Stomach contents	Animals may be killed and food remains identified in the gut. Samples may be taken for a whole population, or selectively for culled problem animals. Alternatively, emetics, stomach pumps or flushing the gut with saline can recover samples without killing animals.	Detailed data are provided, although at the cost of killing or greatly disturbing animals. Differential digestion of foods may bias assessments of diet and in cases where emetics are used animals may develop a conditioned aversion to prey types vomited.	Calver and Porter (1986)
Faecal analysis	Droppings may be obtained from trapped animals, or collected in the field with minimal disturbance to animals. In a related method, regurgitated pellets can sometimes be collected from beneath the roosts of owls or raptors.	Droppings are heavily digested and not all foods may be identified readily.	Calver and Porter (1986) Blankenship and Satakopan (1995)
Tracers	Confirmation of feeding is obtained by recovering radioactive tracers or dyes from the digestive tracts of animals, or using immunological techniques to identify food proteins.	Identifications can be made where visual techniques are unsuccessful, but animals may be killed to collect samples.	Calver and Porter (1986) Calver (1984)
Health and condition studies	Many diseases are transmitted between humans and animals and wildlife tourists may unwittingly do this.	Specialist veterinary knowledge is required.	Fowler and Miller (1999) Franzmann *et al.* (1995) Roffe *et al.* (1996) Harder and Kirkpatrick (1996)

observational and experimental approaches in Williams *et al.*, 2002). The issues that often cause the greatest concern are avoiding animal welfare problems, obtaining independent replicates, choosing an appropriate sample size and deciding on the statistical test for analysing the final data. Cost is often a further factor in choice.

Animal welfare issues

Animal welfare issues must be considered when choosing research techniques. Even activities as apparently innocuous as observation may lower the reproductive success of subjects (Anderson & Keith, 1980; Friend *et al.*, 1996), lead to habituation or other behavioural changes (Butynski & Kalina, 1998), or alter key habitat by trampling, a well-known problem connected with recreation (Tonneson & Ebersole, 1997). More intrusive activities such as marking, radiotracking, trapping and experimental manipulations all raise issues of treatment of study animals, non-target impacts and potential impacts at a population level (Cuthill, 1991; Friend *et al.*, 1996; Putman, 1996; Deutsche *et al.*, 1998). These should be considered explicitly in research designs, with every effort taken to minimise harmful effects to habitat, individual animals and populations.

For example, was it appropriate for Lewis (1998) to damage areas of reef to determine if there are effects on the fish communities? The study was funded by the Great Barrier Reef Marine Park, suggesting that the park authorities decided that the value of the information to be gained outweighed the damage caused. The nature of the design, with extensive sampling before and after the manipulation, may also have reduced the number of sites required. Such detailed justification is often required when ethical issues are involved.

Independent replication

Replication is a further area of concern and it is critical for the ultimate statistical analysis of the results (e.g. Green, 1979). If there is only one treatment observation and one control observation, any difference apparent between them might simply reflect random variation. For example, suppose that it is predicted that whales dive for longer periods when a tourist boat is within 100 m than they would if it was further away. If the length of one dive was measured when a boat was within 100 m and another dive when the boat was more than 100 m away, what can be learned by any difference in the length of the dives? The answer, of course, is nothing: the difference could just be caused by chance alone. However, if multiple dives are measured when the boat is within 100 m (treatment observations) and multiple dives are measured when the boat is beyond 100 m (control observations), investigators can compare the mean diving times for the two groups. Statistical tests can determine if these means are different, because the multiple measurements in each group give an idea of the variability in the length of dives which occurs naturally in each of the groups. However, the replicates must be independent, meaning that there is no possible correlation between them.

The concept of independent replication is easy to grasp in theory, yet often difficult to recognise and apply in practice. For example, it may not be intuitively obvious that littermates are not independent samples because they are genetically related and share a similar rearing environment (e.g. see Parsons *et al.*, 2002). Careful consideration of study design should identify and correct any problems of dependence between replicates. If this is not done and dependent observations are treated as true replicates, the problem of 'pseudoreplication' arises and statistical inferences drawn from the data may be invalid (Hurlbert, 1984). Nevertheless, there may be cases where scarcity of subjects or difficult issues of logistics preclude independent replication. Milliken and Johnson (1989, 2001) provide detailed advice on the design, analysis and interpretation of such studies.

A second problem with replication arises in many behavioural studies, in which many sequential observations are taken on the same subject. These observations are dependent because (1) they are taken from the same animal, which may have its own repertoire of behaviours not necessarily representative of others; and (2) any given behaviour is dependent on that which goes before (a bear which moves away from tourists has a very different range of possible interactions with them compared to a bear that approaches them) (e.g. Hejl *et al.*, 1990; Bell *et al.*, 1990). Here, there is no easy solution. The ornithological literature abounds with advice, because birds are very easy to observe and problems of dependent observations have exercised many minds. Suggestions include: (1) counting a maximum of three observations/individual; (2) counting only the third observation in a series of observations on the same bird (the argument being that the observations that catch your eye and cause you to focus on the bird are likely to be conspicuous behaviours); (3) accept multiple observations as a fact of life in such studies while striving to observe as large a number of individuals as possible (see detailed discussions in Morrison, 1984; Bell *et al.*, 1990; Recher & Glebski, 1990). In summary, the best approach is to follow Green's (1979) advice and use independent replicates wherever possible. If this simply cannot be done, or there are good reasons for using dependent data, then the problem should be admitted and a published study acknowledging the problem used as a model, or specialist texts consulted (e.g. Milliken & Johnson, 1989, 2001).

Choosing an appropriate sample size

How many independent replicates should be taken? It is wasteful to take more than are needed to test the prediction of the study, while too few may lead to the frustration of an ambiguous result (e.g. see the recommendations of Williams *et al.*, 2002 for large sample sizes in assessing tourism impacts on killer whales *Orcinus orca*). A crude rule of thumb is that the greater the level of replication the greater the sensitivity of the test, so that large sample sizes are often needed to detect small changes. However, the question of what sample size to take may be answered more accurately by *a priori* statistical power analysis, which requires:

- a pilot study to give an idea of the likely variability between independent replicates under the study conditions;
- specification of the magnitude of the change or 'effect size' that it is important to detect (either a matter of professional judgement, or specified as a legal requirement);
- choice of the significance level for the statistical test that will be used on the data (conventionally 0.05 in the biological sciences); and
- specification of the desirable power of the test (the probability that, under the specified test conditions, a significant result will be detected if it actually occurs, 80% is often recommended in the life sciences). (Thomas & Juanes, 1996)

Once these requirements are met, the appropriate sample size for testing an effect of the chosen size at the specified significance level and power can be calculated. If a power analysis is omitted, researchers may be forced to admit that a study might have shown more significant effects if sample sizes were larger (e.g. Lewis, 1998). Thomas and Krebs (1997) give a helpful review of software available for power analysis and Steidl and Thomas (2001) discuss the approach from a field biologist's perspective.

Choosing a statistical test

Importantly, decisions about replication and sample size have implications for both data collection and analysis. Thus choice of the statistical test that will be used to determine effects is an integral component of choosing the techniques that will collect the data. This is because all statistical tests make particular assumptions about the properties of the data, so consideration of these at the time techniques are chosen and the research design finalised will enable a smooth transition to analysis. Otherwise, 'As Sir Ronald Fisher once said, perhaps the most a statistician can do after data have been collected is pronounce a postmortem on the effort' (Steidl & Thomas, 2001: 33). Decision charts to assist in selecting an appropriate statistical test are given in several major texts, including Tabachnick and Fidell (1996) and Dytham (2003).

Testing the Prediction: Data Analysis, Drawing Conclusions and Publishing

The high variability inherent in animal behaviour and in the natural environment means that it is rare for studies of the impacts of wildlife tourism to show a clear, unambiguous result by inspection of the data. It is more common to use some form of statistical analysis to determine if a significant effect has in fact occurred, which is why choosing the method of analysis at the same time as the research design is essential. Detailed consideration of the issues relevant to statistical analysis is given in standard biometrics texts such as Sokal and Rohlf (1995); Zar (1999); Fowler *et al.* (1998) and Dytham (2003). However, four issues are likely to be of pressing concern in many studies of wildlife impact: screening data for entry errors and the assumptions of statistical tests before analysis, analysing dependent or non-replicated data, drawing correct conclusions when the null hypothesis of 'no impact' is accepted and publishing the results.

Data screening prior to analysis

Once data are entered into a computer program researchers are often so impatient to see results that they proceed to specify an analysis before carrying out fundamental checks. However, these checks are essential to the credibility of the final analysis. Points to check include:

- Accuracy of the entered data. Obviously, keying errors may distort an analysis.
- Outliers, which are points well outside the range of the rest of the data which may exert a disproportionate influence on an analysis. These can be seen easily by plotting the data. An outlier may indicate a real extreme value or perhaps a data entry error, so it is important to check it carefully.
- Missing data. For example, respondents to a questionnaire may have not indicated their age or their sex, although they have answered most other questions. Be aware of how your computer software will deal with missing data, because some packages may delete all information for any case with missing data irrespective of whether or not you specify the missing variable in the analysis.
- Normality of distribution. Many statistical techniques assume that the variables analysed follow a normal distribution and if they do not the analysis may yield misleading results. Good statistics packages allow easy checking of this assumption.
- Equality of variances. Another common assumption is that the variability of any measured variable is equal across the different groups in the analysis. For example, if a satisfaction index with a wildlife tourism experience is measured for men and women in three different age groups, it would be assumed that the variance of the index would be the same for each of the six possible combinations of age and sex. Again, this assumption can be checked easily in good statistics packages.
- Any specialised assumptions for a particular analysis planned should be checked.

Once data entry anomalies are resolved analysis may proceed if the other assumptions are met. If they are not, the possibilities include:

- Use a different test for analysis that does not make the assumption that is violated (Meddis, 1984; Siegel & Castellan, 1988; and Desu & Raghavarao, 2003 are excellent references).
- Carry out the test as planned, but use a more stringent probability level for significance testing if there are problems with unequal variances (e.g. $p < 0.01$ instead of $p < 0.05$; see Tabachnick and Fidell, 1996: 80).
- Transform the data by converting to a different numerical scale (e.g. by taking logarithms of the values) to conform to the assumption before proceeding with the analysis (Tabachnick & Fidell, 1996, especially Figure 4.6, Sokal & Rohlf, 1995; Zar, 1999).

Failure to screen data seriously risks the embarrassment of erroneous conclusions and incorrect advice to management.

Analysing dependent or non-replicated data

Independence is fundamental to most statistical analyses. However, there are cases in which data are clearly dependent. One example is when multiple measurements are taken on the same individual, as occurs in some before/after studies. The solution is to use an appropriate statistical test which makes explicit allowance for the problem of dependence. For example, Williams *et al.* (2002) used paired *t*-tests in their study of the behavioural responses of killer whales to whale watching boats to compare the responses of the same individuals under different conditions. The paired approach was essential to allow for dependence.

Non-replicated data are another special case. Some studies of wildlife tourism may be expensive to undertake, or special ethical considerations may restrict the number of animals used and preclude replication. Ecologists generally take a dim view of analyses of such data, probably because they are often done incorrectly (e.g. Hurlbert, 1984; Underwood, 1997). However, in some cases valid inferences can be drawn from non-replicated data using the methods described in Milliken and Johnson (1989, 2001). Ideally, this should be a planned step with the non-replication issue recognised when the study was planned, rather than a rescue mission for a badly planned experiment.

What to do when the null hypothesis of 'no impact' is accepted

Statistical interpretation of monitoring or experimental data concerning tourism impacts involves testing a null hypothesis (H_0) of no impact of tourism against an alternative hypothesis (H_a) of an impact occurring, at a pre-chosen level of significance, known as α (commonly 0.05 in the biological sciences). Under these conditions, there is only a 5% chance of concluding incorrectly that tourism has an impact when it does not (known as a Type I error). Thus if the null hypothesis of no impact is rejected, there is a clear case for arguing that an impact has occurred and that ameliorative measures may be necessary. On the other hand, if the null hypothesis cannot be rejected, the standard hypothesis testing approach gives no indication of the probability of a second type of error, the possibility that there was an impact that the test failed to detect (a Type II error).

The potential hidden nature of Type II errors means that studies/monitoring of wildlife tourism impacts where the null hypothesis of no impact is accepted are of special concern. If sample size was not determined via an *a priori* power analysis so that researchers are confident that the test has the required sensitivity, acceptance of the null hypothesis may arise either because there is no effect or because the study/ monitoring lacked the sensitivity to detect a difference that actually occurred (Toft & Shea, 1983; Peterman, 1990).

In this case, a retrospective power analysis may be desirable to determine the magnitude of change that could have been detected by the study (Thomas & Krebs, 1997; Steidl & Thomas, 2001). If the retrospective analysis showed that the study was capable of detecting only large changes, then management may still need to be concerned. However, if the test did have the power to detect small differences, then there is greater confidence that an impact is unlikely. Alternatively, many authors favour using the test data to construct a 95% confidence interval for the range of possible differences that could have occurred (in other words, one can be 95% confident that the real impact lies somewhere between two values) (e.g. Gerard *et al.*, 1998; Steidl & Thomas, 2001). For instance, if sample sizes are small or the data are highly variable, it is possible for the 95% confidence interval for a non-significant test to range from no difference to a very large difference between treatments and managers should be made aware of the possibilities. On the other hand, if the 95% confidence interval for a non-significant test is narrow, management can be much more confident that the impact is negligible. Overall, drawing a conclusion of 'no impact' without either a retrospective power analysis or determination of confidence intervals for the difference between means may be misleading.

Publication

It remains to communicate the findings of the study via peer-reviewed publication. Peer review may correct errors, help authors reach sound conclusions from their data before the work becomes widely available, make significant contributions to style and improve readability (Ratti & Garton, 1996). Work not published in the peer-reviewed literature makes no lasting contribution because it is difficult to access and can be seen as unfinished or even undone (e.g. Malmer, 1990; Ratti & Garton, 1996).

While peer-reviewed publication should remain the goal of serious research, it is a fact of life that some valuable studies do not progress beyond unpublished technical reports of government departments. Indeed, the urgency for relevant information to assist in managing tourism and the delays associated with peer-reviewed publication will ensure ongoing interest in unpublished data and unreviewed publications. However, because such information cannot match the accessibility or the authority of peer-reviewed publications, it should be used cautiously in research and management and researchers should strive to publish in the mainstream peer-reviewed literature (Calver & King, 2000).

Applying Research Results to Adaptive Management of Wildlife Tourism

Research into the impacts of wildlife tourism and management of the tourism experience are intimately connected. Otherwise, it is possible to have standards and procedures for managing tourism that lock in unsustainable practices, because the basic assumptions of the standards and procedures have never been tested by research. Thus managers need to incorporate research on the impacts of wildlife tourism into their planning, but in a reasoned rather than a capricious manner (Noss, 1993). Furthermore, they can often perceive important areas where ignorance or uncertainty could be reduced by research. Such links between research and management can be established through adaptive management.

Adaptive management treats different management actions in space and time as experimental treatments to increase understanding of the system being managed (Walters & Holling, 1990; Boyce, 1997; Lee, 1999). In passive adaptive management a panel of experts guides management decisions, drawing on the results of monitoring and research as they come to hand. This can be extended to active management, in which management interventions are designed deliberately as research studies with the different management options tested (Walters, 1986; Thomas *et al.*, 1990). Thus management and research unite in a feedback loop, with the results of the trials informing management and changes in management policy subject to ongoing testing. Numerous authors concur that such a hypothesis-testing framework, incorporating quantifiable standards that can be falsified, is essential for comparing the long-term effectiveness of different management practices (e.g. Murphy & Noon, 1991; Everett *et al.*, 1994; Norton & May, 1994). There is also a case that non-expert interest groups should also have input into planning and decision-making because values are inevitably involved and the decisions often have widespread social implications (e.g. Kruger *et al.*, 1997).

The adaptive management approach is argued strongly by critics of various resource exploitation industries, with calls such as: ' . . . future forest managers should set explicit operational goals for biodiversity conservation *that can be falsified* and provide a framework such that the prescriptions employed to meet these goals can be tested' (Norton & May, 1994: 23, emphasis is mine; see also Murphy & Noon, 1991; Noss, 1993 and Everett *et al.*, 1994 for endorsements of using quantitative, testable standards in management). It was one of the strong forces behind the development of hypothesis-testing research models as a standard in wildlife biology so it is not surprising that hypothesis-testing models link well with adaptive management. Studies of wildlife tourism with an explicit hypothesis testing foundation should also integrate well with an adaptive approach towards managing the wildlife upon which the tourism depends, as can be seen by revisiting some of the case studies used in this chapter.

Lewis' (1997, 1998) study of the likely impacts of damage caused by dragging anchors on fish species on the Great Barrier Reef is a relevant wildlife tourism example. Although he found that damage similar to that caused by anchor drag had minimal short-term effects on reef fish, he emphasised that the results may not be applicable to other reef habitats or to larger spatial scales and urged further experiments to broaden the findings. Management directions can create such experiments. These might involve designating areas where boats can anchor while implementing a long-term study comparing those areas with control areas where anchoring was forbidden. On the basis of the results, restrictions could be intensified or relaxed, always treating changes as a study question to be evaluated. Similarly, Wrangham's (1974) prediction that aggression during artificial feeding can be reduced by maximising animals' access to the food could be tested via adaptive management. Access could be varied at different sites where provisioning occurred and the incidence of aggression compared. Lastly, Jones' (2000) successful amelioration of carnivore deaths on roads in a Tasmanian park illustrates that successful results can be obtained even when a fully controlled and replicated experiment cannot be attempted.

Such approaches are also consistent with the precautionary principle, where activities may be permitted subject to appropriate monitoring and guidelines for withdrawing permission if thresholds for damage are exceeded (Deville & Harding, 1997). Recommendations under the precautionary principle should be reached after discussions involving all stakeholders. Thus adaptive management should be a basis for constructive dialogue involving not only management and scientific professionals, but tourism operators, wildlife activists and tourists themselves. Dialogue such as this, well informed by research, is a sound foundation for long-term, sustainable wildlife tourism. Strong inference from well-designed studies or monitoring addressing testable predictions is critical for the dialogue to function.

Further reading

Despite its age, Green (1979) remains an excellent introduction to the design of environmental studies. Eberhardt and Thomas (1991) give a concise update, with a more detailed treatment in Krebs (1999) and Scheiner and Gurevitch (2001). Excellent general accounts of both study designs and techniques are given in Berwick and Saharia (1995); Bookhout (1996); Krebs (1999); Lehner (1996) and Sutherland (1996). There are also many fine accounts of statistical analysis, including Bart *et al.* (1998) and in Fowler *et al.* (1998).

Chapter 9

Conclusions

Introduction

This book began by acknowledging the earlier work of Myra Shackley and her ground-breaking book *Wildlife Tourism* published in 1996. Over the ensuing years much has been researched and written on the subject but the basic premise of this book is that overall knowledge is still in its infancy. With the increasing interest in wildlife tourism around the world, there is considerable pressure to initiate and implement wildlife tourism in the wild, often with limited, or even no, thought for the impacts on the wildlife under view. The aim of this book is to give voice to some concerns that we share as we move around the world to observe and enjoy the viewing of wildlife. The story that has been shared is by nature, a subjective one, but one, which is hoped, will resonate with you the reader. It paints an optimistic view of the future and illustrates a variety of understandings and approaches to implement its sustainable development.

A number of key elements emerge. The first is that it is important for us to examine a human view of the world in order to assess the philosophical base from which we approach the natural environment and wildlife as either a set of attributes, resources or both. Secondly, the book dwells on an understanding of ecology as the natural basis from which to interrogate wildlife and wildlife tourism. Planning for wildlife tourism development is then presented as relying on an understanding of the role of stakeholders as opposed to communities as well as their engagement, as opposed to consultation, in the planning process.

Adaptive management is advanced as a key platform in ongoing sustainable management in the uncertain and complex world of wildlife tourism. It is advanced as a deliberate and purposive process in the management of industries where the resultant impacts are not clear. As such it has considerable application for the implementation of successful wildlife tourism.

Linking back to the centrality of ecological understanding in the development of wildlife tourism, the added importance of science and wildlife biology are underscored. The knowledge gained from such research provides a firmer base to make decisions upon which to include or exclude populations and/or habitats for wildlife tourism as well as giving directions for impact management and monitoring.

257

This scientific research must be central to all decision making in regard to future developments. All of these issues are now briefly reviewed together with a final note providing suggestions for future research directions.

World Views

The way the natural world is seen can be split into two main views, that of anthropocentric and ecocentric (Meffe & Carroll, 1997; Miller, 2004). This is important for wildlife tourism as it raises the question of whether wildlife is viewed as an attribute in the lives of people or that a more pragmatic perspective is taken on with wild animals viewed as resources. In this book a more ecocentric perspective is adopted with the recognition that wildlife does not have to be hunted, fished or kept in zoos to be fully 'appreciated' for what it is. In the ecocentric view people's enjoyment of wildlife is more respectful of the animal and this leaves room for animals to be themselves and to be free of the controlling influences of humans.

The natural attributes of wildlife that can be appreciated include their colour (birds and insects); size (e.g. large herbivores and arthropods); their levels of activity (e.g. migrations, herding and flocking behaviour); predatory activities (e.g. raptorial birds, lion hunts); intelligence and anthropomorphic behaviour (primates) and rarity (e.g. rare mammals). In relation to many of these attributes people are becoming increasingly interested in observing these behaviours in natural settings; moreover, some of these behaviours can only be seen in the wild.

The value of seeing wildlife in a relatively undisturbed state is that of a more authentic experience. This includes a sense of discovery, the visitor to natural habitats using more senses while also desiring a greater sense of solitude solitude. This has implications for wildlife tourism in terms of reducing the effects of human intrusion and disturbance to species, modes of access, perceptions of crowding and the delivery of information about wildlife. Visitor satisfaction can be deepened by interpretation where visitor emotions are engaged as part of the wildlife experience. Furthermore, interpretation can be used to manage visitor expectations about a species so that visitors are more respectful and do not attempt to make the animal do something.

Perhaps the biggest issue is managing a diversity of attitude and client behaviours. For some visitors simple observation is not enough and there is a desire for close approach, touching and feeding. It is here that arguably the most work is needed in either catering for these desires or managing them through education and interpretation. Although some visitors desire to be close to and feed animals it is important to promote the advantages of viewing an animal under natural conditions, indeed the evidence is accumulating that visitors do not necessarily require close contact and wildlife feeding situations (e.g. Orams, 2000a). If mangers continue to discourage public feeding in the wild as well as educate the wildlife visitor then feeding wildlife will become increasingly unacceptable over time. Wildlife feeding may be an option under certain circumstances but only when obvious bene fits to wildlife can be demonstrated and when it is carefully managed.

Ecological Base

This book helps to set the scene for ecological research to become an essential component of wildlife tourism. In relation to this a number of problems face ecologists, wildlife managers and tourism researchers because of the wide range of species that are potentially involved in a wide range of tourism situations. In addition to this, there is a lack of baseline data on many species. This is, in part, due to the difficulty of acquiring such information on wild species and in attempting to separate the influence of tourism from natural variation. It is hoped that this book goes a long way in addressing this problem by firstly encapsulating major elements of the 'wildlife tourism situation' and then providing a solid scientific foundation for the investigation of various wildlife tourism scenarios.

The main issues that have been identified involve the difficulties in determining long-term ecological impacts, dealing with the appropriateness of habituation, understanding the varying tolerances of species to human intrusion and dealing with the issues associated with the feeding of wildlife. Resolving problems surrounding the determination of long-term impacts lies in conducting longitudinal studies. It is essential to collect data over different seasons and for a number of years so that the confounding effects of natural variation can be eliminated. There is an increasing body of knowledge (e.g. Romero & Wikelski, 2002; Woodford et al., 2002; Dyck & Baydack, 2004) that identifies habituation as not benign but problematical in that habituated animals may appear to be unaffected but are stressed at the physiological level. The long-term consequences of this may be detrimental in terms of costly energetics and/or the ability of a species to deal with naturally stressful events. The potential contribution of tourism revenue to successful conservation must be balanced against such impacts and there is no simple solution, as evidenced by the ongoing debates over gorilla tourism (contrast Butyniski & Kalina, 1998 with McNeilage et al., 1997).

Because of the actual and potential wide range of species concerned it is important to assess every wildlife tourism situation as a unique case. This does not mean that related studies cannot be applied but awareness must be made that the same species may respond differently in differing geographic locations. This observation can be confounded by the fact that tourism situations differ according to varying visitor expectations, levels of visitor education and awareness, different modes of access, frequency of tourist visits and the numbers of people involved. Management responses therefore have to be tailored according to the specific tourism situation. Appropriate management can sometimes be hampered by lack of knowledge, for example, as in the case of the dearth of ecological knowledge regarding the feeding of wildlife. Understanding the impacts of tourism of wildlife therefore requires answers that are grounded in ecology as well as in the social sciences.

Engaging Stakeholders

Community involvement in the development of wildlife tourism is well accepted and they will sometimes need to make special efforts to promote the inclusion of other relevant players who may not become involved on their own initiative, especially where there are cultural barriers. In addition, there has been a general shift of focus away from the narrower group of 'community' to the involvement of a wider group of 'stakeholders'. This group has been identified in this book as comprising the tourism industry, planners and investors, protected area managers, conservation non-government organisations, tourists, and of course, local communities. In addition it has been noted that stakeholders also comprise any person or group who expresses an interest in the wildlife tourism development in a region.

As well as a wider more inclusive approach to involvement in wildlife tourism development, the emphasis throughout this book has been on the 'engagement' of stakeholders rather than the 'consultation' of community members. This second aspect is an important distinction as it moves away from the prevalent former scenario of developers sharing their plans for tourism development with local community members to the more holistic approach of all stakeholders sharing in a planned future for a region.

A number of processes for including stakeholder involvement in the planning of tourism resources have been identified by Bosselman *et al.* (1999). Their approach is that tourism resources are best planned and managed when viewed as a collective 'common pool' of shared assets with multiple stakeholders. They note that the shared development of resources means making them more useful to humans in an efficient and sustainable manner. All of the processes identified have great application to wildlife tourism planning. They are:

- define boundaries clearly;
- identify the stakeholders;
- let the stakeholders make the rules;
- localise the rules;
- give stakeholders a sense of permanence;
- monitor and mediate rule violations.

Planning of an area for wildlife tourism should commence with the clear identification of its resources and location. A set of spatial and temporal boundaries must be posited but only if the boundaries are consistent with the natural boundaries of the ecological system will decision making be fully effective (Hanna, 1995). Next the stakeholders should be clearly identified, especially those involved in the use of the resource, and rules governing it should be clearly postulated and understood. Repetitive users, for example operators of wildlife tours and/or accommodations, should be encouraged in order to foster a sense of 'ownership' of the geographic region where the tourism is occurring, as it is suggested that repetitive users are more concerned with sustainability. When the various stakeholders are involved in setting the rules of use, it is more likely that they will comply with them and enforce them. A key factor in wildlife tourism stakeholder engagement is to recognise the local issues and address them at this level. This then increases the resiliency of the resource and when conditions change, adaptations can be made more quickly.

The need for continued stakeholder engagement is an important element in the process of planning, managing and monitoring wildlife tourism. To this end it is important that those involved are committed for the 'long haul' in order to give the participants a sense of permanence and ongoing relationship, both to the environment and wildlife as well as to the other stakeholders. Finally, it is essential to include stakeholders in monitoring wildlife tourism development as this tends to ensure a higher level of compliance.

Bosselman *et al.* (1999) argue that if the above processes are followed then a number of positive outcomes will result in the management of a wildlife tourism resource. These include equity, sustainability, efficiency and resilience. An equitable outcome ensures that all stakeholders are involved in the decision-making system which should be fair to all involved. Sustainability should also be a natural goal resulting in protecting the wildlife for future generations through a sense of shared ownership based on an attitude of stewardship. A key attitude is the recognition that wildlife resources are not the preserve of any one group and should be used for tourism in the context of conservation. Naturally there are also some absolutes and while wildlife resources are being addressed here, it should noted that some wildlife groups or habitats need to be preserved and thus are excluded entirely from tourism development.

An efficient approach to wildlife tourism is one which generates economic benefits well in excess of the effort expended to create them, that is, wildlife tourism growth should bring economic benefits for stakeholders that far outweigh its costs. Only when this occurs can financial benefits accrue for wildlife protection and resource conservation. Finally, a resilient wildlife tourism opportunity means that stakeholders have the capacity to continue to function in the face of new and different circumstances. If this is achieved then, by extension, the wildlife tourism region should also move towards a state of ecological resilience.

Adaptive Management

Adaptive management is a central theme of this book. To briefly revisit the material provided earlier, the key characteristics of adaptive management are including the natural and social sciences; recognising uncertainty, complexity and long time-scales; regarding policy and management interventions as objective-driven and experimental, with monitoring an integral part; including stakeholders; and using feedback (Dovers, 2003). Bramwell and Lane (2000c) note that there is growing interest more generally in the tourism planning literature in adaptive approaches. Planning systems need to be able to change and adapt, with learning being critical to this adaptation. Such learning may be in relation to planning features such as goals and objectives, practical activities and actions or institutional arrangements (Hall & Page, 1999). Here the theme of adaptive management is brought together, with comments specific to the sustainable management of wildlife tourism. Part of this drawing together includes comment on the 'barriers and bridges' to achieving adaptive management of wildlife tourism.

Adaptive management is suggested as a suitable policy response (in Chapter 5) given the uncertainties associated with wildlife tourism. Addressing risk and uncertainty are central features of adaptive management (Stankey, 2003). McLain and Lee (1996), in their review of adaptive management, commented that providing devices for addressing uncertainty is a central design feature. In terms of wildlife tourism, these uncertainties relate to a lack of scientific information regarding the impacts of tourism on wildlife, uncertainty about the efficacy of potential policy and management responses, unknown and potentially conflicting interests (Briassoulis, 2002), and uncertainties associated with the tourism industry itself.

Uncertainty in wildlife tourism is also a product of the fugitive, common-pool features of wildlife tourism. As discussed in Chapter 5, this fugitive status means that often wildlife, unless captive, can move freely across the landscape reducing the certainty of where they might be at any time. Also, wildlife are often a common-pool resource and as such it can be impossible to exclude tourists and/or implement management measures (such capping visitor numbers) to reduce impacts. Lastly, rights to the property, the lands or waters on which the wildlife occurs, may not be clear. If ownership is uncertain and no one clearly has the rights to enable them to benefit from tourism income or manage tourists to minimise their impacts, then uncertainty is also highly likely.

The adaptive management theme continues in Chapter 6 on management strategies. Here the concept underpins the emphasis on monitoring (Figure 6.10). Monitoring is discussed as an integral part of management as it is only with monitoring that the success or otherwise of a management strategy can be judged. The feedback provided by monitoring is part of adaptive management. Feedback makes learning, adaptation and change possible.

Adaptive management is, however, more than monitoring. It is 'a deliberative and purposive process through which questions are framed, hypotheses proposed, implementation is designed to enhance learning opportunities, results are critically evaluated, and, if appropriate, subsequent actions and policies are revised and applied . . . in a manner . . . to enhance the continuing process of learning (Stankey,

Plate 9.1 Human–penguin interaction in Antarctica
Source: Ross Dowling

2003: 175). Chapter 8 emphasises the importance of adaptive management for industries, such as wildlife tourism, that have exploitative elements where the associated impacts are largely unknown.

Given the centrality of adaptive management for the sustainable management of wildlife tourism, what are the barriers and opportunities in relation to its realisation in this field? One of the most critical barriers relates to property ownership, a concern flagged by Briassoulis (2002). If those with an interest in sustainably managing wildlife do not have ownership of at least the lands and waters on which the wildlife occurs then it will be impossible to devise, test, monitor and modify management regimes as required for adaptive management. Without ownership, there are few means available to control the levels of tourism use, no acquired rights or authority to do so and no ability to accrue the benefits of improved management (such as entry fees). However, even where uncertainties around rights prevail, adaptive management may still be the best approach (Berkes & Folke, 1998). Such is the situation in Antarctica where tourism development continues and is largely governed by an informal agreement. Tour operators have established their own industry association, the International Association of Antarctica Tour Operators (IAATO), and code of conduct, which includes rules that attempt to minimise the impact visitors have on the environment (Bauer & Dowling, 2003; Plate 9.1).

Barriers may also relate to the skills, commitment and attitudes to risk of those managing the wildlife. Adaptive management requires having the skills to design and test hypotheses as well as establish protocols for the collection and storage of information collected as part of this experimental approach to management. There must also be a commitment to monitoring, a part of management that always seems to fall between the cracks and suffer when resources are limited. And at an institutional or organisational level, there has to be a commitment to adaptive management and a shared understanding of what it entails (Stankey, 2003).

Adaptive management also requires taking risks. Protected area agencies worldwide have become risk-averse in recent years making it difficult for managers to experiment without facing censure (Beckwith & Moore, 2001). One of the most significant sources of learning in adaptive management comes from negative feedback or 'making mistakes' (Stankey, 2003). In relation to wildlife management one of these sources of aversion at least is understandable. If adaptive management is being practised in relation to an endangered species with very low population numbers, then the consequences of a 'mistake' may be irretrievable. Modelling may be the best approach in such circumstances as was done by Brook *et al.* (1997) in their study of possible impacts of increased tourism on the threatened Lord Howe Island Woodhen.

The last barrier to adaptive management is flagged in Chapter 7 where the current schism between scientific research and the management of wildlife tourism is described. Adaptive management relies on research and management uniting in a feedback loop, as described in Chapter 8. Stankey (2003) suggests that adaptive management can help close this gap between managers and scientists, making them partners in formulating problems, developing management strategies and associated monitoring programmes, and evaluating outcomes.

The most promising opportunity in relation to adaptive management and wildlife tourism derives from its multiplicity of stakeholders (see Chapter 4). As mentioned previously, the complexity of wildlife tourism requires an adaptive management approach. However, it is this complexity in relation to the diversity and extent of stakeholder interests that may in turn support adaptive management and make such an adaptive approach succeed when it has failed in many other settings (McLain & Lee, 1996). Adaptive management relies on and embraces wide participation and indigenous knowledge (Berkes & Folke, 1998), both features of wildlife tourism in many parts of the world. These features, which often impede resource management elsewhere, may actually facilitate the desire, through using adaptive management, of achieving sustainable wildlife tourism. Those involved should extend beyond scientists and managers to include any stakeholders whose values are involved or who may be affected by decision making (Kruger *et al.*, 1997).

The Importance of Science and Wildlife Biology

It has long been advanced that political or economic expediency is the driver of resource development, but in recent years a more holistic approach which includes social and environmental considerations, has been embraced through the notion of sustainable development. But the approach presented here goes deeper than this and it has been argued that science generally (including environmental science and ecology), and wildlife biology specifically, should underpin any decisions made in relation to resource development generally, and wildlife tourism, specifically. Thus the scientific method is championed and it should resume its rightful place in providing ecological and biological knowledge which can then assist humans in the understanding of wildlife attributes and consequent decisions about, wildlife resources. Such an approach is based on an integrative view of science that is inclusive of the plethora of science disciplines and seeks to unite them into a useful body of applied knowledge.

However, it is also suggested that science is not value free but rather is open to values and bias just like any other area of human inquiry, including social science (see discussion of these values in Calver *et al.*, 1998). The recognition of this is important because it allows us to examine how scientists have surveyed their subjects, the methods they have used in analysis, and the overall determination of outcomes. All this of course can be of great benefit for the development of wildlife tourism, but at best, science can only predict the most likely consequences of different management actions as it rarely deals in certainties. Notwithstanding the above, the development and management of wildlife tourism is better off with the integration and application of scientific knowledge, then without.

The intersection of science and wildlife tourism occurs through wildlife biology, which is concerned with how animals behave in their natural environment. Through an understanding of the distribution and abundance of particular species, conservation and management decisions can be made. It provides knowledge to strengthen conservation arguments and appropriate methods to determine sustainable management. In addition it underpins education and interpretation as precursors to wildlife viewing. Thus with the rapid increase globally of human–wildlife interactions through wildlife tourism, it is essential that the understanding of wildlife is increasingly advanced and enhanced through scientific research, understanding and knowledge dissemination. To do this it is important to ensure that the research on wildlife through ecology and wildlife biology includes a hypothesis-testing framework for answering questions about the impacts of wildlife tourism. Data collection should move beyond description to explanation by proposing explanations of the phenomenon observed and testing predictions that should be true if the explanation is correct. Once an explanation for a problem has been proposed and a prediction drawn from it for testing, the next step is to choose the actual techniques for collecting the data. Thorough planning and careful analysis is necessary for wildlife impact studies to generate a clear result due to the high variability inherent in animal behaviour as well as the natural environment. Thus care should be taken to ensure accurate and appropriate interpretation of such research outcomes with particular attention to assessing the sensitivity of tests which purport to show no significant impact. The danger of mistaking an insensitive test for 'no impact' is ever present in studies of wildlife tourism and could lead to destruction of the tourism opportunity.

Finally, it is advocated that research into both the impacts of wildlife tourism as well as the management of the tourism experience, should be interrelated. Managers can then incorporate research on the impacts of wildlife tourism into their planning and management decisions for wildlife tourism development. This supports and nurtures the process of adaptive management which treats different spatial and temporal management as experimental actions which advance an understanding of the system being managed. Thus the whole scientific approach should underpin and inform management decisions so that issues such as equity, sustainability, efficiency and resilience can be fostered in the development of wildlife tourism.

Future Directions

All of the above issues provide the basis for future research. Not only are there many elements of wildlife tourism research that is known, but, to use the old cliché, there is obviously much we do not know. So where is the starting point in such a sea of complex confusion. First, it is maintained that more empirical research needs to be carried out in the realm of ecology. While some ecosystems are relatively well researched and understood, others are almost completely unknown. Environmental scientists, like ourselves, are working hard in this area, but dedicated, specific, ongoing studies are required in a multitude of environments. The same is true of wildlife biology. More research on increased numbers of species needs to be conducted. This rigorous scientific approach should not be glossed over in the pursuit of economically expedient applied studies which are often little more than an endorsement of what the developer seeks to establish. More quality, less quantity should be the mantra applied to wildlife tourism research.

Research also needs to be carried out on the engagement of stakeholders for specific wildlife tourism developments. Borrowing from the fields of social science more research should be undertaken on the identification, inclusion and engagement of stakeholders in both the initial and ongoing phases of wildlife tourism development. There also appears to be relatively little research that focuses explicitly on wildlife tourism planning conceived and conducted as an adaptive and creative learning process. Such research is timely and will add much to the future direction of conservation wildlife management.

This book has been about wildlife tourism and its focus has been on the development and management of wildlife tourism in the wild. The authors are passionate advocates of the natural wildlife viewing experience but they have sounded warnings about the lack of appropriate scientific and other knowledge in related decision-making processes. Much remains to be done in order to achieve a wildlife tourism industry that is equitable, sustainable, efficient and resilient. It is felt, however, that this book provides a significant platform in this important area of natural resource management.

References

Acero, J.M. and Aguirre, C.A. (1994) A monitoring plan for tourism in Antarctica. *Annals of Tourism Research* 21 (2), 295–302.

Adams, H.R., Sleeman, J.M. Rwego, I. and New, J.C. (2001) Self-reported medical history survey of humans as a measure of health risk to the chimpanzees (*Pan troglodytes schweinfurthii*) of Kibale National Park, Uganda. *Oryx* 35, 308–12.

Agardy, M.T. (1993) Accommodating ecotourism in multiple use planning of coastal and marine protected areas. *Ocean and Coastal Management* 20, 219–39.

Albers, P.C. and James, W.R. (1988) Travel photography: A methodological approach. *Annals of Tourism Research* 15 (1), 134–58.

Albert, D.M. and Bowyer, R.T. (1991) Factors related to grizzly bear–human interactions in Denali National Park. *Wildlife Society Bulletin* 19, 339–49.

Alcock, D. (1991) Education and extension: Management's best strategy. *Australian Parks and Recreation* 27, 15–17.

Alexander, J. and McGregor, J. (2000) Wildlife and politics: CAMPFIRE in Zimbabwe. *Development and Change* 31, 605–27.

Alexander, S.E. (2000) Resident attitudes towards conservation and black howler monkeys in Belize: The Community Baboon Sanctuary. *Environmental Conservation* 27 (4), 341–50.

Anderson, C.W. (1979) The place of principles in policy analysis. *American Political Science Review* 73, 711–23.

Anderson, D.W. and Keith, J.O. (1980) The human influence on seabird nesting success: Conservation implications. *Biological Conservation* 18, 65–80.

Aronowitz, S. (1988) *Science as Power: Discourse and Ideology in Modern Society*. London: Macmillan Press.

Anon. (1997) What is the World Heritage? *UNESCO Courier* (September 1997), 1–5.

Arnstein, S.R. (1969) A ladder of citizen participation. *American Institute of Planners Journal* 35 (4), 216–24.

ASEAN (Association of South East Asian Nations) (2004) The official website of the Association of South East Asian Nations, The ASEAN Secretariat, Jakarta Indonesia. Online document: http://www.aseansec.org/home.htm (accessed 25 January 2004).

Ashley, C. and Roe, D. (1998) *Enhancing Community Development in Wildlife Tourism: Issues and Challenges*. London, UK: International Institute for Environment and Development.

Au, W.W.L. and Green, M. (2000) Acoustic interaction of humpback whales and whale watching boats. *Marine Environmental Research* 49 (5), 469–581.

Bakeman, R. and Gottman, J.M. (1997) *Observing Interaction: An Introduction to Sequential Analysis*. Cambridge: Cambridge University Press.

Ballantine, J. and Eagles, P.J. (1994) Defining the Canadian ecotourist. *Journal of Sustainable Tourism* 2 (4), 210–14.

Barany, M.E., Hammett, A.L., Shillington, L.J. and Murphy, B.R. (2001) The role of private wildlife reserves in Nicaragua's emerging ecotourism industry. *Journal of Sustainable Tourism* 9 (2), 95–110.

Bart, J., Fligner, M.A. and Notz, W.I. (1998) *Sampling and Statistical Methods for Behavioural Ecologists*. Cambridge: Cambridge University Press.

Basel, J. (1993) An excellent example of ecotourism. In *Proceedings of the World Conference on Adventure Travel and Eco-tourism* (pp. 203–7). Manaus, Brazil: The Adventure Travel Society.

Bates, G. (2002) *Environmental Law in Australia*. Chatswood: Butterworths.

Bauer, T. and Dowling, R. (2003) Ecotourism policies and issues in Antarctica. In D.A. Fennell and R.K. Dowling (eds) *Ecotourism Policy and Planning* (pp. 309–29). Wallingford, UK: CABI Publishing.

Beardsworth, A. and Bryman, A. (2001) The wild animal in late modernity: The case of the Disneyization of zoos. *Tourist Studies* 1, 83–104.

Beck, A.M. (1999) Companion animals and their companions: Sharing a strategy for survival. *Bulletin of Science, Technology and Society* 19 (4), 281–5.

Beckwith, J.A. and Moore, S.A. (2001) The influence of recent changes in public sector management on biodiversity conservation. *Pacific Conservation Biology* 7 (1), 45–54.

Begon, M. (1979) *Investigating Animal Abundance: Capture-Recapture for Biologists*. London: Edward Arnold.

Bell, G.W., Hejl, S.J. and Varner, J. (1990) Proportional use of substrates by foraging birds: Model considerations on first sightings and subsequent observations. In M.L. Morrison, C.J. Ralph, J.Verner and J.R. Jehl, Jr (eds) *Avian Foraging: Theory, Methodology and Applications* (pp. 416–22). Sailorman, CA: Cooper Ornithological Society.

Bell, P.A., Greene, T.C., Fisher, J.D., and Baum, A. (2001) *Environmental Psychology* (5th edn). Fort Worth: Harcourt College Publishers.

Bennett, M. (2003) Perisher Range Resorts EMS – A partnership between government, commercial and not for profit tourism operators, utility providers and nature conservation groups. Paper presented at *2003 Ecotourism Australia 11th National Conference*, Adelaide and Riverland South Australia, 10–14 November 2003.

Bentrupperbäumer, J.M. (1998) Reciprocal ecosystem impact and behavioural interactions between cassowaries, Casarius casuarius, and humans, Homo sapiens: Exploring the natural-human environment interface and its implications for endangered species recovery in North Queensland, Australia. Unpublished PhD thesis, James Cook University of North Queensland.

Bentrupperbäumer, J.M., and Reser, J.P. (2000) Popular cultural images and representations of an endangered species and implications for management. In *EDRA Conference*. Edinburgh .

Bentrupperbäumer, J.M. and Reser, J.P. (2001) *Impacts of Visitation and Use: Psychosocial and Biophysical Windows on Visitation and Use in the Wet Tropics World Heritage Area*. Cairns: Rainforest Cooperative Research Centre.

Bentrupperbäumer, J.M. and Reser, J.P. (2002) *Measuring and monitoring Impacts of Visitation and Use in the Wet Tropics World Heritage Area 2001/2002*. Cairns: Rainforest Cooperative Research Centre.

Bentrupperbäumer, J.M. and Reser, J.P. (2003a) *The Role of the Wet Tropics in the Life of the Community: A Wet Tropics World Heritage Area Survey*. Cairns: Rainforest Cooperative Research Centre.

Bentrupperbäumer, J.M. and Reser, J.P. (2003b) (in preparation) Representing, communicating and managing visitor risk in Northern Australia's World Heritage Areas, the Wet Tropics World Heritage Area and Kakadu.

Bergerud, A.T. (1974) Decline of caribou in North America following settlement. *Journal of Wildlife Management* 38, 757–70.

Berkes, F. and Folke, C. (eds) (1998) *Linking Social and Ecological Systems: Management Practices and Social Mechanisms for Building Resilience.* Cambridge: Cambridge University Press.

Berwick, S.H. and Saharia, V.B. (eds) (1995) *The Development of International Principles and Practices of Wildlife Research and Management: Asian and American Approaches.* Oxford: Oxford University Press.

Binning, C. and Young, M. (1997) *Motivating People: Using Management Agreements to Conserve Remnant Vegetation* (Research Report 1/97: National Research and Development Program on Rehabilitation, Management and Conservation of Remnant Vegetation). Canberra: Land and Water Resources Research and Development Corporation.

Binning, C., Young, M. and Cripps, E. (1999) *Beyond Roads, Rates and Rubbish: Opportunities for Local Government to Conserve Native Vegetation* (Research Report 1/99: National Research and Development Program on Rehabilitation, Management and Conservation of Remnant Vegetation). Canberra: Land and Water Resources Research and Development Corporation.

Birtles, A., Valentine, P. and Curnock, M. (2001) *Tourism Based on Free Ranging Marine Wildlife* (Wildlife Tourism Research Report Series No. 11). Gold Coast, Queensland: Cooperative Research Centre for Sustainable Tourism.

Blane, J.M. and Jaakson, R. (1994) The impact of ecotourism boats on the St Lawrence beluga whales. *Environmental Conservation* 21 (3), 267–9.

Blankenship, L. and Satakopan, S. (1995) Food habits and nutrition. In S.H. Berwick and V.B. Saharia (eds) *The Development of International Principles and Practices of Wildlife Research and Management: Asian and American Approaches* (pp. 327–64). Oxford: Oxford University Press.

Blumstein, D.T., Anthony, L.L., Harcourt, R. and Ross, G. (2003) Testing a key assumption of wildlife buffer zones: Is flight initiation distance a species-specific trait? *Biological Conservation* 110, 97–100.

Bolduc, F. and Guillemette, M. (2003) Human disturbance and nesting success of common eiders: Interaction between visitors and gulls. *Biological Conservation* 110, 77–83.

Bolon, E.G. and Robinson, W. (2003) *Wildlife Ecology and Management* (5th edn). New Jersey: Prentice Hall International.

Bookhout, T.A. (ed.) (1996) *Research and Management Techniques for Wildlife and Habitats.* Bethesda, MD: The Wildlife Society.

Bostock, S. St C. (1993) *Zoos and Animal Rights: The Ethics of Keeping Animals.* London: Routledge.

Bosselman, F.P., Peterson, C.A. and McCarthy, C. (1999) *Managing Tourism Growth: Issues and Applications.* Washington, DC: Island Press.

Botterill, T.D. and Crompton, J. (1996) Two case studies exploring the nature of the tourist's experience. *Journal of Leisure Research* 28 (1), 57–82.

Boyce, M.S. (1995a) Population dynamics. In S.H. Berwick and V.B. Saharia (eds) *The Development of International Principles and Practices of Wildlife Research and Management: Asian and American Approaches* (pp. 277–92). Oxford: Oxford University Press.

Boyce, M.S. (1995b) Population estimation. In S.H. Berwick and V.B. Saharia (eds) *The Development of International Principles and Practices of Wildlife Research and Management: Asian and American Approaches* (pp. 263–76). Oxford: Oxford University Press.

Boyce, M.S. (1997) Population viability analysis: Adaptive management for threatened and endangered species. In S.H. Berwick and V.B. Saharia (eds) *The Development of International Principles and Practices of Wildlife Research and Management: Asian and American Approaches* (pp. 226–38). Oxford: Oxford University Press.

Boyle, S.A. and Samson, F.B. (1985) Effects of nonconsumptive recreation on wildlife: A review. *Wildlife Society Bulletin* 13, 110–16.

Braithwaite, R.W. and Reynolds, P.C. (2002) Wildlife and tourism. In D. Lunney and C. Dickman (eds) *A Zoological Revolution. Using Native Fauna to Assist in its Own Survival* (pp. 108–15). Sydney: Royal Zoological Society of New South Wales, Mosman and Australian Museum.

Bramwell, B. and Lane, B. (2000a) Collaboration and partnerships in tourism planning. In B. Bramwell and B. Lane (eds) *Tourism Collaboration and Partnerships: Politics, Practice and Sustainability* (pp. 1–19). Clevedon, England: Channel View Publications.

Bramwell, B. and Lane, B. (eds) (2000b) *Tourism Collaboration and Partnerships: Politics, Practice and Sustainability*. Clevedon, England: Channel View Publications.

Bramwell, B. and Lane, B. (2000c) Collaborative tourism planning: Issues and future directions. In B. Bramwell and B. Lane (eds) *Tourism Collaboration and Partnerships: Politics, Practice and Sustainability* (pp. 333–41). Clevedon: Channel View Publications.

Bramwell, B. and Sharman, A. (1999) Collaboration in local tourism policymaking. *Annals of Tourism Research* 26 (2), 392–415.

Brewer, L. and Fagerstone, K. (eds) (1998) *Radiotelemetry Applications for Wildlife Toxicology Field Studies*. Brussels and Pensacola, FL: Society of Environmental Toxicology and Chemistry.

Briassoulis, H. (2002) Sustainable tourism and the question of the commons. *Annals of Tourism Research* 29 (4), 1065–85.

Bridgman, P. and Davis, G. (2000) *Australian Policy Handbook*. Crows Nest, NSW: Allen & Unwin.

Bright, A., Reynolds, G.R., Innes, J. and Waas, J.R. (2003) Effects of motorised boat passes on the time budgets of New Zealand dabchick (*Poliocephalus rufopectus*). *Wildlife Research* 30 (3), 237–44.

British Standards Institute (1994) *British Standard for Environmental Management Systems: BS7750*. London: British Standards Institute.

Brodie, S.J. and Biley, F.C. (1999) An exploration of the potential benefits of pet-facilitated therapy. *Journal of Clinical Nursing* 8 (4), 329–37.

Brook, B.W., Lim, L., Harden, R. and Frankham, R. (1997) How secure is the Lord Howe Island Woodhen? A population viability analysis using VORTEX. *Pacific Conservation Biology* 3, 125–33.

Browder, J.O. (2002) Conservation and development projects in the Brazilian Amazon: Lessons from the community initiative program in Rondonia. *Environmental Management* 29 (6), 750–62.

Bryson, J.M. and Crosby, B.C. (1992) *Leadership for the Common Good: Tackling Public Problems in a Shared-Power World*. San Francisco: Jossey-Bass.

Buckley, R.C. (2001) Major issues in tourism ecolabelling. In X. Font and R.C. Buckley (eds) *Tourism Ecolabelling: Certification and Promotion of Sustainable Management* (pp. 19–26). Wallingford, UK: CABI Publishing.

Buckley, R. (2000) Tourism in the most fragile environments. *Tourism Recreation Research* 25 (1), 31–40.

Buckley, R. (2003) *Case Studies in Ecotourism*. Wallingford, UK: CABI Publishing.

Buckley, R.C., Pickering, C.A. and Warnken, J. (2000) Environmental management for alpine tourism and resorts in Australia. In P.M. Godde, M.F. Price and F.M. Zimmermann (eds) *Tourism and Development in Mountain Regions* (pp. 27–45). Wallingford, UK: CABI Publishing.

Burger, J. (1981) The effect of human activity on birds at a coastal bay. *Biological Conservation* 21, 231–41.

Burger, J., Gochfeld, M. and Niles, L.J. (1995) Ecotourism and birds in coastal New Jersey: Contrasting responses of birds, tourists and managers. *Environmental Conservation* 22 (1), 56–65.

Burgman, M.A. and Lindenmayer, D.B. (1998) *Conservation Biology for the Australian Environment*. Chipping Norton, NSW: Surrey Beatty and Sons.

Burns, G.L. and Sofield, T.H.B. (2001) *The Host Community: Social and Cultural Issues Concerning Wildlife Tourism* (Wildlife Tourism Research Report Series No. 4). Gold Coast, Queensland: Cooperative Research Centre for Sustainable Tourism.

Burton, H. and van den Hoff, J. (2002) Humans and southern elephant seals. *Australian Mammalogy* 24, 127–39.

Butler, R.W. (1980) The concept of a tourist area cycle of evolution: Implications for management of resources. *Canadian Geographer* 24 (1), 5–12.

Butynski, T. (1998) Is gorilla tourism sustainable? *Gorilla Journal* 16, June.

Butynski, T.M. and Kalina, J. (1998) Gorilla tourism: A critical look. In E.J. Milner-Gulland and R. Mace (eds) *Conservation of Biological Resources* (pp. 294–313). Oxford: Blackwell Science.

Caldwell, L.K. (1982) *Science and the National Environment Policy Act: Redirecting Policy Through Procedural Reform*. AL: The University of Alabama Press.

CALM (1993) *Monkey Mia Reserve Management Plan*. Department of Conservation and Land Management, Perth, Western Australia.

CALM (1999) *Watching Whales: Rules and tips*. Department of Conservation and Land Management, Perth, Western Australia

Calver, M.C. (1984) A review of ecological applications of immunological techniques for diet analysis. *Australian Journal of Ecology* 9, 19–25.

Calver, M.C. (2000) Lessons from preventive medicine for the precautionary principle and ecosystem health. *Ecosystem Health* 6, 99–107.

Calver, M.C. and King, D.R. (2000) Why publication matters in conservation biology. *Pacific Conservation Biology* 6, 2–8.

Calver, M.C. and Porter, B.D. (1986) Unravelling the food web: Dietary analysis in modern ecology. *Journal of Biological Education* 20, 42–6.

Calver, M.C., Dickman, C.R., Feller, M.C., Hobbs, R.J., Horwitz, P., Recher, H.F. and Wardell-Johnson, G. (1998) Towards resolving conflict between forestry and conservation in Western Australia. *Australian Forestry* 61, 258–66.

Campbell, B., Byron, N., Madzudzo, P.H.E., Matose, F. and Wily, L. (1999) Moving to local control of woodland resources. Can CAMPFIRE go beyond the mega-fauna? *Society and Natural Resources* 12, 501–9.

Campbell, N. (1953) *What is Science?* New York: Dover Publications, Inc.

Cannon, C.E. (1984) Movements of lorikeets with an artificially supplemented diet. *Australian Wildlife Research* 11, 173–9.

Cape Conservation Group (2003) *Turtle Monitoring Field Guide*. Exmouth, Western Australia: Cape Conservation Group.

Carney, K.M. and Sydeman, W.J. (1999) A review of human disturbance effects on nesting colonial waterbirds. *Waterbirds* 22 (1), 68–79.

Cater, C. and Cater, E. (2001) Marine Environments. In D.B.Weaver (ed.) *The Encyclopedia of Ecotourism.* (pp. 265–82). Wallingford: CABI Publishing.

Caughley, G. and Gunn, A. (1996) *Conservation Biology in Theory and Practice.* Cambridge, MA: Blackwell Science.

Caughley, G. and Sinclair, A.R.E. (1994) *Wildlife Ecology & Management.* Cambridge, MA: Blackwell Science.

CDT (Commonwealth Department of Tourism) (1994) *National Ecotourism Strategy.* Canberra: Commonwealth of Australia.

Ceballos-Lascurain, H. (1998) Introduction. In K. Lindberg, M. Epler Wood and D. Engeldrum (eds) *Ecotourism: A Guide for Planners and Managers*, Vol. 2 (pp. 7–10). VT, USA: The Ecotourism Society.

Chalmers, A.F. (1982) *What is this Thing called Science?* Queensland: University of Queensland Press.

Chalmers, A.F. (2000) *What is this Thing called Science?* Queensland: University of Queensland Press.

Chadwick, G. (1971) *A Systems View of Planning.* Oxford: Pergamon Press.

Champ, J.G. (2002). A culturalist-qualitative investigation of wildlife media and value orientations. *Human Dimensions of Wildlife* 7, 273–86.

Chapman, K., Lawes, M. and Macleod, M. (1998) Evaluation of non-lethal control methods on problematic Samango monkeys in the Cape Vidal Recreation Reserve, Greater St Lucia Wetland Park. *South African Journal of Wildlife Resources* 28, 89–99.

Charlesworth, M. (1982) *Science, Non Science and Pseudo Science.* Geelong, Victoria: Deakin United Publisher.

Charters, T. (1995) The state of ecotourism in Australia. In H. Richins, J. Richardson and A. Crabtree (eds) *Proceedings of Ecotourism and Nature Based Tourism: Taking the Next Steps – The Ecotourism Association of Australia National Conference* (pp. 9–17), 18–23 November 1995. Alice Springs, Northern Territory.

Cheney, D.L. and Seyfarth, R.M. (1990) *How Monkeys see the World: Inside the Mind of Another Species.* Chicago: University of Chicago Press.

Ciriacy-Wantrup, S.V. and Bishop, R.C. (1975) 'Common property' as a concept in natural resources policy. *Natural Resources Journal* 15, 713–27.

Clevenger, A.P., Chruszcz, B. and Gunson, K.E. (2001) Highway mitigation fencing reduces wildlife-vehicle collisions. *Wildlife Society Bulletin* 29 (2), 646–53.

Clevenger, A.P., Chruszcz, B. and Gunson, K.E. (2003) Spatial patterns and factors influencing small vertebrate fauna road-kill aggregations. *Biological Conservation* 109, 15–26.

Clutton-Brock, J. (1999) *A Natural History of Domesticated Mammals* (2nd edn). Cambridge: Cambridge University Press.

Coate, K.H. (2001) The development of nature-based tourism in Western Australia. *The Western Australian Naturalist* 23 (1), 39–50.

Cochran, W.G. (1983) *Planning and Analysis of Observational Studies.* New York: John Wiley & Sons.

Cole, D.N. (1995) Wilderness management principles: Science, logical thinking or personal opinion? *Trends* 32 (1), 6–9.

Colman, J. (1998) Whale shark management programme, Western Australia. *Shark News* 11, 5-6.

Constantine, R., Brunton, D. and Dennis, T. (2004) Dolphin-watching tour boats change bottlenose dolphin *(Tursiops truncatus)* behaviour. *Biological Conservation* 117 (3), 299–307.

Cooper, D.E. (1993) Human sentiment and the future of wildlife. *Environmental Values* 2 (4), 335–46.

Cooper, D. (1994) Portraits of paradise: Themes and images of the tourist industry. *Southeast Asian Journal of Social Science* 22, 144–60.

Corkeron, P. (1995) Humpback whales (*Megaptera novaeangliae*) in Hervey Bay, Queensland: Behaviour and responses to whale watching vessels. *Canadian Journal of Zoology* 73, 1290–9.

Cormack, R.M., Patil, G.P. and Robson, D.S. (eds) (1979) *Sampling Biological Populations*. Burtonsville, USA: International Cooperative Publishing House.

Cosgrove, L., Evans, D.G. and Yencken, D. (eds) (1994) *Restoring the Land: Environmental Values, Knowledge and Action*. Carlton, Victoria: Melbourne University Press.

Cowlishaw, G. (1998) The role of vigilance in the survival and reproductive strategies of desert baboons. *Behaviour* 135, 431–52.

Cripps, E., Binning, C. and Young, M. (1999) *Opportunity Denied: Review of the Legislative Ability of Local Governments to Conserve Native Vegetation* (Research Report 2/99). National Research and Development Program on Rehabilitation, Management and Conservation of Remnant Vegetation. Canberra: Land and Water Resources Research and Development Corporation.

Croft, D.B. and Leiper, N. (2001) *Assessment of Opportunities for Overseas Tourism Based on Wild Kangaroos* (Wildlife Tourism Research Report, Series No. 17). Gold Coast, Queensland: Cooperative Research Centre for Sustainable Tourism.

Culick, B.M. and Wilson, R.P. (1995) Penguins disturbed by tourists. *Nature* 376, 301–2.

Culik, B., Adelung, D. and Woakes, A.J. (1990) The effects of disturbance on the heart rate and behaviour of Adelie penguins (*Pygoscelis adeliae*) during the breeding season. In K.R. Kerry and G. Hempel (eds) *Antarctic Ecosystems: Ecological Change and Conservation* (pp. 177–82). Berlin: Springer Verlag.

Cullen, P. (1990) The turbulent boundary between water science and water management. *Freshwater Biology* 24, 201–9.

Cuthill, I. (1991) Field experiments in animal behaviour: Methods and ethics. *Animal Behaviour* 42, 1007–14.

Daigle, J.J., Hrubes, D. and Ajzen, I. (2002) A comparative study of beliefs, attitudes, and values among hunters, wildlife viewers, and other outdoor recreationalists. *Human Dimensions of Wildlife* 7, 1–19.

Davis, D., Tisdell, C. and Hardy, M. (2000) *Wildlife Tourism Research Report 3: The Role of Economics in Managing Wildlife Tourism*. Queensland, CRC for Sustainable Tourism.

Department of Conservation and Land Management (1999) *Watching Whales: Rules and Tips*. Perth, Western Australia: Department of Conservation and Land Management.

Desu, M.M. and Raghavarao, D. (2003) *Nonparametric Statistical Methods for Complete and Censored Data*. Boca Raton, FL: Chapman and Hall/CRC.

Deutsche, C.J., Bonde, R.K. and Reid, J.P. (1998) Radio-tracking manatees from land and space: Tag design, implementation, and lessons learned from long-term study. *Marine Technology Society Journal* 32, 18–29.

Deville, A. and Harding, R. (1997) *Applying the Precautionary Principle*. Sydney: The Federation Press.

Diamond, J. (1993) New Guineans and their natural world. In S.R. Kellert and E.O. Wilson (eds) *The Biophilia Hypothesis* (pp. 251–71). Washington, DC: Island Press.

DITR (Department of Industry, Tourism and Resources) (2003) *Pursuing Common Goals: Case Studies – Opportunities for Tourism and Conservation*. Canberra: Commonwealth of Australia.

Doenier, P.B., Delgiudice, G.D. and Riggs, M.R. (1997) Effects of winter supplemental feeding on browse consumption by white tailed deer. *Wildlife Society Bulletin* 25, 235–43.

Dovers, S. (2003) Processes and institutions for resource and environmental management: Why and how to analyse? In S. Dovers and S. Wild River (eds) *Managing Australia's Environment* (pp. 3–12). Sydney: The Federation Press.

Dowling, R. (1993) An environmentally-based planning model for regional tourism development. *Journal of Sustainable Tourism* 1 (1), 17–37.

Dowling, R.K. (1977) Environmental education. *New Zealand Environment* 16, 24–6.

Dowling, R.K. (1996) The implementation of ecotourism in Australia. In *Proceedings of 2nd International Conference of the Ecotourism Association of Australia: The Implementation of Ecotourism: Planning, Developing and Managing for Sustainability*, 18 21 July 1996, Bangkok, Thailand.

Dowling, R.K. (1999) Developing tourism in the environmentally sensitive North West Cape Region, Western Australia. In T.V. Singh and S. Singh (eds) *Tourism Development in Critical Environments* (pp. 163–75). New York: Cognizant Communication Corporation.

Dowling, R.K. (2001) Environmental tourism. In N. Douglas, N. Douglas and R. Derrett (eds) *Special Interest Tourism: Contexts and Cases* (pp. 283–306). Brisbane: John Wiley & Sons.

Dowling, R.K. (2003) Community attitudes: Tourism development in natural environments. In S. Singh, D.J. Timothy and R. Dowling (eds) *Tourism in Destination Communities* (pp. 205–28). Wallingford: CABI Publishing.

Dowling, R.K. and Wood, J.C. (2003) Ecotourism development in the Indian Ocean Region: The case for shared learning. In R.N. Ghosh, M.A.B. Siddique and R. Gabbay (eds) *Tourism and Economic Development: Case Studies from the Indian Ocean* (pp. 42–62). Oxford: Ashgate Publishing Ltd.

Duffus, D.A. (1996) The recreational use of grey whales in southern Claypot Sound, Canada. *Applied Geography* 16, 179–90.

Duffus, D.A. and Dearden, P. (1990) Non-consumptive wildlife oriented recreation: A conceptual framework. *Biological Conservation*, 53, 213–31.

DuNann Winter, D. (1996) *Ecological Psychology: Healing the Split Between Planet and Self*. New York: Harper Collins College Publishers.

Dunlop, J.N. (1996) Habituation to human disturbance by breeding Bridled Terns *(Sterna anaethetus)*. *Corella* 20, 13–6.

Dunlop, J.N., Klomp, N.I. and Wooller, R.D. (1988) Penguin Island, Shoalwater Bay, Western Australia. *Corella* 12, 93–8.

Dyck, M.G. and Baydack, R.K. (2004) Vigilance behaviour of polar bears (*Ursus maritimus*) in the context of wildlife-viewing activities at Churchill, Manitoba, Canada. *Biological Conservation* 116, 343–50.

Dyson, S.E. and Calver, M.C. (2003) The value of animal ethics committees for wildlife research in conservation biology – an Australian perspective. *Pacific Conservation Biology* 9 (2), 86–94.

Dytham, C. (2003) *Choosing and Using Statistics: A Biologist's Guide*. Malden, MA: Blackwell Science.

EA (Ecotourism Australia) (2003) *EcoCertification: A Certification Program for the Australian Nature and Ecotourism Industry, Launch Summary* (3rd edn). Brisbane: Ecotourism Australia.

Eagly, A.H. and Chaiken, S. (1993) *The Psychology of Attitudes*. Harcourt Brace Jovanovich: Fort Worth.

Eberhardt, L.L. and Thomas, J.M. (1991) Designing environmental field studies. *Ecological Monographs* 61, 53–73.

Eckersley, R. (1995) Markets, the state and the environment: An overview. In R. Eckersley (ed.) *Markets, the State and the Environment: Towards Integration* (pp. 7–45). South Melbourne: Macmillan Education.

Eddy, T.J., Gallup, G.G. and Povinelli, D.J. (1993) Attribution of cognitive states to animals: Anthropomorphism in comparative perspective. *Journal of Social Issues* 49 (1), 87–101.

Edington, J.M. and Edington, M.A. (1986) *Ecology, Recreation and Tourism.* Cambridge, UK: Cambridge University Press.

Edwards, K. (1990) The interplay of affect and cognition in attitude formation and change. *Journal of Personality and Social Psychology* 59 (2), 202–16.

Edwards, V.M. and Steins, N.A. (1999) A framework for analysing contextual factors in common pool resource research. *Journal of Environmental Policy and Planning* 1, 205–21.

Elgar, M.A. (1989) Predator vigilance and group size in mammals and birds: A critical review of empirical evidence. *Biological Review* 64, 13–33.

Elkington, J. (1997) *Cannibals with Forks: The Triple Bottom Line of 21st Century Business.* Oxford: Capstone Publishing Limited.

Ellen, R.F. and Fukui, K. (1996) *Redefining Nature: Ecology, Culture and Domestication.* Oxford: Berg.

Engelhard, G.H., van den Hoff, J., Broekman, M., Baarspul, A.N.J., Field, I., Burton, H. and Reijnders, P.J.H. (2001) Mass of weaned elephant seal pups in areas of low and high human presence. *Polar Biology* 24, 244–51.

Engelhard, G.H., Baarspul, A.N.J., Broekman, M., Creuwels, J.C.S. and Reijnders, P.J.H. (2002) Human disturbance, nursing behaviour and lactational pup growth in a declining southern elephant seal (*Mirounga leonina*) population. *Canadian Journal of Zoology* 80, 1876–86.

Erskine, A.J. (1994) Editorial. *Picoides* 7, 2.

EU (European Union) (2004) The European Union at a glance. Online document: http://europa.eu.int/abc/index_en.htm (accessed 25 January 2004).

Everden, N. (1992) *The Social Creation of Nature.* Baltimore: Johns Hopkins Press.

Everett, R., Oliver, C., Saveland, J., Hessburg, P., Diaz, N. and Irwin, L. (1994) Adaptive ecosystem management. In M.E. Jensen and P.S. Bourgeron (eds) (Vol. II) *Ecosystem Management: Principles and Applications* (Gen. Tech. Rep. PNW-GTR–318). Portland, OR: USDA Forestry Service.

Ewing, S. (2003) Adaptive management – building capacity in our NRM institutions. *Rip Rap* 24, 11–13.

Fabricius, C., Koch, E. and Magome, H. (2001) Towards strengthening collaborative ecosystem management: Lessons from environmental conflict and political change in southern Africa. *Journal of the Royal Society of New Zealand* 31 (4), 831–44.

Farr, R. (1987) Social representations: A French tradition of research. *Journal for the Theory of Social Behavior* 17 (4), 343–70.

Farr, R.M. (1993) Common sense, science and social representations. *Public Understanding of Science* 2, 189–204.

Feinerman, E. and Komen, M.H.C. (2003) Agri-environmental instruments for an integrated rural policy: An economic analysis. *Journal of Agricultural Economics* 54 (1), 1–20.

Fennell, D.A. (1999) *Ecotourism: An Introduction.* Routledge: London.

Fennell, D.A. (2000) Ecotourism on trial: The case of billfish angling as ecotourism. *Journal of Sustainable Tourism* 8 (4), 341–5.

Fennell, D.A. and Dowling, R.K. (eds) (2003) *Ecotourism Policy and Planning.* Wallingford, UK: CABI Publishing.

Fernández-Juricic, E., Jimenez, M.D. and Lucas, E. (2001) Alert distance as an alternative measure of bird tolerance to human disturbance: Implications for park design. *Environmental Conservation* 28 (3), 263–9.

Ferraro, P.J. (2001) Global habitat protection: Limitations of development interventions and a role for conservation performance payments. *Conservation Biology* 15 (4), 990–1000.

Finn, H.C., Maxwell, M. and Calver, M.C. (2002) Why does experimentation matter in teaching ecology? *Journal of Biological Education* 36, 158–62.

Findlay, K.P. (1997) Attitudes and expenditures of whale watchers in Hermanus, South Africa. *South African Journal of Wildlife Research* 27, 57–62.

Floyd, M.F. and Gramann, J.H. (1997) Experience-based setting management: Implications for market segmentation of hunters. *Leisure Sciences* 19, 113–27.

Font, X. (2001a) Regulating the green message: The players in ecolabelling. In X. Font and R.C. Buckley (eds) *Tourism Ecolabelling: Certification and Promotion of Sustainable Management* (pp. 1–17). Wallingford: UK: CABI Publishing.

Font, X. (2001b) Conclusions: A strategic analysis of tourism labels. In X. Font and R.C. Buckley (eds) *Tourism Ecolabelling: Certification and Promotion of Sustainable Management* (pp. 259–69). Wallingford, UK: CABI Publishing.

Font, X. and Buckley, R.C. (2001) (eds) *Tourism Ecolabelling: Certification and Promotion of Sustainable Management*. Wallingford, UK: CABI Publishing.

Font, X., Flynn, P., Tribe, J. and Yale, K. (2001) Environmental management systems in outdoor recreation: A case study of a forest enterprise (UK) site. *Journal of Sustainable Tourism* 9 (1), 44–60.

Ford, E.D. (2000) *Scientific Method for Ecological Research*. Cambridge: Cambridge University Press.

Forrest, C.J. and Mays, R.H. (1997) *The Practical Guide to Environmental Community Relations*. New York: John Wiley & Sons.

Fossey, D. (2000) *Gorillas in the Mist* (5th edn). Boston: Houghton Mifflin.

Fowler, G.S. (1999) Behavioural and hormonal responses of Magellanic Penguins (*Spheniscus magellancus*) to tourism and nest site visitation. *Biological Conservation* 90, 143–9.

Fowler, J., Cohen, L. and Jarvis, P. (1998) *Practical Statistics for Field Biology*. New York: John Wiley & Sons.

Fowler, M.E. and Miller, R.E. (1999) *Zoo and Wild Animal Medicine: Current Therapy*. Philadelphia: W.B. Saunders.

Frankfort-Nachmias, C. and Nachmias, D. (1996) *Research Methods in the Social Sciences*. London: Arnold.

Franklin, A. and White, R. (2001) Animals and modernity: Changing human–animal relations, 1949–1998. *Journal of Sociology* 37 (3), 219–38.

Franzmann, A.W., Cook, R., Singh, C.M. and Cheeran, J.V. (1995) Health and condition evaluation of wild animal populations: The animal indicator concept. In S.H. Berwick and V.B. Saharia (eds) *The Development of International Principles and Practices of Wildlife Research and Management: Asian and American Approaches* (pp. 65–402). Oxford: Oxford University Press.

Friend, M., Toweill, D.E., Brownell, R.L.J., Nettles, V.F., Davis, D.S. and Foreyt, W.J. (1996) Guidelines for proper care and use of wildlife in field research. In T.A. Bookhout (ed.) *Research and Management Techniques for Wildlife and Habitats* (pp. 96–105). Bethesda, MD: The Wildlife Society.

Frohoff, T.G. (2000) Behavioral indicators of stress in odontocetes during interactions with humans: A preliminary review and discussion, International Whaling Commission Scientific Committee: SC/52/WW2.

Fulton, G.R. and Ford, H.A. (2001) The conflict between animal welfare and conservation. *Pacific Conservation Biology* 7, 152–3.

Gabrielsen, G.W. and Smith, E.N. (1995) Physiological responses of wildlife to disturbance. In R.L. Knight and K.J. Gutzwiller (eds) *Wildlife and Recreationists: Coexistence through Management and Research*. Washington, DC, USA: Island Press.

Galdikas, B.M.F. (1995) *Reflections of Eden: My Life with the Orangutans of Borneo*. London: Victor Gollancz.

Gales, N., Hindell, M. and Kirkwood, R. (2003) *Marine Mammals: Fisheries, Tourism and Management Issues*. Collingwood, Australia: CSIRO Publishing.

Galicia, E. and Baldassarre, G.A. (1997) Effects of motorised tour boats on the behaviour of non-breeding American Flamingos in Yucatan, Mexico. *Conservation Biology* 11 (5), 1159–65.

Gampell, J. (1999) To save the turtles. *Readers Digest*, May, Asia Issue.

Garrison R.W. (1997) Sustainable nature tourism: California's regional approach. In *World Ecotour '97 Abstracts Volume* (pp. 180–2). Rio de Janiero, Brazil: BIOSFERA.

Garrod, B. and Fennell, D.A. (2004) An analysis of whalewatching codes of conduct. *Annals of Tourism Research* 31, 334–52.

GBRMPA (Great Barrier Reef Marine Park Authority) (1997) *Guidelines for Managing Visitation to Seabird Breeding Islands*. Townsville, Australia: Great Barrier Reef Marine Park Authority.

Gerard, P.D., Smith, D.R. and Weerakoddy, G. (1998) Limits of retrospective power analysis. *Journal of Wildlife Management* 62, 801–7.

Gilbert, F.F. and Dodds, D.G. (1992) *The Philosophy and Practice of Wildlife Management*. FL: Krieger Publishing Company.

Gill, A.J., Norris, K. and Sutherland, W.J. (2001) Why behavioural responses may not reflect the population consequences of human disturbance. *Biological Conservation* 97, 265–8.

Gilmore, D. and Fisher, R. (1992) *Villages, Forests and Foresters: The Philosophy, Process and Practice of Community Forestry in Nepal*. Kathmandu: Shayogi Press.

Goodall, J. (1990) *Through a Window: My Thirty Years with the Champanzees of Gombe*. Boston: Houghton Mifflin.

Goodwin, H., Kent, I., Parker, K. and Walpole, M. (1998) *Tourism, Conservation and Sustainable Development: Case Studies from Asia and Africa*. London: International Institute for Environment and Development.

Government of Western Australia (2003) *Hope for the Future: The Western Australian State Sustainability Strategy*. Perth: Department of Premier and Cabinet.

Grauman, C.F. and Kruse, L. (1990) The environment: Social construction and psychological problems. In H.T. Himmelweit and G. Gaskell (eds) *Societal Psychology* (pp. 212–29). London: Sage.

Green, R.H. (1979) *Sampling Design and Statistical Methods for Environmental Biologists*. New York: John Wiley & Sons.

Green, R.J. and Higginbottom, K. (2000) The effects of non-consumptive wildlife tourism on free-ranging wildlife: A review. *Pacific Conservation Biology* 6, 183–97.

Green, R. and Higginbottom, K. (2001) *The Negative Effects of Wildlife Tourism on Wildlife* (Wildlife Tourism Research Report Series No. 5). Gold Coast, Queensland: Cooperative Research Centre for Sustainable Tourism.

Green, R., Higginbottom, K. and Northrope, C. (2001) *A Tourism Classification of Australian Wildlife* (Wildlife Tourism Research Report Series No. 7). Gold Coast, Queensland: Cooperative Research Centre for Sustainable Tourism.

Greiner, R., Stoeckl, N. and Schweigert, R. (2004) Estimating community benefits from tourism: The case of Carpentaria Shire. Paper presented to the *48th Annual Conference of the Australian Agricultural and Resource Economics Society*, Melbourne, 11–13 February.

Griffin, D.R. (1992) *Animal Minds*. Chicago: University of Chicago Press.

Griffiths, M. and Van Schaik, C.P. (1993) The impact of human traffic on the abundance and activity periods of Sumatran rain forest wildlife. *Conservation Biology*, 7 (3), 623–6.

Guerrera, W., Sleeman, J.M., Jasper, S.B., Pace, L.B., Ichiose, T.Y. and Reif, J.S. (2003) Medical survey of the local human population to determine possible health risks to the mountain gorillas of Bwindi impenetrable forest national park, Uganda. *International Journal of Primatology* 24, 197–207.

Gunningham, N. and Sinclair, D. (1998) Designing environmental policy. In N. Gunningham, P. Grabosky and D. Sinclair (eds) *Smart Regulation: Designing Environmental Policy* (pp. 375–453). Oxford: Clarendon Press.

Hairston, Sr, N.G. (1989) *Ecological Experiments: Purpose, Design and Execution*. Cambridge: Cambridge University Press.

Hall, C.M. (2000a) *Tourism Planning: Policies, Processes and Relationships*. Harlow, England: Prentice-Hall.

Hall, C.M. (2000b) Rethinking collaboration and partnership: A public policy perspective. In B. Bramwell and B. Lane (eds) *Tourism Collaboration and Partnerships: Politics, Practice and Sustainability* (pp. 143–58). Clevedon: Channel View Publications.

Hall, C.M. (2003) Institutional arrangements for ecotourism policy. In D.A. Fennell and R.K. Dowling (eds) *Ecotourism Policy and Planning* (pp. 21–38). Wallingford, UK: CABI Publishing.

Hall, C.M. and Page, S.J. (1999) *The Geography of Tourism and Recreation: Environment, Place and Space*. London: Routledge.

Hammitt, W.E. and Cole, D.N. (1998) *Wildland Recreation: Ecology and Management*. New York: John Wiley & Sons.

Hammitt, W.E. and Symmonds, M.C. (2001) Wilderness. In D.B.Weaver (ed.) *The Encyclopedia of Ecotourism* (pp. 327–43). Wallingford: CABI Publishing.

Hanna, S. (1995) *Property Rights and the Environment: Social and Ecological Issues*. Washington, DC: The World Bank.

Harder, J.D. and Kirkpatrick, R.L. (1996) Physiological methods in wildlife research. In T.A. Bookhout (ed.) *Research and Management Techniques for Wildlife and Habitats* (pp. 275–306). Bethesda, MD: The Wildlife Society.

Hardin, G. (1968) The tragedy of the commons. *Science* 162, 1243–8.

Hartig, T. and Evans, G.W. (1993) Psychological foundations of nature experience. In T. Gärling and R.G. Golledge (eds) *Behavior and Environment: Psychological and Geographical Approaches*. New York: Elseview Science Publishers.

Hautaluoma, J.E. and Brown, P.J. (1979) Attributes of the deer hunting experience: A cluster analytic study. *Journal of Leisure Research* 10, 271–87.

Hejl, S.J., Verner, J. and Bell, G.W. (1990) Sequential versus initial observations in studies of avian foraging. In *Avian Foraging: Theory, Methodology and Applications*. Asilomar, California, Cooper Ornithological Society.

Hendee, J.C. and Schoenfeld, C. (1990) Wildlife in wilderness. In J.C. Hendee, G.H. Stankey and R.C. Lucas (eds) *Wilderness Management* (2nd edn) (revised) (pp. 215–39). Golden, CO: North American Press.

Higginbottom, K., Green, R. and Northrope, C. (2003) A framework for managing the negative impacts of wildlife tourism on wildlife. *Human Dimensions of Wildlife* 8, 1–24.

Higginbottom, K., Green, R.J., Leiper, N., Moscardo, G., Tribe, A. and Buckley, R. (2001a) *Evaluation of Organized Tourism involving Wild Kangaroos* (Wildlife Tourism Research Report Series No. 18). Gold Coast, Queensland: Cooperative Research Centre for Sustainable Tourism.

Higginbottom, K., Northrope, C. and Green, R.J. (2001b) *Positive Effects of Wildlife Tourism on Wildlife* (Wildlife Tourism Research Report Series No. 6). Gold Coast, Queensland: Cooperative Research Centre for Sustainable Tourism.

Higginbottom, K., Rann, K., Moscado, G., Davis, D. and Muloin, S. (2001c) *Status Assessment of Wildlife Tourism in Australia: An Overview.* (Wildlife Tourism Research Report Series No. 1). Gold Coast, Queensland, Cooperative Research Centre for Sustainable Tourism.

Higham, J.E.S. (1998) Tourists and albatrosses: The dynamics of tourism at the Northern Royal Albatross Colony, Taiaroa Head, New Zealand. *Tourism Management* 19 (6), 521–31.

Higham, J.E.S. (2001) Managing ecotourism at Taiaroa Head albatross colony. In M. Shackley (ed.) *Flagship Species: Case Studies in Wildlife Tourism Management* (pp. 17–31). Burlington, VT: The International Ecotourism Society.

Higham, J. and Luck, M. (2002) Ecotourism: A contradiction in terms? *Journal of Ecotourism* 1 (1), 36–51.

Hill, M. (1997) *The Policy Process in the Modern State*. London: Prentice-Hall, Harvester Wheatsheaf.

Hjalager, A.M. (1996) Tourism and the environment: The innovation connection. *Journal of Sustainable Tourism* 4 (4), 201–17.

Hobbs, R. (1998) Ecologists in public. In R. Wills and R. Hobbs (eds) *Ecology for Everyone* (pp. 20–5). Chipping Norton, New South Wales: Surrey Beatty & Sons.

Hodge, A. (2002) Ecotourist trap: Don't feed the animals. *The Weekend Australian Magazine*, November 16–17: 38–42.

Hoelscher, S. (1998) The photographic construction of tourist space in Victorian America. *Geographical Review* 88 (4), 548–71.

Hogan, L., Metzger, D. and Peterson, B. (1998) *Intimate Nature: The Bond between Women and Animals*. New York: The Ballantine Publishing Group.

Holden, A. (2000) *Environment and Tourism*. London: Routledge.

Holland, S., Ditton, R. and Graefe, A. (1998) An ecotourism perspective on billfish fisheries. *Journal of Sustainable Tourism* 6 (2), 97–116.

Holland, S., Ditton, R. and Graefe, A. (2000) A response to 'Ecotourism on trial: The case of billfish angling as ecotourism'. *Journal of Sustainable Tourism* 8 (4), 346–51.

Holling, C.S. (1978) *Adaptive Environmental Assessment and Management*. Chichester: John Wiley & Sons.

Hollis, T. and Bedding J. (1994) Can we stop the wetlands from drying up? *New Scientist* 143, 30–3.

Honey, M. (1999) *Ecotourism and Sustainable Development: Who Owns Paradise?* Washington DC: Island Press.

Horwich, R.H., Murray, D., Saqui, E., Lyon, J. and Godrey, D. (1993) Ecotourism and community development: A view from Belize. In K. Lindberg and D.E. Hawkins (eds) *Ecotourism: A Guide for Planners and Managers* (pp. 52–168). North Benninton, VT: The Ecotourism Society.

Horwitz, P. and Calver, M. (1998) Credible science? Evaluating the regional forest agreement process in Western Australia. *Australian Journal of Environmental Management* 5, 213–25.

Hosier, P.E., Kochhar, M. and Thayer, V. (1981) Off-road vehicle and pedestrian track effects on the sea-approach of hatchling loggerhead turtles. *Environmental Conservation* 8, 158–61.

Howard, J., Lipscombe, N. and Poter, A. (2001) The tourist, the dingo, and interpretation on Fraser Island, Queensland. Paper presented at the *IAA Conference*. Albury: Charles Sturt University, Albury.

Howlett, M. and Ramesh, M. (1995) *Studying Public Policy: Policy Cycles and Policy Subsystems*. Ontario: Oxford University Press.

Hoyt, E. (1996) Whale watching: A global overview of the industries rapid growth and some implications and suggestions for Australia. In K. Colgan, S. Prasser and A. Jeffery (eds) *Encounters with Whales: 1995 Proceedings*. Canberra: Australian Nature Conservation Agency.

Hoyt, E. (2000) *Whale-watching 2000: Worldwide Tourism Numbers, Expenditures, and Expanding Socioeconomic Benefits*. Crowborough: International Fund for Animal Welfare.

Hughes, M. (pers comm, 2004) Research Officer, Tourism Programme, Murdoch University, Perth, Western Australia.

Hughes, M., Newsome, D. and MacBeth, J. (in press) Case study: Visitor perceptions of captive wildlife tourism in a Western Australian natural setting. *Journal of Ecotourism*.

Hughes, P. (2001) Animals, values and tourism: Structural shifts in UK dolphin tourism provision. *Tourism Management* 22, 321–9.

Huijser, M.P. and Bergers, P.J.M. (2000) The effect of roads and traffic on hedgehog (*Erinaceus europaeus*) populations. *Biological Conservation* 95, 11–116.

Hunter, M.L. (1990) *Wildlife, Forests and Forestry: Principles of Managing Forests for Biological Diversity*. NJ: Prentice-Hall, Englewood Cliffs.

Hurlbert, S.H. (1984) Pseudoreplication and the design of ecological field experiments. *Ecological Monographs* 54, 187–211.

IIWDT (Hebridean Whale and Dolphin Trust) (2003) HWDT Wins Major Tourism Award. Online document: http://whales.gn.apc.org/news_awards.html (accessed 2 December 2003).

IAATO (International Association of Antarctic Tourism Operators) (2003a) *Guidance for Those Organising and Conducting Tourism and Non-governmental Activities in the Antarctic*. Online document: http://www.iaato.org/tourop_guide.html (accessed 4 December 2003).

IAATO (International Association of Antarctic Tourism Operators) (2003b) *Guidance for Visitors to the Antarctic*. Online document: http://www.iaato.org/visitor_guide.html (accessed 4 December 2003).

Ikuta, L.A. and Blumstein, D.T. (2003) Do fences protect birds from human disturbance? *Biological Conservation* 112, 447–52.

Ittelson, W.H., Proshansky, H.M., Rivlin, L.G. and Winkel, G.H. (1974) *An Introduction to Environmental Psychology*. New York: Holt, Rinehart and Winston.

IUCN (International Union for the Conservation of Nature) (1980) *World Conservation Strategy: Living Resource Conservation for Sustainable Development*. Gland, Switzerland: International Union for Conservation of Nature and Natural Resources, United Nations Environment Programme and the World Wildlife Fund.

Jacobson, S.K. and Lopez, A.F. (1994) Biological impacts of ecotourism: Tourists and nesting turtles in Tortuguero National Park, Costa Rica. *Wildlife Society Bulletin* 22 (3), 414–9.

Jafari, J. (ed.) (2000) *Encyclopedia of Tourism*. London: Routledge.

Jarman, P.J. and Brock, M.A. (1996) Collaboration of science and management in endangered species recovery. In S. Stephens and S. Maxwell (eds) *Back from the Brink: Refining the Threatened Species Recovery Process* (pp. 74–8). Chipping Norton, NSW: Surrey Beatty & Sons.

Jewell, S.D. (2000) Multi-species recovery plans. *Endangered Species Bulletin* 25 (3), 30–1.

Jim, C.Y. (1989) Visitor management in recreation areas. *Environmental Conservation* 16 (1), 19–32 + 40.

Johns, B.G. (1996) Responses of chimpanzees to habituation and tourism in the Kibale Forest, Uganda. *Biological Conservation* 78, 257–62.

Johnson, D.H. (1996) Population analysis. In T.A. Bookhout (ed.) *Research and Management Techniques for Wildlife and Habitats*. Bethesda, MD: The Wildlife Society.

Johnson, D.H., Haseltine, S.D. and Cowardin, L.M. (1994) Wildlife habitat management on the northern prairie landscape. *Landscape and Urban Planning* 28, 5–21.

Johnson, S.A., Bjorndal, K.A. and Bolten, A.B. (1996) Effects of organized turtle watches on loggerhead (*Caretta caretta*) nesting behavior and hatchling production in Florida. *Conservation Biology* 10 (2), 570–7.

Johnstone Strait Killer Whale Interpretive Society (2004) Online document: http://www.Killerwhalecentre.org/home/contact_society.html (accessed 5 March 2004).

Jones Lang Wootton (1993) *North West Cape Tourism Development Study*. Perth, Western Australia: Jones Lang Wootton.

Jones, D.N. and Buckley, R.C. (2001) *Birdwatching Tourism in Australia* (Wildlife Tourism Research Report Series No. 10). Gold Coast, Queensland: Cooperative Research Centre for Sustainable Tourism.

Jones, M.E. (2000) Road upgrade, road mortality and remedial measures: Impacts on a population of eastern quolls and Tasmanian devils. *Wildlife Research* 27, 289–96.

Kahlenborn, W. and Domine, A. (2001) The future belongs to international ecolabelling schemes. In X. Font and R.C. Buckley (eds) *Tourism Ecolabelling: Certification and Promotion of Sustainable Management* (pp. 247–58). Wallingford, UK: CABI Publishing.

Kahn, P.H. (1997) Developmental psychology and the biophilia hypothesis: Children's affiliation with nature. *Developmental Review* 17, 1–61.

Kahn, P.H. (1999) *The Human Relationship with Nature: Development and Culture*. Cambridge: The MIT Press.

Kamal, K.B., Boug, A. and Brain, P.F. (1997) Effects of food provisioning on the behaviour of commensal Hamadryas, baboons, *Papio hamadryas*, at Al Hada Mountain in western Saudi Arabia. *Zoology in the Middle East* 14, 11–22.

Kaplan, R. and Kaplan, S. (1989) *The Experience of Nature: A Psychological Perspective*. New York: Cambridge University Press.

Katcher, A. and Wilkins, G. (1993) Dialogue with animals: Its nature and culture. In S.R. Kellert and E.O. Wilson (eds) *The Biophilia Hypothesis* (pp. 173–200). Washington, DC: Island Press.

Keller, V. (1989) Variations in response of great crested grebe *Podiceps cristatus* to human disturbance – a sign of adaptation? *Biological Conservation* 49, 31–45.

Kellert, S.R. (1993) The biological basis for human values of nature. In S.R. Kellert and E.O. Wilson (eds) *The Biophilia Hypothesis* (pp. 42–72). Washington, DC: Island Press.

Kellert, S.R. (1996) *The Value of Life: Biological Diversity and Human Society*. Washington, DC: Island Press.

Kellert, S.R. and Wilson, E.O. (eds) (1993) *The Biophilia Hypothesis*. Washington, DC: Island Press.

Kerley, L.L., Goodrich, J.M., Miquelle, D.G., Smirnov, E.N., Quickley, H.B. and Hornocker, N.G. (2002) Effects of roads and human disturbance on amur tigers. *Conservation Biology* 16, 97–108.

King, J.M. and Heinen, J.T. (2004) An assessment of the behaviors of overwintering manatees as influenced by interactions with tourists at two sites in central Florida. *Biological Conservation* 117 (3), 227–34.

Kinnaird, M.F. and O'Brien, T.G. (1996) Ecotourism in the Tangkoko Duasudara Nature Reserve: Opening Pandora's Box? *Oryx* 30 (1), 65–73.

Kirkwood, R., Boren, L., Shaughnessy, P., Szteren, D., Mawson, P., Huckstadt, L., Hofmeyr, G., Oosthuizen, H., Schiavini, A., Campagna, C. and Berris, M. (2003) Pinniped-focussed tourism in the Southern Hemisphere: A review of the industry. In N. Gales, M. Hindell and R. Kirkwood (eds) *Marine Mammals*. Collingwood, Australia: CSIRO Publishing.

Klein, M.L. (1993) Waterbird behavioural responses to human disturbances. *Wildlife Society Bulletin* 21, 31–9.

Klein, M.L., Humphrey, S.R. and Percival, H.F. (1995) Effects of ecotourism on distribution of waterbirds in a wildlife refuge. *Conservation Biology* 9 (6), 1454–65.

Knight, R.L. and Cole, D.N. (1995) Factors that influence wildlife responses to recreationists. In R.L. Knight and K.J. Gutzwiller (eds) *Wildlife and Recreationists: Coexistence through Management and Research* (pp. 71–9). Washington, DC: Island Press.

Knight, R.L. and Gutzwiller, K.J. (1995) *Wildlife and Recreationists: Coexistence through Management and Research*. Washington, DC: Island Press.

Knight, R., Mattson, D., Blanchard, B. and Eberhardt, L. (1988) Mortality patterns and population sinks for Yellowstone grizzly bears, *Wildlife Society Bulletin* 16, 121–5.

Knopf, R. (1987) Human behavior, cognition, and affect in the natural environment. In D. Stokols and I. Altman (eds) *Handbook of Environmental Psychology* Vol. 2. (pp. 783–826). New York: John Wiley & Sons.

Knowlton, F.F. (1995) Radio telemetry as a wildlife research tool. In S.H. Berwick and V.B. Saharia (eds) *The Development of International Principles and Practices of Wildlife Research and Management: Asian and American Approaches* (pp. 81–106). Oxford: Oxford University Press.

Kraft, M.E. and Vig, N.J. (1997) *Environmental Policy in the 1990s*. Washington, DC: CQ Press.

Krebs, C.J. (1988) The experimental approach to rodent population dynamics. *Oikos* 52, 143–9.

Krebs, C.J. (1999) *Ecological Methodology*. Menlo Park, California: Addison-Wesley Longman,

Krebs, J.R. and Davies, N.B. (eds) (1977) *Behavioural Ecology: An Evolutionary Approach*. Cambridge, MA. Blackwell Science.

Kruger, F.J., van Wilgen, B.W., Weaver, A.v.B. and Greyling, T. (1997) Sustainable development and the environment: Lessons from the St Lucia environmental impact assessment. *South African Journal of Science* 93, 23–33.

Kuhn, T.S. (1970) *The Structure of Scientific Revolutions*. University of Chicago Press.

Kutay, K. (1993) Brave new role: Ecotour operators take centre stage in the era of green travel. In *Going Green: The Ecotourism Research for Travel Agents*. Supplement to *Tour & Travel News*. October 25: 80.

Lancia, R.A., Nichols, J.D. and Pollock, K.H. (1996) Estimating the number of animals in wildlife populations. In T.A. Bookhout (ed.) *Research and Management Techniques for Wildlife and Habitats* (pp. 215–53). Bethesda, MD: The Wildlife Society.

Lanjouw, A. (2001) Against the odds. *New Scientist* 2303, 42–5.

Lanjouw, A. (2002) Mountain gorillas: A challenge for modern conservation. *Fauna and Flora* April, 7–12.

Lawrance, K. and Higginbottom, K. (2002) *Behavioural Responses of Dingoes to Tourists on Fraser Island* (Wildlife Tourism Research Report Series No. 27). Goldcoast, Queensland: Cooperative Research Centre for Sustainable Tourism.

Lazarus, R.S. (1991) *Emotion and Adaptation*. New York: Oxford University Press.

Lee, K.N (1999) Appraising adaptive management. *Conservation Ecology* 3 (2), 3.

Lehner, P.N. (1996) *Handbook of Ethological Methods*. Cambridge: Cambridge University Press.

Lewis, A.R. (1997) Effects of experimental coral disturbance on the structure of fish communities on large patch reefs. *Marine Ecology Progress Series* 161, 37–50.

Lewis, A.R. (1998) Effects of experimental coral disturbance on the population dynamics of fishes on large patch reefs. *Journal of Experimental Marine Biology and Ecology* 230, 91–110.

Lewis, A. and Newsome, D. (2003) Planning for stingray tourism at Hamelin Bay, Western Australia: The importance of stakeholder perspectives. *International Journal of Tourism Research* 5, 331–46.

Liddle, M. (1997) *Recreation Ecology: The Ecological Impact of Outdoor Recreation and Ecotourism*. London, UK. Chapman & Hall.

Lilieholm, R. J. and Romney, L.R. (2000) Tourism, national parks and wildlife. In R.W. Butler and S.W. Boyd (eds) *Tourism and National Parks: Issues and Implications* (pp. 137–51). Chichester: John Wiley & Sons Ltd.

Lima, S.L. (1994) On the personal benefits of anti-predatory vigilance. *Animal Behaviour* 48, 734–6.

Lindenmayer, D.B. and Franklin, J.F. (2002) *Conserving Forest Biodiversity: A Comprehensive Multiscaled Approach*. Island Press, Washington, USA.

Lindsay, A.R., Gillum, S.S. and Meyer, M.W. (2002) Influence of lakeshore development on breeding bird communities in a mixed northern forest. *Biological Conservation* 107, 1–11.

Litchfield, C. (2001) Responsible tourism with great apes in Uganda. In S.F. McCool and R.N. Moisey (eds) *Tourism, Recreation and Sustainability*. Oxford, UK: CABI Publishing.

Litvaitus, J.A., Titus, K. and Anderson, E.M. (1996) Measuring vertebrate use of terrestrial habitats and foods. In T.A. Bookhout (ed.) *Research and Management Techniques for Wildlife and Habitats* (pp. 54–74). Bethesda, MDThe Wildlife Society.

Luck, M. (2003) Education on marine mammal tours as agent for conservation – But do tourists want to be educated? *Ocean and Coastal Management* 46, 943–56.

Lutkebohle, T. (1995) Dolphin movements and behaviour in the Kessock Channel and how these are influenced by boat traffic. *Scottish Natural Heritage*, December 1995.

MacLellan, L.R. (1999) An examination of wildlife tourism as a sustainable form of tourism development in North West Scotland. *International Journal of Tourism Research* 1 (5), 375–87.

Mallick, S.A. and Driessen, M.M. (2003) Feeding of wildlife: How effective are the 'Keep Wildlife Wild' signs in Tasmania's National Parks? *Ecological Management and Restoration* 4, 199–204.

Malmer, N. (1990) The new editor-in-chief gets the floor. *Oikos* 57, 3–5.

Manfredo, M.J. (1989) Human dimensions of wildlife management. *Wildlife Society Bulletin* 17 (4), 447–9.

Manfredo, M.J. (ed.) (2002) *Wildlife Viewing in North America: A Management Planning Handbook*. Corvallis, Oregon: Oregon State University Press.

Mann, J. and Kemps, C. (2003) The effects of provisioning on maternal care in wild bottlenose dolphins, Shark Bay, Australia. In N. Gales, M. Hindell and R. Kirkwood (eds) *Marine Mammals*. Collingwood, Australia: CSIRO Publishing.

Mason, P. (2000) Zoo tourism: The need for more research. *Journal of Sustainable Tourism* 8, 333–9.

Mason, P. (2003) *Tourism Impacts, Planning and Management*. Oxford: Butterworth-Heinemann.

Mason, P.A. and Legg, S.J. (1999) Antarctic tourism: Activities, impacts, management issues, and a proposed research agenda. *Pacific Tourism Review* 3, 71–84.

Mason, P., Johnston, M. and Twynam, D. (2000) The World Wide Fund for Nature Arctic Tourism project. *Journal of Sustainable Tourism* 8 (4), 305–23.

McCarthy, J. (forthcoming) *The Fourth Circle: A Political Ecology of Sumatra's Rainforest Frontier*. Stanford, USA: Stanford University Press.

McLain, R.J. and Lee, R.G. (1996) Adaptive management: promises and pitfalls. *Environmental Management* 20 (4), 437–48.

McLaren, D. (1998) *Rethinking Tourism and Ecotravel: The Paving of Paradise and What You Can Do to Stop It*. CT: Kumarian Press.

McNeilage, A., Plumptre, A.J., Brock-Doyle, A. and Vedder, A. (1997) Bwindi Impenetrable National Park, Uganda: Gorilla Census 1997. *Oryx* 35, 39–47.

Mead, R.J. (1990) *The Design of Experiments: Statistical Principles for Practical Application*. Cambridge: Cambridge University Press.

Meddis, R. (1984) *Statistics Using Ranks: A Unified Approach*. Oxford: Basil Blackwell.

Medeiros de Araujo, L. and Bramwell, B. (2000) Stakeholder assessment and collaborative tourism planning: The case of Brazil's Costa Dourada project. In B. Bramwell and B. Lane (eds) *Tourism Collaboration and Partnerships: Politics, Practice and Sustainability* (pp. 272–94). Clevedon: Channel View Publications.

Medio, D., Ormond, R.F.G. and Pearson, M. (1997) Effect of briefings on rates of damage to corals by SCUBA divers. *Biological Conservation* 79, 91–5.

Medlik, S. (2003) *Dictionary of Travel, Tourism and Hospitality* (3rd edn). Oxford: Butterworth Heinemann.

Meffe, G.K. and Carroll, R.C. (eds) (1997) *Principles of Conservation Biology*. New York: Sinauer Associates.

Merritt, D.J. and Baker, C. (2001) *A Biological Basis for Management of Glow-Worm Populations of Ecotourism Significance* (pp. 1–61). Gold Coast, Queensland: CRC for Sustainable Tourism.

Merton, R.K. (1973) *The Sociology of Science: Theoretical and Empirical Investigations*. Chicago: The University of Chicago Press.

Mignucci-Giannoni, A.A., Montoya-Ospina, R.A., Jiménez-Marrero, N.M., Rodriguez-López, M.A., Williams Jr, E.H. and Bonde, R.K. (2000) Manatee mortality in Puerto Rico. *Environmental Management* 25 (2), 189–98.

Mihalic, T. (2003) Economic instruments of environmental tourism policy derived from environmental theories. In D.A. Fennell and R.K. Dowling (eds) *Ecotourism Policy and Planning* (pp. 99–120). Wallingford, UK: CABI Publishing.

Mikola, J., Miettinen, M., Lehikoinen, E. and Lehtilä, K. (1994) The effects of disturbance caused by boating on survival and behaviour of velvet scoter *Melanitta fusca* ducklings. *Biological Conservation* 67, 119–24.

Miller Jr, G.T. (2004) *Living in the Environment – Principles, Connections, and Solutions* (13th edn). CA: Thomson Brooks/Cole.

Milliken, G.A. and Johnson, D.E. (1989) *Analysis of Messy Data: Vol. 2 Non-replicated Experiments*. London: Van Nostrand Reinhold (International).

Milliken, G.A. and Johnson, D.E. (1992) *Analysis of Messy Data: Vol. 1: Designed Experiments*. New York: Chapman & Hall.

Milliken, G.A. and Johnson, D.E. (2001) *Analysis of Messy Data. Vol. 3: Analysis of Covariance*. Boca Raton: Chapman & Hall.

Moore, S.A. (2001) Social and economic influences on restructuring rural landscapes for biodiversity conservation: Remnant vegetation in the West Australian wheatbelt as a case study. Paper presented at the *Restructuring Rural Landscapes in the WA Wheatbelt and Austria Workshop, CSIRO Floreat, WA, 22–23 February 2001*. School of Environmental Science, Murdoch University and Ministry of Environment, Austria.

Moore S.A. and Wooller, S. (2003) Review of landscape, multi- and single species recovery planning for threatened species (unpublished report prepared for WWF Australia, August 2003). Perth, Western Australia: School of Environmental Science, Murdoch University.

Moore, S.A., Smith, A.J. and Newsome, D. (2003) Environmental performance reporting for natural area tourism: Contributions by visitor impact management frameworks and their indicators. *Journal of Sustainable Tourism* 11, 348–75.

Morrison, A., Hsieh, S. and Wang, C.Y. (1992) Certification in the travel and tourism industry: The North American experience. *The Journal of Tourism Studies* 3 (2), 32–40.

Morrison, M.L. (1984) Influence of sample size and sampling design on avian foraging behaviour. *Condor* 86, 146–50.

Morrison, M.L., Ralph, C.J., Verner, J. and Jehl Jr, J.R. (eds) (1990) *Avian Foraging: Theory, Methodology and Applications.* Asilomar, CA: Cooper Ornithological Society.

Moscardo, G. and Woods, B. (1998) Managing tourism in the Wet Tropics World Heritage Area: Interpretation and the experience of visitors on Skyrail. In E. Laws, B. Faulkner and G. Moscardo (eds) *Embracing and Managing Change in Tourism: International Case Studies* (pp. 285–306). London: Routledge.

Moscardo, G., Woods, B. and Greenwood, T. (2001) *Understanding Visitor Perspectives on Wildlife Tourism.* Gold Coast, Queensland: CRC for Sustainable Tourism.

Muir, F. and Chester, G. (1993) Case study: Managing tourism of a seabird nesting island. *Tourism Management* April, 99–105.

Mulkay, M.J. (1991) *Sociology of Science: A Sociological Pilgrimage.* Milton Keynes: Open University Press.

Mullner, A., Linsenmair, K.E. and Wikelski, M. (in press) Exposure to ecotourism reduces survival and affects stress response in hoatzin chicks (*Opisthocomus hoazin*). *Biological Conservation.*

Murphy, D.D. and Noon, B.D. (1991) Coping with uncertainty in wildlife biology. *Journal of Wildlife Management* 55, 773–82.

Mvula, C.D. (2001) Fair trade in tourism to protected areas: A micro case study of wildlife tourism to South Luangwa National Park, Zambia. *International Journal of Tourism Research* 3, 393–405.

Myers, N., Mittermeier, R.A., Mittermeier, C.G., da Fonesca, G.A.B. and Kent, J. (2000) Biodiversity hotspots for conservation priorities. *Nature* 403, 853–8.

Nash, R.F. (1990) *The Rights of Nature: A History of Environmental Ethics.* Leichardt, NSW: Primavera Press.

Nature Based Tourism Strategy (1997) *Nature Based Tourism Strategy for Western Australia.* Perth, WA: Nature Based Tourism Advisory Committee of the Western Australian Tourism Commission.

Needham, J. (1969) *The Grand Titration: Science and Society in East and West.* Toronto: Allen & Unwin.

Nellemann, C., Jordhoy, P., Stoen, O.G. and Strand, O. (2000) Cumulative impacts of tourist resorts on wild reindeer (*Rangifer tarandus tarandus*) during winter. *Arctic* 53 (1), 9–17.

Nelson, D.R., Johnson, R.R., McKibben, J.N. and Pittenger, G.G. (1986) Antagonistic attacks on divers and submersibles by grey reef sharks (*Carcharhinus amblyrhynchos*): antipredatory or competitive? *Bulletin of Marine Science* 38 (1), 68–88.

Nepal (2000) Tourism, national parks and local communities. In R.W. Butler and S.W. Boyd (eds) *Tourism and National Parks: Issues and Implications.* (pp. 73–94). Chichester, England: John Wiley & Sons Ltd.

Neuman, W.L. (2000) *Social Research Methods: Qualitative and Quantitative Approaches*. Boston: Allyn & Bacon.

Newsome, D.N. (2000) Spotlighting excursion, Punda Maria Rest Camp, Kruger National Park.

Newsome, D., Moore, S.A. and Dowling, R.K. (2002) *Natural Area Tourism: Ecology, Impacts and Management*. Clevedon, England: Channel View Publications.

Newsome, D., Lewis, A. and Moncrieff, D. (2004) Impacts and risks associated with developing, but unsupervised, stingray tourism at Hamelin Bay, Western Australia. *International Journal of Tourism Research* 6 (5), 305–23.

Ng, S., Dole, J., Sauvajot, R., Riley, S. and Valone, T. (2004) Use of highway undercrossings by wildlife in southern California. *Biological Conservation* 115, 499–507.

NHMRC (National Health and Medical Research Council) (1997) *Australian Code of Practice for the Care and Use of Animals for Scientific Purposes*. Canberra: Australian Government Publishing Service.

Nianyong, H. and Zhuge, R. (2001) Ecotourism in China's Nature Reserves: Opportunities and challenges. *Journal of Sustainable Tourism* 9 (3), 228–42.

Nielsen, C. (2003) *Tourism and the Media: Tourist Decision-Making, Information, and Communication*. Melbourne: Hospitality Press.

Nietfeld, M.T., Barrett, M.W. and Silvy, N. (1996) Wildlife marking techniques. In T.A. Bookhout (ed.) *Research and Management Techniques for Wildlife and Habitats* (pp. 140–68). Bethesda, MD: The Wildlife Society.

Nisbet, I.C.T. (2000) Disturbance, habituation and the management of waterbird colonies. *Waterbirds* 23, 312–32.

Norton, T.W. and May, S.A. (1994) Towards sustainable forestry in Australian temperate eucalypt forests: Ecological impacts and priorities for conservation, research and management. In T.W. Norton and S.R. Dovers *Ecology and Sustainability of Southern Temperate Ecosystems* (pp. 10–30). Collingwood, Australia: CSIRO Publishing.

Noss, R.F. (1993) Sustainable forestry or sustainable forests? In G.H. Aplet, N. Johnson, J.T. Olson and V.A. Sample (eds) *Defining Sustainable Forestry* (pp. 17–43). Washington, DC: Island Press.

OECD (Organisation for Economic Co-Operation and Development) (2003) *Voluntary Approaches for Environmental Policy: Effectiveness, Efficiency and Usage in Policy Mixes*. Paris: Organisation for Economic Co-Operation and Development.

Olindo, P. (1991) The old man of nature tourism in Kenya. In T. Whelan (ed.) *Nature Tourism: Managing for the Environment* (pp. 23–38). Washington, DC: Island Press.

Olliff, T., Legg, K. and Keading, B. (1999) *Effects of Winter Recreation on Wildlife of the Greater Yellowstone Area: A Literature Review and Assessment* (Report to the Greater Yellowstone Coordinating Committee). Wyoming: Yellowstone National Park.

Orams, M.B. (1996) A conceptual model of tourist-wildlife interaction: The case for education as a management strategy. *Australian Geographer* 27 (1), 39–51.

Orams, M. (1999) *Marine Tourism: Development, Impacts and Management*. London: Routledge.

Orams, M.B. (2000a) *The Economic Benefits of Whale-Watching in Vava'u, The Kingdom of Tonga*. Albany, New Zealand: Centre for Tourism Research, Massey University at Albany.

Orams, M.B. (2000b) Tourists getting close to whales: Is it what whale-watching is all about? *Tourism Managment* 21, 561–9.

Orams, M.B. (2001) From whale hunting to whale watching in Tonga: A sustainable future? *Journal of Sustainable Tourism* 9 (2), 128–47.

Orams, M.B. (2002) Feeding wildlife as a tourism attraction: A review of issues and impacts. *Tourism Management* 23, 281–93.

Orams, M.B., Hill, G.J.E. and Baglioni Jr, A.J. (1996) 'Pushy' behavior in a wild dolphin feeding program at Tangalooma, Australia. *Marine Mammal Science* 12, 107–17.

Orsini, J-P. (2004) Human impacts on Australian sealions (*Neophoca cinera*) hauled out on Carnac Island (Perth, Western Australia): Implications for wildlife and tourism management. Unpublished MSc thesis, Murdoch University, Western Australia.

Ostrom, E., Burger, J., Field, C.B., Norgaard, R.B., Policansky, D. (1999) Revisiting the commons: Local lessons, global challenges. *Science* 284, 278–82.

Page, S.J. and Dowling, R.K. (2002) *Ecotourism*. Harlow: Pearson Education.

Parsons, B.C., Short, J.C. and Calver, M.C. (2002) Evidence for male-biased dispersal in a reintroduced population of burrowing bettongs *Bettongia lesueur* at Heirisson Prong, Western Australia. *Australian Mammalogy* 24, 219–24.

Parsons, R. (1991) The potential influences of environmental perception on human health. *Journal of Environmental Psychology* 11, 1–23.

PATA (Pacific Asia Tourism Association) (1991) *PATA Code for Environmentally Responsible Tourism: An Environmental Ethic for the Travel and Tourism Industry*. San Francisco: Pacific Asia Tourism Association.

PATA (Pacific Asia Tourism Association) (2004) What is PATA? Pacific Asia Travel Association: On-line document: http://www.pata.org/frame.cfm?pageid=8 (accessed 25 January 2004).

Patterson, M.E. and Williams, D.R. (1998) Paradigms and problems: The practice of social science in natural resource management. *Society and Natural Resources* 11, 279–95.

Paton, D.C., Dorward, D.F. and Fell, P. (1983) Thiamine deficiency and winter mortality in Red Wattlebirds, *Anthochaera carunculata* (Aves: Meliphagidae) in suburban Melbourne. *Australian Journal of Zoology* 31, 147–54.

Perrine, D. (1989) Reef fish feeding; amusement or nuisance? *Sea Frontiers* 35 (5), 272–9.

Peterman, R.M. (1990) Statistical power analysis can improve fisheries research and management. *Canadian Journal of Fisheries and Aquatic Science* 47, 2–15.

Peterson, D. and Goodall, J. (1993) *Visions of Caliban: On chimpanzees and people*. Boston: Houghton Mifflin.

Pinkola Estés, C. (1992) *Women who Run with the Wolves*. London: Random House Group Ltd.

Plous, S. (1993a) The role of animals in human society. *Journal of Social Issues* 49 (1), 1–9.

Plous, S. (1993b) Psychological mechanisms in the human use of animals. *Journal of Social Issues* 49 (1), 11–52.

Pratkanis, A.R., Breckler, S.J. and Greenwald, A.G. (eds) (1989) *Attitude Structure and Function*. Hillsdale, NJ: Lawrence Erlbaum Associates.

Primack, R.B. (1998) *Essentials of Conservation Biology*. Sunderland, MA: Sinauer Associates.

Pugsley, C.W. (1984) Ecology of the New Zealand glow-worm, *Arachnocamp luminosa diptera*: Keroplatidae, in the glow-worm cave, Waitomo. *Journal of the Royal Society of New Zealand* 14, 387–407.

Putman, R.J. (1996) Ethical considerations and animal welfare in ecological field studies. In N.S. Cooper and R.C.J. Carling (eds) *Ecologists and Ethical Judgements* (pp. 123–36). London: Chapman & Hall.

Quenette, P.Y. (1990) Functions of vigilance behaviour in mammals: A review. *Acta Oecologica* 11, 801–18.

Rapoport, R.W. (1993) Environmental values and the search for a global ethic. *Journal of Environmental Psychology* 13, 173–82.

Rasmussen, P.W., Heissey, D.M., Nordheim, E.V. and Frost, T.M. (2001) Time-series intervention analysis: Unreplicated large-scale experiments. In S.M. Scheiner and J. Gurevitch (eds) *Design and Analysis of Ecological Experiments* (pp. 158–77). Oxford: Oxford University Press.

Ratti, J.T. and Garton, E.O. (1996) Research and experimental design. In T.A. Bookhout (ed.) *Research and Management Techniques for Wildlife and Habitats* (pp. 1–23). Bethesda, Maryland: The Wildlife Society.

Raven, P.H. and Johnson, G.B. (1991) *Understanding Biology*. St Louis: Mosby Year Book Inc.

Recher, H.F. (1992) Simple journalists or simple scientists? Are environmental issues too complex for the media? *Australian Zoologist* 28, 19–23.

Recher, H.F. (1998) Public and political: The challenge for ecologists. In R. Wills and R. Hobbs (eds) *Ecology for Everyone* (pp. 9–15). Chipping Norton, NSW: Surrey Beatty & Sons.

Recher, H.F. and Glebski, V. (1990) Analysis of the foraging ecology of eucalypt forest birds: Sequential versus single-point observations. *Avian Foraging: Theory, Methodology and Applications*. Asilomar, CA: Cooper Ornithological Society.

Recher, H.F., Gowing, G. and Armstrong, T. (1985) Causes and frequency of deaths among birds mist-netted for breeding studies at two localities. *Australian Wildlife Research* 12, 321-6.

Reed, M.G. (2000) Collaborative tourism planning as adaptive experiments in emergent tourism settings. In B. Bramwell and B. Lane (eds) *Tourism Collaboration and Partnerships: Politics, Practice and Sustainability* (pp. 247–71). Clevedon: Channel View Publications.

Regal, J. and Putz, K. (1997) Effect of human disturbance on body temperature and energy expenditure in penguins. *Polar Biology* 18(4), 246–53.

Reser, J. and Bentrupperbäumer, J. (2000) Unpackaging the nature and management implications of 'environmental concern'. Paper presented at the International Symposium on Society and Resource Management, Western Washington University, Bellingham, Washington, USA (17–22 June). Book of Abstracts (p. 259).

Reser, J.P. and Scherl, L.M. (1988) Clear and unambiguous feedback: A transactional and motivational analysis of environmental challenge and self encounter. *Journal of Environmental Psychology* 8, 269–86.

Reynolds, P.C. and Braithwaite, R.W. (2001) Towards a conceptual framework for wildlife tourism. *Tourism Management* 22, 31–42.

Rice, N. (1996) A precautionary approach to whale watching is needed. *African Wildlife* 50 (6), 22.

Richards, G. and Hall, D. (2000) *Tourism and Sustainable Community Development*. London: Routledge.

Richards, S. (1983) *Philosophy and Sociology of Science*. Oxford, England: Basil Blackwell.

Ritchie, J.R.B. (2000) Interest based formulation of tourism policy for environmentally sensitive destinations. In B. Bramwell and B. Lane (eds) *Tourism Collaboration and Partnerships: Politics, Practice and Sustainability* (pp. 44–77). Clevedon: Channel View Publications.

Rivera J. (2002) Assessing a voluntary environmental initiative in the developing world: The Costa Rica certification for sustainable tourism. *Policy Sciences* 35, 333–60

Rodger, K. and Moore, S.A. (2004) Bringing science to wildlife tourism: The influence of managers' and scientists' perceptions. *Journal of Ecotourism* 3 (1), 1–19.

Rodgers, J.A. and Smith, H.T. (1995) Set-back distances to protect nesting bird colonies from human disturbance in Florida. *Conservation Biology* 9 (1), 89–99.

Rodgers, J.A. and Smith, H.T. (1997) Buffer zone distances to protect foraging and loafing waterbirds from human disturbance in Florida. *Wildlife Society Bulletin* 25 (1), 139–45.

Roe, D., Leader-Williams, N. and Dalal-Clayton, D. (1997) *Take Only Photographs, Leave Only Footprints: The Environmental Impacts of Wildlife Tourism*. London: Environmental Planning Group, International Institute for Environment and Development.

Roffe, T.J., Friend, M. and Locke, L.N. (1996) Evaluation of causes of wildlife mortality. In T.A. Bookhout (ed.) *Research and Management Techniques for Wildlife and Habitats* (pp. 324–48). Bethesda, MD: The Wildlife Society.

Romero, L.M. and Wikelski, M. (2002) Exposure to tourism reduces stress-induced corticosterone levels in Galápagos marine iguanas. *Biological Conservation* 108, 371–4.

Romesberg, H.C. (1981) Wildlife science: Gaining reliable knowledge. *Journal of Wildlife Management* 45, 293–313.

Ronconi, R.A. and St Clair, C.C. (2002) Management options to reduce boat disturbance on foraging black guillemots (*Cepphus grille*) in the Bay of Fundy. *Biological Conservation* 108, 275–81.

Rose, G. (2000) Practising photography: An archive, a study, some photographs and a researcher. *Journal of Historical Geography* 26 (4), 555–71.

Ross, H., Buchy, M. and Proctor, W. (2002) Laying down the ladder: A typology of public participation in Australian Natural Resource Management. *Australian Journal of Environmental Management* 9 (4), 205–17.

Ryan, C. (1998) Saltwater crocodiles as tourist attractions. *Journal of Sustainable Tourism* 6, 314–27.

Ryel. R, and Grasse, T. (1991) Marketing ecotourism: Attracting the elusive ecotourist. In T. Whelan (ed.) *Nature Tourism Managing for the Environment* (pp. 164–86). Washington, DC: Island Press.

Sagan, D. and Margulis, L. (1993) God, Gaia, and biophilia. In S.R. Kellert and E.O. Wilson (eds) *The Biophilia Hypothesis* (pp. 345–64). Washington, DC: Island Press.

Samuel, M.D. and Fuller, M.R. (1996) Wildlife radiotelemetry. In T.A. Bookhout (ed.) *Research and Management Techniques for Wildlife and Habitats* (pp. 370–418). Bethesda, MD: The Wildlife Society

Samuels, A., Bejder, L., Constantine, R. and Heinrich, S. (2003) Swimming with wild cetaceans, with a special focus on the Southern hemisphere. In N. Gales, M. Hindell and R. Kirkwood (eds) *Marine Mammals* (pp. 277–303). Collingwood, Australia: CSIRO Publishing.

Saprolsky, R.M., Romero, L.M. and Munck, A.U. (2000) How do glucocorticoids influence stress-responses? Integrating permissive, suppressive, stimulatory, and adaptive actions. *Endocrine Reviews* 21, 55–89.

Saunders, D.A. and Ingram, J.A. (1998) Twenty-eight years of monitoring a breeding population of carnaby's cockatoo. *Pacific Conservation Biology* 4 (3), 261–70.

Scarpaci, C., Dayanthi, N. and Corkeron, P.J. (2003) Compliance with regulations by 'swim-with-dolphins' operations in Port Phillip Bay, Victoria, Australia. *Environmental Management* 31, 342–7.

Schanzel, H.A. and McIntosh, A.J. (2000) An insight into the personal and emotive context of wildlife viewing at the Penguin Place, Otago Peninsula, New Zealand. *Journal of Sustainable Tourism* 8 (1), 36–52.

Scheiner, S.M. and Gurevitch, J. (2001) *Design and Analysis of Ecological Experiments*. Oxford: Oxford University Press.

Schemnitz, S.D. (1996) Capturing and handling wild animals. In T.A. Bookhout (ed.) *Research and Management Techniques for Wildlife and Habitats* (pp. 106–24). Bethesda, MD: The Wildlife Society.

Scheyvens, R. (2002) *Tourism for Development: Empowering Communities*. Harlow, England: Prentice-Hall, Pearson Education.

Sekercioglu, C.H. (2002) Impacts of bird watching on human and avian communities. *Environmental Conservation* 29(3), 282–9.

Shackley, M. (1992) Manatees and tourism in southern Florida: Opportunity or threat? *Journal of Environmental Management* 34, 257–65.

Shackley, M. (1996) *Wildlife Tourism*. London: International Thomson Business Press.

Shackley, M. (1998) 'Stingray City': Managing the impact of underwater tourism in the Cayman Islands. *Journal of Sustainable Tourism* 6 (4), 328–38.

Shackley, M. (ed.) (2001) *Flagship Species: Case Studies in Wildlife Tourism Management*. Burlington, VT, USA: The International Ecotourism Society.

Shafer, C.S. and Inglis, G.J. (2000) Influence of social, biophysical, and managerial conditions on tourism experiences within the Great Barrier Reef World Heritage Area. *Environmental Management* 26, 73–87.

Shepard, P. (1996) *The Others: How Animals made us Human*. Washington, DC: Island Press.

Sherwood, B., Cutler, D. and Burton, J. (2002) *Wildlife and Roads: The Ecological Impact*. Imperial College Press: London, UK.

Shrader-Frechette, K.S. and McCoy, E.D. (1995) *Method in Ecology*. Cambridge, UK: Cambridge University Press.

Sibley, R.M. and Smith, R.H. (1998) Identifying key factors using l-contribution analysis. *Journal of Animal Ecology* 67, 17–24.

Siegel, S. and Castellan Jr N.J., (1988) *Nonparametric Statistics for the Behavioral Sciences*. New York: McGraw-Hill.

Simmons, I.G. (1993) *Interpreting Nature: Cultural Constructions of the Environment*. London: Routledge.

Sinclair, M.T. (1992) Tourism, economic development and the environment: Problems and policies. *Progress in Tourism and Hospitality Management* 4, 75–81.

Singer, C. (1950) *A History of Biology: A General Introduction to the Study of Living Things*. London: H.K. Lewis & Co. Ltd.

Singer, P. (1995) *Animal Liberation*. London: Random House.

Singh, S., Timothy, D.J. and Dowling, R.K. (2003) *Tourism in Destination Communities*. Clevedon: Channel View Publications.

Sinha, C. (2001) Wildlife tourism: A geographical perspective. Paper presented at the *Geography Curriculum Inservice Conference. Tourism Geography: Issues, Challenges and the Changing Nature of Contemporary Tourism*, University of Western Sydney, Hawkesbury Campus, National Parks and Wildlife Service.

Sirakaya, E. and Uysal, M. (1997) Can sanctions and rewards explain conformance behaviour of tour operators with ecotourism guidelines? *Journal of Sustainable Tourism* 5, 322–32.

Skalski, J.R. and Robson, D.S. (1992) *Techniques for Wildlife Investigations: Design and Analysis of Capture Data*. San Diego: Academic Press.

Skeat, H. (2003) Encouraging high standards in the Great Barrier Reef tourism industry. Paper presented at *2003 Ecotourism Australia 11th National Conference*, Adelaide and Riverland, South Australia, 10–14 November 2003.

Skira, I. and Smith, S. (1991) Feeding wildlife in national parks. In *Proceedings of 5th Australian Seminar on National Parks and Wildlife* (pp.1882–6). Tasmania, Australia.

Smith, A.J. (1998) Environmental impacts of recreation and tourism in Warren National Park, Western Australia and appropriate management planning. Unpublished Honours Thesis, Department of Environmental Science, Murdoch University, Western Australia.

Smolker, R. (2001) *To Touch a Wild Dolphin: The Lives and Minds of the Dolphins of Monkey Mia*. Milsons Point, New South Wales: Random House Australia.

Sokal, R.R. and Rohlf, F.J. (1995) *Biometry*. New York: W.H. Freeman and Company.

Sontag, S. (1977) *On Photography* (3rd edn). Toronto: McGraw-Hill Ryerson Ltd.

Soulé, M.E. (1993) Biophilia: Unanswered questions. In S.R. Kellert and E.O. Wilson (eds) *The Biophilia Hypothesis* (pp. 441–55). Washington, DC: Island Press.

Southwood, T.R.E. and Henderson, P.A. (2000). *Ecological Methods*. Malden, MA: Blackwell Science.

Spellerberg, I.F. (2002) *Ecological Effects of Roads*. Enfield, USA: Science Publishers Inc.

Stankey, G.H. (2003) Adaptive management at the regional scale: Breakthrough innovation or mission impossible? A report on an American experience. In B.P. Wilson and A. Curtis (eds) *Agriculture for the Australian Environment* (pp. 159–77). Albury, NSW: The Johnstone Centre, Charles Sturt University.

Stankey, G.H., Cole, D.N., Lucas, R.C., Peterson, M.E. and Frissell, S.S. (1985) *The Limits of Acceptable Change (LAC) System for Wilderness Planning* (General Technical Report INT–176). Ogden, UT: US Department of Agriculture, Forest Service, Intermountain Forest and Range Experiment Station.

Steidl, R.J. and Thomas, L. (2001) Power analysis and experimental design. In S.M. Scheiner and J. Gurevitch (eds) *Design and Analysis of Ecological Experiments* (pp. 3–13). Oxford: Oxford University Press.

Stern, P.C., Dietz, T. and Kalof, L. (1993) Value orientations, gender and environmental concern. *Environment and Behaviour* 25, 322–48.

Stokes, T., Hulsman, K., Ogilvie, P. and O'Neill, P. (1996) Management of human visitation to seabird islands of the Great Barrier Reef Marine Park region. *Corella* 20, 1–13.

STTI (Sustainable Travel and Tourism Innovations) (2002) *GREEN GLOBE 21. Sector Benchmarking Indicators for Accommodation*. Brisbane: Green Globe Asia Pacific.

Sutherland, W.J. (1996) *Ecological Census Techniques: A Handbook*. Cambridge: Cambridge University Press.

Swabe, J. (1996) *Animals, Disease and Human Social Life: The Human-Animal Relationship Reconsidered*. Amsterdam: Amsterdam University.

Tabachnick, B.G. and Fidell, L.S. (1996) *Using Multivariate Statistics*. New York: Harper Collins Publishers.

Taber, R.D. and Saharia, V.B. (1995) Comparative approaches to wildlife management: The setting for the workshop. In S.H. Berwick and V.B. Saharia (eds) *The Development of International Principles and Practices of Wildlife Research and Management: Asian and American Approaches* (pp. 3–10). Oxford: Oxford University Press.

TFS (The Fletcher School) (2003) Multilaterals Project – Edward Ginn Library, The Fletcher School of Law and Diplomacy, Tufts University, Medford, Massachusetts – Online document: http://fletcher.tufts.edu/multilaterals.html (accessed 1 December 2003).

The Ecotourism Society (1998) *Ecotourism Statistical Fact Sheet*. VT: The Ecotourism Society.

Theodoropoulous, D.I. (2003) *Invasion Biology: Critique of a Pseudoscience*. Blythe, CA: Avaar Book.

The Orangutan Foundation (2003) Orangutan study and support tour: Online document: www.orangutan.org.uk.

The Whale and Dolphin Conservation Society (2004) Online document: http://www.responsiblewhalewatching.org/links.html (accessed 5 March 2004).

Thomas, J.W., Forsman, E.D., Lint, J.B., Meslow, E.C., Noon, B.R. and Verner, J. (1990) *A Conservation Strategy for the Northern Spotted Owl* (a report to the Interagency Scientific Committee to address the conservation of the northern spotted owl). Portland, OR: US Forest Service, Bureau of Land Management, US Fish and Wildlife Service, National Park Service.

Thomas, L. and Juanes, F. (1996) The importance of statistical power analysis: An example from *Animal Behaviour*. *Animal Behaviour* 52, 856–9.

Thomas, L. and Krebs, C.J. (1997) A review of statistical power analysis software. *Bulletin of the Ecological Society of America* April 1997, 126–39.

Thompson, K. and Foster, N. (2003) Ecotourism development and government policy in Kyrgyzstan. In D.A. Fennell and R.K. Dowling (eds) *Ecotourism Policy and Planning* (pp. 169–86). Wallingford, UK: CABI Publishing.

Thompson, M.J. and Henderson, R.E. (1998) Elk habituation as a credibility challenge for wildlife professionals. *Wildlife Society Bulletin* 26 (3), 477–83.

Thompson, W.L., White, G.C. and Gowan, C. (1998) *Monitoring Vertebrate Populations*. San Diego, USA: Academic Press.

Tilden, F. (1982) *Interpreting our Heritage*. Chapel Hill, NC: University of North Carolina Press.

Timothy, D.J. (1999) Participatory planning: A view of tourism in Indonesia. *Annals of Tourism Research* 26 (2), 371–91.

Tisdell, C. and Wilson, C. (2002) Economic, educational and conservation benefits of sea turtle based ecotourism: A study focussed on Mon Repos (Wildlife Tourism Research Report, Series No. 20). Gold Coast, Queensland: Cooperative Research Centre for Sustainable Tourism.

Todd, S.E. and Williams, P.W. (1996) From white to green: A proposed environmental management system framework for ski areas. *Journal of Sustainable Tourism* 4 (3), 147–73.

Toft, C.A. and Shea, P.J. (1983) Detecting community-wide patterns: Estimating power strengthens statistical inference. *American Naturalist* 122, 618–25.

Tonnesen, A.S. and Ebersole, J.J. (1997) Human trampling effects on regeneration and age structure of *Pinus edulis* and *Juniperus monosperma*. *Great Basin Naturalist* 57, 50–6.

Tremblay, P. (2001) Wildlife tourism consumption: Consumptive or non-consumptive? *International Journal of Tourism Research* 3, 81–6.

Tremblay, P. (2002) Tourism wildlife icons: Attractions or marketing symbols? *Journal of Hospitality and Tourism Management* 9, 164.

Trombulak, S.C. and Frissell, C.A. (2000) Review of ecological effects of roads on terrestrial and aquatic communities. *Conservation Biology* 14, 18–30.

Tuite, C.H., Hanson, P.R. and Owen, M. (1984) Some ecological factors affecting winter wildfowl distribution on inland waters in England and Wales, and the influence of water-based recreation. *Journal of Applied Ecology* 21, 41–62.

Ulrich, R.S. (1983) Aesthetic and affective response to natural environment. In I. Altman and J.F. Wohlwill (eds) *Human Behavior and Environment: Advances in Theory and Research* (Vol. Six) (pp. 85–125). New York: Plenum Press.

Ulrich, R.S. (1984) View through a window may influence recovery from surgery. *Science* 224, 420–1.

Ulrich, R.S. (1993) Biophilia, biophobia, and natural landscapes. In S.R. Kellert and E.O. Wilson (eds) *The Biophilia Hypothesis* (pp. 73–137). Washington, DC: Island Press.

Ulrich, R.S., Dimberg, U. and Driver, B.L. (1991) Psychophysiological indicators of leisure benefits. In B.L. Driver, P.J. Brown and G.L. Peterson (eds) *Benefits of Leisure* (pp. 73–89). Venture Publishing: State College, PA.

Underwood, A.J. (1997) *Experiments in Ecology: Local Design and Implementation using Analysis of Variance*. Cambridge: Cambridge University Press.

UNEP (United Nations Environment Programme) (2003) UNEP Tourism Programme: Why is UNEP Concerned with Tourism? Online document: http://www.uneptie.org/pc/tourism/about-us/why-tourism.htm (accessed 1 December 2003).

Urry, J. (1990) *The Tourist Gaze: Leisure and Travel in Contemporary Societies*. London: Sage Publications.

Urry, J. (1995) *Consuming Places*. London: Routledge.

Van Gelder, J.J. (1973) A quantitative approach to the mortality resulting from traffic in a population of Bufo bufo. *Oecologia,* 13, 93–5.

Vaske, J.J., Decker, D.J. and Manfredo, M.J. (1995) Human dimensions of wildlife management: An integrated framework for coexistence. In R.L. Knight and K.J Gutzwiller (eds) *Wildlife and Recreationists: Coexistence Through Management and Research*. Washington, DC: Island Press.

Virtanen, P. (2003) Local management of global values: Community-based wildlife management in Zimbabwe and Zambia. *Society and Natural Resources* 16, 179–90.

Visser, N. and Njuguna, S. (1992) Environmental impacts of tourism on the Kenya coast. *Industry and Environment* 15 (3), 42–51.

Waayers, D. and Newsome, D. (2003) *A Management Framework for the Conservation of Endangered Turtles* (unpublished final report to Environment Australia). Murdoch, Western Australia: Murdoch University.

Walters, C. (1986) *Adaptive Management of Renewable Resources*. New York: Macmillan.

Walters, C.J. and Holling, C.S. (1990) Large-scale management experiments and learning by doing. *Ecology* 71, 2060–8.

Warnken, J. and Buckley, R. (2000) Monitoring diffuse impacts: Australian tourism developments. *Environmental Management* 25 (4), 453–61.

WATC and CALM (Western Australian Tourism Commission and Western Australian Department of Conservation and Land Management) (1997) *Nature Based Tourism Strategy for Western Australia*. Perth: Government of Western Australia.

WCED (World Commission on Environment and Development) (1987) Our Common Future (Report of the World Commission on Environment and Development) (The Brundtland Commission). Oxford: Oxford University Press.

Wearing, S. and Neil, J. (1999) *Ecotourism Impacts, Potentials and Possibilities*. Melbourne: Butterworth-Heinemann.

Wearing, S. and Wearing, M. (1999) Decommodifying ecotourism: Rethinking global-local interactions with host communities. *Society and Leisure* 22 (1), 39–70.

Weaver, D. (2001a) *Ecotourism*. Milton, Queensland: John Wiley & Sons.

Weaver, D.B. (2001b) Ecotourism in the context of other tourism types. In D.B.Weaver (ed.) *The Encyclopedia of Ecotourism* (pp. 73–83). Wallingford: CABI Publishing.

Wegner, A. (2001) Improving consideration of biodiversity in environmental impact assessment in Western Australia. Unpublished Honours thesis, Murdoch University, Western Australia.

Weiler, B. (1995) Ecotourism Association of Australia. In R. Harris and N. Leiper (eds) *Sustainable Tourism: An Australian Perspective* (pp. 63–7). Chatswood: Butterworth-Heinemann.

Wet Tropics Management Authority (WTMA) (1997) *Protection Through Partnerships: Policies for Implementation of the Wet Tropics Plan*. Cairns, Queensland: Wet Tropics Management Authority.

Wienecke, B.C., Wooller, R.D. and Klomp, N.I. (1995) The ecology and management of Little Penguins on Penguin Island, Western Australia. In P. Dann, I. Norman and P. Reilly (eds) *The Penguins* (pp. 440–67). Chipping Norton, New South Wales: Surrey Beatty and Sons.

Wicks, B.E. and Schuett, M.A. (1991) Examining the role of tourism promotion through the use of brochures. *Tourism Management* 12 (4), 301–12.

Wilkie, D.S. and Carpenter, J.F. (1999) Can nature tourism help finance protected areas in the Congo Basin? *Oryx* 33, 332–8.

Williams, D.R. (2001) Sustainability and public access to nature: Contesting the right to roam. *Journal of Sustainable Tourism* 9 (5), 361–71.

Williams, I.D. and Polunin, N.V.C. (2000) Differences between protected and unprotected reefs of the western Caribbean in attributes preferred by dive tourists. *Environmental Conservation* 27, 382–91.

Williams, R., Trites, A.W. and Bain, D.E. (2002) Behavioural responses of killer whales (*Orcinus orca*) to whale-watching boats: Opportunistic observations and experimental approaches. *Journal of Zoology* 256, 255–70.

Williams, T.D., Cooke, F., Cooch, E.G. and Rockwell, R.G. (1993) Body condition and gosling survival in mass-banded lesser snow geese. *Journal of Wildlife Management* 57, 555–62.

Wilson, B. (1994) Review of Dolphin Management at Monkey Mia. Unpublished report to Department of Conservation and Land Management. Perth, Western Australia.

Wilson, E.O. (1984) *Biophilia*. Cambridge: Harvard University Press.

Wilson, C. and Tisdell, C. (2001) Sea turtles as a non-consumptive resource especially in Australia. *Tourism Management* 22, 279–88.

Wilson, R.F. (2000) The impact of anthropogenic disturbance on four species of arboreal folivorous possums in the rainforest of north-eastern Queensland, Australia. Unpublished PhD thesis, Department of Tropical Environment Studies and Geography, James Cook University of North Queensland, Australia.

Wolcott, T.G. and Wolcott, D.L. (1984) Impact of off-road vehicles on macro-invertebrates of a Mid-Atlantic beach. *Biological Conservation* 29 (3), 217–40.

Wolmer, W. and Ashley, C. (2003) Wild resources management in Southern Africa: Participation, partnerships, ecoregions and redistribution. *IDS Bulletin* 34 (3), 31–40.

Woodford, M.H., Butynski, T.M. and Karesh, W.B. (2002) Habituating the great apes: The disease risks. *Oryx* 36 (2), 153–60.

Woods-Ballard, A.J., Parsons, E.C.M., Hughes, A.J., Velander, K.A., Ladle, R.J. and Warburton, C.A. (2003) The sustainability of whale-watching in Scotland. *Journal of Sustainable Tourism* 11 (1), 40–55.

Worboys, G., Lockwood, M. and De Lacy, T. (2001) *Protected Area Management: Principles and Practice*. Melbourne: Oxford University Press.

Wrangham, R.W. (1974) Artificial feeding of chimpanzees and baboons in their natural habitat. *Animal Behaviour* 22, 83–93.

WTO (World Tourism Organization) (1998) Hot tourism trends for 21st century. *World Tourism Organization News* 4, 1–3.

WTTC (World Travel and Tourism Council) (2003) About WTTC. Online document: http://www.wttc.org/framesetaboutus.htm (accessed 1 December 2003).

Wynberg, R. (2002) A decade of biodiversity conservation and use in South Africa: Tracking progress from the Rio Earth Summit to the Johannesburg World Summit on Sustainable Development. *South African Journal of Science* 98, 233–43.

Yalden, P.E. and Yalden, D.W. (1990) Recreational disturbance of breeding golden plovers (*Plusialis apricarius*). *Biological Conservation* 51, 243–62.

Young, M.D. and Gunningham, N. (1997) Mixing instruments and institutional arrangements for optimal biodiversity conservation. In P. Hale and D. Lamb (eds) *Conservation Outside Nature Reserves* (pp. 123–35). Brisbane: Centre for Conservation Biology, The University of Queensland.

Zar, J.H. (1999) *Biostatistical Analysis*. NJ: Prentice-Hall International.

Ziman, J. (1984) *An Introduction to Science Studies: The Philosophical and Social Aspects of Science and Technology*. Cambridge, Cambridge University Press.

Zinn, H.C., Manfredo, M.J. and Barro, S.C. (2002) Patterns of wildlife value orientations in hunters' families. *Human Dimensions of Wildlife* 7, 147–62.

Index

Locations